THE INNER CITADEL

THE INNER CITADEL

The *Meditations* of Marcus Aurelius

❧

Pierre Hadot

Translated by Michael Chase

HARVARD UNIVERSITY PRESS

Cambridge, Massachusetts
London, England

First Harvard University Press paperback edition, 2001

Publication of this book has been aided by
a grant from the French Ministry of Culture.

Originally published as *La Citadelle Intérieure: Introduction aux "Pensées" de Marc Aurèle* by
Pierre Hadot, copyright © 1992 Librairie Arthème Fayard.

Library of Congress Cataloging-in-Publication Data

Hadot, Pierre.
[Citadelle intérieure. English]
The inner citadel : the Meditations of Marcus Aurelius / Pierre
Hadot ; translated by Michael Chase.
p.   cm.
Includes bibliographical references (p.   ) and index.
ISBN 0-674-46171-1 (cloth)
ISBN 0-674-00707-7 (pbk.)
1. Marcus Aurelius, Emperor of Rome, 121–180.   Meditations.
2. Ethics.   3. Stoics.   4. Life.   I. Title.
B583.H3313   1998
188—dc21
97-46971

CONTENTS

꧁꧂

PREFACE

✵

Soon, you will have forgotten everything.
Soon, everybody will have forgotten you!

Meditations, VII, 21

Marcus Aurelius was wrong. Eighteen centuries—almost two millen-
nia—have passed, and the *Meditations* are still alive. Nor have their pages
been reserved to a few aristocrats of the intellect, like Shaftesbury,
Frederick II, or Goethe: on the contrary, for centuries they have brought
reasons to live to innumerable unknown people, who have been able to
read them in the multiple translations of the *Meditations* which have been
made in every corner of the earth; and they still do so today.

The *Meditations* are an inexhaustible source of wisdom; an "eternal
Gospel," in Renan's words. Apparently, the *Meditations* do not hold any
particular difficulties in store for their readers. Aphorisms and brief dissertations follow one another without any apparent order, and as the
reader leafs through the book, he or she winds up finding a striking or
moving formula which seems to speak by itself, and to need no exegesis.
It is not a book to be read in one sitting. One must return to it often, in
order to discover in it, day by day, some nourishment which suits the
momentary states of our soul. The modern reader can perfectly well
understand a given aphorism by Marcus Aurelius, like the one I have
quoted as an epigraph. This is what is always attractive about the *Meditations:* their sayings, whose limpidity can never grow old.

And yet, what a deceptive limpidity! For besides these formulas, there
are others which are much more obscure, and which have been understood by historians in widely varying ways. The overall meaning of the
book, its purpose, and some of its affirmations are very hard for us to
grasp. Nor is this the case only with Marcus Aurelius. For all kinds of
reasons, of which chronological distance is not the most important, our
understanding of ancient works has grown more and more dim. To gain
access to them once more, we will have to practice a kind of spiritual

exercise or intellectual ascetics, in order to free ourselves from certain prejudices and rediscover what is, for us, almost another way of thinking. This is what we shall attempt to do throughout the present work. Before we set out upon this itinerary, however, it may be helpful to become aware of these prejudices and illusions, which threaten to cause the modern reader to go astray when reading a work from antiquity.

In the first place, the reader will perhaps imagine that the text has remained constant since the distant era in which it appeared, as do our contemporary printed texts. But we must not forget that ancient texts were, precisely, not printed: for centuries they were copied by hand, and copying errors were thereby constantly introduced. We can hardly blame the ancient scribes for this, if we think of our modern books, which, although they are printed, are often filled with printer's errors, which sometimes deform the author's thought to the point of rendering it unintelligible. That, however, is another question. It cannot be overemphasized that it is thanks to the efforts of the scholars who investigate and classify the manuscripts in which ancient works have been preserved, and who attempt, using the critical method of the classification of errors, to reconstitute the original state of the text, that we can now read the works of antiquity in a state which is more or less satisfactory, but can never be perfect. I feel I must insist upon this point, which is sometimes completely ignored by some scientific authorities or historians of philosophy, who imagine that one can hold forth about the theories of a particular ancient author without knowing what he really wrote. In the case of Marcus Aurelius, the greatest uncertainty often reigns with regard to certain words of his text. This does not affect the totality of the work, but it nevertheless remains true that some passages present almost insurmountable difficulties, and we should not be surprised if these difficulties are reflected in the translations which have been made of this author.

The modern reader tends too often to imagine that there is only one possible translation of a Greek text, and he or she may be surprised to find considerable differences. This fact should, however, make the reader aware of the distance that separates us from the ancients. Translation presupposes, first of all, a choice with regard to the Greek text, in those cases in which this text is sometimes uncertain. But the translators' hesitations often also correspond to the difficulties they have in understanding the text, and to the sometimes radically different interpretations of it which they propose. In the case of Marcus Aurelius, for example, many have not been able to render in an exact manner the technical terms, peculiar to the Stoic system, which are found on every page of the

Meditations. Moreover, in the case of Marcus, the division of the text into chapters is very uncertain, and often the limits of each "meditation" are not absolutely clear. Thus, the very appearance of the text can vary widely.

Finally, the modern reader might imagine—and no one is safe from this error—that the ancient author lives in the same intellectual world as he does. The reader will treat the author's affirmations exactly as if they came from a contemporary author, and will therefore think he has immediately understood what the author meant. In fact, however, this understanding will be anachronistic, and the reader will often run the risk of committing serious mistranslations. To be sure, it is fashionable nowadays to affirm that, in any case, we cannot know exactly what an author meant, and that, moreover, this does not matter at all, for we can give the works any meaning we please. For my part, and without entering into this debate, I would say that before we discover "unintentional" meanings, it seems to me both possible and necessary to discover the meaning which the author intended. It is absolutely indispensable to go in the direction of a basic meaning, to which we can then refer in order to uncover, if we should so wish, those meanings of which the author was perhaps not conscious. It is true, however, that this reconstitution is extremely difficult for us, because we project attitudes and intentions proper to our era into the past. In order to understand ancient works, we must relocate them within their context, in the widest sense of the term, which can signify the material, social, and political situation as well as the political and rhetorical universe of thought. In particular, we must recall that the mechanisms of literary composition were very different then from what they are now. In antiquity, the rules of discourse were rigorously codified. In order to say what he wanted to say, an author had to say it in a specific way, in accordance with traditional models, and according to rules prescribed by rhetoric or philosophy. Marcus Aurelius' *Meditations,* for instance, are not the spontaneous outpourings of a soul that wants to express its thoughts immediately, but rather an exercise, accomplished in accordance with definite rules. As we shall see, they presuppose a pre-existing canvas, upon which the philosopher-emperor could only embroider. Often, Marcus says certain things only because he *has* to say them, by virtue of the models and precepts imposed upon him. The meaning of the *Meditations* can, therefore, only be understood once we have discovered, among other things, the prefabricated schemes which have been imposed upon it.

My intention, which is to offer the modern reader an introduction to

the reading of the *Meditations,* will thus perhaps not be without usefulness. I will try to discover what Marcus wanted to accomplish by writing
them, to specify the literary genre to which they belong, and, especially,
to define their relationship with the philosophical system which inspired
them. Finally, without trying to produce a biography of the emperor, I
will try to determine how much of him is visible in his work.

I have chosen to quote the *Meditations* abundantly. I hate those mono-
graphs which, instead of letting the author speak and staying close to the
text, engage in obscure elucubrations which claim to carry out an act of
decoding and reveal the "unsaid" of the thinker, without the reader's
having the slightest idea of what that thinker really "said." Such a
method unfortunately permits all kinds of deformations, distortions, and
sleight of hand. Our era is captivating for all kinds of reasons: too often,
however, from the philosophical and literary point of view, it could be
defined as the era of the misinterpretation, if not of the pun: people can,
it seems, say anything about anything. When I quote Marcus Aurelius, I
want my reader to make contact with the text itself, which is superior to
any commentary. I would like him to see how my interpretation tries to
base itself on the text, and that he can verify my affirmations directly and
immediately. The translation I offer is completely original. I have been
working on Marcus Aurelius for more than twenty years, in particular on
a new edition and translation of the *Meditations,* which will be published
within the next few years. In the course of this work, interpretation and
translation have gone hand in hand, and this is why I could not illustrate
my arguments by referring the reader to existing translations, which
would have been different from mine, and which might not have corresponded exactly with my idea of the philosopher-emperor's work.

I should like to thank Michael Chase for his sensitive and philologi-
cally astute translation, as well as Angela Armstrong. Finally, my thanks
go to Margaretta Fulton and Mary Ellen Geer at Harvard University
Press, as well as Brian Stock at the University of Toronto, for their
patient and helpful advice.

Note on Transliteration and Quotation

I have sometimes found it useful to allude to certain Greek technical terms which are peculiar to Stoic philosophy. I have tried to transliterate them as simply as possible, using the letter ē to represent the Greek letter eta, and ō to represent the letter omega.

In order not to multiply my notes unnecessarily, the references for the quotations from Marcus Aurelius and the *Discourses* of Epictetus have been indicated in parentheses within the text. In both cases, the first number refers to the number of the book, the second to the chapter number, and the third to the paragraph number within the chapter. Unless I indicate otherwise, the references given in Chapters 4 and 5 always refer to the text of the *Discourses* of Epictetus.

The Greek text of Marcus Aurelius on which my translations are based is generally that of W. Theiler, *Marc Aurel, Wege zu sich selbst* (Zurich: Artemis Verlag, 1974).

Translator's Note

I have used the following procedure in rendering Pierre Hadot's translations: I first literally translated Hadot's French version, and then compared it with the original Greek or Latin texts. We have exchanged correspondence about doubtful cases, and this process has resulted in a number of corrections with regard to the 1992 French edition of this work. The final result is, I hope, a translation which, insofar as is possible, is faithful both to Pierre Hadot and to the Greek and Latin authors to whom he has so fruitfully dedicated his life. Finally, all notes enclosed in square brackets are my own.

THE INNER CITADEL

THE EMPEROR-PHILOSOPHER

A happy youth, a tormented reign

The future Marcus Aurelius, who was to receive this name later on, as a result of his adoption by the emperor Aurelius Antoninus Pius, was born in Rome in 121, and was initially named Marcus Annius Verus. The families of his mother and father possessed a number of brick factories,[1] which represented an enormous fortune and a considerable investment of capital. Such wealth allowed its holders to exercise political influence, and the factory owners often attained positions from which they could influence construction programs, as was the case for Marcus Aurelius' grandfather.

After his grandfather died during his early childhood, Marcus was noticed, protected, and favored by the emperor Hadrian. Just before his death in 138, the latter, in order to ensure his succession, adopted Antoninus—uncle-in-law of the future Marcus Aurelius—and asked him to adopt Marcus as well as Lucius Verus, the son of Aelius Caesar, whom Hadrian had initially chosen as his successor, but who had just died.

On July 10, 138, Hadrian was succeeded by Antoninus. One year later, the future Marcus Aurelius, at the age of eighteen, was raised to the dignity of Caesar. In 145, he married Faustina, daughter of Antoninus. The couple had thirteen children, of whom only six survived beyond childhood: five daughters and one son, the future emperor Commodus.[2]

The correspondence which Marcus exchanged with his rhetoric teacher Fronto, which lasted nearly thirty years—from 139 to 166/167, the date of Fronto's death[3]—provides us with precious details on this period of Marcus Aurelius' life, as well as on the atmosphere at the court of the Antonines: family life, children's illnesses, wine-making, the future emperor's studies and readings, the rhetorical homework which he punctually sent to Fronto, and the tender friendship which linked not only the master and the student, but also the families of Marcus Aurelius and of Fronto. At the death of Antoninus (161), Marcus Aurelius, then thirty-nine years old, became emperor, and he immediately had equal power conferred upon his adoptive brother, Lucius Verus.

In the same year as their common accession to the throne, the Parthians invaded the eastern provinces of the Empire. The campaign began with a disaster for the Roman army, whereupon Lucius was sent east, where, under the command of two seasoned warriors, Statius Priscius and Avidius Cassius, the Roman troops regained the upper hand (163–166). They invaded the Parthian kingdom, and seized Ctesiphon and Seleucia.

No sooner had the ceremonies celebrating the two emperors' victory of 166 ended when most alarming news arrived from another border of the Empire. The Marcomanni and the Quadi, Germanic peoples from the region of the Danube, were threatening the North of Italy. The two emperors were obliged to come and restore order to the situation, and spent the winter at Aquileia. At the beginning of the year 169, however, Lucius died in the carriage in which he was riding along with Marcus Aurelius. From 169 to 175, the Emperor then had to carry out military operations in the region of the Danube.

In 175, at the very moment when he was beginning to enjoy some success, Marcus received word of the rebellion of Avidius Cassius, who, as a result of a plot which had spread through several provinces of the East and of Egypt, had himself proclaimed Emperor. Marcus Aurelius was probably saved on this occasion by the loyalty of Martius Verus, the governor of Cappadocia. At any rate, as the Emperor was preparing to leave for the East, he learned of the assassination of Avidius Cassius, which put an end to this tragic episode.

Marcus Aurelius nevertheless decided to travel to the eastern provinces, accompanied by Faustina and their son Commodus; he went to Egypt, Syria, and Cilicia, where Faustina died. Ancient historians loved to linger over Faustina's numerous adulteries; whatever may be the truth behind this gossip, the Emperor was profoundly affected by her loss, and it is with deep emotion that, in the *Meditations* (I, 17, 18), he evokes the memory of his wife, so "docile, so loving, and so upright."

On his way back to Rome, the Emperor passed through Smyrna and then Athens, where, together with Commodus, he was initiated into the Eleusinian Mysteries. The festivities celebrating the victories over the Germans and the Sarmatians took place at Rome, on December 23, 176, but Marcus Aurelius had to leave once again for the Danubian front in 178. He died at Sirmium or at Vienna in 180.

The Empire was ravaged by natural catastrophes even more than by wars during this period: floodings of the Tiber (161), earthquakes at Cyzicus (161) and at Smyrna (178), and above all the terrible plague epidemic brought back from Asia by Roman troops returning from the Parthian war (166). As J. F. Gilliam has shown,[4] this plague did not perhaps bring about the vast depopulation which has been described by certain historians, who have made it the decisive cause of the decline of Rome, but it certainly did have serious consequences for the social and economic life of the Empire.

What a tormented reign it was! No sooner had Marcus Aurelius ascended the throne than he was suddenly overwhelmed by natural disasters, military and political difficulties, and family cares and mournings, which forced him to engage in a battle every day.

The sober—albeit partial—judgment of Cassius Dio[5] is one of the most just that have been made on the subject of Marcus: "He didn't have the luck which he deserved . . . but was confronted, throughout his reign, by a multitude of disasters. That is why I admire him more than any other, for it was amidst these extraordinary and unparalleled difficulties that he was able to survive, and to save the Empire."

As Ferdinand Lot has written,[6] "The Roman world saw a series of sovereigns succeed to the throne the likes of which history has never seen since, and this happened precisely at the time first of the stagnation, and then of the decline of the ancient world." After enumerating the examples of Marcus Aurelius, Septimius Severus, Diocletian, Julian, and Theodosius, among others, he continues: "Statesmen, legislators, warriors, they sped from Brittany to the Rhine, from the Rhine to the Danube, from the Danube to the Euphrates, in order to defend the Roman world and civilization against the Germanic or Sarmatian Barbarians, against the Parthians, and then against the Persians. They all knew that their lives were constantly threatened . . . And they abandoned themselves fearlessly to their tragic destiny as supermen. For if ever supermen have existed, we have to look for them among the emperors of the second to the fourth century." Such is the perspective within which we must situate the personality of Marcus Aurelius, if we hope to catch a glimpse of it.

Evolution toward philosophy

In this work, however, the goal is not to write the biography of one of these "supermen."[7] Our task shall only be to ask how Marcus Aurelius came to write the *Meditations;* and this is the same as asking how he became a philosopher, and how the *Meditations* could represent for him a part of his philosophical activity.

First, it is perhaps not inappropriate to recall that a philosopher in antiquity was not necessarily a theoretician of philosophy, as is all too often supposed. In antiquity, a philosopher was someone who lived like a philosopher—that is, who led a philosophical life. Cato the Younger, a statesman of the first century B.C., was a Stoic philosopher, but he did not write a single philosophical treatise. Rogatianus, a statesman of the third century A.D., was a Platonic philosopher, the disciple of Plotinus, and yet he wrote no philosophical treatise. Neverthless both men considered themselves philosophers, because they had adopted a philosophical way of life. Let it not be said, moreover, that they were amateur philosophers. In the view of the masters of ancient philosophy, authentic philosophy was not that which discoursed upon theories or commented upon authors. In the words of Epictetus (III, 21, 5), a Stoic who had a considerable influence upon Marcus Aurelius: "Eat like a man, drink like a man, get dressed, get married, have children, lead the life of a citizen. . . . Show us all this, so that we can see whether or not you have really learned something from the philosophers."[8]

Ancient philosophers thus had no need to write. If, moreover, they did write, it was not necessary for them to invent a new theory, or develop any specific part of a system. It was enough for them to formulate the fundamental principles of the school in favor of which they had made their choice of life. When Marcus was writing the *Meditations,* he did not invent anything new, and did not bring about any progress within Stoic doctrine. This, however, is not to say that he was not a philosopher, and especially not a Stoic philosopher.[9]

On the other hand, the fact of having taken some philosophy courses did not necessarily mean that one was a philosopher. Lucius Verus, Marcus Aurelius' adoptive brother, received instruction from the same philosophy teachers as his brother, but no one would think of calling him a philosopher.[10] The Latin author Aulus Gellius, Marcus' contemporary, was a student of the Platonic philosopher Taurus at Athens. There is no doubt that Gellius was interested in philosophy, and he cites many philosophical texts in his works, but he makes no claim to lead a philosophical life. Rhetoricians and statesmen found in philosophy courses training for dialectics, and material to develop commonplaces in their discourses. As Fronto wrote to Marcus: "Philosophy will give you the substance of your discourse, and rhetoric its form."[11] They did not, however, feel obliged to live like philosophers. This is why the *Discourses* of Epictetus, as reported by Arrian, constantly remind the philosopher's audience that philosophy does not consist in dialectical skillfulness or beautiful language, but in the way one lives day-to-day life. To be a philosopher was not to have received a theoretical philosophical education, or to be a professor of philosophy. Rather, it was to profess, as a result of a conversion which caused a radical change of life-style, a way of life different from that of other people.

It would be extremely interesting to know, in all its details, the manner in which Marcus' conversion to philosophy took place. Yet many points remain obscure.

We possess two documents of capital importance on Marcus Aurelius' evolution. The first is the correspondence between Marcus and his rhetoric teacher Fronto, of which I have already spoken; unfortunately, it has come down to us in a palimpsest discovered in the nineteenth century; thus this collection of letters has been covered over by other writing, and the chemical products which were used to make it legible have caused irreparable deterioration of the manuscript, which contains gaps and is often unreadable. The second piece of evidence comes from the Emperor himself, who, as he wrote the first book of his *Meditations,* mentioned all he owed to his parents, teachers, and friends; this is an extremely concise text, which leaves us terribly unsatisfied. Still, with the help of the meager indications we can glean from these sources, we can distinguish a certain number of phases in Marcus' evolution toward philosophy. Although later hagiographers asserted that he was "serious" from childhood on,[12] we can discern an initial period of carefree youth, which seems to have continued until the age of twenty, that is, into the period when he was already Caesar. It is possible, however, that under the influence of Diognetus, one of the teachers Marcus speaks about in his *Meditations* (I, 6), the desire to live as a philosopher may have touched him already at this period.

Marcus' conversion to philosophy seems to have been the work of Junius Rusticus, who revealed to him the teachings of Epictetus, and his conversion can probably be dated to the years 144–147. In any case, when Marcus was twenty-five, in 146–147, he wrote Fronto a letter which leaves no doubt as to his new state of mind. Besides, throughout the first years of Marcus' elevation to the throne, Fronto makes almost constant allusions to the philosophical way of life of his Imperial student.

Carefree life of a young prince and dreams of a life of austerity

Marcus' letters to Fronto—particularly those he wrote when he was still a young eighteen- or twenty-year-old Caesar—allow us to catch a glimpse of the simple, familiar way of life which was led at the court of Marcus' adoptive father Antoninus, particularly in the Imperial villas, far away from Rome, to which Antoninus often liked to withdraw. The family took part in the labors of the grape harvests, and there was no luxury in the meals served, or even in the heating. The future emperor liked physical exercise—especially hunting—which he seems to have practiced without any particular scruples with regard to his subjects. This, at least, is what we can glimpse from a letter which could date from the years 140–143, only the first part of which has been preserved:

> . . . When my father came back home from the vineyards, I went riding, as usual. I got started and we gradually moved away. Suddenly, in the middle of the road, there was a big flock of sheep, and the place was deserted: there were four dogs, two shepherds, and nothing else. When they saw this group of horsemen coming, one of the shepherds said to the other, "Watch out for these horseman; they're the kind that usually cause the most trouble." No sooner did I hear this than I spurred my horse and headed him straight for the flock; the terrified beasts scattered, running every which way, bleating and in the utmost confusion. The shepherd threw his staff at me, but it landed on the rider who was following me, and we fled. Thus, he who was afraid of losing a lamb wound up losing his staff! Do you think I made this story up? No, it's true. I'd write you still more about it, but they're coming to get me for my bath.[13]

In this childish prank, we catch the future emperor in an act of foolishness and senselessness. We are a long way from the philosopher who will later try, among other things, to render justice with the utmost scrupulousness. Most of the time, moreover, the tone of these letters to Fronto is very playful. It appears as though the young Caesar, that passionate reader, who was no doubt trying his hardest to polish his skills at rhetoric, was not thinking about anything else.

It does seem, however, that even in his childhood Marcus Aurelius had seen what the ideal of a philosophical life could be. In the first book of his *Meditations* (I, 6), he attributes this aspiration for a life of austerity to the influence of a certain Diognetus.[14] The latter was one of the first teachers Marcus had; he had taught him to write dialogues "while he was still a child," and had turned him away from a game which had long been practiced by young Greeks: mentioned by Aristophanes and Plato, it consisted essentially in playing with quails by striking them lightly on the head.[15] It was Diognetus, said Marcus, who gave him his love for philosophy and inspired in him "the desire to sleep on a cot and a simple animal-skin, and for things of this sort which belong to the 'Hellenic' way of life." We shall return to this last phrase. For the moment, let us note the correspondence between this note from the *Meditations* and the indications given us by *The Life of Marcus Aurelius* in the *Historia Augusta*:[16] "At the age of twelve, he adopted the costume of a philosopher, and a little later the endurance of one, too. He used to study dressed in a pallium—that is, a philosophers' cloak—and sleep on the ground; his mother had all kinds of difficulty in getting him to stretch out on a bed covered with animal skins."

A short cloak and a hard bed were the symbols of the Stoic philosophical life. We find them in Seneca, who advises his disciple Lucilius to practice this austerity from time to time, evoking Demetrius the Cynic lying on his cot; in the younger Pliny, who speaks of the jurist Aristo—more of a philosopher than the so-called philosophers—whose bed called to mind the simplicity of life of the ancients; and finally in the Stoic Musonius, teacher of Epictetus, who declared that a cot and a simple animal-skin are enough for sleeping.[17]

On this topic, we can well wonder whether "Hellenic way of life *(agōgē)*," the reading of the manuscripts of the *Meditations,* ought to be preserved, or whether we should emend the reading to "Laconian way of life *(agōgē)*." For among the ancients, the "Hellenic way of life" tended rather to designate Greek culture and civilization, both in its spiritual and in its material forms: literature and philosophical discourses, to be sure, but also the gymnasia and social way of life.[18] The expression "Laconian way of life," by contrast, traditionally designated the "rough life" which characterized at the same time Spartan education and philosophical *askēsis*. The word *agōgē* was, moreover, often used by itself to designate the life-style of the Lacedaemonians.[19] In his life of the Spartan legislator Lycurgus, Plutarch[20] describes the way in which Spartan children were brought up: once they reached the age of twelve, they lived without any tunic, received only one cloak for the whole year, and slept on mattresses which they themselves had made out of reeds.

The model of this style of life was strongly idealized by the philosophers, especially the Cynics and Stoics. This was what F. Ollier[21] has

termed the "Spartan mirage," and it was all the more a mirage in that
Sparta was a warlike, totalitarian state which "fashioned its citizens to
become the docile instruments of its will," whereas the Cynics and Stoics
considered personal moral value as the only goal of life. From Spartan
education, they retained only its training for perseverance, its return to a
natural life, and its contempt for social conventions. To cite only one
example: the Stoic Musonius considered that a disciple "educated Spartan style" was in a better condition to receive philosophical instruction,
and he had praised at length the Lacedaemonians' frugal life-style.[22] One
might add that the philosophers' cloak (Greek *tribōn,* Latin *pallium*) worn
by the young Marcus Aurelius was none other than the Spartan cloak,
made of coarse cloth, that had been adopted by Socrates, Antisthenes,
Diogenes, and the philosophers of the Cynic and Stoic tradition.[23]

How did Diognetus transmit to Marcus the desire for the austere life
of the philosophers and the Spartans? We do not know. Did he boast to
him of the free life of the Cynic or Stoic philosophers? Following the
example of Plutarch, did he tell him about the life of Lycurgus or of
Cleomenes? Be this as it may, he brought about in his student what we
might call an initial conversion toward philosophy.

Nevertheless, in the letters from Marcus to Fronto which date from
before the years 146–147, we do not perceive the slightest trace of this
youthful—or rather, childish—enthusiasm for the Spartan-style philosophical way of life. No doubt it had been short-lived; and yet this fire,
though apparently extinguished, continued to smolder, and it would not
be long before it flared up once again.

Junius Rusticus

Ancient historians are unanimous in recognizing the vitally important
role played by Junius Rusticus in Marcus' evolution toward philosophy.
"His favorite teacher," says the *Historia Augusta,*[24] "was Junius Rusticus,
whose disciple he was and for whom he had the greatest respect. This
Rusticus was as effective in war as he was in peace, and he was a great
practitioner of the Stoic way of life. Marcus Aurelius consulted him on
all his business, whether public or private; he used to greet him with a
kiss even in front of the Praetorian prefect; honored him with a second
consulate, and, after his death, requested that the Senate raise statues of
him." The *Historia Augusta* could, moreover, have added that Rusticus'
first consulate, in 162 (the year after Marcus became emperor), was
certainly intended as a sign of the disciple's gratitude toward his master.
When the historian Cassius Dio[25] speaks of Marcus' philosophy teachers,

he mentions only Junius Rusticus and Apollonius of Chalcedon, both of whom he depicts as Stoics. Later, in the fourth century, Themistius still speaks of the privileged relationship between Junius Rusticus and the Emperor.[26]

It will come as no surprise that a statesman, who was to become Prefect of the City from 162 to 168, should be at the same time a philosophy teacher. There was nothing extraordinary about this in antiquity: Cicero and Seneca were also statesmen, and they too did not hesitate to present themselves as philosophy teachers. There were two reasons for this: in the first place, ancient philosophy was not restricted to specialists and professionals, so that statesmen could perfectly well live as philosophers and master philosophical discourse. Moreover, as has been well shown by I. Hadot,[27] there was at Rome an old tradition according to which young people attached themselves to older and more experienced personages who initiated them into political life, but also into ethical life. This was in particular the way they studied law—as Cicero did under Scaevola—but young people could also be initiated into the philosophical life in this way. From this perspective, we may say that Junius Rusticus gave Marcus Aurelius private philosophy lessons, and that he was at the same time his friend and his spiritual guide.

The first book of the *Meditations* renders him an extended homage— the longest of any, in fact, except for that accorded to Marcus' adoptive father, the emperor Antoninus (I, 7):

From Rusticus. To have had some idea of the need I had to straighten out my moral condition, and to take care of it.

That I did not let myself be dragged into sophistical ambition, or to compose treatises on philosophical theorems, to declaim fine exhortatory speeches, or, finally, to try to strike my audience's imagination by parading myself ostentatiously as a man who practices philosophical exercises, or is generous to a fault.

To have given up rhetoric, poetry, and refined expressions.

Not to walk around in a toga while I'm home, and not to let myself go in such matters.

To write letters simply, just like the letter he himself wrote to my mother from Sinuessa.

To be disposed, with regard to those who are angry with you and offend you, in such a way as to be ready to respond to the first call, and to be reconciled as soon as they themselves wish to return to you.

To study texts with precision, without being content just to skim over them in a general, approximate way; and not to give my assent too quickly to smooth talkers.

To have been able to read the notes taken at the courses of Epictetus, which he lent to me from his own library.

What Marcus learned from Rusticus was thus, in a sense, the opposite of what he had learned from Diognetus. As Epictetus[28] had said, the goal of philosophy is not to wear a cloak, but to reason correctly. Philosophy does not consist in sleeping on the ground, nor in writing dialogues, but in rectifying one's character. It resides neither in sophistry, bookish dissertations, nor pretentious declamations, nor in ostentatiousness, but rather in simplicity. In this text, we can glimpse the conflict that separated Fronto and Rusticus in the orientation of Marcus' education: "To have given up rhetoric, poetry, and refined expressions." Fronto himself referred to this opposition when, declaring himself delighted to see that the new Emperor had spoken eloquently in public, although it had been several years since he had refused to continue his rhetorical studies, he wrote to him: "Of all the people I have known, I have never found anyone gifted with a greater natural gift for eloquence. . . . My dear Rusticus, our Roman, who would give his life or sacrifice it willingly to save your little finger, was then forced to concede—much against his will, and with a disgusted look on his face—that what I used to say about your rhetorical talents was right."[29]

His role as spiritual guide cannot always have been easy for Rusticus. The mention of Rusticus' attitude toward those who got angry with him does seem to be an allusion to the attitude of Marcus himself: in the same first book of his *Meditations,* Marcus thanks the gods for having brought it about that, although he frequently became angry with Rusticus, he never went so far as to do something he might later regret (I, 17, 14). No doubt relations between the two men were stormy, both during Marcus' youth, when Rusticus pointed out to his disciple that he needed to reform his character (I, 7, 1), and during the period when Rusticus was one of the Emperor's advisers. Thus, Rusticus, by his indulgence and his gentleness, showed Marcus the attitude that he too should adopt vis-à-vis those who became irritated with him. It does seem as though one of the Emperor's principal character defects was his tendency to become irritated easily.

Marcus Aurelius does not say a word about the Stoic doctrines taught to him by Junius Rusticus. There is nothing surprising about this, for although the first book of the *Meditations* draws up a list of what the Emperor has received from his parents, his teachers, his friends, and the gods, it is a list of the models and practical advice which have been offered to him, and not the description of a purely intellectual itinerary. From this perspective, however, the mention of the notes taken during the classes of Epictetus is sufficient, for compared to Epictetus, all the Stoic teachers of Marcus' time were mere epigones. As far as Stoicism is concerned, the figure of Epictetus dominated the entire second century. For Marcus, this was the greatest benefit he had received from Rusticus, for his *Meditations* were to be no more than variations—often superbly orchestrated—on themes proposed by the philosopher-slave.

The reading of "Aristo"

Conversions are often thought to be events that happen instantaneously in unexpected circumstances. History is filled with anecdotes of this kind, whether they be about Polemon, after a night of debauchery, stumbling by chance into the class of the Platonic philosopher Xeno-crates; Augustine hearing a child's voice telling him to "take this and read it"; or Saul blinded on the road to Damascus. It would be nice to find the traces of a sudden conversion to philosophy in the case of our philoso-pher-emperor as well, and they have long been thought to have been discovered in a letter from Marcus to his teacher Fronto,[30] in which he says that he is so upset that he is sad and is no longer eating.

At the beginning of this letter, Marcus mentions—in a half-joking tone and without entering into details—a discussion he had had with his friend Aufidius Victorinus, Fronto's son-in-law. Aufidius is bursting with pride at having been a judge during an arbitration; he boasts—certainly less than seriously—that he is the most just of all the men who had come to Rome from Umbria, and he considers himself superior to Marcus Aurelius, who is only an assessor and is happy just to sit and yawn beside the judge. As Caesar—we learn from the rest of the letter that Marcus was twenty-five years old at the time—Marcus had to assist the emperor Antoninus in his judicial activity, and it is to this function that Aufidius is probably alluding.[31]

After telling this story, Marcus moves on to another topic. Fronto is coming to Rome, intending, as was his custom, to check on his pupil's literary work. To be sure, Marcus is happy at the thought of his master's visit, but he is extremely upset that he has not read the texts Fronto had assigned to him (Plautus and Cicero, it would seem), and especially that he has not written a rhetorical argument in which he was to plead for both the pro and the contra side.

The reason for his falling behind, says Marcus, is his reading of Aristo:

> Aristo's books are a joy for me, and at the same time a torture. They
> are a joy, in that they teach me better things; but when they show
> me to what extent my inner dispositions *(ingenium)* are distant from
> these better things, then all too often your disciple blushes and is
> angry with himself because, at the age of twenty-five, I have not yet
> assimilated into my soul any of the salutary dogmas and purest
> reasonings. This is why I am tormented, angry, and jealous, and I no
> longer eat.

In the third part of his letter, Marcus announces to Fronto that he is
going to follow the advice of an ancient orator: under certain circumstances, the laws must be allowed to sleep. He will therefore let Aristo's
books sleep a little, and devote himself to the rhetorical work he had
promised his teacher. However, in his current state of mind, it would be
impossible for him to argue simultaneously for and against some matter—that is, we are to understand, as if the justice or injustice of the
matter in question were indifferent to him.

Traditionally, this letter has been considered as the story of Marcus'
conversion, which would thus have occurred at the age of twenty-five,
and the Aristo spoken of here has consequently been identified with
Aristo of Chios, a Stoic of the third century B.C. On this interpretation, it
was the reading of this author which brought about this sudden transformation.

E. Champlin has recently expressed his doubts about this interpretation.[32] This author starts off from the observation that the beginning and
end of the letter allude to jurisprudence, with the beginning evoking
Aufidius' pride as a judge, and the end speaking, à propos of Aristo's
books, of "letting the laws sleep," and he concludes that the middle part
of the letter is also to be interpreted in the context of jurisprudence. The
books mentioned by Marcus would therefore be those not of Aristo of
Chios, but of Titus Aristo, a Roman jurisconsult of the time of Trajan,
whose ascetic image had been evoked in one of the letters of Pliny the
Younger. When he describes the effect made on him by these works,
therefore, Fronto's student is not at all speaking of his regrets at not yet
being a philosopher, but of his sadness at not yet having sufficiently
studied jurisprudence. This is why at the end of the letter, the books of
Aristo are identified with the laws which must sometimes be allowed to
sleep.

This interpretation has been criticized by R. B. Rutherford, H. Görgemanns, and myself.[33] In the first place, it seems completely unlikely that, at the age of twenty-five, Marcus could cry out, à propos of some books on jurisprudence: "At the age of twenty-five, I have not yet assimilated into my soul any of the salutary dogmas and the purest reasonings," and that he could speak of the distance of his "inner dispositions" as compared to the ideal he has discovered. Moreover, the irritation, sadness, and loss of appetite,[34] even when we take rhetorical amplification into account, would seem highly exaggerated if they were the result of a temporary passion for jurisprudence.

Second, it is somewhat facile to attempt to interpret the letter as if it dealt with the one theme of jurisprudence, and with that theme alone. The story of Aufidius Victorinus forms a whole, independent of what follows it. Finally, the formula "to let the laws sleep" was a proverbial expression,[35] meaning that, in cases of serious crises, we must sometimes resign ourselves to silencing our moral principles.

Champlin bases his argument on the fact that, already in antiquity, all the works of Aristo of Chios were considered to be apocryphal. To be sure, it is virtually certain that this philosopher, like many others from Socrates down to Epictetus, gave only oral instruction and wrote nothing. Yet the list of his "works" as it existed in antiquity enumerated, for the most part, such titles as *hypomnēmata, scholai,* and *diatribai,* which designated notes taken during class by students.[36] This is also how the teachings of Epictetus have come down to us: thanks to the notes taken by Arrian, a statesman of the beginning of the second century A.D. It is not impossible that Marcus had access to these notes taken at Aristo's classes, or to extracts from the letter preserved in the Stoic schools. He may also have read a collection of "Comparisons" *(Homoiōmata)* by the same Aristo, which was popular down to the end of antiquity, and which moreover does seem authentic, since it accords with what we know of Aristo's teaching from other sources. For instance, we know that he considered dialectics to be useless, and we find sayings in this collection which illustrate this view. The reasonings of the dialecticians, says Aristo, are like spiders' webs: completely useless, but ingenious. Those who conduct advanced studies of dialectics are like people eating crayfish: they struggle with a lot of shell for very little nourishment. Dialectics is like mud on the road: it is completely useless, and it makes those who walk fall down. We should also note the following remark on the brevity of life: the time and life accorded to men are very short; sleep, like a tutor, takes away half of it from us.[37] It should be noted as well that

Marcus could have known Aristo through Cicero and Seneca, who had spoken about him.[38]

In the final analysis, however, our problem is not that of knowing which Aristo Marcus read. According to the testimony of Pliny, the jurisconsult Titus Aristo used to live like a philosopher, and he too can perfectly well, after all, have written philosophical works. The only thing we can say with certainty is that the letter reveals the complete upheaval that his reading of philosophical books brought about in Marcus.

It is nevertheless difficult to admit that it was the mere reading of Aristo of Chios—if the books in question were genuinely by him—that brought about Marcus' conversion and had a considerable influence on his thought, for the characteristics which, according to ancient tradition, distinguished the teaching of Aristo of Chios are not found in the *Meditations* of Marcus Aurelius. On this point, I must correct an interpretation which I had proposed in a previous study, and I shall return later to this doctrinal problem.[39]

Marcus states quite clearly in the first book of his *Meditations* that the decisive influence on him came from his reading of the *Discourses* of Epictetus, which Junius Rusticus had obtained for him. We must imagine Marcus' conversion rather as a slow evolution, brought about by his frequenting of Junius Rusticus, and of other philosophers of whom I shall speak shortly. Besides, we must not forget that many of Marcus' letters to Fronto are lost. It is probable that, in other missives, the student let his teacher know that he was becoming more and more detached from rhetoric, and that he wanted to devote himself to the improvement of his inner dispositions. He tried to do so with delicacy, and a bit of self-deprecating irony, as in the present letter. Marcus' reading of Aristo, whoever he may have been, represents only a moment and a milestone in a long process. Marcus certainly read many other authors, just as he listened to different philosophy teachers. What is of interest here, however, is that the first evidence we have of his adherence to philosophy may be dated approximately from his twenty-fifth year.

Professors and friends

In addition to Junius Rusticus, Marcus and the ancient historians name other philosophy teachers, in particular Apollonius of Chalcedon and Sextus of Chaeronea. Junius Rusticus was the spiritual guide who was very close to his disciple, whereas Apollonius and Sextus were professors in charge of a school, where Marcus had to go hear their lectures. According to the *Historia Augusta,* Apollonius—whom the ancient historians depict as a Stoic—refused to come to the palace to give lessons to his royal student: "The disciple must come to the master," he is supposed to have said, "and not the master to the disciple." The emperor Antoninus Pius, who had had him sent for at great expense from distant Chalcedon to teach the young Caesar Stoicism, remarked on this occasion[40] that it was easier to get Apollonius to come from Chalcedon to Rome than to get him to come from his house to the palace.

In the first book of the *Meditations* (I, 8), Marcus mentions Apollonius immediately after Rusticus. Here again, Marcus makes no allusion to the content of Apollonius' teaching; rather, what he retains from his teacher are moral attitudes and practical advice: on freedom; on the art of reconciling extremes—for example, to come to a decision after lengthy reflection, but without putting it off; to be on the alert but at the same time relaxed;[41] not to consider oneself bound by the favors one has received, but not to disdain them either. In Marcus' eyes, Apollonius was a teacher who did not give himself the airs of a great professor. He did not consider the experience and teaching skills he had acquired to be his main qualities, and he did not go in for nitpicking when it came to the explanation of texts. When Apollonius died before Marcus became emperor, the latter was deeply grieved, and wept abundantly. The courtiers reproached Marcus for his demonstration of affection, probably because they considered his philosophical pretensions to be a joke, and wanted to show him that he was being unfaithful to his own principles. However, the emperor Antoninus Pius said to them: "Let him be a man. Neither philosophy nor the Empire can uproot affections."[42]

Marcus, then, attended the school of Apollonius while he was still a young Caesar. It seems, however, that it was after he became emperor, when Marcus was already growing old, that he attended the lectures of Sextus of Chaeronea. The latter was, according to the *Historia Augusta,*[43] a Stoic, whereas the collection known as the *Souda*[44] calls him a skeptic, no doubt confusing him with the famous skeptic Sextus Empiricus. According to the *Souda,* Marcus frequently took Sextus along as his assessor when he had trials to judge. The story was told that a certain Lucius, a philosopher of Marcus' time famous for his uninhibited speech, asked Marcus why he went to Sextus' school. Marcus replied: "Learning is a good thing, even for one who is growing old. From Sextus the philosopher I shall learn what I do not yet know." Lucius raised his hands skyward: "Oh Zeus," he cried, "the aging Emperor of the Romans is hanging tablets around his neck in order to go to school, while my king Alexander died at the age of thirty-two!"[45]

Sextus also appears in the first book of Marcus' *Meditations* (I, 9), right after Apollonius. Among other things, what Marcus retained from Sextus were his benevolence, the way in which he directed his household, the model he provided of a life in accordance with nature, his simple gravity, his gift of guessing his friends' feelings, his patience, his ability to adapt himself to each person, and to join together impassibility and tenderness. At the same time, however, Marcus also evokes part of Sextus' teachings, for instance his ability to set in order "the fundamental principles *(dog-mata)* necessary for life, with evidence and method," and above all "the idea of a life in conformity with nature." This last detail does seem to confirm that Sextus was a Stoic.

We have no way of knowing whether there were any differences between the teachings of Apollonius and those of Sextus. It is likely that there were few, and that the Stoics of the time were all more or less dependent upon the teachings of Musonius Rufus and his student Epictetus. Fronto, at least, considered that the famous philosophers of his day—Euphrates, Dion, Timocrates, and Athenodotus—were all disciples of Musonius Rufus.[46] Besides, if Marcus followed a regular course of study in the schools of Apollonius and of Sextus, this means that he studied the three parts of philosophy: not only ethics, but also the theory of nature and dialectics. When, in a letter to Marcus, Fronto reproaches him[47] for studying dialectics and the refutation of sophisms, it is perhaps not a case of rhetorical exaggeration.

Apart from these philosophers in charge of schools, whose classes Marcus attended, we find among his teachers Roman statesmen who professed philosophy. It seems to me that this is clearly apparent from the plan of the first book of the *Meditations,* in which Marcus evokes successively his parents; the educators he had during his childhood, in particular Diognetus; the dominant figure of his spiritual guide Junius Rusticus, who, for Marcus, was linked to his conversion to philosophy; Apollonius and Sextus, the two professors whose schools he attended; Alexander the Grammarian and Fronto, his grammar and rhetoric teachers; and Alexander the Platonist,[48] a rhetorician who became Marcus' secretary for Greek correspondence about 170. The Emperor considered the last-named figure as a "friend," and retained from him some lessons about moral conduct.

The three names which follow—Catulus, Severus, and Maximus—

form a group not of professors but of friends. They were no doubt older men who, like Junius Rusticus, either were statesmen or least had had a political career, but who also had an influence on the development of Marcus' philosophical life. The Maximus in question was Claudius Maximus, proconsul of Africa and philosopher, whom Apuleius mentions in his *Apology*. The *Historia Augusta* presents Claudius Maximus and Cinna Catulus as Stoics, and there is no good reason to doubt this testimony, since the same *Historia Augusta* is perfectly well aware that Severus—that is, Claudius Severus Arabianus, consul in 146—was an Aristotelian.[49] The son of this individual, also a consul, was also an Aristotelian; this is explicitly stated by Galen,[50] who tells how Severus' son used to attend the public sessions of anatomy, with commentary, which the famous doctor had organized for the Roman nobility.[51]

Marcus then goes on to evoke the Emperor Antoninus (I, 16), of whom Marcus paints, as it were, the portrait of the ideal prince that he himself would have liked to be. Philosophy is not absent from this description, for Antoninus is compared to Socrates, who was able both to enjoy pleasures and to abstain from them, according to the circumstances.

Book I concludes with Marcus recalling all the benefits he has received from the gods, foremost among which, he says, were his encounters with the philosophers Apollonius, Rusticus, and Maximus. The final lines of this first book do seem to allude to chapter 7, in which the Emperor had expressed his gratitude to Rusticus for having dissuaded him from sophistical ambition, bookish dissertations, and pretentious declamations, and for having thus revealed to him that philosophy was a way of life.

According to his own testimony in Book I, then, it was to Junius Rusticus that Marcus owed his discovery of true philosophy and of the thought of Epictetus. The Stoic teachings of Apollonius and of Sextus were then added to this decisive contribution, while from his "friends" Alexander the Platonist, Claudius Maximus, Claudius Severus, and Cinna Catulus he received the advice and the examples which helped him to live his philosophical life.

The philosopher-emperor

When, on March 7, 161, Marcus became emperor, it was an unexpected and extraordinary event. Rome now had an emperor who professed to be a philosopher—not only that, but a Stoic philosopher. Fronto, for one, was less than reassured to see such a man governing the Empire: philosophy, he felt, could be a bad inspiration. In a letter to Aufidius Victorinus about a juridical problem Marcus was facing concerning the will of his extremely wealthy aunt Matidia, Fronto wrote: "I was greatly afraid that his philosophy might persuade him to make the wrong decision."[52] For Fronto, moreover, Stoic philosophy as Marcus understood it was the enemy of eloquence, which Fronto held to be indispensable for a sovereign. He wrote to the Emperor:

> Even should you attain the wisdom of Cleanthes or of Zeno, you shall still be obliged, like it or not, to wear the purple pallium, and not that of the philosophers, made of coarse wool.[53]

". . . and so," we are to understand, "you are darned well going to have to speak in public, and remember my rhetoric classes."

Throughout the years in which Marcus was weighed down by the heavy burdens of the Empire, Fronto was to become the advocate of common sense, as opposed to philosophical rigor. For example, he advised the Emperor to relax and take a real vacation during his stay on the coast at Alsium: "Even your Chrysippus himself, they say, used to get plastered every day."[54] When Fronto speaks of "your Chrysippus," by the way, it should be noted that although some modern historians—no doubt fond of paradoxes—have wondered whether or not Marcus considered himself a Stoic,[55] his friend Fronto certainly had no such doubts. When he speaks of the Emperor's philosophy, he spontaneously brings up the great names of Stoicism: Cleanthes, Zeno, and Chrysippus. It is clear that Marcus made no secret of his Stoic affinities.

Sometimes, Fronto is content to smile at the Emperor's infatuation: in keeping with his dogmas *(instituta tua),* says Fronto, Marcus must have remained imperturbable in a situation in which his life was threatened.[56] On another occasion, speaking about the Emperor's children whom he had just visited, Fronto observed that one of them was holding a piece of black bread in his hand, just like a real philosopher's son.[57]

The people, both in Rome and throughout the Empire, seem to have been aware that the Emperor was a philosopher. Thus when, during his reign, at the height of the Danubian wars, Marcus was forced to enlist the gladiators, the current joke in Rome was that Marcus wanted to make the people renounce their pleasures and constrain them to philosophy.[58] In this regard, the dedications of the *Apologies* that some Christian apologists used to send to the Emperor are interesting. The emperors' titles usually included the names they gave themselves after a victory, but in Marcus' case we see that the Christian apologist Athenagoras added the title of "philosopher" to the list: "To the Emperors Marcus Aurelius Antoninus and Lucius Aurelius Commodus, Armenians, Sarmatians, and above all philosophers." Here Commodus, Marcus' unworthy son, benefits from his father's reputation. The same holds true for Marcus' adoptive brother Lucius Verus, in the dedication—unfortunately corrupt in its present state—which Justin placed at the beginning of his *Apology*. In any case, Marcus, then still a Caesar, is called "philosopher" in it, together with Lucius Verus. The reason these dedications mention the title of "philosopher" is that the Apologists' arguments ran as follows: Christianity is a philosophy—indeed the best of all philosophies. Therefore, a philosopher-emperor must tolerate it.

In order to govern, the Emperor surrounded himself with philosophers. I have already spoken of his Stoic "friends": Junius Rusticus, consul in the year 162, Prefect of Rome around 165; Claudius Maximus, proconsul of Africa; and Cinna Catulus. But there were not only Stoics; there were also convinced Aristotelians like Claudius Severus, consul in 173 and Marcus' son-in-law, as well as all those whom Galen mentions in the context of his sessions of dissection. Above all, there was the circle which gravitated around the Peripatetic philosopher Eudemus of Pergamon: Sergius Paulus, consul in 168, proconsul of Asia in 166–167, Prefect of Rome around 168; Flavius Boethius, Governor of Palestinian Syria around 166–168, who had been the student of the Peripatetic Alexander of Damascus, and finally M. Vetulenus Civica Barbarus, consul in 157, who had accompanied Marcus' daughter Lucilla on her trip to Antioch, where she was to marry Lucius Verus.[59]

Galen's testimony allows us to glimpse an intense philosophical activity in the circles of the Roman aristocracy of Marcus' time, and it must be emphasized once more that these philosophical statesmen were not amateurs, vaguely interested in philosophical doctrines, but that they had consciously chosen their philosophical school. Some were enthusiastic Aristotelians, others Stoics. Thus, it was not just one philosopher who governed the Empire at that time, but several philosophers. Galen recounts, moreover, that there was a radical opposition between the court of Marcus Aurelius and that of his adoptive brother Lucius Verus. Around Marcus, it was the fashion to have one's head shaved, Stoic-style: the poet Persius had referred to the adepts of this school as "sheared youths,"[60] who slept and ate but little. At Lucius Verus' court, by contrast, the fashion was to wear one's hair long; and Lucius used to call

Marcus' entourage "mimologoi," or mimes, probably because he thought they were playing at being philosophers in order to imitate the Emperor.[61] Cassius Dio, for his part, writes that under the reign of Marcus Aurelius, many people gave the appearance of being philosophers, in the hopes of attracting the Emperor's liberality.[62]

We have so far attempted, albeit too briefly, to glimpse how Marcus became a philosopher. We now must ask ourselves how he came to write the *Meditations*.

2

A FIRST GLIMPSE OF

THE *MEDITATIONS*

❧

The fate of a text

In our time, now that the printing and distribution of books are banal, everyday operations, we no longer realize to what extent the survival of any work of antiquity represented an almost miraculous adventure. If, after having been dictated or written onto relatively fragile materials, and then having been more or less disfigured by copyists' mistakes, a text managed to survive until the birth of printing, it was only because it had the good fortune not to be burned in one of the numerous library fires of antiquity, or else simply did not fall into useless pieces. The odyssey of Marcus Aurelius' *Meditations* seems to have been particularly risky.

In all probability, the Emperor wrote for himself and his own private use, rather than by dictation. At his death, the notes Marcus wrote in this way were saved and conserved by a family member, a friend, or an admirer. Was it ever published, that is to say, copied down and distributed to bookstores? It is difficult to say. Some scholars have thought that they recognize analogies between the *Meditations* and the speech which, according to the historian Cassius Dio, writing a few years after the Emperor's death, Marcus delivered before his soldiers on the occasion of the rebellion of Avidius Cassius.[1] In fact, however, the analogies in expression are not very specific; these were formulas which were fairly widespread in the philosophical and literary tradition.

It does seem that, two centuries after Marcus, the philosopher Themistius knew of the existence of the work: he speaks of *paraggelmata*[2] or "exhortations" written by Marcus. The historian Aurelius Victor and the *Historia Augusta* claim that Marcus, before leaving on his expedition to the Danubian front, had publicly set forth the precepts of his philosophy in the form of a series of exhortations.[3] This is an interesting detail, for it reveals that the writing of the *Meditations* was linked in a confused way with the wars against the Germans, which is not completely false. Much later, in the fourteenth century, it would be imagined that the work was a book composed with a view to the education of Marcus' son Commodus.[4] In any case, it seems that none of these authors had direct access to the book of which they were speaking.

It was not until the Byzantine tenth century that we find testimonies to the reading and copying of Marcus' works. The great Byzantine lexicon entitled the *Souda,* which dates from that period, contains several extracts from the *Meditations,* and specifies that Marcus Aurelius' work consists of twelve books.[5] In addition, the bishop Arethas, in a letter of 907 addressed to Demetrius, metropolitan of Heraclea, speaks of a copy of the philosopher-emperor's work in his possession, which is readable but in poor condition. He has had it recopied, he writes, and can thus bequeath it to posterity in renewed condition.[6] There are, moreover, several literal quotations from the *Meditations* in Arethas' works.[7] In the Byzantine world, the *Meditations* were read throughout the following centuries.[8]

In the West, we do not find quotations from Marcus until the beginning of the sixteenth century: the *De arte cabalistica* of Johannes Reuchlin, published in 1517, contains quotations of two passages from the *Meditations,* probably taken from a manuscript in Reuchlin's possession.[9] It was not until 1559 that a printed edition appeared, brought out by Andreas Gesner of Zurich. Based on a now-lost manuscript, this edition was accompanied by a Latin translation made by Xylander (Wilhelm Holzmann). Besides this edition, we have only one complete manuscript of the Emperor's works: the *Vaticanus Graecus* 1950, which dates from the fourteenth century.

We can thus surmise that it is only a matter of luck that we happen to know the *Meditations* of Marcus Aurelius. We must admit, however, that in the case of a number of passages—fortunately not very numerous—the state of the text as we now possess it is less than satisfactory; and given the small number of manuscripts, it is difficult to improve upon the text. In order to reestablish the text with the highest degree of probability, therefore, we are sometimes reduced to making conjectures.

The text, is, in any event, rather difficult to understand, and the reader should not be surprised if he finds that the original translation I am proposing is sometimes rather different from other extant translations. Moreover, it is because my interpretation of the thought of Marcus Aurelius is based upon my way of translating the text that I have found it necessary to include lengthy quotations from his work.

Neither in the manuscripts nor in the first edition, moreover, is there any division of the work into chapters; and there are few paragraphs. The first editors and translators who, in the sixteenth and seventeenth centuries, worked with the first edition proposed a variety of divisions; but the modern numeration is that of the Latin translation by Thomas Gataker, published in Cambridge in 1652.[10] Gataker's division, however, is in need of complete revision. Some chapters must be reunited, and, above all, many others must be subdivided, since a number of passages with very different subject matter have been unjustifiably grouped together. The reader should not be surprised, therefore, to encounter the divisions I have introduced into a particular text, which will seem different from those found in the other extant translations.

The title

As we have seen, it was the edition of 1559 which revealed Marcus Aurelius to the West. The work quickly became a huge success, with editions of the Greek text, and translations into Latin and the various European languages, coming fast and furious. Soon, however, the following question arose: under which genre should the work be classified? In antiquity, a book's title allowed its readers to recognize immediately in which category it should be situated. Moreover, it was not usually the philosopher who gave the title to his writings: more often than not, the classes he had written entered his school's library without a title. Then, for convenience, his disciples and successors got the habit of referring to the work by the part of philosophy or the specific question with which it dealt—for example, *Classes on Physics*—sometimes accompanied by the name of the addressee (*Nichomachean Ethics*). No doubt Plato chose the titles of dialogues himself, but they are usually taken from the names of the protagonists of the discussion: *Charmides, Phaedo, Philebus*. A book's title was not then, as it is now, an invention of the author, by means of which he tries to show off his originality and attract the reader by the unusual nature of his formulations, as in *The Bald Soprano, The Dancer and the Chatterton, The Cook and the Man-eater*.[11]

It is highly likely that when Marcus was writing what we now call the *Meditations*, he had no idea of giving a title to these notes intended only for himself. In antiquity, moreover, as long as a book remained unpublished—through a public reading, for instance—it was almost always the case that the author did not give it a title. Thus, we find the physician Galen and the philosopher Plotinus entrusting their texts to friends, without providing them with titles.[12] Their works, which they had given to their entourage, were in the state of what the ancients used to call *hypomnēmata:* that is to say, notes not yet quite revised for publication, and lacking a title. This is all the more true if, as is probably the case, Marcus' work was made up of a collection of strictly personal and private notes. When Arethas[13] (ninth to tenth centuries), to whom we no doubt owe the preservation of our precious text, describes the condition of his manuscript, he merely designates it as "the very profitable book of the Emperor Marcus." The fact that he does not give it a title may well lead us to believe that the manuscript did not bear one. Likewise, the epigram dedicated to Marcus' book, perhaps composed by Theophylactus Simocattes (seventh century), does not give any title.[14] When Arethas wrote his scholia on Lucian, he quotes the work as follows: Marcus in "the ethical writings addressed to himself" *(ta eis heauton Ethika).* The Byzantine dictionary called the *Souda*[15] says of Marcus: "He consigned the rule *(agōgē)* of his personal life in twelve books." Finally, let us recall that Themistius, in the third century, made extremely vague allusions to some *paraggelmata,* or "exhortations" of Marcus Aurelius.

The Vatican manuscript gives no title to the Emperor's work. Some manuscript collections of extracts from it do bear the notice: *ta kat' heauton,* which could be translated: "Writing concerning Himself," or "Private Writing."

After the publication of the Greek text in 1559, various translations, corresponding to various theories and interpretations, were given to the work. Xylander's translation, which accompanied the Greek text in 1559, proposed the title *De seipso seu vita sua* ("On Himself or on His Life"). In the editions of Strasburg (1590) and of Lyon (1626), the title was *De vita sua* ("On his life"). When Meric Casaubon published his Graeco-Latin edition in London in 1643, he preferred the title *De seipso et ad seipsum* ("About Himself and to Himself"); but when the English translation appeared in 1634, he had entitled it *Meditations concerning himselfe.* Thomas Gataker, another English humanist of the same period, placed the following formula at the beginning of his Latin translation with commentary: *De rebus suis sive de eis quae ad se pertinere censebat* ("On His Private Affairs, or the Matters which He Thought Concerned Him").

Thus, the work was to receive all kinds of titles, in all sorts of languages. In Latin: *De officio vitae* ("On the Duty of Life"); *Pugillaria* ("Tablets"); *Commentaria quae ipse sibi scripsit* ("Notes which He Wrote for Himself"). In French: *Pensées morales* ("Moral Thoughts"); *Pensées*

("Thoughts"); *A moi-même* ("To Myself"). In English: *Conversations with Himself; Meditations; Thoughts; To Himself; Communings with Himself;* and in German, *Betrachtungen über sich selbst* or *mit sich selbst* ("Reflections on Himself" or "with Himself"); *Selbstbetrachtungen* ("Reflections on Himself"); *Wege zu sich selbst* ("Paths toward Himself").

Hypotheses on the work's literary genre

Many historians and readers of the *Meditations* did not understand, and still do not understand, what Marcus Aurelius' intentions were in writing them down. Consequently, they have projected back upon him, in a totally anachronistic way, the prejudices and literary habits of their own time. The first editor, "Xylander" (Holzmann), noting that the text he was publishing lacked the fine structure of a dialogue by Plato or a treatise by Cicero, had already conjectured that the *Meditations,* in the state in which they existed in the manuscript he was editing, were only loose extracts from the works of Marcus Aurelius, and that the Emperor's book had come down to us mutilated, incomplete, and in utter disorder.[16] It seemed to him inconceivable that Marcus could have left these obscure, disorderly texts to posterity, since in this period the systematic treatise was considered the perfect form of philosophical production.

Meric Casaubon, who translated Marcus Aurelius into English and Latin in the seventeenth century (1634 and 1643 respectively), seems to have been much better informed about the variety of literary genres in antiquity. In the Preface to his Latin translation, he reminds his readers that there then existed the literary genre of the aphorism—used, for example, by Theognis and Phocylides—which consisted in expressing one's thoughts in the form of short sayings; he added that Epictetus' *Manual,* as composed by Arrian, was presented entirely in this way. Moreover, he adds, if one is able to discern the real unities that make up the text, one will be better able to understand both the flow of ideas within each passage and the themes which often recur throughout the work.

Besides, Casaubon went on, we must not forget that Marcus was writing for himself, and was not seeking clarity, as an author would who was addressing himself to the public. This gives Casaubon[17] the opportunity to criticize the custom that had arisen in his time of quoting Marcus' work by the title *De vita sua* ("On His Life"). True, he writes, some emperors—such as Augustus—did write books about their lives; but their subject was the acts and events of their public and private lives.

With Marcus this is not the case; rather, as the *Souda* indicated, what we have is a writing dealing with "the rule of his own life." Some editors had expressed this idea by means of the title *De officio suo* ("On His Duty"); but this did not render the specificity of the title *Eis heauton*, which, in order to be rendered with exactitude, must be translated as *De seipso et ad seipsum* ("About Himself and to Himself"). Thus, the work is a dialogue Marcus had with himself and about himself. Casaubon here reminds the reader that Solon was supposed to have written some "Instructions for Himself" *(hypothēkas eis heauton)*; above all, he reminds the reader that, for the Platonists and the Stoics, the "self" was the soul or the spirit.

Thomas Gataker defines the specific character of the work even more precisely. He opposes the *Discourses* of Epictetus—transmitted to us by his disciple Arrian, who was thus their editor, just as the Evangelists were in the case of Christ—to the writings of Marcus, which emanated from his own notes. Gataker uses the word *adversaria,* meaning "that which is always in front of one," or "the rough draft which one always has handy." The Emperor's mind, says Gataker, was always devoted to philosophical occupations, and he developed the habit of writing down the thoughts that came to him in the course of his meditations, without feeling compelled to put them into any kind of order. They were arranged solely in accordance with the places and times in which he had either composed them himself, or encountered them in the course of his readings and conversations. This is shown, moreover, by such remarks as "In the Land of the Quades" and "At Carnutum," placed at the beginning of Books II and III. This resulted in some inconsistencies and repetitions, and a style that is often elliptical or abrupt: sufficient to allow the Emperor to recall such-and-such an idea, but liable to lead to a great deal of obscurity. These were notes intended for Marcus' personal use.[18]

As early as the beginning of the seventeenth century, however, the philologist Caspar Barth,[19] writing in 1624, emphasized that traces of organization, and sometimes even long chains of reasoning, could be found in Marcus' writings. Barth thus returned to the theory of Xylander, according to which the text, in the state in which it had been preserved, represented mere extracts *(eclogai)* taken from a vast systematic treatise on ethics which the Emperor was supposed to have composed.

In the eighteenth century, an analogous opinion was set forth by Jean-Pierre de Joly, who edited and translated the *Meditations* in 1742 and again in 1773. Marcus, said Joly, had composed a systematic treatise on ethics, written on tablets which were dispersed after his death; an editor then published them in their state of disorder. The task of the modern editor, then, was to rediscover the systematic order of the treatise; and this is what Joly attempted to do by publishing a systematic presentation of the *Meditations,* divided into thirty-five sections.[20]

In the twentieth century, A. S. L. Farquharson published, in 1944, an edition, English translation, and commentary on Marcus' text which was remarkable in every respect. He took up the hypothesis of Barth and Joly from another angle: for a period of ten to fifteen years, he thought, Marcus had accumulated materials of every variety with a view to the composition of "a work of consolation and of encouragement." Indeed, certain meditations do show signs of highly conscientious literary composition. After the Emperor's death, it was perhaps a secretary who made a choice from among these notes. Their present disorder could be the result either of the fact that the secretary left them as they were, or that he introduced into them an order which does not satisfy us, or the fact that the text has been mutilated or disorganized by scribes through the course of the years. In any event, Marcus' intention was to write a handbook of useful advice for the philosophical life. In Farquharson's view, Marcus' *Meditations* can be compared to the *Meditations* of Guigues of Chartres, the well-known *Religio Medici* of Thomas Browne, and above all the *Pensées* of Pascal.[21]

The apparent lack of order of the *Meditations* did not disturb nineteenth-century readers at all. In the century of Romanticism, it was thought that the work was the Emperor's own "journal intime." "It is probable," wrote Renan,[22] "that Marcus kept a private diary of his inner states starting from an early age. In it, he would inscribe in Greek the maxims to which he had recourse in order to fortify himself, reminiscences from his favorite authors, passages from those moralists who most impressed him, the principles which had sustained him throughout the day, and sometimes the reproaches which his scrupulous conscience thought it had to address to itself." I should state right away that, if we understand by "diary" notes which one writes for oneself and which accumulate day after day, then we can indeed say, with G. Misch in his *History of Autobiography,*[23] that the Emperor did write a "diary," or, in the words of P. Brunt[24] in his excellent study entitled "Marcus Aurelius in his *Meditations,*" a "spiritual diary." If, however, we understand by "diary" a writing to which one consigns the outpourings of one's heart and spiritual states, then the *Meditations* are not a "diary," and the fact that Marcus Aurelius wrote his *Meditations* does not allow us, as Renan claimed, to know whether or not the Emperor had an uneasy soul. Renan was too much inclined to imagine the philosopher-emperor as a kind of Amiel or Maurice de Guérin, expressing their worries and sufferings every day. Following Renan, twentieth-century historians have taken pleasure in the image of Marcus finding consolation from reality by exhaling his resignation, pessimism, or resentment into his *Meditations*.

A strange work

We must try to imagine the state in which the first humanists discovered the manuscript containing the copy of Marcus Aurelius' book. They were faced with a work without a title, which began with a list of the examples or advice which Marcus had received from his parents, his teachers, his friends, and from the emperor Antoninus Pius, as well as a list of the favors which the gods had accorded to him. After this enumeration—in the manuscript, at any rate, which was used for the establishment of the *editio princeps*—one could read a note which was both geographical and chronological in nature: "Written in the land of the Quades, on the banks of the Gran." Then there came a series of reflections, several pages long, which sometimes contained divisions, marked by a paragraph and by capital letters, which do not always correspond to our modern-day division of the work into chapters. At the beginning of what we now call chapter III, we find the following indication: "Written in Carnutum." The reflections then begin again, and continue until the end of the work. In the *Vaticanus,* the books are not numbered: the most this manuscript contains is a two-line separation between what are today Books I and II; between today's Books II and III; between today's Book IV and Book V; between today's Book VIII and Book IX; and a dividing mark between today's Book XI and Book XII. This means that the divisions between Books III and IV; V and VI; VI and VII; VII and VIII; and IX and X are not indicated.

Who is responsible for remarks like "in the land of the Quades" or "in Carnutum?" Was it Marcus himself, who wanted to remind himself of the circumstances in which a specific group of notes had been written? Or was it some secretary responsible for preserving the Emperor's documents, who added a kind of tag to the package that had been entrusted to him? The first hypothesis is the more likely; but if so it is, I believe, something unique in the entire history of ancient literature, and well suited to show to what extent we are dealing with writings recorded day by day and linked, not perhaps to precise circumstances, but to the variations in the spiritual state of their author. Did such geographical indications exist among the other books, and did they then become lost? Or was the greater part of the book written at Carnutum? Was it Marcus himself who gave up supplying such indications? We do not know. Did the twelve books which we distinguish today correspond to twelve groups which represented, in the view of their author, sequences of thoughts having their own unity and different from one another? Or was this division purely accidental, due, for instance, to the form and dimensions of the physical materials of Marcus' writing? Again, were the books separated by an editor, either just after Marcus' death, or by Arethas, when he produced an edition of the text in the tenth century? We have seen that the breaks between books, at any rate in the *Vaticanus,* were faintly marked, if not nonexistent.

The contents of the work are rather disconcerting as well. After Book I, which presents an undeniable unity in its evocation of all those, gods and men, to whom Marcus is expressing his gratitude, the rest of the work is nothing but a completely incoherent series—at least in appearance—of reflections which are not even composed in accordance with the rules of the same literary genre. We encounter many very short sentences, often quite striking and well written, for example:

Soon you will have forgotten everything, and soon everyone will have forgotten you (VII, 21).

Everything is ephemeral, that which remembers and that which is remembered (IV, 35).

The best way to get even with them is not to resemble them (VI, 6).

Alongside these short formulas, we find a certain number of longer developments, which vary in length from twenty to sixty lines; they may have the form of a dialogue with a fictitious interlocutor, or of one that Marcus carries out with himself. In them, Marcus exhorts himself to follow a specific moral attitude, or else he discusses certain general philosophical problems: if souls survive after death, for instance, where can they be located (IV, 21)? In most of these passages, whether they are long or short, Marcus' individuality can scarcely be discerned; most of the time, we have to do with exhortations addressed to a moral person. We also find, however, some passages in which Marcus speaks to himself as an Emperor (VI, 30, 1; VI, 44, 6); or in which he speaks of his attitude toward life at court (V, 16, 2; VI, 12; VIII, 9); about the way he must express himself in the Senate (VIII, 30); about his faults (V, 5, 1); or about his entourage (X, 36). He also evokes the people he has known in his life (VIII, 37, 1; X, 31, 1), in imaginatory exercises in the course of which, in order to prepare himself for death, he represents to himself the fragility of all things human, and the continuity of the processes of metamorphosis, which will not spare anyone in his entourage.

In addition to these various literary forms, we must also add two collections of quotations in Books VII (32–51) and XI (22–39). Borrowed from the tragedians, Plato, and Epictetus, they have obviously been chosen for their moral efficacy.

How, then, are we to define this work, which, by its multiple aspects and unusual tone, seems to be the only example of its genre in all of antiquity?

The *Meditations* as personal notes *(hypomnēmata)*

It's time to stop rambling. You will no longer reread the notes *(hypomnēmatia)* that you had taken, the great deeds of the ancient Greeks and the Romans, or the extracts from the works you had been putting aside until your old age (III, 14).

Here we can catch a glimpse of the intellectual activity to which Marcus devoted himself all his life. Already in his youth, when still the student of Fronto, he assiduously copied out extracts from Latin authors.[25] He must later have gone to the trouble of making up "for his old age" an anthology of edifying quotations, of which we can discover traces in some pages of the *Meditations.* He had also put together a historical collection: "the great deeds of the ancient Greeks and Romans." Finally, Marcus also speaks of his "personal notes," using the diminutive word *hypomnē-matia.* It has often been suggested that these notes should be identified with the *Meditations.*[26] It is extremely difficult to give a definitive judgment on this point; nevertheless, with the help of other ancient parallels, we can at any rate imagine the way in which the *Meditations* were composed.

In the first place, it seems that, as he wrote the *Meditations,* Marcus decided to change completely the finality of his literary activity. In Books II and III, we find numerous allusions both to the imminence of death weighing upon Marcus, who was then engaged in the military campaigns of the Danube, and to the urgency of the total conversion he felt he was about to undergo, and the change in his literary activity which would be a necessary result of this:

> Leave your books alone. Don't let yourself be distracted any longer; you can't allow yourself that any more (II, 2, 2).

> Throw away your thirst for reading, so that when you die, you will not be grumbling, but will be in true serenity, thanking the gods from the bottom of your heart (II, 3, 3).

Marcus is no longer to disperse himself by gathering extracts from authors in the course of his readings, for he no longer has time to read. He is no longer, out of intellectual curiosity or speculative interest, to write great quantities of "note-cards," as we would call them nowadays: rather, he is to write only in order to influence himself, and concentrate on the essential principles (II, 3, 3):

> Let these thoughts be enough, if they are life-principles *(dogmata)* for you.

Marcus, then, is to keep on writing. From now on, however, he will write only efficacious thoughts: that is, those which totally transform his way of living.

As he wrote these texts, which were to become our *Meditations,* Marcus no doubt used these "note-cards" which he was afraid he would no longer have the time to reread; just as he no doubt had recourse to his collections of extracts in order to take from them the quotations from authors which he reproduced in several books of the *Meditations.*

Formally, then, Marcus' literary activity did not change. He continued to write down for himself all kinds of notes and reflections *(hypomnē-mata);* but the finality of these intellectual exercises had become completely modified. From the point of view of the imminence of death, one thing counts, and one alone: to strive always to have the essential rules of life present in one's mind, and to keep placing oneself in the fundamental disposition of the philosopher, which consists essentially in controlling one's inner discourse, in doing only that which is of benefit to the human community, and in accepting the events brought to us by the course of the Nature of the All.

Thus, the *Meditations* belong to that type of writing called *hypomnēmata* in antiquity, which we could define as "personal notes taken on a day-to-

day basis." This was a very widespread practice, and on this point we
have the remarkable testimony of Pamphila, a married woman who lived
at the time of Nero in the first century A.D., who had published her
hypomnēmata. In the introduction she had placed at the beginning of this
collection—now unfortunately lost—she tells the reader that, during the
course of thirteen years of married life, which "was not interrupted for a
day nor even for an hour," she noted down what she learned from her
husband, from visitors who came to the house, and from the books she
read. "I wrote them down," she said, "in the form of notes *(hypomnēmata),* in no special order, and without sorting them out and distinguishing them according to their subject matter. Rather, I wrote them down
at random, in the order in which each matter presented itself to me." She
could, she adds, have ordered them by subject matter with a view to their
publication, but she found variety and the absence of a plan more pleasant and more graceful. All that she wrote under her own name was an
overall introduction and, apparently, a few transitional passages. The
notes she had gathered together dealt with the lives of philosophers,
history, rhetoric, and poetry.[27]

In the following century, the Latin author Aulus Gellius also published
his personal notes, under the title of *Attic Nights.* In his preface, he writes:
"Whether I was reading a Greek or a Latin book, or whether I had heard
someone say something worthy of being remembered, I jotted down
what interested me, of whatever kind it was, without any order, and I
then set it aside, in order to support my memory [this is the etymological
meaning of *hypomnēmata*]". The book he is now offering to the public,
he adds, will preserve the same variety and disorder as his notes.[28]

At the beginning of his treatise *On the Tranquillity of the Soul,* Plutarch
explains to the work's addressee that, since he was in a hurry to hand
over his manuscript to the mail-courier who was just about to leave for
Rome, he had not had the time to put together a well-written treatise,
but had merely communicated to him the notes *(hypomnēmata)* that he
had gathered together on this theme.[29]

It is probable that many educated people—and especially philosophers—were in the habit of making such collections of all kinds of notes
for their personal use: both in order to inform themselves, and also in
order to form themselves; that is, to ensure their spiritual progress. It was
no doubt with this goal in mind that Plutarch had put together his
collection on the tranquillity of the soul.

This, then, is the genre of writings among which we should place the
Meditations of Marcus Aurelius. It is important to emphasize, however,

that in his case, most of these notes were exhortations to himself, or a dialogue with himself, usually composed with the utmost care.

Inner dialogue gave rise to a highly particular literary genre, of which we know only one written and published example: the *Soliloquies* of Augustine. For him the writer's ego is no longer situated—as is often the case with Marcus—at the level of Reason, exhorting the soul. Rather, Augustine's ego takes the place of the soul listening to Reason:

> For a long time, I had being going over a thousand thoughts in my mind; indeed, for many days I had been ardently searching for myself and my good, and for that evil which I had to avoid, when suddenly I was told (was it I who was speaking, or someone, either outside me or within me, I do not know; that is precisely what I am trying with all my strength to find out); at any rate, I was told. . . .

What the voice tells Augustine is that he must write down what it is going to make known to him. He himself is to write, not dictate, for it is not fitting to dictate things so intimate: they demand absolute solitude.[30]

Let us pause for a moment and consider this extremely interesting remark. Throughout antiquity, authors either wrote themselves, or else they dictated their works. For instance, we know from Porphyry that Plotinus wrote his treatises by hand.[31] There were many drawbacks to dictation, as was pointed out by that great user of secretaries, St. Jerome: "It is one thing to twirl one's pen around in its ink several times before one writes, and thus to write only that which is worthy of being retained; but it is another to dictate to a secretary everything that comes into one's head, for fear of falling silent, because the secretary is waiting."[32] Augustine, however, allows us to glimpse a wholly other point of view: it is only in the presence of ourselves, he implies, that we can reflect upon that which is most intimate to us. The presence of another, to whom one speaks or dictates, instead of speaking to oneself, makes inner discourse in some way banal and impersonal. This, in all probability, is why Marcus too wrote his *Meditations* in his own hand, as he also did in the case of the letters he wrote to his friends.[33]

Tiziano Dorandi[34] has recently drawn attention to the variety of stages leading to the completion of a literary work in antiquity. As a first stage, the author might compose rough drafts, written on tablets of wax or of wood. Alternatively, he might, either at the outset or after this stage, compose a provisional version of his work. Then, in the third stage, came the definitive revision of the work, which was indispensable before its final publication. Now, Marcus was clearly writing only for himself, and we must imagine that he probably never envisaged this third stage. All our evidence points to the conclusion that Marcus, as he wrote down his thoughts from day to day, always remained at the first stage. He probably used tablets *(pugillares),* or some other medium useful for handwritten notes, such as leaves *(schedae).*[35] At what point was this material copied and corrected by a scribe? Possibly during Marcus' lifetime, for his own personal use. It is also possible, however, and perhaps more probable, that it was after his death; and on this hypothesis we may imagine, without having recourse to the destruction postulated by Joly,[36] that the tablets or leaves may not have been copied down in the precise order in which they were written. It is perhaps not irrelevant in this context that our Book I, which was in all probability written later and independently from the others, was placed at the beginning of the collection. Nevertheless, the essential part seems to be in order. Each book is characterized, at least in part, by a specialized vocabulary and by its emphasis on certain themes; this allows us to suppose that each book has its own unity, and was written during a period when the Emperor's attention was concentrated on a specific question.

Obviously, it is difficult, and even impossible, to obtain a clear idea of what really happened. We must, it would seem, be content with three certainties: first of all, the Emperor wrote *for himself.*[37] Second, he wrote *day by day,* without attempting to write a unified work, destined for the public. This is to say that his works remained in the state of *hypomnēmata* or personal notes, perhaps written on a "mobile" kind of medium like tablets. In the third place, Marcus took the trouble to write down his thoughts, aphorisms, and reflections *in a highly refined literary form,* since it was precisely the perfection of the formulas which could ensure their psychological efficacy and persuasive force.

These characteristics suffice to distinguish the personal notes of Marcus Aurelius from those of Pamphila or of Aulus Gellius, or even from the "note-cards" assembled by Plutarch in order to compose his treatise on the tranquillity of the soul—as well as from the notes taken by Arrian at the classes of Epictetus. It seems, in fact, that unlike these other *hypomnēmata,* the *Meditations* of Marcus Aurelius were spiritual exercises, practiced in accordance with a specific method. We must now explore what this means.

3

THE *MEDITATIONS* AS SPIRITUAL EXERCISES

※※

"Theory" and "practice"

The *Meditations* have only one theme: philosophy. We can see this from passages such as the following:

> What is it that can escort you in order to protect you in this life? Only one thing: philosophy. It consists in keeping your inner god free from pollution and from damage (II, 17, 3).

> Be careful of becoming "caesarized" . . . Keep yourself simple, good, pure, grave, natural, a friend of justice. Revere the gods, be benevolent, affectionate, and firm in accomplishing your duties. Fight in order to remain as philosophy has wished you to be (VI, 30, 1–3).

For the ancients in general, but particularly for the Stoics and for Marcus Aurelius, philosophy was, above all, a way of life. This is why the *Meditations* strive, by means of an ever-renewed effort, to describe this way of life and to sketch the model that one must have constantly in view: that of the ideal good man. Ordinary people are content to think in any old way, to act haphazardly, and to undergo grudgingly whatever befalls them. The good man, however, will try, insofar as he is able, to act justly in the service of other people, to accept serenely those events which do not depend on him, and to think with rectitude and veracity (VII, 54):

> Always and everywhere, it depends on you piously to be satisfied with the present conjunction of events,

to conduct yourself justly toward whatever other people are present, and

to apply the rules of discernment to the inner representation you are having now, so that nothing which is not objective may infiltrate its way into you.

Many of the *Meditations* present these three rules of life—or one or another of them—in a variety of forms. But these practical rules manifest a global attitude, a vision of the world, and a fundamental inner choice, which is expressed in a "discourse," or in universal formulas which Marcus, following Epictetus,[1] calls *dogmata* (Marcus Aurelius II, 3, 3; III, 13, 1; IV, 49, 6). A dogma is a universal principle which founds and justifies a specific practical conduct, and which can be formulated in one or in several propositions. Our word "dogma" has, moreover, retained something of this meaning, for instance in Victor Hugo: "Liberty, Equality, Fraternity: these are dogmas of peace and of harmony. Why should we make them seem frightening?"[2]

In addition to the three rules of life, then, the *Meditations* formulate, in every possible way, those dogmas which express, in discursive form, the indivisible inner disposition that manifests itself in the three rules of action.

Marcus himself gives us good examples of the relationship between general principles and rules of life. We have seen that one of the rules of life he proposes consists in consenting with serenity to events willed by Destiny, which do not depend on us. But he also exhorts *himself*, in the following terms (IV, 49, 6):

On the occasion of everything that causes you sadness, remember to use this "dogma": not only is this not a misfortune, but it is a piece of good fortune for you to bear up under it courageously.

This dogma is deduced from the fundamental dogma of Stoicism, which is the foundation for all Stoic behavior: only moral good, or virtue, is a good, and only moral evil, or vice, is an evil.[3] Marcus formulates this explicitly elsewhere (VIII, 1, 6):

What does happiness consist of? It consists of doing that which the nature of mankind desires. How shall we do this? By possessing those dogmas which are the principles of impulses and of action. Which dogmas? Those which pertain to the distinction of what is good from what is bad: there is no good for mankind but that which renders him just, temperate, courageous and free, and there is no evil for mankind, except that which brings about in him the contrary vices.

Marcus also employs the word *theōrēma* to designate the "dogmas," inasmuch as every art entails principles, and consequently so too does that art of living called philosophy (XI, 5):

What art do you practice? That of being good. How can you practice this except by starting out from theorems, some of which concern the Nature of the All, and others of which deal with the constitution proper to mankind?

Dogmas, as Marcus says (VII, 2), run the risk of dying out, if one does not constantly reignite those inner images, or *phantasiai,* which make them present to us.

Thus, we can say that the *Meditations*—with the exception of Book I—are wholly made up of the repeated, ever-renewed formulation of the three rules of action which we have just seen, and of the various dogmas which are their foundation.

Dogmas and their formulation

These dogmas, or foundational and fundamental rules, were the subject of demonstrations within the Stoic schools. Marcus learned such demonstrations from his Stoic teachers Junius Rusticus, Apollonius, and Sextus, to whom he renders homage in the first book of the *Meditations*. Above all, he read about them in the *Discourses* of Epictetus as collected by Arrian. In his *Meditations,* Marcus mentions "the large number of proofs by which it is demonstrated that the world is like a City," or else the teachings he has received on the subject of pleasure and pain, and to which he has given his assent (IV, 3, 5, 6).

With the aid of these demonstrations, the dogmas imposed themselves upon Marcus with absolute certainty, and he usually restricts himself to formulating them in the form of a simple proposition, as he does in Book II, 1, 3. The nature of the good, he says there, is moral good *(to kalon);* while that of evil is moral evil *(to aischron).* This condensed form is sufficient to evoke the theoretical demonstration of which they were the subject, and it allows the inner disposition which was a result of his clear view of these principles—that is, the resolution to do good—to be re-awakened within his soul. To repeat the dogmas to oneself, or write them down for oneself, is "to retreat," as Marcus says (IV, 3, 1), "not to the countryside, the seashore, or the mountains," but within oneself. It is there that one can find the formulas "which shall renew us." "Let them be concise and essential," Marcus continues, in order that their efficacy be complete. This is why, in order to be ready to apply the three rules of action, Marcus sometimes gathers together a series of chapter-heads *(kephalaia),* extremely brief in form, which constitute an enumeration of points which, by their very accumulation, can increase their psychic efficacy (II, 1; IV, 3; IV, 26; VII, 22, 2; VIII, 21, 2; XI, 18; XII, 7; XII, 8; XII, 26). I cannot quote these lists in their entirety, but I shall take one example (XII, 26) in which eight *kephalaia,* or fundamental points, pro-vide a group of resources with a view to the practice of that rule of action which prescribes that we must serenely accept that which happens to us, but does not depend on our will:

> If you are annoyed at something, it is because you have forgotten:
> (1) that everything happens in accordance with universal Nature;
> (2) that whatever fault was committed is not your concern;
> (3) and, moreover, that everything that happens has always hap-pened thus and will always happen thus, and is, at this very mo-ment, happening thus everywhere;
> (4)how close is the relationship between man and the whole human race: for this is no community of blood or of seed, but of the intellect.
> You have also forgotten:
> (5)that the intellect of each person is God, and that it has flowed down here from above;
> (6) and that nothing belongs to any of us in the strict sense, but that our child, our body and our soul come from above;
> (7)and that everything is a judgment-value;
> (8) and the only thing each of us lives and loses is the present.

All the points presented here in the form of a laconic *aide-mémoire,* which does nothing but evoke demonstrations with which Marcus is familiar from elsewhere, can be found separated from one another throughout the *Meditations:* they are repeated, ruminated upon; but also explained and sometimes demonstrated. If we assemble these series of *kephalaia* (II, 1; IV, 3; IV, 26; VII, 22, 2; VIII, 21, 2; XI, 18; XII, 7; XII,

8; XII, 26) we can thus discover almost all the themes announced or developed in the *Meditations*. By connecting them to the most fundamental dogmas of Stoicism, we can present, in a structured form, the whole ensemble of doctrines which constitute the essential core of the *Meditations*.

From the absolutely primary principle according to which the only good is moral good and the only evil is moral evil (II, 1, 3), it follows that neither pleasure nor pain are evils (IV, 3, 6; XII, 8); that the only thing shameful is moral evil (II, 1, 3); that faults committed against us cannot touch us (II, 1, 3; XII, 26); that he who commits a fault hurts only himself (IV, 26, 3); and that the fault cannot be found elsewhere than within oneself (VII, 29, 7; XII, 26). It further follows that I can suffer no harm whatsoever from the actions of anyone else (II, 1, 3; VII, 22, 2).

From the general principles

1. only that which depends on us can be either good or evil; and
2. our judgment and our assent depend on us (XII, 22),

it follows that the only evil or trouble there can be for us resides in our own judgment; that is to say, in the way we represent things to ourselves (IV, 3, 10; XI, 18, 11); and that people are the authors of their own problems (IV, 26, 2; XII, 8). Everything, therefore, is a matter of judgment (XII, 8; XII, 22; XII, 26). The intellect is independent of the body (IV, 3, 6), and things do not come inside us in order to trouble us (IV, 3, 10). If everything is a matter of judgment, every fault is in fact a false judgment, and proceeds from ignorance (II, 1, 2; IV, 3, 4; XI, 18, 4–5).

In the enumeration of *kephalaia* in Book XI (XI, 18, 2), Marcus tells himself:

Go higher up still, starting from the principle that if we reject atoms, it must be Nature which governs the All.

In the list in Book IV, he says:

Remember the disjunction: either providence or atoms.

These brief mentions of a principle, which it is assumed is known, allow us to glimpse that Marcus is here again alluding to teachings he has received, which placed face to face the Epicurean position (atoms) and the Stoic position (Nature and providence), to conclude in favor of the latter. I shall return to this point. For the moment, suffice it to say that from the dogma that affirms a unity and rationality of the world, many consequences may be drawn, to which Marcus alludes in his series of *kephalaia*. Everything comes from universal Nature and in conformity with the will of universal Nature (XII, 26)—even the malevolence of mankind (XI, 18, 24), which is a necessary consequence of the gift of liberty. Everything occurs in conformity with Destiny (IV, 26, 4): thus, it is in conformity with the order of the universe that all things undergo continuous metamorphosis (IV, 3, 11; XII, 21), but are also ceaselessly repeated (XII, 26), and that we must die (IV, 3, 4; XI, 18, 10). Universal Reason gives form and energy to matter that is docile, but without strength; this is why we must always and everywhere distinguish the causal (reason) and the material (XII, 8; XII, 18). It is from universal Reason that comes that reason which is common to all mankind and assures its relatedness, which is not a community of blood or of seed (II, 1, 3; XII, 26). This is why people are made for one another (II, 1, 4; IV, 3, 4; XI, 18, 1–2).

One last series of *kephalaia* can be grouped around the grandiose vision of the immensity of universal Nature, and the infinity of space and of time (IV, 3, 7; XII, 7). From this perspective, the whole of life seems to be of minuscule duration (VIII, 21, 2; IV, 26, 5; XII, 7); the instant seems infinitesimal (II, 14, 3; XII, 26); the earth seems like a point (IV, 3, 8; VIII, 21, 2); current fame and posthumous glory seem completely vain (IV, 3, 8; VIII, 21, 3; XII, 21; IV, 3, 7), all the more so since they can only be obtained from people who contradict themselves and each other (IV, 3, 8; VII, 21, 3), and whom one cannot respect, if one sees them as they really are (XI, 18, 3).

All these "dogmas" can, then, be deduced from more fundamental dogmas. Yet they all become crystallized around the three rules or disciplines of life, which we have distinguished. The discipline of thought, for example, obviously presupposes the dogmas which concern freedom of judgment; the discipline of action presupposes those which affirm the existence of a community of reasonable beings; and the discipline of consent to events presupposes the dogma of the providence and rationality of the universe. We can glimpse a similar grouping in IV, 3.

Lists of *kephalaia* or fundamental points: such is the first mode of formulation of dogmas in the *Meditations*. Yet these fundamental points are also taken up by themselves and frequently repeated throughout the course of the work. Thus the invitation, formulated in one of the series of *kephalaia* (XII, 8), to discern what is causal in each thing, is repeated eight times in isolated form, without any commentary or explanation, in the body of the *Meditations* (IV, 21, 5; VII, 29, 5; VIII, 11; IX, 25; IX, 37; XII, 10; XII, 18; XII, 29). Likewise, the affirmation "All is judgment," which figures in two lists of *kephalaia* (XII, 8 and XII, 26) is found twice by itself, either without commentary or accompanied by a very brief explanation (II, 15; XII, 22). Above all, the dogma according to which our troubles come only from our judgments, and that things do not penetrate within us (IV, 3, 10), recurs eighteen times in the course of the *Meditations,* sometimes repeated almost word for word, and sometimes in slightly different form (V, 19; VI, 52; VII, 2; VIII, 47; IX, 13; IX, 15; XI, 11; XI, 16; XII, 22; XII, 25; IV, 7; IV, 39, 2; V, 2; VII, 14; VII, 16; VIII, 29; VIII, 40; VIII, 49).

Let us now consider another theme which we have encountered in the series of *kephalaia:* that of the eternal repetition of all things both in universal Nature and in human history (XII, 26, 3). This, too, is a point which is dear to Marcus, and which he goes over indefatigably. It does not matter, he writes, whether one attends the spectacle of the world for a short or a long time, since the totality of being is present at each instant and in each thing. All things are thus *homoeideis;* that is, they have the same content, and therefore repeat themselves infinitely.

From all eternity, all things have identical contents, and pass through the same cycles (II, 14, 1).

Everything is of the same kind, and of identical contents (VI, 37).

From all eternity, all things are produced with identical contents, and for all infinity there will be other things of this kind (IX, 35).

In a sense, a man of forty—if he is not devoid of intelligence—has seen all that has been and all that shall be, once he recognizes that all things have identical contents (XI, 1, 3).

It would be tedious to cite other examples of the many repetitions which one finds all throughout the work. It suffices to note that most of the *Meditations* take up again—often in a highly elaborate and striking form—these various *kephalaia* and dogmas, the list of which Marcus gives us several times in the course of his work.

It is, however, not enough to "retreat," returning frequently to these dogmas to reorient one's actions; after all, in the art of living, we must do nothing which is not in conformity "with the theorems of the art" (IV, 2). Rather, we must often return to their theoretical foundations. Marcus clearly explains this need, in a passage which has been misunderstood by many interpreters (X, 9). Within it, we must distinguish two different lines of thought. The first is a concentrated and brutal description of the unhappiness of the human condition, when it is not guided by reason:

> Buffoonery and bloody struggles; torpor and agitation; the slavery of every day![4]

Then there comes another thought, completely independent from the first, which has to do with the importance of theory:

> All your fine sacred dogmas, which you think without founding them on a science of Nature, and then abandon: they will disappear rapidly. From now on, you must see and practice everything, so that that which is required by the present circumstances is accomplished, but, at the same time, the theoretical foundation of your actions is always present in an efficacious way, and that you always maintain within yourself—latent, but not buried—that self-confidence which is procured by science, applied to each particular case.

We must, then, not only act in conformity with the theorems of the art of living and the fundamental dogmas, but also keep present to our consciousness the theoretical foundations which justify them. This is what Marcus means by the "science of Nature," because, in the final analysis, all of life's principles merge in the knowledge of Nature.[5] Without this, the formulations of dogmas will become devoid of sense, no matter how often they are repeated.

This is why Marcus uses a third method of formulating dogmas. Here the technique involves reconstructing the arguments used to justify them, or even reflecting upon the difficulties to which they may give rise. For instance, Marcus alludes, without citing them, to all the proofs which demonstrate that the world is like a City (IV, 3, 5); and this formula entailed a quite specific attitude vis-à-vis events and other people. Elsewhere, however, he bases this formula on a complex series of rationalizations, and we can summarize the sorites he constructs as follows: a city is a group of beings subject to the same laws. Now, the world is a group of beings subject to the same laws: the law of Reason. Therefore, the world is a City (IV, 4). This reasoning was traditional in Stoicism; traces of it can be found, for example, in Cicero.[6] Yet elsewhere, Marcus remarks that we must imbibe our spirit with the help of reasoning—that is, the linkages between representations (V, 16, 1)—and he proposes further demonstrations, one of which also has the form of a sorites.

This theoretical work does not, however, consist solely in reproducing a simple series of reasonings. It may take on several forms: either that of literary or rhetorical-sounding developments, or of more technical discussions concerning *aporiai*. The dogma according to which "Everything happens in conformity with universal Nature" (XII, 26, 1), for instance, is presented in what one might call a highly orchestrated manner in V, 8, as well as in VII, 9:

> All things are linked together mutually, and their linkage is sacred.
> Nothing, so to speak, is foreign to anything else, for everything is
> coordinated and everything contributes to the order of one single
> world. One single world is the result of all things, and one single
> God penetrates throughout them all; there is one single substance,
> and one single law which is the Reason common to all intelligent
> beings; there is one truth.

This theme of the unity of the world, based on the unity of its origin, is often repeated in analogous terms (VI, 38; XII, 29); but it is also discussed critically, sometimes in schematic fashion, but at other times in a more diluted way, particularly in the numerous passages in which we find what Marcus calls the "disjunction": either atoms (that is, Epicurean dispersion), or one Nature (Stoic unity; cf. IV, 27; VI, 10; VI, 44; VII, 75; VIII, 18; IX, 28; IX, 39; X, 6–7).

Many other major points are discussed in comparatively long developments: for instance, the mutual attraction that reasonable beings feel for one another, which explains that people are made for one another (IX, 9); or the dogma that nothing can constitute an obstacle for intellect or reason (X, 33).

The three rules of life or disciplines

As we have seen, practical conduct obeys three rules of life which determine the individual's relationship to the necessary course of Nature, to other people, and to his own thought. As in the case of his exposition of the dogmas, Marcus' exposition of these rules is highly structured. The three rules of life or discipline correspond to the three activities of the soul: judgment, desire, and impulse; and to the three domains of reality: our individual faculty of judgment, universal Nature, and human nature. This can be seen in the following diagram:

activity	domain of reality	inner attitude
(1) judgment	faculty of judgment	objectivity
(2) desire	universal Nature	consent to Destiny
(3) impulse toward action	human Nature	justice and altruism

We encounter this ternary model very frequently throughout the *Meditations*. I shall cite a few important passages:

Always and everywhere, it depends on you
—piously to rejoice in the present conjunction of events (2);
—to conduct yourself with justice toward whatever people are present (3);
—to apply the rules of discernment to your present representation (1), so that nothing nonobjective may infiltrate its way in (VII, 54).

The following are enough for you:
—your present value-judgment (1), as long as it is objective;
—your present action (3), as long as it is accomplished in the service of the human community;
—your present inner disposition (2), as long as it finds its joy in every conjunction of events brought about by the external cause (IX, 6).

Reasonable nature is indeed following its proper path
—if, with regard to its *representations* (1), it gives its assent neither to what is false, nor to what is obscure;
—if it directs its *impulses* (3) only toward those actions which serve the human community;
—if it has *desire* (2) and aversion only for that which depends on us; while it joyfully greets all that which is granted to it by universal Nature (VIII, 7).

Again,

Erase your *representation (phantasia)* (1);
Stop your *impulse toward action (hormē)* (3)
Extinguish your *desire (orexis)* (2);
Have your guiding principle *(hēgemonikon)* within your power
(IX, 7).

What must you practice?
One thing only:
—thought devoted to justice and *actions* accomplished in the service
of the community (3);
—*speech* which can never deceive (1);
—an *inner disposition* (2) which lovingly greets each conjunction of
events, recognizing it as necessary, familiar, and flowing forth from
so great a principle, and so great a source (IV, 33, 3).

In addition to these explicit formulations, we find numerous allusions to
the three disciplines, in various forms. Thus, Marcus lists as a triad of
virtues: "truth," "justice," and "temperance" (XII, 15); or "unhurried-
ness in judgment," "love of people," and "the disposition to place oneself in the cortege of the gods" (III, 9, 2)—which correspond to the three
rules of life. It sometimes happens that only two or even only one of the
disciplines appears, as for instance in IV, 22:

To accomplish justice on the occasion of each impulse toward
action, and, on the occasion of each representation, retain only that
part of it which exactly corresponds to reality (here we can recognize the disciplines of action and of judgment).

In X, 11, 3:

He is content with two things: to accomplish the present action
with justice, and to love the fate which has, here and now, been
allotted to him.

And again, in VIII, 23:

Am I accomplishing some action? I accomplish it, relating it to the
well-being of mankind. Is something happening to me? I greet it,
relating what happens to me to the gods and to the source of all

things, whence is formed the framework of events (here we recognize the disciplines of action and of desire).

Often, only one theme is evoked, as for instance the discipline of
desire (VII, 57):

—   Love only the event which comes upon us, and which is linked to
     us by Destiny.

or the discipline of judgment (IV, 7):

Suppress the value-judgment (which you add), and the "I've been
hurt" is also suppressed. Suppress the "I've been hurt," and the
harm is suppressed.

or, finally, the discipline of impulses (XII, 20):

In the first place: nothing at random, and nothing unrelated to some
goal or end. Second, don't relate your actions to anything except an
end or goal which serves the human community.

The *Meditations,* then, take up the various *dogmas* one by one, either
briefly or in more developed form, and different chapters give longer lists
of them than others. Likewise, they tirelessly repeat, either concisely or
in more extended form, the formulation of the three *rules of life,* which
can be found gathered together in their entirety in certain chapters. As
we shall see, Book III attempts to give a detailed, ideal portrait of the
good man, and the three rules of life, which correspond precisely to the
good man's behavior, are set forth in great detail. On the other hand, we
can also find the three rules of life—mixed together with other related
exhortations—presented in a form so concise that it makes them almost
enigmatic:

Erase this representation [discipline of judgment].
Stop dancing around like a puppet [discipline of action].
Circumscribe the precise moment of time.
Recognize what is happening to you or to someone else [disci-
pline of the consent to Destiny].
Divide the object and analyze it into "causal" and "material."
Think about your last hour.

As for the wrong committed by so-and-so: leave it right where the fault was committed (VII, 29).

These three disciplines of life are the true key to the *Meditations* of Marcus Aurelius, for the various dogmas I have discussed crystallize around them. The dogmas affirming our freedom of judgment, and the possibility for mankind to criticize and modify his own thought, are linked to the discipline of judgment, while all the theorems on the causality of universal Nature are grouped around that discipline which directs our attitude toward external events. Finally, the discipline of action is fed by all the theoretical propositions concerning the mutual attraction which unites rational beings.

In the last analysis, we realize that behind their apparent disorder, we can discern a highly rigorous conceptual system in Marcus' *Meditations*. I shall now turn to a detailed description of its structure.

Imaginative exercises

The *Meditations* do not just formulate the rules of life and the dogmas by which they are nourished; for it is not only reason which is exercised in them, but the imagination as well. For example, Marcus does not restrict himself to saying that life is short and that we all must soon die, by virtue of the laws of metamorphosis imposed by Nature. Instead, he brings to life before his eyes (VIII, 31)

the court of Augustus; his wife, his daughter, his descendants, his progeny, his sister, Agrippa, his relatives, his acquaintances, his friends Arius and Maecenas, his doctors, his sacrificers, the death of an entire Court . . .

Yet it is not only the disappearance of a court that he tries to represent to himself, but that of a whole generation (IV, 32):

For instance, imagine the time of Vespasian. You'll see all of that: people getting married, raising a family, falling ill, dying, going to war, celebrating festivals, doing business, working the fields; there'll be flatterers, arrogant or suspicious people, conspirators; there'll be people who desire the death of others; others who grumble about present events; there'll be lovers, misers, others who lust after consulate or kingship. That life of theirs: is it not true that it is nowhere now?

At other times, Marcus thinks of the great men of the past: Hippocrates, Alexander, Pompey, Caesar, Augustus, Hadrian, Heraclitus, Democritus, Socrates, Eudoxus, Hipparchus, and Archimedes. "All of them long dead!" he writes (VI, 47); "No more and nowhere!" (VIII, 5). By so doing, Marcus takes his place in the great literary tradition which, from Lucretius to François Villon,[7] has evoked the famous dead: "Where are the snows of yesteryear?" "Where are they?" Marcus had already asked (X, 31, 2); "Nowhere; no matter where!"

Such imaginative exercises recur rather often in the *Meditations* (IV, 50; VI, 24; VII, 19, 2; VII, 48; VIII, 25; VIII, 37; IX, 30; XII, 27). It is by this means that Marcus attempts vigorously to place the dogma of universal metamorphosis before his eyes.

Life itself, however, is a kind of death, when it is not illuminated by virtue, by the practice of the rules of life, and by the knowledge of those dogmas which provide knowledge of things human and divine. This is what explains those descriptions of the vanity of human life—worthy of a Cynic—which we sometimes find in the *Meditations,* as in the following extraordinary passage (VII, 3):

> The vain solemnity of a procession; dramas played out on the stage; troops of sheep or goats; fights with spears; a little bone thrown to dogs; a chunk of bread thrown into a fish-pond; the exhausting labor and heavy burdens under which ants must bear up; crazed mice running for shelter; puppets pulled by strings. . . .

And we have already encountered the following brief but striking note (X, 9):

> Buffoonery and bloody struggles; torpor and agitation; the slavery of every day.

Writing as a spiritual exercise

As we have seen throughout these analyses, the *Meditations* appear to be variations on a small number of themes. The result of this is the large number of repetitions they contain, which are sometimes almost verbatim. We have already encountered several examples of this, and the following ones can be added:

> How could that which does not make a man worse, make life worse? (II, 11, 4)

> That which does not make a man worse than he is, does not make his life worse, either. . . . (IV, 8).

> All is ephemeral: that which remembers, and that which it remembers (IV, 35).

> Ephemeral . . . is he who remembers and that which he remembers (VIII, 21, 2).

> Nothing is so capable of producing greatness of soul (III, 11, 2).

> Nothing is so capable of producing greatness of soul (X, 11, 1).

Many more examples could be cited, including long developments such as VIII, 34 and XI, 8, both of which are structurally parallel, and are devoted to the power which man has received from God to reunite himself with the All from which he has separated himself.

The advice on distinguishing within each thing "that which is causal" from "that which is material" is repeated almost ten times, with only very slight variations. Here we can recognize one of the fundamental structures of Stoic physics,[8] and therefore—once again—the technical nature of the formulas Marcus uses. But Marcus does not merely repeat this distinction as if he were reproducing something he had learned in a Stoic school; for him, it has an existential meaning. To distinguish the causal element is to recognize the presence within oneself of the *hēgemonikon*, that is, the principle which directs all being. This is that principle of thought and judgment which makes us independent of the body, and the principle of liberty which delimits the sphere of "that which depends on us," as opposed to "that which does not depend on us."

Marcus does not say this; however, we can deduce it from the overall structure of his system. He is content merely to recommend to himself to apply this distinction, without ever giving an example which might help us to understand what this exercise might mean. The reason is that Marcus has no need of examples; he knows perfectly well what he's talking about. These formulas, which are repeated throughout the *Meditations,* never set forth a doctrine. Rather, they serve only as a catalyst which, by means of the association of ideas, reactivates a series of representations and practices, about which Marcus—since he is writing only for himself—has no need to go into detail.

Marcus writes only in order to have the dogmas and rules of life always present to his mind. He is thus following the advice of Epictetus, who, after having set forth the distinction between what does and does not depend on us—the fundamental dogma of Stoicism—adds:

> It is about this that philosophers ought to meditate; this is what they should *write down* every day, and it should be the subject of their exercises (I, 1, 25).

> You must have these principles at hand *(procheira)* both night and day; you must *write them down;* you must read them (III, 24, 103).

The Stoic philosophical life consists essentially in mastering one's inner discourse. Everything in an individual's life depends on how he represents things to himself—in other words, how he tells them to himself in inner dialogue. "It is not things that trouble us," as Epictetus said *(Manual,* §5), "but our judgments *about* things," in other words, our inner discourse about things. I will have a great deal to say later on about the *Discourses* of Epictetus, which were collected by his disciple Arrian. They depict Epictetus speaking with his students during his philosophy classes, and, as Arrian says in his brief preface, "When he spoke, he certainly had no other desire than to set the thoughts of his listeners in motion toward what is best . . . when Epictetus spoke these words, his audience could not help feeling just what this man wanted them to feel."

Epictetus' speech, then, was intended to modify his audience's inner discourse. We are thus in the presence of two therapies: one was that of the word, practiced in a variety of forms, by means of striking or moving formulas and with the help of logical and technical rational processes, but also with the help of seductive and persuasive imagery. Another was the therapy of writing for oneself, which, for Marcus, consisted in taking up the dogmas and rules of action as they were stated by Epictetus—all the while addressing himself—and assimilating them, so that they might become the principles of his inner discourse. Therefore, one must constantly rekindle the "representations" *(phantasiai)* within oneself, in other words, those discourses which formulate dogmas (VII, 2).

Such writing exercises thus lead necessarily to incessant repetitions, and this is what radically differentiates the *Meditations* from every other work. Dogmas are not mathematical rules, learned once and for all and then mechanically applied. Rather, they must somehow become achievements of awareness, intuitions, emotions, and moral experiences which have the intensity of a mystical experience or a vision. This spiritual and affective spirituality is, however, quick to dissipate. In order to reawaken it, it is not enough to reread what has already been written. Written pages are already dead, and the *Meditations* were not made to be reread. What counts is the reformulation: the act of writing or talking to oneself, right now, in the very moment when one needs to write. It is also the act of composing with the greatest care possible: to search for that version which, at a given moment, will produce the greatest effect, in the moment before it fades away, almost instantaneously, almost as soon as it is written. Characters traced onto some medium do not fix anything: everything is in the act of writing. Thus, we witness a succession of new attempts at composition, repetitions of the same formulas, and endless variations on the same themes: the themes of Epictetus.

The goal is to reactualize, rekindle, and ceaselessly reawaken an inner state which is in constant danger of being numbed or extinguished. The task—ever-renewed—is to bring back to order an inner discourse which becomes dispersed and diluted in the futility of routine.

As he wrote the *Meditations,* Marcus was thus practicing Stoic spiritual exercises. He was using writing as a technique or procedure in order to influence himself, and to transform his inner discourse by meditating on the Stoic dogmas and rules of life. This was an exercise of writing day by day, ever-renewed, always taken up again and always needing to be taken up again, since the true philosopher is he who is conscious of not yet having attained wisdom.

"Greek" exercises

It is not surprising to the modern reader that the *Meditations* were written in Greek. One might, however, wonder why the Emperor, whose mother tongue was Latin, chose to use Greek to write personal notes intended only for himself.

First of all, we must note that Marcus was completely bilingual, having studied Greek rhetoric with Herodes Atticus and Latin rhetoric with Fronto. More generally, the population of Rome was made up of the most diverse elements, who had converged upon the Empire's metropolis for a wide variety of reasons, and the two languages were in constant use. In the streets of Rome, the Greek doctor Galen could rub elbows with the Christian apologist Justin, or else with some Gnostic. All these figures taught in Rome and had students from the educated classes.[9]

Even in Rome, Greek was the language of philosophy. The rhetorician Quintillian, writing at the end of the first century A.D., notes that few Latin writers had ever dealt with philosophy: he cites only Cicero, Brutus, Seneca, and a few others. He could also have included the name of Lucretius. Be that as it may, in the first century A.D. Cornutus, Musonius Rufus, and Epictetus all wrote in Greek, which allows us to infer that, from then on, educated Romans accepted that even in Rome, the official language of philosophy should be Greek.

One might have thought that Marcus would have preferred to talk to himself in Latin. As we have seen, however, the *Meditations* are not spontaneous effusions, but exercises carried out in accordance with a program which Marcus had received from the Stoic tradition, and in particular from Epictetus. Marcus was working with pre-existing materials, and painting on a canvas given him by someone else. This fact entails several consequences.

In the first place, this philosophical material was associated with a technical vocabulary, and the Stoics, in particular, were renowned for the technical nature of their terminology. Translators must, by the way, be aware of this peculiarity of Marcus' vocabulary, and pay the closest possible attention when they encounter such words as *hypolēpsis* ("value-judgment"); *katalēptikos* ("objective"; "adequate"); *phantasia* ("representation," not "imagination"), *hēgemonikon* ("directing principle"); *epakolouthēsis* ("necessary but nonessential consequence"); and *hypexairesis* ("reserve clause"), to cite only a few examples. Such technicalities go to show that Marcus was no amateur, and that it was not the case that Stoicism was just "a religion" for him.[10]

It was difficult to translate these terms into Latin. It could be said that Lucretius, Cicero, and Seneca had done quite well when faced with the same kind of challenge. But the goal of these authors was popularization: they wanted to make Greek philosophy accessible to a Latin audience. Marcus' project was different: he was writing for himself. To translate or to adapt terminology would distract him from his goal. What is more, if they were translated into Latin, the technical terms of Greek philosophy would lose a part of their meaning. In the same way, when Aulus Gellius,[11] a contemporary of Marcus who had studied philosophy at Athens, translates a passage from the *Discourses* of Epictetus as reported by Arrian, he feels obliged to transcribe technical Greek words, in order to explain his choice of the Latin words which he has chosen to correspond to them. Modern translators of Heidegger are often forced to do the same. In the final analysis, philosophy, like poetry, is untranslatable.

In any case, Marcus had no time to indulge in the literary work of translation. In the urgency of conversion and the imminence of death, he searched for immediate effects: words and phrases which would dissipate worry or anger immediately (IV, 3, 3). He felt the need to plunge back into the atmosphere of philosophical instruction, and to remember the exact phraseology of Epictetus, which supplied him with the themes upon which he developed his variations.

4

THE PHILOSOPHER-SLAVE AND
THE EMPEROR-PHILOSOPHER

Memories of philosophical readings

Some quotations from philosophers appear occasionally in the *Meditations*.[1] It is possible that Marcus may have read some of these authors, but he may also have come across them in the course of his Stoic readings.

The Stoics considered Heraclitus, for instance, as their great ancestor.[2] Several passages from the Ephesian philosopher appear in the *Meditations*, but it is difficult to distinguish the authentic passages from the paraphrases which the Emperor gives of them, perhaps because he is quoting them from memory. It is possible that Marcus' allusion to "people who speak and act while asleep," and thus live in a state of unconsciousness (IV, 46, 4), is only a development of the first fragment of Heraclitus, which also alluded to the unconsciousness of the majority of mankind, analogous to sleep.[3]

At any rate, the theme of the sleep of unconsciousness made a deep impression on Marcus. He makes a possible allusion to the Heraclitean fragment[4] which speaks of a person so drunk he no longer knows where he is going: "he who forgets where the road leads," as Marcus puts it (IV, 46, 2). More significantly, Marcus affirms—still under the inspiration of Heraclitus[5]—that those who are asleep and unconscious also contribute, in their own way, to the fabrication of the world, and he draws from this the following conclusion (VI, 42, 1):

We are all working together in order to complete one work; some of us knowingly and consciously, and the others unconsciously.

Thus, even when we oppose ourselves to the will of universal Reason, each of us collaborates with it, for the course of Nature also has need of those who refuse to follow it. After all, Nature has integrated freedom into her plan, as well as all that it implies: including unconsciousness or resistance. In the drama which Nature makes us play, sleepers and opponents are precisely what she has to foresee.

For these people, asleep or unconscious, who are "in discord with the *logos*"[6] (IV, 46, 3), "what they encounter every day seems foreign to them"[7] (IV, 46, 3). It could be that this Heraclitean theme was all the more dear to Marcus because of the great importance he attached to the notion of "familiarity" with Nature, and therefore with the *logos*. It is this familiarity which allows us to recognize as familiar or natural, and not foreign, all those events which occur by the will of Nature (III, 2, 6).

The death of the elements into one another[8]—an eminently Heraclitean theme—could not fail to attract the Emperor's attention (IV, 46, 1); after all, Stoicism had accustomed him to meditate upon universal metamorphosis.[9]

Together with Heraclitus we find Empedocles, one of whose verses Marcus cites (XII, 3). The "pure-orbed" *Sphairos* which this poet-philosopher had imagined was the traditional model for the Sage.[10]

Without naming its author, Marcus quotes and criticizes (IV, 24) a fragment of Democritus which advises people not to get involved in too many things, if they want to keep their peace of mind. In fact, among those authors—especially Stoics—who dealt with this virtue, it was a tradition to refuse the Democritean invitation to inaction.[11]

In the collection entitled "The Sentences of Democratus," sometimes attributed to Democritus,[12] Marcus found an aphorism which, one could say, sums up his own thought (IV, 3, 11):

> The world is nothing but metamorphosis *(alloiōsis)*, and life is nothing but an opinion (or a judgment: *hypolēpsis*).

In this formulation, Marcus no doubt recognized Epictetus' idea according to which it is not things that trouble us, but the representations and judgments which we make about them (*Manual,* §5).

Elsewhere (VII, 31, 4), Marcus criticizes another Democritean text, which affirmed that true reality consists of atoms and the void, and that everything else was only "by convention" *(nomisti)*. As Galen explains,[13] this meant that "in itself," there is nothing but atoms; but that "with regard to us," there is a whole world of colors, odors, and tastes, which we assume is real, but which in fact is only subjective. Marcus corrects the Democritean formula, but interprets it in a Stoic sense. He denies the infinite number of atoms which, on this theory, are the only real princi-

ples, but he admits the word *nomisti,* on the condition that it be understood not in the sense of "by convention," but as if it meant "by a law."
For Marcus, then, only half of Democritus' formula is true: "Everything
is *nomisti.*" Its meaning, however, is that "everything happens by the
law," that is, the law of universal Nature. The other part of Democritus'
formula, which asserted that the true reality is the multiplicity of atoms
which constitute the principles, is false; for if everything comes about by
the laws of Nature, then the number of principles is quite restricted. In
fact, it is reduced to one: the *logos;* or to two: the *logos* and matter. Such,
at least, is one interpretation of this difficult and probably corrupt text.[14]
One might also consider that Marcus understands "Everything is *nomisti*"
in the same sense as the sentence of Democritus cited above: "Everything
is subjective; that is, everything is judgment." In other words, Marcus
may have understood it in the light of Epictetus' idea that everything is in
our representations.[15] This does not mean that we do not know reality,
but that we attribute to it values of good or of evil which have no basis in
reality.

Marcus also thinks he recognizes this doctrine in the formula of a
Cynic (II, 15):

> "Everything is matter of judgment." No doubt what people used to
> say in opposition to Monimus the Cynic is obvious; but the useful-
> ness of what he said is obvious too, as long as we receive what is
> profitable in what he said, while remaining within the limits of what
> is true.

According to the comic playwright Menander,[16] Monimus the Cynic
used to declare that all human opinion *(to hypolēphthen)* is only vanity
(tuphos). Marcus believed he was penetrating to the deepest truth of the
formula cited by Menander: in the final analysis, everything is a matter of
opinion; what troubles us are our value-judgments, and they are only
vanity *(tuphos).*

As Monimus said, it is usually precisely our vanity—*tuphos* in the sense
of "emptiness," "smoke," but also "pride"—which perverts our value-
judgments (VI, 13):

> Pride is a dreadful sophist, and it is just at the moment when you
> think you are devoting yourself to serious matters that it enchants
> you the most. Look, for instance, at what Crates says about a man
> like Xenocrates.

In antiquity, Platonists like Xenocrates had the reputation of being vain, proud, and haughty, so it is not surprising that Crates—who, like Monimus, was a Cynic—should have reproached him for his *tuphos,* or puffed-up vanity.[17]

There is no doubt that, either directly or indirectly, Marcus was familiar with other Cynic texts. There is nothing surprising about this: on the one hand, Cynicism and Stoicism were very close to each other with regard to their conceptions of life; and on the other, as we have seen in the case of Democritus and Monimus, our philosopher-emperor had the gift of recognizing Stoic doctrines in the texts which retained his attention.

We also find several Platonic texts in the *Meditations,* taken from the *Apology* (28b; 28d), the *Gorgias* (512d–e), the *Republic* (486a), and the *Theaetetus* (174d–e). Once again, this is not surprising, because the Plato whom Marcus quotes is, so to speak, a "pre-Stoic" Plato—that is, one who has Socrates speak in terms the Stoics would not have denied. For this Plato/Socrates, the important questions are not those dealing with life and death, but those that deal with justice and injustice, or good and evil (VII, 44); we must remain at the post which has been assigned to us (VII, 45); what matters is not to save one's life, but to spend it in the worthiest way possible (VII, 46); he who embraces in one glance the totality of time and of substance is not afraid of death (VII, 35). Finally, Marcus finds in the *Theaetetus* (174d–e) a description of the difficult situation of a king, bereft of the leisure he needs to think and to philosophize, like a shepherd shut up with his flock "in a pasture in the midst of the mountains" (X, 23). What Marcus recognized in all these quotations was Stoicism, not Platonism.[18]

Marcus also read a text by Theophrastus, the student of Aristotle, which he alone mentions of all the authors of antiquity. The passage probably interested the judge in Marcus, responsible for assessing guilt, since it raises the question of degrees of responsibility. According to Theophrastus, crimes committed with pleasure, and resulting from the attraction of pleasure, are more serious than those one is forced to commit because of the suffering caused by an injustice we have borne, which pushes us on to anger. Marcus approves of this theory (II, 10), and it has been maintained that he was thereby unfaithful to Stoicism, since the Stoa held that all faults are equal.[19] Now, it is true that the Stoics considered wisdom to be an absolute perfection. The slightest fault, therefore, estranged a person from this perfection just as much as the most serious one did. One was either a sage or not, and there was no intermediate status. In theory, therefore, there was no such thing as a more or less serious fault. Yet, for all that, the Stoics did allow for the possibility of moral progress in the case of the non-sage, and consequently they also admitted degrees of moral progress. Different degrees of the gravity of faults could therefore also be allowed in the case of the non-sage.[20] Epictetus himself, for that matter, also appears to consider that certain faults are more easy to pardon than others (IV, 1, 147): the passion of love, for example, is easier to pardon than that of ambition.

Marcus also mentions the "Pythagoreans," who ordained that we should raise our eyes toward the heavens at dawn, in order to remind ourselves of that model of order and purity represented by the stars (XI, 27).[21]

Epicurean maxims and passages from Epicurus are also to be found in the *Meditations*. Marcus rewrites them into a Stoic vocabulary when he quotes them, and he retains from them advice which a Stoic could legitimately practice: be happy with the present, without regretting that which we do not possess and could not possess (VII, 27); pain cannot be simultaneously both unbearable and eternal (VII, 33; VII, 64); we should always keep the virtues of the ancients in mind (XI, 26); and finally, in every circumstance, we must remain on the level of philosophy, and not let ourselves be dragged down into sharing the anthropomorphic view-points of those who do not practice philosophy (IX, 41).[22] The commentary Marcus gives on this last-mentioned passage—a letter written by Epicurus while he was ill or on his deathbed—allows us to understand how Stoics such as Seneca and Epictetus could find, even in Epicureanism, maxims capable of nourishing their own meditation. We must not assume that they were eclectics, rather than dyed-in-the-wool Stoics: they knew perfectly well that there was a radical opposition between Stoic and Epicurean doctrines, as well as between the practical attitude of the Stoics and the Epicureans. They were also aware, however, that Epicureanism, Stoicism, Platonism, and Aristotelianism were merely the different and opposing forms of a single phenomenon: the philosophical style of life. Within the latter, there could be points held in common by several—or even all—of the schools, as Marcus states expressly with regard to the letter of Epicurus (IX, 41):

It is common to all the schools not to depart from philosophy under any circumstances, and not to let oneself be dragged into the chatter of the vulgar, that is, of those who do not practice the science of Nature.

In particular, the Stoics and the Epicureans shared a specific attitude with regard to time. They insisted on concentration on the present moment,[23] which allows us both to grasp the incomparable value of the present instant, and to diminish the intensity of pain, as we become conscious of the fact that we only *feel* and *live* this pain within the present moment.

When all is said and done, it was as a Stoic, and as a disciple of Epictetus, that Marcus read the texts of the philosophers whom he quotes. For it is above all the reading of Epictetus, and the knowledge of his teachings, which explain the *Meditations*.

The teachings of Epictetus

In the course of the preceding pages, we have encountered the name of Epictetus more than once. Nor is this surprising, given that he is mentioned many times in the *Meditations*. For instance, Marcus expresses his gratitude to his Stoic teacher Rusticus for having passed along to him notes taken at Epictetus' classes. Marcus often quotes texts explicitly from Epictetus, and places him on the same level as those whom the Stoics considered the greatest of masters (VII, 19, 2):

> How many men—like Chrysippus, like Socrates, like Epictetus—has Eternity swallowed up!

Epictetus was, at the time, considered to be *the* great philosopher. His image and teachings were mentioned throughout the literature of the second century A.D., and he was to remain a model for philosophers down to the end of antiquity. The Latin author Aulus Gellius, who had studied at Athens, mentions a conversation he had witnessed there in which the rhetorician Herodes Atticus quoted a passage from the *Discourses* of Epictetus, as collected by Arrian. He also informs us that, in another conversation, the philosopher Favorinus had reported several of the Master's sayings. In the course of a sea voyage, Aulus Gellius himself had met another philosopher, who pulled the *Discourses* out of his travel-bag and read him a passage from them. Elsewhere in Gellius' *Attic Nights,* we find allusions to details about Epictetus' life: his initial condition as a slave; his expulsion from Rome by the emperor Domitian; and his eventual settling down in Nicopolis.[24] The satirist Lucian, who also lived under the reign of Marcus, tells how an admirer once bought "the clay lamp of the Stoic Epictetus" for 3,000 drachmas. "No doubt he hoped," remarks Lucian,[25] "that if he read at night by the light of this lamp, the wisdom of Epictetus would come upon him all of a sudden during his sleep, and he would be just like that admirable old man." Marcus' doctor, Galen, alludes to a dialogue which Favorinus of Arles had directed against Epictetus, and which Galen himself refuted.[26] Even Christians such as Origen, who wrote in the third century, speak of Epictetus in terms of respect.[27]

Epictetus was born in the first century A.D., in Phrygian Hierapolis (Pammukale in modern Turkey). Sometime during the second half of the century, he was brought to Rome as the slave of Epaphroditus, one of Nero's freedmen. Epictetus mentions his master Epaphroditus several times in the *Discourses;* he allowed his slave to attend the classes of the Stoic philosopher Musonius Rufus. Musonius had a tremendous influence on Epictetus; the latter frequently reproduces his teacher's sayings in the *Discourses,* and describes his teaching as follows (III, 23, 29): "When we sat before him, each of us felt as though someone had denounced our faults to him. Such was the exactitude with which he hit upon our current state, and placed everyone's faults before his eyes."

After having been set free by Epaphroditus, Epictetus opened his own philosophy school in Rome, but was expelled from the city, together with all other philosophers, by the emperor Domitian in 93–94. He then set himself up at Nicopolis, in Epirus on the Greek coast, a town which served as a jumping-off point for the sea voyage across the Adriatic to Italy. There he opened a new philosophy school. The Neoplatonist Simplicius relates that Epictetus was so poor that the house he lived in at Rome had no need for a lock, since it contained nothing other than the mattress and the mat on which he used to sleep. The same author reports that Epictetus had adopted an orphan, and had taken in a woman in order to bring him up,[28] but he never married.[29] The precise date of his death is not known.

Epictetus wrote nothing. If we can still get some idea of his teachings, it is thanks to Arrian of Nicomedia, a politician who, as a young man about 108 A.D., had attended Epictetus' classes in Nicopolis, and later published the "notes" he had taken at these classes. Arrian of Nicomedia is an attractive character.[30] It should be pointed out right away that his contemporaries considered him a philosopher: inscriptions dedicated to him during his lifetime at Athens and Corinth designate him by this title.[31] The historian Cassius Dio had apparently written a "Life of Arrian the Philosopher."[32] Arrian did, indeed, leave philosophical works behind him. In addition to his notes which report the *Sayings* or *Discourses* of Epictetus, one must add a little work which was of much greater importance in the history of western thought: the so-called *Manual* of Epictetus (in Greek, *Encheiridion*). The word *Encheiridion* ("that which one has at hand") alludes to a requirement of the Stoic philosophical life—a requirement to which Marcus, too, had tried to respond by composing his *Meditations*. In every one of life's circumstances, it was necessary to have "at hand" the principles, "dogmas," rules of life, or formulas which would allow a person to place himself in that inner disposition most conducive to correct action, or to accept his fate. The *Manual* is a selection of passages taken from the *Sayings* of Epictetus.[33] It is a kind of anthology of striking maxims aimed at illuminating the philosopher in the course of his actions. Arrian also seems to have written a book on celestial phenomena, or what was called *meteorology* in antiquity.[34] As we have seen, however, a philosopher in antiquity was not someone who wrote philosophical books, but someone who led a philosophical life, and we have every reason to believe that Arrian, although he remained a politician like Marcus' teacher Rusticus, tried to live like a philosopher. We can surmise this from the end of his preface to Epictetus' *Discourses;* by publishing them, Arrian wanted to produce in his readers the same effect that Epictetus had on his auditors: to raise them up toward the Good. His model, moreover, was Socrates' famous disciple Xenophon, who had also had a military and political career at the same time as a literary one. Arrian wanted to be known as the "new Xenophon"; he imitates the latter both in style and in the subject matter of his works, and, like Xenophon, he too wrote a treatise on hunting. Above all, however, Arrian wrote the *Discourses,* which are as it were the *Memorabilia* of Epictetus, the new Socrates.[35] He certainly did not have in mind a mere literary model, but a model for life: that of the philosopher in action. Two centuries later, the philosopher Themistius[36] would praise Junius Rusticus and Arrian for having abandoned their books and placed themselves at the service of the common good, not only like Cato and other Romans, but especially like Xenophon and Socrates himself. For Rusticus and Arrian, Themistius goes on, philosophy did not stop with pen and ink: they were not content merely to write about courage, and they did not shrink from their duty of serving the interests of the State.

Arrian did, indeed, enjoy a brilliant career as a statesman: he was proconsul of the province of Beltica around 123 A.D., *consul suffectus*[37] in 129 or 130, and governor of Cappadocia from 130 (or 131) to 137 (or 138). In this last capacity, he repulsed an invasion of the Alani in 135, made an inspection of the coasts of the Black Sea, and presented a report on his trip to the emperor Hadrian.

In the preface he addressed to his friend Lucius Gellius, Arrian explains the way he had gathered together his notes taken at the classes given by Epictetus: "I did not compose them in a literary style, as could have been done in the case of sayings of this kind, and I did not publish them myself, precisely because I did not compose them." In antiquity, it was in principle only works carefully composed according to the rules of style and composition that were made public, either by means of a public reading, or by giving the text over to booksellers.

> Yet I tried to write down everything I heard while he was speaking, in the same words that he used, in order to preserve for myself, in the future, "notes to help me remember" *(hypomnēmata)* his thought and his freedom of speech. It is therefore natural that these notes should have the appearance of a spontaneous, man-to-man conversation, and not at all that of a composition intended to be read later.

What Arrian means is that he has reproduced, insofar as was possible, the spontaneity of an exhortation or a dialogue, and this is how he explains his use of popular language *(koinē)* throughout the work, instead of the literary style he had used in his other books. He continues: "I do not know how notes which were in such a state have managed to find their way into the public domain, unbeknownst to me and against my wishes." The same thing probably happened to Arrian as had happened to Galen: class notes, initially confided to friends, were gradually copied in a wide variety of circumstances and were thus, for all intents and purposes, "published." "I don't particularly care if people think me incapable of properly composing a work." Here, by despising literary glory, Arrian shows himself to be a good student of Epictetus.

> As for Epictetus: it is not important in his case either, if it is true that he held discourses in contempt. When he spoke, the only thing he wanted was to set the thoughts of his listeners in motion toward better things. If that is indeed the result of these discourses, then they will certainly not fail to produce the effect that the discourse of philosophers should produce. If the contrary should occur, then at least may those who read them know that when they were spoken by Epictetus himself, the person listening to them necessarily felt what that man wanted him to feel. If these discourses fail to produce this effect, perhaps I am to blame; perhaps, however, things just had to be that way.

I shall not go into detail about the discussions to which this passage has given rise among historians. Some are of the opinion that Arrian has preserved for us in his work the very words of Epictetus, taken down by stenography. For others, on the contrary, Arrian, in his desire to imitate Xenophon's *Memorabilia,* carried out a much more extensive editorial activity than he gives us to understand in his letter to Gellius: he often reconstituted Epictetus' sayings, since their literary form is much more refined than Arrian was willing to admit. In any case, unless we suppose that Arrian was capable of developing an original philosophical discourse himself and attributing it to Epictetus, we have no alternative but to concede that, as far as the main points are concerned, Arrian's work is closely connected with the living teaching of Epictetus.[38]

We must not conclude from this, however—as has been done by the majority of historians and commentators—that *all* of Epictetus' teachings are contained in the *Discourses* as reported by Arrian. As we read them, we find allusions to parts of the course which were not included by Arrian. In fact, as has been shown by Souilhé,[39] the greatest part of Epictetus' course, as was the case for all philosophy courses from at least the first century A.D. on, was devoted to the explanation of texts by the founders of the school—that is, in the case of the Stoics, Zeno and Chrysippus. The master would explain these texts, but this was also sometimes the task of the auditors. Now, although Arrian did not reproduce one single bit of this technical aspect of Epictetus' pedagogical activity, he does sometimes allude to it. For instance, he relates a scene in which one of Epictetus' students is explaining, under the guidance of a more advanced student, a Stoic text concerning the logical problem of syllogisms (I, 26, 13); similarly, he speaks of Epictetus getting up in the morning and thinking about how he will direct the exercise of textual explanation in his class later that day (I, 10, 8).

This part of the class, then, which consisted of "reading"[40] would become the *lectio* of the Middle Ages, and finally our "lesson." It made up the most essential part of Epictetus' teachings, but is completely absent from the *Discourses* of Epictetus. What they do preserve for us, however, is what could be termed the nontechnical part of the course. All philosophy courses—at least since the beginning of the first century A.D.—contained as an essential element the explanation of texts; yet they could also end in a moment of free discussion between the philosopher and his auditors. Aulus Gellius, writing a few decades after Arrian, tells how his Platonic teacher had the habit, after the *lectio* or textual explanation, of suggesting that his auditors question him on a topic of their choice. The *Discourses* narrated by Arrian thus correspond to those more relaxed moments in which the Master entered into a dialogue with his students, or developed remarks which he considered useful for the practice of the philosophical life.[41]

It is most important to emphasize this point, for it means that we cannot expect to find technical and systematic expositions of the whole of Stoic doctrine in Epictetus' *Discourses* as reported by Arrian. This does not mean, however, that Epictetus did not, in that part of course devoted to theoretical instruction, tackle the Stoic system as a whole by means of the explanation of texts. In other words, we should not say that, of the three parts of Stoic philosophy—physics, ethics, and logic—Epictetus ignores physics, or that part of this discipline which described physical phenomena; for we have no idea which Stoic texts Epictetus read during his classes, nor of the explanation he gave of them. All we can say is that he does not mention physical problems in those discourses with his disciples which have come down to us. It does appear that Arrian himself wrote a book on comets, which is unfortunately now lost to us. If this is true, we can presume that Arrian had been initiated by Epictetus into the philosophical treatment of this kind of question. The way Photius describes the contents of the work even allows us to see what Arrian had retained from the lessons of Epictetus—that is, the moral significance that was to be attributed to physical investigations:[42] "Arrian, who wrote a little work on the nature, formation, and apparitions of comets, tries to show in a number of discussions that appearances such as this do not foretell anything, either good or evil."

We shall have occasion to return to Epictetus' conception of the tripartite division of philosophy. For the moment, it is sufficient to say that it would be utterly false to conclude, on the basis of the content of the *Discourses* as they have come down to us, that Late Stoicism underwent an impoverishment in its theoretical teaching.[43] In the first place, as we have seen, the *Discourses* only reproduce—certainly in a highly fragmentary way—that part of the course which was, by definition, neither theoretical nor technical. Second, they are only the echo of the remarks that Arrian heard over a period of one or two years, during the time of his stay at Nicopolis. Epictetus, by contrast, taught for twenty-five or thirty years. Finally, we must not forget that only the first four books of the *Discourses* have been preserved. This means that one or more books have been lost: Aulus Gellius quotes a long passage from book V.[44] Thanks to Marcus Aurelius, we can also get a glimpse of the existence of Epictetan texts otherwise unknown to us. Thus we can see that the

Discourses, at least in the condition in which they have come down to us, do not by any means give us an idea of everything that Epictetus said, much less of what he did not say.

We know from Book I of the *Meditations* (chapter 7) that Marcus came to know Epictetus thanks to Junius Rusticus, who had instructed Marcus in Stoic doctrine before going on to become one of his counselors. Marcus tells us that Rusticus lent him his personal copy of the *hypomnē-mata* of Epictetus, that is, of notes taken at his classes. This assertion can be interpreted in two ways: in the first place, we might think that the writings in question were a copy of the work by Arrian. Arrian himself, in his letter to Lucius Gellius mentioned above, represented his work as *hypomnēmata,* or notes designed to serve as an *aide-mémoire.* The letter to Gellius was probably written after the death of Epictetus, which took place sometime between 125 and 130 A.D. The book was probably in circulation by 130. Aulus Gellius tells us that during the year he spent studying at Athens around 140, he was present at a discussion in the course of which the famous millionaire Herodes Atticus had brought from the library a copy of what Gellius calls the *dissertationes* of Epictetus, put into order *(digestae)* by Arrian.[45] He also tells how, on a sea voyage from Cassiopoiea to Brindisium, he had encountered a philosopher who was carrying this work in his traveler's sack; what is more, the philosopher had read him a passage from the now-lost book V. Thus, thanks to Rusticus, Marcus was able to read a copy of the *Discourses* as composed by Arrian, and this copy was more complete than the ones known by our modern editions.

Another hypothesis, proposed by Farquharson,[46] could also be envisaged. The notes passed on by Rusticus to Marcus might have been Rusticus' own, which he himself had taken at the classes of Epictetus. From the point of view of chronology, if we assume that Epictetus died between 125 and 130 A.D., and that Rusticus was born at the beginning of the second century (as can be surmised from his official *cursus*), it is entirely possible that he may have been Epictetus' student around 120 A.D. Moreover, since the *Discourses* of Epictetus as reported by Arrian were widely known in Greece around 140, it is difficult to imagine that in the Rome of about 145–146 A.D.—at the time when Marcus had become converted to philosophy—no copy of the work was to be found. Marcus represents Rusticus' gift as something exceptional, so we are entitled to wonder if the gift was indeed Rusticus' own notes. If this were the case, then these notes may have revealed to Marcus an Epictetus quite different from the one we know thanks to Arrian. After all,

Epictetus certainly did not say the same things, every year, to all of his students.

It is, in any case, virtually certain that Marcus did read Arrian's work, since the *Meditations* contain several literal quotations taken from it. Whether Marcus read only the *Discourses* as composed by Arrian, or whether he also had access to the notes of Rusticus, one thing is certain: Marcus was familiar with more texts pertaining to the teachings of Epictetus than we are today. We now possess only a part of Arrian's work; and the notes of Rusticus—if indeed they did exist—might well have revealed to Marcus teachings of Epictetus other than those reported by Arrian. As we shall see, it is thanks to Marcus that we have access to several fragments of Epictetus which are otherwise unknown.

Quotations of Epictetus in the *Meditations*

You are a little soul carrying around a corpse, as Epictetus has said (IV, 41).

When you kiss your child, says Epictetus, you must say to yourself: "perhaps you will be dead tomorrow . . ." (XI, 34).

These are the two explicit quotations of Epictetus which are to be found in the *Meditations*.[47] The first text is not to be found in the four books of Epictetus' *Discourses* reported by Arrian which we possess today, and came to Marcus, as I have said, by some other channel. The "soul carrying around a corpse" also reappears in IX, 24, in one of a series of descriptions of the miserable condition into which human life is plunged when it is not in conformity with Nature and with Reason:

Infantile rages, infantile games! Souls carrying corpses around! In order that the scene of the Evocation of the dead be before your eyes in a yet more striking way.

In the other quotation from Epictetus (XI, 34), we can recognize a text from book III of the *Discourses* (III, 24, 88).

Yet it often happens that Marcus repeats whole passages from Epictetus, without quoting him. When Marcus (VII, 63) quotes a passage from Plato (*Republic,* 412e–413a), for example, he gives the text in the form which had been given it by Epictetus (I, 28, 4):

Each soul is deprived of the truth against its will.

We encounter this quote again, moreover, in the long series of *kephalaia* against anger (XI, 18, 5).

Epictetus alluded to the Stoic theory of suicide as follows (I, 25, 18):

So there's some smoke in the house? If there's not too much, I'll stay; if there's too much, I'll leave. For what you must never forget, and keep firmly in mind, is that the door is wide open.

Marcus echoes Epictetus as follows (V, 29, 2):

Smoke? Then I'm leaving!

Epictetus gave the following recommendation to his disciple (III, 3, 14):

As soon as you go out in the morning, and whatever it is you see or hear, carry out this test. You respond, as if we were having an argument by questions and answers:
    —What did you see?
    —A handsome man, or a good-looking woman.
Then apply the rule *(epage ton kanōna),* [and ask yourself]:
    —Does their beauty depend upon their will, or not?
    —It does not depend upon their will.
    —Then reject it.

Once more, Marcus picks up the tune (V, 22):

That which does not harm the State does not harm its citizen either. Each time you imagine you have been injured, *apply this rule (epage touton ton kanōna).*

In both cases, we see a theoretical position or dogma (the distinction between what does and does not depend on us, or the identity of interest between the State and the citizen) represented as a rule *(kanōn)* which must be applied to each particular case.

The whole final part of Book XI (chapters 33–39) appears to be a series of passages from Epictetus. First, as we have seen, Epictetus is cited explicitly in chapter 34. Chapter 33 also gives an anonymous summary of a passage from book III of the *Discourses* (III, 24, 86), while chapters

35–36 cite still more texts from book III (III, 24, 92–93; III, 22, 105). In fact, it is as though we had before us a collection of notes that Marcus had taken while reading book III of the *Discourses*.

The following chapter (XI, 37) is introduced by the phrase "he says," which gives us every right to suppose that Marcus is continuing to quote the same author as in the preceding chapters—that is, Epictetus. This text has no parallel in the *Discourses,* but it comes without any doubt from the lost portion of Epictetus. In it, we can recognize Epictetus' usual vocabulary *(topos peri tas hormas, hypexairesis, kat'axian, orexis, ekklisis),* and above all one of his fundamental teachings: that of the three rules of life, or the disciplines of judgment, of desire, and of action, of which I shall be speaking throughout the present work.

Chapter 38 is also introduced by "he says," which can only designate Epictetus. It is perhaps a rather free paraphrase of a text (III, 25, 3) in which Epictetus affirms that the fight for virtue is no small matter, since what is at stake is nothing less than happiness. Marcus remarks (XI, 38):

> The struggle, then, is not about winning just any old prize, but about deciding whether one will be sane or insane.

The last chapter (XI, 39) is supposed to transmit various sayings of Socrates, but since chapters 33 to 38 are taken from Epictetus, it is quite likely that this passage should also be attributed to Epictetus.

There may be still other anonymous quotations from Epictetus in the *Meditations.* H. Fränkel[48] thought, with good reason, that IV, 49, 2–5 was one such quotation:

> —I'm so unlucky that such-and-such a thing has happened to me!
> —Not at all! On the contrary, you should say: "How lucky I am, since now that such-and-such a thing has happened to me, I remain free from grief: I neither let myself be broken by the present, nor do I fear what is going to happen! For this event could have happened to anyone, but not everyone would have remained free from grief.
> —Why, moreover, should we say that this particular event is a misfortune, while that one is a piece of good fortune? In general, do you call anything a "misfortune" for man which does not cause the nature of man to deviate from its goal? And do you think that that which is not contrary to the will of Nature causes the nature of man to deviate from its goal?
> —What, then, is the will of Nature?

—You've learned it. Does the event which has happened to you prevent you from being just, from possessing greatness of soul, from being temperate and prudent, without haste in your judgments, without falsity in your speech, reserved, and free, and everything else such that, when they are present together, the nature of man possesses that which is proper to it?

Fränkel bases his contention on lexical and grammatical particularities which are quite convincing.[49] It could perhaps be objected—quite rightly—that this passage basically does nothing but express in dialogue form the fundamental dogma of Stoicism: that the only evil is moral evil, in other words, that which prevents us from practicing the virtues. This is true, but it does not alter the fact that the tone and form of this passage are in stark contrast with the rest of the *Meditations*. Normally, when Marcus uses the word "I," he is speaking either about himself, or about the good man, speaking to himself. Here, by contrast, the "I" represents the interlocutor of a dialogue which Marcus is reporting. It is highly probable that this is a dialogue which Epictetus has imagined before his auditors, as he often does in the *Discourses,* and that Marcus has copied it down. It should be noted that, elsewhere in his *Discourses* (I, 4, 23), Epictetus tells his auditors that what is truly worthwhile is to work at eliminating all "Alas!" and "How unhappy I am!" from one's life.

It is thus probable that we have here an unrecognized fragment of Epictetus. Are there others? I think it likely that there are some. In general, moreover, we should not exclude the hypothesis that a given passage of the *Meditations* may be utilizing a text from an unknown author, or at any rate may be a paraphrase thereof. As far as Epictetus is concerned, however, we must bear in mind the fact that Marcus had read so much of him as to become impregnated with his vocabulary, his stylistic habits, and especially his ideas. This situation was recognized perfectly by the unknown fourteenth-century humanist who copied extracts from Books I to IX in a manuscript now kept at Darmstadt. At the beginning of Book II, he wrote: *antikrus epiktetizei* ("He is openly Epictetizing"; that is, he is following and imitating Epictetus).

The three rules of life or disciplines according to Epictetus

We have already seen the important role played in the *Meditations* by what I have called the triple rule of life, which proposes a discipline of representations or judgments, of desire, and of action. This very tripartition of the acts and functions of the soul, and the entire distinction between judgment, desire, and impulse, is a doctrine which is peculiar to Epictetus, and which is not found in Stoicism prior to him. Its presence in Marcus Aurelius is, nevertheless, unmistakable. In VIII, 7, for example, Marcus clearly draws an opposition between representations *(phantasiai)*, desires *(orexeis)*, and impulses toward action *(hormai)*, and he does so again in VIII, 28:

> Every judgment, every impulse to action, and every desire or aversion are within the soul, and nothing else can enter therein.

We have already encountered a brief maxim which also makes use of the same schema:

> Erase your representation *(phantasia)*, check your impulse to action *(hormē)*, extinguish your desire *(orexis)*. Keep your directing principle *(hēgemonikon)* within your power (IX, 7).

The three rules of life propose an *askēsis,* or discipline, for these three acts of the soul. In the context of the cento of passages from Epictetus (XI, 33–39) which we have already seen, Marcus himself cites an Epictetan passage which we know only through his intermediary (XI, 37):

> We must discover the rule to be applied in the case of the assent [to be given to representations and judgments],
> —while in the matter of exercises relating to impulses to action, we must never relax our attention, in order that these impulses to action may be accompanied by a reserve clause, that their goal be to serve the community, and that they be proportionate to value,
> —and, finally, we must abstain completely from desire, and pay no attention to things that do not depend on us.

Discipline of representations and judgment, discipline of impulsive action, discipline of desire: Epictetus formulates these three rules of life not only in this text, but in several chapters of his *Discourses.* Moreover, they correspond precisely to the three rules of life formulated by Marcus, which are in a sense the key to his *Meditations.*

The influence of Aristo

In the context of Marcus' conversion to philosophy, I alluded to the influence that the reading of the works of the third century B.C. Stoic Aristo of Chios may have exerted on the Emperor. I had once thought I could recognize an echo of Aristo's teachings in some of the Emperor's sayings. Aristo had defined the supreme goal of life in the following terms: "To live in a disposition of indifference with regard to indifferent things." Marcus, for his part, writes (XI, 16):

> To spend one's life in the best way: the power to do this resides within the soul, if one is indifferent to indifferent things.

I was once struck by the similarity of these formulas.[50] In fact, however, Aristo was not the only Stoic to speak of indifference to indifferent things; moreover, Marcus, as a faithful adherent to the Stoicism of Epictetus and of Chrysippus, did not understand this principle in the same sense as Aristo, and interpreted it in a wholly different way.

The principle of all Stoicism is, moreover, precisely indifference to indifferent things. This means, in the first place, that the only value is moral good, which depends on our freedom, and that everything that does not depend on our freedom—poverty, wealth, sickness, and health—is neither good nor bad, and is therefore indifferent. Second, it means that we must not make any distinction between indifferent things; in other words, we must love them equally, since they have been willed by universal Nature. This indifference to indifferent things can be found, for example, in a passage from Philo of Alexandria,[51] which describes the exercise of wisdom—that is to say, philosophy—without there having been any particular influence by Aristo on Philo: "Accustomed no longer to pay attention to bodily and external evils, exercising ourselves to be indifferent to indifferent things, armed against pleasures and desires . . . for such people, all of life is a festival."

As a matter of fact, the difference between Aristo and the other Stoics bore precisely on the very notion of "indifferent." For Aristo, that which was indifferent was completely "undifferentiated,"[52] and no element of daily life had any importance in and of itself. Such a view ran the risk of leading to a skeptical attitude such as that of Pyrrho, who was also indifferent to everything. Orthodox Stoics, while they recognized that the things which do not depend on us are indifferent, nevertheless admitted that we could attribute to them a moral value, by conceding the existence of political, social, and family obligations, linked to the needs of human nature in accordance with reasonable probability. This was the realm of the *kathēkonta,* or duties, of which I shall have more to say later. Marcus Aurelius, like Epictetus, allowed for the existence of this entire order of obligations and duties, which Aristo had denied. In fact, Marcus uses the technical term *kathēkon* in the Stoic sense a total of five times.[53] There can thus be no question of any influence by Aristo on Marcus as far as the doctrine of indifference is concerned.

Moreover, Aristo rejected the physical and logical parts of philosophy as useless.[54] At first glance, Marcus appears to incline toward a similar attitude; for example, he thanks the gods for not having allowed him to be carried away with resolving syllogisms or studying celestial phenomena (I, 17, 22). Elsewhere, he admits that he no longer hopes to excel in dialectics or in the philosophy of nature (VII, 67). Here again, however, the underlying sense is wholly different. For Aristo, logic and physics are strictly useless. For Marcus, by contrast, it is the *theoretical discourse* of logic and physics which is no longer a matter of concern. He did, however, intend to practice a *lived* logic (the discipline of judgment) and a *lived* physics (the discipline of desire). As he says explicitly (VIII, 13):

> Continuously, and, if possible, on the occasion of every representation which presents itself to you, practice physics, pathology, and dialectics.

We are thus forced to conclude that there is no trace of Aristo's doctrines to be found in the *Meditations* of Marcus Aurelius.[55]

5

THE STOICISM OF EPICTETUS

❧

The general characteristics of Stoicism

It is probably scarcely necessary to remind the reader that when we speak of the doctrines of a philosopher from the period we are studying, we must not imagine that we have to do with a system invented lock, stock, and barrel by the philosopher in question. Ancient philosophy had nothing in common with our contemporary philosophers, who imagine that philosophy consists, for each philosopher, in inventing a "new discourse" or new language, all the more original the more it is incomprehensible and artificial. In general, ancient philosophy was situated within a tradition, and attached to a school. Now, Epictetus was a Stoic; this means that for him philosophy consisted in explicating the texts of Zeno and Chrysippus, the founders of the school, and above all in practicing himself, and having his disciples practice, the way of life peculiar to the Stoic school. This does not mean that Epictetus' teaching was devoid of its own characteristic features. These features, however, did not modify the fundamental dogmas of Stoicism, or the essential choice of a way of life. On the contrary, they are to be found within his form of teaching, in his way of presenting the doctrine, and in the definition of certain specific points (for instance, the distinction between desire and impulse), or else within the particular color and tonality which permeate the Stoic way of life proposed by the philosopher.

By the time Epictetus taught, it had been some four centuries since Zeno of Citium had founded the Stoic school at Athens. One can say that Stoicism was born of the fusion of three traditions: the Socratic ethical tradition, the Heraclitean physical and "materialistic" tradition, and the dialectical tradition of the Megareans and of Aristotle. The Stoic choice of life was analogous to the Socratic choice of life, according to which moral good or virtue is the only value, to which everything else must be subordinated. As Socrates says in Plato's *Apology* (41d): "For a good man, no evil is possible, whether he be dead or alive." "No evil is possible," precisely because such a man, since he is good, is a stranger to moral evil. Since for him there is no other evil than moral evil, he believes that all those things which appear to be evil in the eyes of men—death, illness, the loss of wealth, insults—are not evils for him. This transmutation of values, however, can only be carried out by means of an operation which is, at the same time, both intellectual and ethical: it consists in examining oneself in a dialogue, a *logos,* or a process of reasoning which one develops either with someone else or with oneself. The spirit of Socratism is thus the affirmation of the absolute value of moral good, as discovered by reason; it is also the idea according to which the moral life is a matter of judgment and of knowledge.

Prima facie, it does not appear that the physical tradition of Heraclitean "materialism" has anything to do with the Socratic ethical tradition. We shall soon see, however, that the originality of Stoicism consists precisely in the intimate and indissoluble fusion of these two traditions. For the moment, it is sufficient to emphasize the influence of Heraclitus upon the Stoic vision of a universe in perpetual transformation, of which the original element is fire, and which is set in order by a *logos* or Reason, in accordance with which events are linked by mutual necessity.

Finally, it is not surprising that Stoicism is situated as well within the dialectical tradition of the Megarians, but also within that of the Platonic Academy and of Aristotle. In this period, instruction in philosophy consisted above all in training for discussion and argumentation, and consequently in dialectical exercises. Here again, we encounter a *logos:* this time it is human discourse, but one which is rational and just, insofar as it imitates that *logos* which maintains the universe in order.

We can thus glimpse the extraordinary unity which held the parts of the Stoic system together. It is the unity of one single *logos,* or Reason, which permeates all things. In the words of Émile Bréhier:

> It is one single, unique reason which, in dialectics, links consequent propositions to their antecedents; which, in nature, links together all causes; and which, in human conduct, establishes perfect concord between acts. It is impossible that a good man should not be a physicist and a dialectician; it is impossible for rationality to be realized separately in these three areas; it is impossible completely to grasp the reason within the course of events in the universe without, at the same time, realizing reason within one's own behavior.[1]

Stoicism is a philosophy of self-coherence, based upon a remarkable intuition of the essence of life. From the very first moment of its existence, every living being is instinctively attuned to itself; that is, it tends to preserve itself, to love its own existence, and to love all that can preserve this existence. This instinctive accord becomes a moral accord with oneself, as soon as man discovers by means of his reason that the supreme value is not those things which are the objects of this instinct for self-preservation, but the reflective choice of accord with oneself, and the *activity of choice itself*. This is because voluntary accord with oneself coincides with the tendencies of universal Reason, which not only makes each living being into a being in accord with itself, but makes the entire world as well a being in accord with itself. In the words of Marcus Aurelius (IV, 23):

All that is in accord with you is in accord with me, O World.

Human society, which is the society of those who participate in one single *logos* or Reason, also forms—at least in principle—an ideal City, whose Reason, which is the Law, ensures its accord with itself. Finally, it is obvious that the Reason of each individual, in the mutual linkage of its thoughts or speech, demands logical and dialectical coherence with itself.

This coherence with oneself is thus the fundamental principle of Stoicism. For Seneca,[2] all wisdom may be summed up in the formula: "Always want the same thing, and always refuse the same thing." There is no need, Seneca continues, to add the tiny restriction "as long as what one wants is morally good." Why? Because, he says, "One and the same thing can be universally and constantly pleasing only if it is morally right." This is nothing but the distant echo of the formulas by which Zeno, the founder of Stoicism, used to define the sovereign Good: "Live in a coherent way *(homologoumenōs)*;[3] that is to say, live in accordance with a rule of life which is one and harmonious, because those who live in incoherence are unhappy."

This coherence with oneself is, as we have seen, based on the self-coherence of universal Reason or Nature. The well-known Stoic theme of the Eternal Return is only one other aspect of this theme. Universal Reason wishes this world to be as it is: that is to say, arising from the original fire, and returning to this original fire, and therefore having a beginning and an end. Nature's will, however, is always the same; and the only thing its continuous action can accomplish is the repetition of this world, with precisely this beginning, precisely this end, and the entire course of events situated between these two moments. Thus, this world returns eternally: "There will be another Socrates, a Plato, and every man with the same friends and the same fellow-citizens . . . and this renewal will not happen once, but several times; rather, all things will be repeated eternally."[4] This is why the sage, like universal Reason, must intensely wish for each instant: he must wish intensely for things to happen eternally exactly as they do happen.

I have just mentioned the figure of the sage. It was characteristic of Stoic philosophy to make of this figure a transcendent norm, which can only be realized in rare and exceptional cases. Here we encounter an echo of Plato's *Symposium* (204d), where Socrates appears as the figure who knows that he is not a sage. Socrates' situation places him between the gods, who are wise and know that they are wise, and men, who think they are wise but do not realize that they are not. This intermediary situation is that of the philosopher: he who loves and aspires to wisdom precisely because he knows that he lacks it. It is also the situation of Eros, who loves Beauty because he knows he lacks it; neither man nor god, Eros is therefore a *daimōn,* intermediary between the two. The figure of Socrates thus coincides both with that of Eros and with that of the philosopher.[5]

Similarly, the Stoic sage is the equal of God, since God is nothing other than universal Reason, producing in self-coherence all the events of the universe. Human reason is an emanation or part of this Universal Reason. It can, however, become obscured and deformed as a result of life within the body, owing in particular to the attractions of pleasure. It is only the sage who is able to make his reason coincide with universal Reason. Such perfect coincidence, however, can only be an ideal, for the sage is necessarily an exceptional being. There are very few of them— perhaps only one, or perhaps none at all. He is an almost inaccessible ideal, and, in the last analysis, more of a transcendent norm than anything else, which the Stoics never tire of describing, even as they enumerate all its paradoxes. Philosophy is not wisdom, but only the exercise of wisdom, and if the philosopher is not a sage, he is necessarily a non-sage. There is thus a contradictory opposition between sage and non-sage: either one is a "sage" or one is not, and there is no middle term. There are no degrees of unwisdom, relative to wisdom. As the Stoics used to say, it doesn't matter much if you are one cubit below the surface of the water, or five hundred fathoms: you'll drown in the one case just as much as in the other. Since, then, the sage is extremely rare, all humanity is out of its mind, and men suffer from an almost universal corruption of or deviation from Reason. Yet the Stoics still urge people to philoso-phize—that is, to train themselves for wisdom. They therefore believe in the possibility of spiritual progress.

The explanation of this apparent paradox is that, although it is true that there is a contradictory opposition between wisdom and unwisdom, and therefore that there are no degrees of unwisdom as opposed to wisdom, it is nevertheless the case that, as in Plato's Symposium, there are two categories of people within the state of unwisdom itself: those non-sages who are not conscious of their state—these are the foolish ones—and those non-sages who *are* aware of their state, and who attempt to progress toward inaccessible wisdom. Those in the latter category are philoso-phers.

Thus, from the point of view of logic, we have here a contrary oppo-sition between the sage and the foolish, who are unaware of their state. This opposition does, however, admit of a middle term: the non-foolish non-sages—in other words, philosophers.[6]

The ideal sage would thus be one who could, at each moment and definitively, make his reason coincide with that universal Reason which is the Sage that thinks and produces the world.

An unexpected consequence of this Stoic theory of the sage is that Stoic philosophy—and I do mean Stoic philosophy; that is, the theory and the practice of training for wisdom—allows for a great deal of uncer-tainty and simple probability. After all, only the Sage possesses a perfect, necessary, and unshakable knowledge of reality; the philosopher does not. The goal, project, and object of Stoic philosophy are thus to allow the philosopher to orient himself or herself within the uncertainties of daily life, by proposing probable choices which our reason can accept, even if it is not always sure it ought to. What matters are not results or efficiency, but the *intention* to do good. What matters is to act out of one motive alone, without any other considerations of interest or pleasure: that of the moral good. This is the only value, and the only one we need.

The Stoics on the parts of philosophy

By the time Zeno founded the Stoic school, the custom of distinguishing various parts of philosophy, and of determining their mutual relationship, was already traditional within the teaching provided by the philosophical schools. Since the time of Plato, and especially since that of Aristotle, philosophers had been paying the most careful attention to questions concerning the different types of knowledge, and the various methods which characterize them.[7]

We can presume that within the Platonic school, also known as the Old Academy, there was already a distinction between three parts of philosophy: dialectics, physics, and ethics. Dialectics was the noblest part of philosophy, inasmuch as, in the sense that Plato had given to this term, it corresponded to the discovery of the Ideas or Forms (for example, the notion of Justice or of Equality). This discovery was brought about by a "dialectical" method of discussion; that is to say, for the Platonists, by means of rigorous argumentation. Physics, as the study of the visible world, was an inferior part of philosophy, but it did have as its object, to some degree at least, celestial phenomena, or the necessary, eternal movement of the stars. Ethics was lower still, inasmuch as its objects were the uncertain, contingent actions of mankind. Thus, the division of the parts of philosophy reflects the hierarchy which the Platonists had introduced among the various degrees of reality.

The Stoics, at the same time as they took up this division, transformed it completely. Their terminology appears to remain the same, but it no longer corresponds to the hierarchy of the Platonists, but rather to the dynamic, unitary conception of the world which was peculiar to the Stoa. Among physics, ethics, and dialectics, there was no longer any preeminence of one discipline over the others, for all three were related to the same *logos* or divine Reason. This Reason was equally present in the physical world, in the world of social life—since society is based upon the reason common to all mankind—and in human speech and thought; that is, within the rational activity of judgment.

Moreover, from the point of view of perfect action, which is that of the sage, these three disciplines mutually imply one another, since it is one and the same *logos* or Reason which is to be found within nature, the human community, and individual reason. This is why, to return once more to the remarks of Émile Bréhier, "it is impossible for a good man [that is, one who practices ethics] not to be a physician and a dialectician; it is impossible for rationality to be realized separately in these three areas, and, for instance, to grasp reason fully in the course of events in the world, without at the same time realizing reason within one's own conduct."[8] The perfect exercise of any one of these disciplines implies that of all the others. The sage practices dialectics by maintaining coherence in his judgments; he practices ethics by maintaining coherence in his will, and in the actions which result from it; and he practices physics by behaving like a part which is coherent with the whole to which it belongs. For the Stoics, the parts of philosophy are virtues[9] which—like all virtues, in their view—are equal and mutually imply one another: to practice one of them is necessarily to practice all of them.

Thus, from this point of view, there is a sense in which logic, physics, and ethics are not really distinct from one another; no one of them precedes the others, and they are all mixed up together. The Platonic-Aristotelian model of a hierarchy of knowledge and of levels of reality is thus replaced by the representation of an organic unity, in which there is complete compenetration. For the Platonists and the Aristotelians, the whole of reality is heterogeneous, and is composed of zones in which substantiality and necessity are completely different. For the Stoics, on the contrary, all reality is homogeneous, and the sequence of events wholly necessary. The distinction between physics, as the science of the sensible world, and a science of the transcendent world of Ideas (that is, Platonic dialectics) or of the gods (theology) is completely abolished. *Physis* or nature, which, for the Platonists and the Aristotelians, was only a small part—and the lowest part at that—of the whole of reality, becomes all of reality.

The word "dialectics" also changes its meaning. It no longer denotes, as it does for Plato, a method of reasoning which starts from notions common to all mankind, and rises, by means of questions and answers, to the discovery of those essences which make reasoning and language possible. Nor does it denote, as it did for Aristotle, a method of reasoning which starts from notions which are common to all mankind—and therefore not scientific—and makes possible, by means of questions and answers, the attainment of *probable* conclusions in every area of reality. Although Stoic dialectics also takes its point of departure in common notions, it is able to obtain true and necessary conclusions because it reflects the necessary interrelation of causes within the sensible world.

To be sure, for the Stoics, physics, ethics, and dialectics are—formally at least—to be related to three different sectors of reality: the physical world, human conduct, and the functioning of thought. Nevertheless, the Stoics did not consider these three parts as corpora of theoretical doctrines, but as inner dispositions and practical conduct of the sage, and hence of the philosopher in training for wisdom. From this perspective, the living exercise of physics, ethics, and dialectics, and the practice of these three virtues, in fact corresponds to one attitude: the single act of placing oneself in harmony with the *logos,* whether it be the *logos* of universal Nature, the *logos* of rational human nature, or the *logos* as it is expressed in human discourse.

Although physics, ethics, and dialectics are practically merged together into a single act when it comes to the concrete exercise of philosophy, they must nevertheless be well distinguished when it comes to teaching them. Philosophy must be set forth and described before the disciple. Thus, philosophical discourse introduces a temporal dimension which has two aspects: there is the "logical" time of the discourse itself, and then there is the psychological time which the disciple requires to assimilate what he or she is being taught. Logical time corresponds to the inner requirements of theoretical discourse: there must be a series of arguments, which must be presented in a specific order, and this is logical time. All expositions of doctrine, however, are addressed to an auditor, and the auditor introduces another component: the stages of his spiritual progress; and here we are dealing with a time which is purely psychological. Until the auditor has assimilated a given doctrine inwardly and spiritually, it is either useless or impossible to speak to him or her about anything else. There is, moreover, a kind of conflict between these two times, for it is often difficult to safeguard the logical order while still taking the auditor's spiritual state into account.

Thus, from the point of view of that discourse which transmits philosophical instruction, the Stoics distinguished very sharply and clearly between the three parts of philosophy, and tried to establish among them not only a logical order, but also a pedagogical one. There was much discussion on this topic within the school, for there was no agreement on the order which was to be established between physics, ethics, and logic or dialectics. We know that the Stoics used to compare the parts of philosophy to the parts of organic totalities such as an egg, a garden, or a living being. However, although logic was always presented in these comparisons as the part which ensures self-defense and solidity, the innermost and most precious part was sometimes presented as ethics, and sometimes as physics.

In his treatise *On Stoic Self-Contradictions,* Plutarch[10] reproaches Chrysippus with having sometimes placed physics as the end-point of philosophical instruction, as if it were the supreme initiation which transmitted teachings about the gods, and at other times placing physics before ethics, since the distinction between good and evil was only possible on the basis of the study of universal Nature and the organization of the world. In fact, these hesitations correspond to the various types of educational program which could be chosen. According to the *logical* order of exposition, physics should precede ethics, in order to give it a rational foundation. According to the *psychological* order of education, however, physics must follow ethics, because it is by practicing ethics that one prepares oneself for the revelation of the divine world, that is, of universal Nature.

It was in order to get past these difficulties that some Stoics, while continuing to profess their own theory concerning the ideal priority of a given part of philosophy within the overall educational program, urged that the parts of philosophy be presented simultaneously within the context of instructional philosophical discourse: "Some Stoics held that no part of philosophy had any priority, but that they were all mixed together; and they made their teaching mixed, too."[11] The parts of philosophy were "inseparable."[12] How, indeed, could one wait until one finished the complete program for one part, before beginning the study of another? Above all, how could one wait to practice philosophy itself, in all its three aspects? Chrysippus himself seems to have recommended this type of "mixed" instruction, for he writes: "He who begins with logic must not abstain from the other parts, but must participate in the other studies, when the opportunity arises."[13] In fact, the method of teaching must be integral at each of its moments, since we are not trying to acquire three distinct theoretical bodies of knowledge, separate from one another, but rather to train ourselves for that unique act of wisdom which is, indissolubly, the practice of physics, of ethics, and of logic.

In view of the preceding considerations, we are now better able to understand how the Stoics distinguished between *philosophy* and discourse *concerning* philosophy. They affirmed that logic, physics, and ethics—which up until now I have been calling, in accordance with common usage, the parts of philosophy—were not in fact parts of philosophy properly so called, but parts of discourse concerning philosophy.[14] The only time physics, logic, and ethics appear as distinct, separate, and perhaps even successive, is within the context of the philosophical teaching discourse.

It is this teaching discourse which requires a theoretical exposition of logic, in the form of an abstract study of the rules of reasoning. It also requires a theoretical exposition of physics, that is to say, an abstract study of the structure and coming-to-be of the cosmos. Finally, it requires a theoretical exposition of ethics—in other words, an abstract study of human behavior, and of the rules which it ought to obey. Chrysippus used to say explicitly that these were the "three kinds of *theōrēmata* proper to philosophy."[15] In philosophy itself, by contrast, understood as the exercise of wisdom, physics, ethics, and logic are mutually implicated within and interior to one another, in that act—at once multiple and unique—which is the exercise of physical virtue, ethical virtue, and logical virtue. At this point, we are no longer concerned with producing abstract theories of logic—that is, theories of the art of speaking and writing well; rather, we are concerned with speaking and writing well in reality. We no longer construct abstract theories of ethics, or of acting well; instead we are concerned about whether we are in fact acting well. Finally, at this level we are no longer interested in developing abstract theories about physics, in order to prove that we are a part of the cosmic All; rather, we try to live as a true part of the cosmic All.

These three exercises mutually imply one another, and in fact they constitute one single act or disposition, which is differentiated only insofar as it is oriented toward the three aspects of reality: the Reason of human discourse, the Reason of human society, and the Reason of the cosmos.

Thus, logic, physics, and ethics are distinguishable when we *talk about* philosophy, but not when we *live* it.

The three acts of the soul and the three exercise-themes according to Epictetus

From Zeno (332–262 B.C.) and Chrysippus (c. 281–204 B.C.) to Epictetus (died c. 125 A.D.), the formulation of Stoic doctrine evolved—particularly as a result of its polemics with other philosophical schools—and sometimes the rigor of the positions of the school's founders was somewhat attenuated. Yet its fundamental dogmas never changed.

Epictetus himself, at any rate—perhaps because of his teaching methods, which obliged him to explicate the works of the founding fathers—went back to the origins. As Bréhier used to say, Epictetus cannot be too highly recommended to anyone wishing to understand the Old Stoa.[16] Already in 1894, in two remarkable studies devoted to Epictetus, A. Bonhöffer had reached similar conclusions.[17] It can be said that Epictetus subscribes to the most orthodox Stoic tradition: that which, beginning with Chrysippus, apparently continues through Archedemus and Antipater;[18] he makes no allusions to Panetius or to Posidonius. Through Epictetus, Marcus Aurelius was able to go back to the purest Stoic sources, and the following exposition of the Stoicism of Epictetus may consequently be regarded as a preliminary sketch of the Stoicism of Marcus Aurelius.

It is true that, in the sayings of Epictetus as recorded by Arrian, we nowhere find a systematic exposition of the totality of Stoic doctrine; the reasons for this have been explained above. The subjects of the *Discourses* were inspired by occasional circumstances, such as the questions raised by his students, or the visit of a specific personage. Epictetus' sayings are essentially anecdotal; but it is all the more precious to be able to observe within them the presence of a highly structured theme, which frequently recurs and can be said to summarize the essential points of Stoicism.

There is one highly structured theme that integrates right at the outset something which, it would seem, Epictetus is the only one within the Stoic tradition, besides Marcus Aurelius, to distinguish: the three activities or operations of the soul. These are the desire to accumulate that which is good, the impulse to act, and judgment on the value of things.

Basing his view on the traditional and fundamental Stoic distinction between those things which do not depend upon our will and those which do, Epictetus enumerates these three psychological operations as follows:

> What depends on us are value-judgments *(hypolēpseis)*, impulses toward action *(hormē)*, and desire *(orexis)* or aversion; in a word, everything which is our own business. What does not depend on us are the body, wealth, honors, and high positions in office; in a word, everything which is not our own business.[19]

Here, we can glimpse one of the Stoics' most fundamental attitudes: the delimitation of our own sphere of liberty as an impregnable islet of autonomy, in the midst of the vast river of events and of Destiny. What depends on us are thus the acts of our soul, because we can freely choose them. We can judge or not judge, or judge in whatever manner we please; we can desire or not desire; will or not will. By contrast, that which does not depend on us—Epictetus lists our body, honors, riches, and high positions of authority—is everything that depends upon the general course of nature. Our body, first: it is true that we can move it, but we are not completely in control of it. Birth, death, sickness, involuntary movements, sensations of pleasure or of pain: all these are completely independent of our will. As for wealth and honors: we can, to be sure, attempt to acquire them, yet definitive success does not depend upon us, but upon a series of human factors and events which are exterior to us; they are imponderable and do not depend upon our will. Thus, the Stoic delimits a center of autonomy—the soul, as opposed to the body; and a guiding principle *(hēgemonikon)* as opposed to the rest of the soul. It is within this guiding principle that freedom and our true self are located. It is also there, and only there, that moral good and evil can be found, for the only moral good and evil are voluntary good and evil.

The soul or guiding principle thus has three fundamental activities. In the first place, as it receives the images which come from bodily sensations, it develops an inner discourse, and this is what constitutes *judgment*. The soul tells itself what a given object or event is; in particular, it tells itself what the object is *for* the soul, that is, what it is in the soul's view. Here we have the central node of the whole of Stoicism: that of inner discourse, or judgments expressed on the subject of representations. As Epictetus and Marcus Aurelius never tire of saying, everything is a matter of judgment. It is not things themselves that trouble us, but our representations of these things, the ideas we form of them, and the inner discourse which we formulate about them. Desire and impulses to action are the necessary results of this inner discourse: if we desire something, it is because we have told ourselves that the thing in question is good; likewise, if we want to do something, it is because we have told ourselves that it was a good thing.

As is well known, the Stoics held that only those representations should be accepted into the mind which they called *kataleptikai,* a term which is usually translated as "comprehensive." This translation gives the impression that the Stoics believed a representation to be true when it "comprehends," or seizes the contents of reality. In Epictetus, however, we can glimpse a wholly different meaning of the term: for him, a representation is *kataleptikē* when it does not go beyond what is given, but is able to stop at what is perceived, without adding anything extraneous to that which is perceived. Rather than "comprehensive representations," then, it would be better to speak of "adequate representations."

Here is a translation—slightly paraphrased, in order to make it more comprehensible—of a vital passage from the *Discourses* of Epictetus. It shows in action the inner discourse, or the soul's dialogue with itself, on the subject of representations (III, 8, 1–2):

> In the same way as we train ourselves in order to be able to face up to sophistical interrogations, we ought also to train ourselves to face up to representations *(phantasiai),* for they too ask us questions.

For example, let's say we formulate within ourselves the contents of the representation: "So-and-so's son is dead."

This representation is asking you a question, and you should reply: "That does not depend on the will, and is not something bad."

"So-and-so's father has disinherited him. What do you think of that?" Reply: "That doesn't depend on the will, and is not something bad."

"He was very hurt by it." Reply: "That *does* depend on the will, and is something bad."

"He put up with it bravely." "That depends on the will, and is something good."

Epictetus continues:

If we acquire this habit, we will make progress; for we will give our assent only to that of which there is an adequate *(kataleptike)* representation.

It is quite remarkable that Epictetus here is representing moral life as a dialectical exercise, in which we engage in a dialogue with events, as they ask us questions.

Epictetus then goes on to give the following examples, in which representations ask us questions. "Her son is dead" is an inner representation which we formulate, and it asks us the question: "What happened?" This could lead us to enunciate a value-judgment, of the type "a great misfortune," but we must reply: "Her son is dead." The representation, however, is not satisfied; it asks "Nothing more?" to which the soul responds: "nothing more." Epictetus then continues along the same lines:

"His ship sank."
"What happened?"
"His ship sank."

"He was sent to prison." But if you add the proposition "a terrible thing happened to him," then that is coming from you.

What Epictetus means is that the idea according to which a certain event is a misfortune—as well as the consequences that such a representation may have on the desires and tendencies of the soul—is a representation which has no basis in reality; rather, it goes beyond an adequate vision of reality, by adding to it a false value-judgment. Such a representation can arise only in a soul which has not yet assimilated the fundamental dogma of Stoicism: happiness is only to be found in moral good, or virtue; and misfortune is only to be found in moral evil, in faults and in vice.

If the only good is moral good, and the only evil is moral evil, how can the Stoic live his daily life, in which there are many things which are morally neither good nor evil, but are "indifferent," to use a term from the Stoic vocabulary? A person must, after all, eat, sleep, work, raise a family, and fulfill his or her role within the community. The Stoic, too, must act; and he or she has an impulse—both instinctive and rational—to act. Thus, the second of the soul's proper functions, coming after the activity of representations, judgments, and assent, must be just this impulse to *act,* as well as action itself. The domain of the latter includes what Epictetus and the Stoics call the *kathēkonta;* that is, those actions which, in all probability and for good reason, may be considered as "appropriate" to human nature. These are the actions which conform to the deep-rooted instinct which urges rational human nature to act in order to preserve itself. Thus, both the active impulse and action itself will be exercised above all in the domain of society, of the state, of the family, and of relations between human beings in general.

Human action cannot, however, hope to be completely effective; it does not always attain its goal. Mankind is, therefore, reduced to hoping and to desiring that what suits him actually happens, and that that which he fears does not. *Desire* is thus the third activity proper to the human soul, and its domain is not that which one does oneself, but rather that which happens—in other words, the events which happen to us by virtue of Destiny, and the course of universal Nature. He who desires does not act, but is in a certain disposition of waiting. As was the case with the impulse to action, desire depends on us, and the soul is free either to desire a given object, or not to desire it.

The philosopher, then, must train himself in these three domains of activity: judgment, impulse toward action, and desire (III, 2, 1–2):

> There are three domains in which he who would become perfect must train himself:
> —the domain concerning *desires* and aversions, so that he may not find himself frustrated in his desires, and may not encounter that which he was seeking to avoid;
> —the domain concerning active impulses and repulsions, and in general, the domain which concerns what is appropriate *(kathēkon)* for our nature, so that he may act in an orderly way, in accordance

with rational probability, and without negligence;
—the domain in which what matters is to preserve oneself from error and insufficient reasons; and, in general, that which concerns the assent [which we give to judgments].

If we gather together all the indications concerning this theme contained in Epictetus' sayings, we can present this theory of the three forms or domains[20] of philosophical exercise as follows:

The first domain is that of *desires* and *aversions*. Humans are unhappy because they desire things which they consider good, but which they may either fail to obtain or else lose; and because they try to avoid things which they consider as evils, but which are often inevitable. The reason is that these apparent goods and evils—wealth and health, for example, or on the contrary poverty and sickness—do not depend on us. Thus, the exercise of the discipline of desire will consist in gradually renouncing these desires and aversions, so that we may finally desire only that which does depend on us—in other words, moral good—and may avoid only that which depends on us—in other words, moral evil. That which does not depend on us is to be considered as indifferent, which means that we are not to introduce any preferential order among such things, but accept them as willed by the will of universal Nature, which Epictetus sometimes designates by the term "gods" in general. To "follow the gods" means to accept their will, which is identical with the will of universal Nature (I, 12, 8; I, 20, 15). The discipline of desire thus has as its object the passions *(pathē)*, or the emotions which we feel when events present themselves to us.

The second domain of exercises is that of *impulses to action*. As we have seen, it is the field of those actions which are "appropriate" *(kathēkonta)* to our rational nature. These are actions—and therefore something which depends on us—that have an effect on things which do not depend on us, such as other human beings, politics, health, family life, and so forth. All of these areas are, in themselves, "indifferent" in the Stoic sense of the term; but they may, in accordance with a rational justification or reasonable probability, be considered as corresponding to reasonable nature's instinct for self-preservation. Since such actions are directed exclusively toward other people, and have their foundation in that community of reasonable nature which unites humankind, they must be guided by our intention to place ourselves in the service of the human community, and bring about the reign of justice.

The third domain of exercises is that of *assent (sunkatathesis)*. Each representation *(phantasia)* which presents itself to us must be subjected to criticism, so that our inner dialogue and the judgment we enunciate with regard to it may not add anything "subjective" to that which, within the representation, is "adequate" to reality; only thus will we be able to give our assent to a true judgment. We have already seen the importance of this theme in Stoicism, for which good and evil are not to be found anywhere else than in our faculty of judgment.

It is tempting to compare the three acts of the soul as distinguished by Epictetus—rational activity of judgment and assent, impulse to action, and desire—with the three parts of the soul recognized by the Platonists. Following Plato, they distinguished between the rational part of the soul, its "choleric" part, which is the seat of action, and the "desiring" part, which is the principle of pleasure and of passion. This comparison is all the more attractive in that Plato, like Epictetus, based his system of virtues, and therefore, in a sense, his "ascetic" system, on his distinction of the parts of the soul. For Epictetus, as we have seen, there is a discipline of the soul's intellectual activity, a discipline of impulses and tendencies to action, and a discipline of desire. In Plato's *Republic,* justice is the inner harmony of the individual as well as of the state, and it consists in the union of three elements: the first is wisdom, which, in the soul, reigns over the rational part, and in the state is the characteristic of the philosopher-kings. Within the soul, courage reigns over the "choleric" and impulsive part; whereas within the state it pertains to the class of warriors. Finally, that temperance which is to be found within the soul reigns over the "desiring" part; whereas within the state it must be the characteristic of the lowest class: that of the artisans.[21]

In spite of these analogies, however, the schemes of Plato and of Epictetus are radically and completely different. For Plato, there is a hierarchy among the parts of the soul analogous to that which is established between the classes of society in the *Republic:* rulers, warriors, and artisans. The philosopher-kings impose their rule upon the warriors and artisans, who are their inferiors. In the same way, good reason imposes its law upon the inferior parts of the soul.

For Epictetus, by contrast, both active impulse and desire are acts of the rational soul, or the "guiding principle" within each human being. There is thus no opposition or difference of level between rational activity, impulses to action, and desire. Impulses and desire are located within the rational soul itself; and this is all the more true in that impulse and desire, even if they do have affective repercussions upon the soul, are, according to Stoic teaching, essentially judgments made by the rational soul. Reason is not essentially good; rather, like impulses and desire, it can be either good or bad, according to whether it emits true or false judgments, which then determine conduct. A passage from Plutarch[22] provides a good summary of Stoic doctrine as we find it in Epictetus:

> For the Stoics, virtue is a disposition of the ruling part of the soul . . . or rather it is reason when the latter is coherent with itself, firm, and constant. They do not believe that the passionate and irrational parts of the soul differ from the rational faculty by means of a natural difference; but that it is the same part of the soul, which they call *dianoia* and *hēgemonikon* (the faculty of reflection and the directing principle) which changes and is completely transformed in the passions and the transformations which it undergoes, either in its state or in its dispositions, and that it becomes vice or virtue. In itself, however, there is nothing irrational about this faculty, but it is called irrational when, owing to excessive impulses, it becomes very strong and triumphant, and is consequently led to something inappropriate and contrary to the choice of reason. Passion, thus, is reason, but reason which is vitiated and depraved, and which, owing to the effect of bad and perverted judgment, has acquired strength and vigor.

For Plato, we can say that the essence of human beings resides in reason; and reason is necessarily right, but the life of the concrete individual does not necessarily coincide with it. For Epictetus, by contrast, as for the Stoics in general, the essence of mankind does consist in reason, the principle of freedom, and the power to choose. Precisely because it is the power to choose, however, it can be either good or bad and is not necessarily right.

Impulse and desire are thus located within the "directing principle," or center of the human soul's freedom. For this reason, they are on the same level as the rational faculty of judgment and of assent. Obviously, however, judgment, impulse, and desire are not interchangeable. Each impulse and each desire has its foundation and its origin in a judgment. It is as a function of its inner discourse that the soul feels a certain impulse to action, or a certain inner disposition of desire.

The three exercise-themes and the three parts of philosophy

For the Stoics, as we have seen, there is not only a discourse about logic, but a lived logic. Likewise, there is not only a discourse about ethics, but also a lived ethics; there is not only a discourse about physics, but also a

lived physics. In other words, philosophy, insofar as it is the conduct of
life, is indissolubly logic, ethics, and physics. We can recognize this lived
logic, ethics, and physics in the three exercises of Epictetus which we
have just examined.

It is worth noting that, in order to designate these exercises,
Epictetus[23] uses the word *topos,* a term traditionally used by the Stoics—at
least since the time of Apollodoros of Seleucia, who flourished at the end
of the second century B.C.—to designate the parts of philosophy.[24] When
the Stoics spoke of the parts of philosophical discourse, they were probably using the word *topos* in a rhetorical and dialectical sense, in which it
signified a thesis, or a "general question which is put up for discussion."[25]
In the same way as a rhetorical or dialectical *topos* was a theme for
exercises in the area of discourse, so Epictetus' three *topoi* are three
themes of intellectual exercise, which correspond to the three parts of
philosophical discourse. At the same time, however, they are also three
themes of lived exercise, which put the principles formulated in philosophical discourse into action, in the area of life.

It is obvious that, for Epictetus, the discipline of judgment and of
assent corresponds to the logical part of philosophy, while the discipline
of impulses corresponds to the ethical part of philosophy. This equivalence comes out clearly in a passage in which Epictetus opposes logic, on
the one hand, as a part of theoretical discourse, and on the other the
discipline of assent, as a lived logic. He then goes on to contrast ethics, as
a part of theoretical discourse, and the discipline of impulses, as a lived
ethics. The context is a section of the *Discourses* (IV, 4, 11–18) in which
Epictetus is criticizing the false philosopher, who is content merely to
read theoretical discourses about philosophy. Epictetus reminds his audience that "Life is made up of other things besides books," and then
proceeds as follows:

> It is as if, in the domain *(topos)* of the exercise of assent, when we are
> in the presence of representations of which some are "adequate"
> *(kataleptikai)* and the others are not, we were to refuse to distinguish
> the ones from the others, but preferred to read treatises entitled *On
> Comprehension.* What, then, is the reason for this? It is because we
> have never read, and we have never written, so as to be capable, in
> a context of action, to use the representations which actually do
> present themselves to us in a manner in conformity with nature.
> Rather, we have confined ourselves to learning what is said, and
> being able to explain it to someone else; we've learned how to
> resolve a syllogism and how to examine a hypothetical argument.

As we can see, Epictetus is here opposing two kinds of logic; theoretical logic, as it is contained in treatises with titles like *On Comprehension,* gives us only a theoretical knowledge and technical skill in argumentation, which bears no relationship to reality. Opposed to this stands lived logic, which consists in criticizing, and entering into dialogue with, the representations which actually do present themselves to us in the course of everyday life. Similarly, Epictetus goes on, we should not be concerned with reading treatises entitled *On Impulses,* in order to find out what people have to say about impulses, but rather we should get busy and act. Here, the theoretical ethics contained in treatises on impulse and—Epictetus adds—on duty is placed in relation to the exercise of the discipline of impulse.

The correspondence between logic and the discipline of assent, then, can be easily admitted; as can that between ethics and the discipline of impulses. What, however, shall we say about the discipline of desire? The structure of the Stoic scheme of the three parts of philosophy seems to require that it correspond to physics. Is this possible? Seemingly not; in the first place, Epictetus makes no allusion to any particular relationship between physics and the discipline of desire in the passage quoted above, although he does relate the discipline of judgment to logic, and the discipline of impulses to ethics. Instead, he merely speaks of theoretical treatises entitled *On Desire and Aversion,* which seem to be ethical treatises. If it is true, however, that the abstract theory of "desire" itself, insofar as it is an act of the soul, is situated within the domain of ethics, nevertheless the lived practice of the discipline of desire implies, in the last analysis, a specific attitude toward the cosmos and nature. I have already hinted at this point in my account of the content of the three disciplines, but must now be more specific. The discipline of desire has as its goal to bring it about that we never desire things of which we might be frustrated, and that we never flee that which we might undergo against our will. This discipline therefore consists in desiring only the good which depends upon us—the only thing that is truly good, for the Stoics—and just as much in fleeing only moral evil. As for that which does not depend on us: we are to accept it, as willed by universal Nature (II, 14, 7):

Here is approximately what we think the philosopher's task is. He must adapt his own will to events, in such a way that, among all events which occur, there may be none which occur when he did not want them to occur, and that, of all events which do not occur, there may be none which does not occur when he wanted it to happen. The result, for those who have undertaken this task, is that they are not frustrated in their desires, and that they are not forced to undergo that for which they have an aversion.

The continuation of this passage still describes the task of the philosopher, but now with regard to his relations with others. We have here, then, a very clear linkage between the discipline of desire and the consent willed by destiny. Such consent presupposes that mankind recognize himself as a part of the All, and that he understand that events are necessarily linked to one another by the will of universal Reason. Whatever happens, Epictetus recommends, one should not become irritated

> against the events that have been disposed by Zeus himself [that is to say, by universal Reason]; he has defined them and placed them in order in cooperation with the Moirae [i.e., the Fates], who were present at your birth and have woven your destiny. Don't you know how tiny a part you are, compared to the All? (I, 12, 25).

Elsewhere, Epictetus writes in the same vein (II, 17, 25):

> Let your desires and your aversions become attached to Zeus, and to the other gods; give them to them, let them govern them, and let this desire and this aversion be ranged in accordance with them.

Consent to destiny and obedience to the gods—the essential components of the discipline of desire—presuppose that man become aware of his place within the All, and consequently that he practice physics. "The consent to Destiny," writes A.-J. Voelke,[26] "requires first of all that the universe be understood, thanks to an effort of thought in which intellectual power bases itself upon sense-representations. . . . The result of this methodical elucidation is that, little by little, we arrive at the rational certainty that we are living in a cosmos which is good, and set in harmonious order by a supreme Providence." We shall see later that, in the writings of Marcus Aurelius, this theme of the link between the discipline of desire and physics lived as a spiritual exercise is orchestrated even more richly than in the sayings of Epictetus which have come down to us.[27]

Sometimes Epictetus places the three disciplines on the same level, but he also sometimes seems to establish a hierarchy among them. Consequently, he sometimes enumerates the three disciplines without establishing any determinate order among them, as for example when he begins with the discipline of assent (I, 17, 22; IV, 4, 14ff; IV, 6, 26). Elsewhere, by contrast, he speaks of first, second, and third themes of exercise *(topoi):* the first being that of desires, the second that of impulses, and the third that of assent. In Epictetus' view, this order corresponds to different phases of spiritual progress. From this perspective, it is the discipline of desire, and then that of impulses, which must come first and which are the most necessary (I, 4, 12). The discipline of assent now comes only in third place, and is reserved for those who are making progress (III, 2, 5; III, 26, 14; IV, 10, 13), since it ensures them firmness in their assenting. Nevertheless, we can sense that for Epictetus, the disciplines of desire and of impulse are fused together into the discipline which criticizes representations, and therefore in the discipline of judgment and assent. After all, for Epictetus, who is here being entirely faithful to Stoic orthodoxy, the cause of our passions—that is to say, of our desires—as well as of our actions—that is, of our impulses—is nothing other than representations *(phantasiai)*—in other words, the ideas we form of things. All the tragedies and dramas in the world are the simple result of the false ideas of events that the heroes of these tragedies and dramas have formed for themselves (I, 28, 10–33). If this is true, however, the exercise-theme which has as its object the criticism of representations and judgment ought to come first.

In fact, this apparent confusion is, once again, the result of differences in perspective: differences introduced, on the one hand, by the concrete, lived practice of philosophy, and on the other by the orderly progression demanded by the teaching of philosophy. In practice, it is indeed the criticism of our representations, and the correction of the false ideas which we form about things, which is the most urgent task, because it conditions the control of our desires and our impulses. We cannot wait to practice the discipline of judgment and of assent until, at the end of our program of studies, we have begun the study of texts on theoretical logic, or the examination of hypothetical syllogisms and sophisms. The urgency of life does not permit such niceties, and, in the words of Epictetus, "life is made up of other things besides books." In everyday life, the discipline of desire, the discipline of impulses, and the discipline of judgment are inseparable, and are but three aspects of one activity, which Epictetus calls "the right way of using *(chrēsis)*" representations (II, 19, 32; 22, 29); that is to say, the right way of examining the value and correctness of the ideas which we form of things, which are the causes of our desires and impulses.

And yet these three disciplines are taught, which means they are the object of a theoretical discourse which, if it is well assimilated by the disciple, contributes to his spiritual progress. Here again the matter is urgent—but from another point of view. The exercise-themes which are to be given top priority are those which will allow the disciple to live philosophically: the discipline of desire, which delivers us from "worries, agitations, and grief" (III, 2, 3), and the discipline of impulse, which teaches us to live within our family and our city. "These," says Epictetus (I, 4, 12), "are the exercise-themes which must come first, and which are the most necessary." In theoretical teaching, then, the discipline of desire, which is the first exercise-theme, will correspond to physics; the second—the discipline of active impulses—will correspond to ethics, and in particular to the theory of appropriate duties and actions *(kathēkonta)*.

Once again, then, we return to the relationship between theoretical physics and that lived physics which we have identified as the discipline of desire. In order for the philosopher to be able to discipline his desires, he must understand the Stoic theory of nature. As Chrysippus[28] himself had already said:

> There is no more appropriate way to arrive at the theory of goods and of evils, virtues and wisdom, than by starting out from universal Nature and the organization of the world . . . for the theory of goods and evils must be connected to these subjects . . . and physics is taught only so that we may be able to teach the distinction which must be established between goods and evils.

It is precisely upon this distinction between goods and evils that the discipline of desire is based, and this is why we encounter this intimate link between physics and the theme of the exercice of desire in Epictetus. Epictetus, moreover, also makes an explicit reference to Chrysippus (I, 10, 10):

> Please examine what, according to Chrysippus, is the administration of the world, and what place rational animals occupy therein. Then, from this point of view, consider who you are, and what good and evil are for you.

In the *Discourses* of Epictetus as reported by Arrian, we do not find lengthy considerations of this series of questions, which must have corresponded to an entire program of studies. Often, however, we can recognize in passing Epictetus' allusions to this essential part of the discourse on the teaching of physics, such as the following passage (IV, 7, 6):

> God has made everything that is in the universe and the universe in its entirety, free of constraint and independent; but he made the parts of the Whole for the sake of the Whole. Other beings lack the capability of understanding the divine administration; but rational beings possess the inner resources which allow them to reflect upon this universe. They can reflect that they are a part of it, and on what kind of a part they are; and that it is good for the parts to yield to the Whole.

Becoming aware, by means of the study of physics, of our situation as parts of the Whole does not just serve the function of providing a theoretical and rational foundation for the discipline of desire, which, as we have seen, requires that, precisely because we are parts of the Whole, we must desire everything that happens as a result of the natural course of Nature. On the contrary, it also means enjoying the spectacle of the entire universe, and looking at the world with the vision of God himself. In another passage, Epictetus describes the solitary meditation of God at the moment when, at the end of one of the periodic cycles of the Universe, he remains alone, since for a moment all things have been reabsorbed into him—that is to say, into the original fire which is at the same time the *logos* which produces the world—and he urges us to imitate him (III, 13, 7):

> As Zeus is with himself, rests in himself, thinks about the way in which he administers the world, and is plunged in thoughts worthy of himself; so too should we converse with ourselves: with no need of others, and without being worried about how to keep our lives busy. We, too, should reflect on the way in which God administers the world, and on our relation to the rest of the world; we should consider what our attitude has been, up until now, toward things that happen; and on what it is now; we should consider what are the things that cause us pain, and how we could best remedy them. . . .

Here we switch, with complete naturalness, from a vision of the universe to an examination of conscience. The latter is related to the discipline of desire, and to our attitude with regard to the events that happen to us by virtue of the general movement of the universe. As Epictetus says later on (IV, 1, 100–101):

> This body made of mud: how could God have created it free of impediments? He therefore submitted it to the revolution of the Universe, as he did with my possessions, my furniture, my house, my children, and my wife. Why, then, should I fight against God? Why should I wish for things that ought not to be wished for?

It is thus no good complaining, and blaming him who has given us all for taking away from us that which he has given (IV, 1, 103–4):

> Who are you, and why have you come here? Isn't it God who has introduced you down here? Isn't it he who has made the light shine for you . . . and who has given you reason and the senses? In what condition, moreover, has he introduced you down here? . . . Was it not so as to live on earth with a miserable piece of flesh and, for a little while, to contemplate his government, follow his procession, and celebrate a festival with him?

Good people, therefore, will say when they are dying (III, 5, 10):

> I leave full of gratefulness to you, for you have judged me worthy of celebrating the festival with you, of contemplating your works, and of following together with you the way in which you govern the world.

Finally, the discipline of desire, insofar as it is a lived physics, consists not only in accepting what happens, but in contemplating the works of God with admiration (I, 6, 19–25):

> God introduced humankind down here in order to contemplate both him and his works . . . For us, nature's final accomplishment is contemplation, becoming aware, and a way of living in harmony with nature. Make sure, then, that you do not die without having contemplated all these realities . . . will you never realize, then, who you are, why you were born, and what this spectacle is to which you have been admitted?

The first theoretical instruction in the education of a philosopher must therefore be in physics, which forms the basis of the distinction between good and evil, and hence the discipline of desire. The second subject of theoretical teaching is in ethics, which is the basis of the discipline of impulses. Theoretical instruction in logic, which corresponds to what Epictetus calls the "exercise-theme of assent," comes third.

We have here a good example of the way in which Epictetus viewed two kinds of exercises as somehow fundamentally identical: *intellectual exercises,* as practiced in the exposition of a given part of philosophical discourse—in this case, logic—and *lived exercises,* as practiced in everyday life—here, as the exercise-theme *(topos)* of judgment and assent. Epictetus does, after all, use the same term, "the exercise-theme of assent," to designate both lived logic (the criticism of our representations and of the ideas which we form of things) and, on the other hand, theoretical logic (that is to say, the theory of syllogisms).

On the one hand, Epictetus affirms (III, 12, 14–15):

The third exercise-theme concerns assent, and in particular seductive and attractive representations. Just as Socrates used to say that an unexamined life is not worth living, so we must never accept an unexamined representation.

Thus, in this description of lived logic, or logic put into practice, we recognize the proper use of representations which is, in fact, the basis and foundation of all the other exercise-themes. Let me repeat: from this lived and concrete point of view, the three themes are necessarily simultaneous; and if Epictetus speaks of the "third theme," it is only for the sake of clarity of exposition.

On the other hand, there are other passages in which the exercise-theme of assent really *is* the third theme: it comes last after all the others, and is reserved for those who are making progress (III, 2, 5). In this case, what is under discussion is theoretical/scholarly discourse about logic, conceived as reasoning-processes which change in value—those which end in one of the premises, hypothetical syllogisms, and deceptive reasoning (III, 2, 6).[29] Epictetus insists upon the absolute necessity of this teaching; for instance, he responds as follows to an auditor who asks to be persuaded of the usefulness of logic (II, 25, 1): "Without logic, how will you know whether or not I am deceiving you with a sophism?" For Epictetus, it is indispensable to be able to provide, by means of the art of uncovering sophisms and errors in reasoning, the dogmas one has received via instruction in physics and ethics with an unshakably firm foundation. Such logic may be sterile (I, 17, 10); it is a purely critical

discipline, which teaches no dogma, but examines and criticizes everything else.

In the final analysis, one gets the impression that, for Epictetus, the
place of logic in a philosophical education is situated at two moments:
the beginning and the end. It has its place at the beginning, because, as
we have seen, in order to be able to practice the three themes of philosophical exercise, it is indispensable to learn, as soon as possible, how to
criticize one's representations, and how to give one's assent only to those
which are adequate. "This," says Epictetus, "is the reason why we place
logic at the beginning" (I, 17, 6). Logic also, however, has its place at the
end of the curriculum, in its more technical form of the theory of
syllogisms; this is what gives unshakable certainty to the dogmas, which
are the principles of action (III, 26, 14). The danger of this technical
study, however, is that it may remain purely technical, and become an
end in itself or a means of showing off (III, 2, 6; I, 26, 9; II, 19, 5). In such
a case, the third exercise-theme may become deleterious to a philosophical education.

As we can see, reconciling the demands of concrete philosophical life
with those of pedagogical and theoretical education was very difficult for
Epictetus, as it was for the other Stoics as well. He probably restricted
himself to the combined teaching of all three disciplines. Nevertheless,
the doctrine of the three *topoi,* or lived exercise-themes, appears in
Epictetus' teachings as the final development of the Stoic theory of the
three parts of philosophy. Epictetus enunciates a philosophical discourse
on the subject of these three parts, but at the same time he also finds
them within the everyday life of philosophers. Here, they assume the
form of three exercise-themes, linked to the three activities of the soul;
for the discipline of desire is possible only by means of that awareness by
virtue of which the philosopher considers himself as a part of the cosmic
All. Likewise, the discipline of impulses is possible only by means of that
awareness by virtue of which the philosopher discovers his place within
the human community; while the discipline of assent is possible only
thanks to the awareness by means of which the philosopher simultaneously discovers, on the one hand, his liberty with regard to representations, and, on the other, the rigorous laws of Reason.

The coherence of the All

Most historians of philosophy mention Epictetus' doctrine of the three
exercise-themes. For instance, they have recognized that Arrian used this

scheme of the three exercise-themes in order to group together those sayings of Epictetus which he collected in the summary of the Master's teachings which he entitled the *Manual*.[30] Scholars have also sought to discover traces of analogous schemes in Seneca or Cicero,[31] but it appears that we shall never arrive at decisive results concerning this point. Despite all these efforts, however, scholars have perhaps not sufficiently emphasized the human significance of this doctrine.

The discipline of desire essentially consists in re-placing oneself within the context of the cosmic All, and in becoming aware of human existence as being a part, one that must conform to the will of the Whole, which in this case is equivalent to universal Reason. The discipline of impulses and of actions consists essentially in re-placing oneself within the context of human society; this entails acting in conformity with that Reason which all human beings have in common, and which is itself an integral part of universal Reason. Finally, the discipline of judgment consists in allowing oneself to be guided by the logical necessity which is imposed upon us by that Reason which is within ourselves; this Reason, too, is a part of universal Reason, since logical necessity is based upon the necessary linkage of events.

Thus, the scheme of Epictetus' exercise-themes has exactly the same goal as did the three aspects of lived philosophy—physics, ethics, and logic—for the Stoics: to live "in accordance with Reason." There is nothing surprising about this, since, as we have seen, Epictetus holds that the three exercise-themes *are* the three aspects of lived philosophy. The philosopher must abandon his partial, egoistic vision of reality, in order, by way of physics, to rise to the point of seeing things as universal Reason sees them. Above all, the philosopher must intensely wish the common good of the universe and of society, by discovering that a part can possess no other proper good than the common good of the All. The philosopher is a citizen of the world (I, 9, 1; II, 10, 3); but he or she is also a citizen of the human City (II, 5, 26), which is nothing other than a smaller image of the cosmic City. If one's individual consciousness can be expanded as far as the utmost limits of the cosmic event, and wills this wholly and completely, this still does not prevent one from assuming the responsibilities of social duties, nor from having a profound love for the human community. If my Reason has come forth from universal Reason, then so has that of all other human beings. All people are brothers and sisters since they share in the same Reason; and even a slave is thus his master's brother (I, 13, 3).

Epictetus' three disciplines, therefore, guide and direct the relations between human beings and the universe, other human beings, and humankind's own reason. Thus, the totality of human existence is situated in relation to the whole of reality. For the Stoics, moreover, totality is precisely what characterizes living beings; in their view, to be a whole is to be coherent with oneself. By means of the three disciplines, people freely cooperate with a totality and a coherence which will necessarily be actualized, whether they like it or not, for it is only the totality of the cosmos which is assured of a perfect, unbreakable coherence. Although humankind's freedom confers upon it the privilege of being able to conform, freely and voluntarily, to this rational coherence of the cosmos, it also exposes humanity to the risk of allowing incoherence to infiltrate its thought, its affectivity, and the human City as a whole. Humankind's adherence to the coherence of cosmic Reason is always fragile and in doubt, but the divine plan will be realized of necessity.

The doctrine of the three exercise-themes, disciplines, or rules of life thus contains within itself the whole essence of Stoicism, recapitulated in a grandiose way. It invites humankind to a complete reversal of its vision of the world and its usual way of living. The philosopher-emperor Marcus Aurelius, as the distant disciple of the philosopher-slave, would magnificently develop and orchestrate these richly-harmonied themes in his *Meditations*.

6

THE INNER CITADEL, OR
THE DISCIPLINE OF ASSENT

※

The discipline of assent

As we have seen, the *Meditations* are Stoic spiritual exercises. We can, however, be more specific: by means of these exercises, Marcus Aurelius wished to establish within himself the inner discourse and the profound dispositions which would allow him to practice concretely—in the midst of his imperial life—the three exercise-themes or rules of life set forth by Epictetus. The *Meditations* return constantly to the formulation of these exercise-themes, and of the dogmas which serve as their foundation. The structure underlying the *Meditations* is the very same ternary structure that we have just seen in the case of Epictetus, and we must now turn to examining the form which this structure takes on in the *Meditations*.

The objective or adequate representation *(phantasia kataleptikē)*

The discipline of assent consists essentially in refusing to accept within oneself all representations which are other than objective or adequate. In order to understand what Marcus Aurelius means by this, it is necessary to specify the meaning of the technical Stoic vocabulary which the Emperor uses in this context.

In the first place, sensation *(aisthēsis)* is a corporeal process which we have in common with animals, and in which the impression of an exterior object is transmitted to the soul. By means of this process, an image *(phantasia)* of the object is produced in the soul, or more precisely in the guiding part *(hēgemonikon)* of the soul.

The *phantasia* has a double aspect. On the one hand, it replaces the object, and in a sense becomes identified with it, since it is an image of the object. On the other hand, it is a modification *(pathos)* of the soul, brought about by the action of an exterior object. Marcus Aurelius, for instance, asks himself the following question (III, 11, 3; XII, 18): "What is the nature of the object which is producing this *phantasia* within me?"

In the summary of Stoic logic which the historian Diogenes Laertius has preserved for us, we read the following: "The *phantasia* comes first, and then reflection *(dianoia)* which enunciates what it feels as a result of the *phantasia,* and expresses it in discourse."[1] The presence of this image in the soul is thus accompanied by an inner discourse; that is to say, a phrase, proposition, or series of phrases and propositions which enunciate the nature, quality, and value of the object which has given rise to the *phantasia* in question. It is to these enunciations that we may either give or withhold our assent. Like exterior objects, the *phantasia* is corporeal, but the inner discourse to which we give our assent is incorporeal, insofar as it possesses a meaning. By contrast with the passive nature of the *phantasia*—the image or representation produced by exterior objects—this inner discourse represents an activity of the guiding part of the soul. The soul, moreover, can also produce representations *(phantasiai)* when it combines the images it has received.[2]

This double aspect of the cognitive process—passive and active, constrained and free—can be observed in a passage by Epictetus quoted by Aulus Gellius.[3] It deserves to be cited in its entirety, since it gives a good description of the mechanism of assent:

> These representations of the soul, which the philosophers call *phantasiai,* by which a person's spirit is momentarily moved, at the first glimpse of the thing which presents itself to the soul: they do not depend upon the will, and are not free. Rather, by means of some kind of force which is peculiar to them, they throw themselves upon people, in order to be known.
>
> Assents, by contrast, which are called *sunkatatheseis,* by means of which these representations are recognized and judged, are voluntary and take place through human freedom.
>
> This is why, when a terrifying sound is heard—whether it comes from the heavens or from the collapse of some building, or whether it announces some kind of danger, or anything else of that nature— it is necessary that the soul of the sage, too, be also slightly moved and constricted and terrified; not because he judges that some form of evil is present, but because of the rapid and involuntary movements, which usurp the proper task of the mind and of reason.
>
> The sage, however, does not give his assent immediately to such representations which terrify his soul; he does not approve them,

but brushes them aside and rejects them, and it seems to him that there is nothing to fear from such things. This is the difference between the sage and the foolish person: the foolish person thinks that things are as they appear to the first emotion of his soul—that is to say, atrocious and frightful, and the foolish person approves by his assent these first impressions, which appear to justify his fear.

But the sage, although the color of his face was briefly and rapidly altered, does not give his assent, but maintains the force and solidity of the dogma which he has always had about such representations: that they are not at all to be feared, but they terrify people by means of a false appearance and an empty terror.

This text provides a fairly clear distinction between the image (*phantasia*—in this case, the thunderclap which resounds within the soul); the judgment (which Marcus calls a *hypolēpsis*), which is an inner discourse of the form: "This is awful and terrible!"; and finally the assent *(sunkatathesis),* which either approves or fails to approve the judgment.

Marcus has a frequent tendency to confuse judgment and representation; in other words, he identifies representations with the inner discourse which enunciates their content and their value. We may omit the passage in Book V, 16, 2, where Marcus speaks of a chain of representations, even though what is being discussed is a syllogism, and hence a chain of judgments: for in this particular case one can admit that he is speaking of those *phantasiai logikai,* or abstract representations, which I have alluded to above as the result of intellectual operations. Elsewhere, however, we find Marcus saying either (VIII, 29): "Erase your representations *(phantasiai),*" or else (VIII, 40): "Suppress your judgment," without there being any apparent difference in meaning. And yet Marcus is sometimes quite capable of distinguishing the inner discourse—and hence the judgment—which the soul develops *about* a given representation, from the representation itself (VIII, 49):

Don't tell yourself anything more than what your primary representations tell you. If you've been told, "So-and-so has been talking behind your back," then this is what you've been told. You have *not,* however, been told that "Somebody has done a wrong to you."

Here, we can recognize the stages of the process. In the first place, we have the exterior event: someone announces to Marcus that so-and-so has been saying negative things about him. Next, we have the representation produced within him, which is called "primary" because as yet, nothing has been added to it. In the third place, there is the discourse which enunciates the contents of this primary representation: "So-and-so has been saying negative things about you"; this is what is announced by the primary representation. Finally, there is yet another enunciation, which is no longer content merely to describe the situation, but emits a value-judgment: "I have been wronged."

Here we encounter once again the notion of an "adequate" or "objective" representation *(phantasia kataleptikē)*, as we have seen it defined by Epictetus. An objective or adequate representation is one which corresponds exactly to reality, which is to say that it engenders within us an inner discourse which is nothing other than the pure and simple description of an event, without the addition of any subjective value-judgment (Arrian, *Discourses,* III, 8, 5):

> He was sent to jail.
> What happened? He was sent to jail. But "He is unhappy" is added
> by oneself [i.e., subjectively].

Thus, both Marcus and Epictetus draw a clear distinction between "objective" inner discourse, which is merely a pure description of reality, and "subjective" inner discourse, which includes conventional or passionate considerations, which have nothing to do with reality.

The "physical" definition

> One must always make a definition or description of the object which is presented in a representation, so as to see it in itself, as it is in its essence, in its nakedness, in its totality, and in all its details. One must say to oneself the name which is peculiar to it, as well as the names of the parts which compose it, and into which it will be resolved (III, 11).

Marcus Aurelius gives us several examples of what he means by this kind of definition (VI, 13):

> How important it is to represent to oneself, when it comes to fancy dishes and other such foods: "This is the corpse of a fish, this other thing the corpse of a bird or a pig." Similarly, "This Falernian wine is just some grape juice," and "This purple vestment is some sheep's

hair moistened in the blood of some shellfish." When it comes to sexual union, we must say, "This is the rubbing together of abdomens, accompanied by the spasmodic ejaculation of a sticky liquid." How important are these representations *(phantasiai)* which reach the thing itself and penetrate right through it, so that one can see what it is in reality.

Here again, Marcus uses the term *phantasia* to designate that inner discourse which describes the object of representations. Yet these representations, which appear to be discourses which "strike reality and penetrate it through and through," correspond to "objective" or "adequate" representations, as these are conceived by Epictetus and Marcus Aurelius. They do not add anything to reality; rather, they define it in its nudity, by separating it from the value-judgments which people feel obliged to add to it, whether by habit, under the influence of social prejudices, or out of passion.

We can call this kind of definition "physical," since it frees our representations from every kind of subjective and anthropomorphic consideration, as well as from every relation to the human point of view, in order to define them, as it were, scientifically and physically. Once again we note that, according to Stoic philosophy, all is in all. Although the criticism of representations and the search for objective representations are a part of logic, they can nevertheless only be achieved if we adopt a physical point of view, by situating events and objects within the perspective of universal Nature. It is for this reason that it will be necessary to speak of this kind of definition once again, when we are dealing with the discipline of desire.

The Inner Citadel

Things Cannot Touch the Soul

Things cannot touch the soul.

They have no access to the soul.

They cannot produce our judgments.

They are outside of us.

They themselves know nothing, and by themselves they affirm nothing.
(Marcus Aurelius, *Meditations,* IV, 3, 10; V, 19; VI, 52; IX, 15)

Marcus insists strongly and repeatedly on the total exteriority of things with respect to us, and he does so in striking terms which do not appear in the sayings of Epictetus which Arrian has preserved. When Marcus says that "things cannot touch the soul," he does not mean that they are not the *cause* of the representations *(phantasiai)* which are produced within the soul. One could argue that, since the relationship between things and their representations is that of cause and effect, it is a part of the necessary linkage of Destiny. But the blow which sets the inner discourse of the guiding principle in motion is only the opportunity for this guiding principle to develop its inner discourse. The discourse itself, however, remains entirely free:

> Just as when you push a cylinder, says Chrysippus,[4] you have caused it to begin its movement, but you have not given it the property of rolling, so likewise a representation will no doubt mark and imprint its form upon the soul; and yet our assent will still remain within our power. Just like the cylinder, our assent may be pushed from without, but then it will move by its own force and nature.

The skeptic Sextus Empiricus[5] confirms this twofold aspect of perception, in the context of his criticism of the Stoics:

> Perception *(katalēpsis)* consists, according to them, in giving one's assent to an objective *(kataleptikē)* representation, and this seems to be a twofold matter: there is something involuntary it, as well as something voluntary, which depends upon our judgment. The act of receiving a representation, for instance, is involuntary; it does not depend upon the person receiving the representation, but upon the *cause* of the representation. . . . Giving one's assent to such a psychological movement, however, *is* within the power of the person receiving the representation.

In order to understand what Marcus Aurelius means when he says that things cannot touch the soul and are outside of us, we must bear in mind that the word "soul" could have two meanings for the Stoics. In the first place, it was a reality made of air *(pneuma)* which animates our body and receives the impressions, or *phantasiai,* from exterior objects. This is often what Marcus means by "soul." Here, however, when he speaks about "us" and about the soul, he is thinking of that superior or guiding part of the soul which the Stoics called the *hēgemonikon.* It alone is free, because it alone can give or refuse its assent to that inner discourse which enunciates what the object is which is represented by a given *phantasia*. This borderline which objects cannot cross, this inviolable stronghold of freedom, is the limit of what I shall refer to as the "inner citadel." Things cannot penetrate into this citadel: that is, they cannot produce the discourse which we develop about things, or the interpretation which we give of the world and its events. As Marcus says, the things outside of us "stay still"; they "do not come to us"; rather, in a way, "it is we who go toward them" (XI, 11).

These assertions must obviously be understood in a psychological and moral sense. Marcus does not mean that things stay immobile in a physical sense, but that they are "in themselves," in the sense in which "in itself" could be opposed to "for itself." Things do not care about us: they do not try to influence us, penetrate within us, or trouble us. Besides, "they know nothing about themselves and affirm nothing about themselves." It is rather we who are concerned about things, who try to get to know them, and who are worried about them. It is human beings who, thanks to their freedom, introduce trouble and worry into the world. Taken by themselves, things are neither good nor evil, and should not trouble us. The course of things unfolds in a necessary way, without choice, without hesitation, and without passion.

> If you are grieving about some exterior thing, then it is not that thing which is troubling you, but your judgment about that thing (VIII, 47).

Here we encounter an echo of a famous saying by Epictetus:

> What troubles people is not things, but their judgments about things (*Manual*, §5).

Things cannot trouble us, because they do not touch our ego; in other words, they do not touch the guiding principle within us. They remain on the threshold, outside of our liberty. When Marcus and Epictetus add that "what troubles us is our judgment about things," they are clearly alluding to the discourse which it is within our power to pronounce within ourselves, in order to define for ourselves the meaning of a given event. It is this latter judgment which may trouble us, but this is where the fundamental dogma of Stoicism comes in: there is no good but moral good, and there is no evil but moral evil. That which is not moral—that is to say, that which does not depend on our choice, our liberty, or our judgment—is indifferent, and ought not to bother us. If our judgment about things is troubling us, the reason is that we have forgotten this fundamental dogma. The discipline of assent is thus intimately linked to the doctrine of good, bad, and indifferent things (XI, 16):

> To live one's life in the best way: the power to do this resides within our soul, if we are capable of being indifferent to indifferent things. And we *can* be indifferent to indifferent things if we consider each of these things, in each of its parts and in its totality, remembering that none of them can produce within us a value-judgment about them, nor can they reach us. Rather, things remain immobile, whereas it is we who engender judgments about them, and, as it were, write them down within ourselves. But it is possible for us not to write them down; it is also possible, if we have not succeeded in this, to erase them instantaneously.

The soul is free to judge as it pleases

Things, therefore, should not have any influence upon the guiding principle. Both Epictetus and Marcus Aurelius agree that the guiding principle alone is responsible, whether it is troubled by things, or whether, on the contrary, it is at peace. It is the guiding principle itself which modifies itself, as it chooses this or that judgment about things, and consequently this or that representation of the world. In the words of Marcus Aurelius (who here uses the word "soul" to designate the superior, guiding part of the soul; V, 19): "the soul modifies itself." This concept was a part of Stoicism well before the time of Epictetus and Marcus, as is shown by the following passage in Plutarch:[6]

> It is the same part of the soul, which they call *dianoia* (faculty of reflection) and *hēgemonikon* (guiding principle), which changes and is totally transformed in the passions and transformations which it undergoes . . . they affirm that passion itself is reason, but depraved and vicious reason, which, as a result of bad and mistaken judgment, grows strong and vigorous.

Here we encounter another Stoic dogma: there is no opposition, as the Platonists had held, between one part of the soul which is rational and good in and of itself, and another part which is irrational and bad. Rather, it is reason—and the ego itself—which *becomes* either good or bad, as a function of the judgments which it forms about things. "It is the soul which changes itself, according to whether it knows things, or fails to know them."[7] This means that it is by its own judgment and decision that the soul is in the right, or in error.

It must be understood that, for Epictetus and Marcus Aurelius, all of the preceding must be situated in the order of the value which is attributed to things, and not in the order of being. In order to clarify this, we can use an example set forth by Marcus (VIII, 50): the cucumber that I want to eat is bitter. Consequently, there is impressed upon my soul the representation of a bitter cucumber, and the soul's guiding principle should have only one thing to say about this representation: the assertion "This cucumber is bitter." Here we can recognize an instance of the objective and adequate representation *(phantasia kataleptike)*. The entire discipline of assent will therefore consist in my accepting only this one objective representation. If, however, I were to add the question: "Why are there such things in the world?" or the exclamation "Zeus is wrong to allow such things!" then I am adding, freely and of my own accord, a value-judgment which no longer corresponds to the adequate content of my objective representation.

In Arrian's *Manual* (§5), the saying "It is not things that trouble people, but their judgments about things" is well explained by the following commentary: "For instance, there is nothing fearful about death . . . rather, it is because of the judgment which we bring to bear upon death—i.e., that it is fearful—that is what is fearful about death." Once again, we have here a value-judgment which is added on in a purely subjective way.

It is in the area of value-judgments that the power of the guiding principle, and of its faculty of assent, comes into play. It is this power that introduces value differences into a world which is indifferent and "in itself." Nevertheless, the only value-judgments which are authentic and true are those which recognize that the good is moral good, that evil is moral evil, and that that which is neither morally good nor bad is indifferent, and therefore valueless. In other words, the Stoic definition of good and evil has as its consequence the total transformation of one's vision of the world, as it strips objects and events of the false values which people have the habit of attributing to them, and which prevent them from seeing reality in its nudity (VII, 68):

True judgment says to that which presents itself: "this is what you are in essence, even though you may appear to common opinion to be something else."

However, although

the guiding principle has the power to bring it about that every event appears to it in the way it wills (VI, 8),

this does not mean that the guiding principle can imagine anything it pleases about reality, but rather that it is free to attribute what value it wishes to the objects it encounters. In order to suppress the false value which we attribute to these objects, it is enough to suppress our false discourse about the value of these objects. If we suppress the inner discourse which says "I have been harmed," then the harm disappears and is suppressed (IV, 7). As Epictetus had said (IV, 1, 110): "Do not tell yourself that indifferent things are necessary to you, and they will no longer be so."

Thus, when Epictetus and Marcus Aurelius speak of "judgments" (*hypolēpsis*), they are thinking of "value-judgments." This is why I have usually translated *hypolēpsis* as "value-judgment."

Critical idealism?

It is thus misleading to compare, as does Victor Goldschmidt,[8] the affirmations of Epictetus and Marcus Aurelius to a kind of "Kantian idealism," completely different from the theory of the objective or comprehensive representation proposed by Chrysippus. For Chrysippus, writes Goldschmidt, "comprehension was the natural consequence of assent—accorded voluntarily but necessarily—to the comprehensive representation. Now, as in Kantianism, comprehension applies more to appearances than to the thing in itself. It is we who elaborate upon the appearance brought about by the object, and it is therefore this subjectivity, deforming reality as it does, which we must study and criticize, much more than reality itself . . . it is as if the representation, which is no longer comprehensive immediately and as a result only of the object, was now rendered such by the activity of the subject." Goldschmidt, however, failed to see that, for Epictetus and Marcus Aurelius, the activity of the subject does not consist in *producing* a comprehensive or objective representation, but rather in sticking to that which is objective within the objective representation, without adding to it any value-judgment which might deform it. According to Epictetus (III, 12, 15), we must say to each of our representations:

> Let's see some identification! Do you have the sign from nature which every representation must have, in order to be approved?

This interrogation is not directed toward the objective and adequate representation to which we spontaneously give our consent, but rather to the other representations or judgments: those inner discourses we pronounce not about the reality of the event or thing, but about its value. It is the latter which lack the "ID" and the "sign" of an objective and adequate representation.

The reason Goldschmidt gave this interpretation of Epictetus and of Marcus Aurelius is that he has misunderstood a passage from Epictetus. This passage is, to be sure, highly enigmatic at first sight (*Manual*, I, 5):

> Every time you are in the presence of an unpleasant representation, practice saying to yourself: "You're only a representation *(phantasia)*, and *not quite* what you represent *(to phainomenon)*."

This, at any rate, is the translation proposed by Goldschmidt, but it is incorrect. What is under discussion here is an "unpleasant" representation—that is, one which gives the impression that an object or event is painful, injurious, or terrifying. What this means is that the *value*-judgment "this is unpleasant" has been added on to the objective representation of an object or event. The representation is consequently no longer objective, but subjective. A more accurate translation of Epictetus' Greek would thus be "You are only a subjective representation," which is to say, "You are merely a pure representation" (or "a mere product of my imagination," as we would put it today), "and you are *not at all*" ("not at all,"[9] and not "not quite," as Goldschmidt translated) "what really presents itself." Here, then, *to phainomenon* designates the object as it is when it presents itself within an objective and adequate representation—in other words, what is truly perceived.

The simultaneous discovery of oneself and of the world

In the last analysis, then, the discipline of assent appears as a constant effort to eliminate all the value-judgments which we bring to bear upon those things which do not depend upon us, and which therefore have no moral value. The phenomena of nature and the events of the world, once they are stripped of all the adjectives—"terrifying," "frightening," "dangerous," "hideous," "repulsive"—which humankind, in its blind anthropomorphism, applies to them, appear in their nudity and all their savage beauty. All reality is then perceived from the perspective of universal Nature, as within the flow of eternal metamorphoses of which our individual life and death are only the tiniest waves. And yet, in the very act by which we transform the way we used to look at things, we also become aware of our ability to transform this way of seeing. Hence, we become aware of the inner power which we possess to see things—and by "things," let us always understand the *value* of things—as we want to see them. In other words, thanks to the discipline of assent, the transformation of our consciousness of the world brings about a transformation of our consciousness of ourselves. And although Stoic physics makes it seem as if events are woven inexorably by Fate, the self becomes aware of itself as an island of freedom in the midst of a great sea of necessity. This awareness consists in delimiting our true self, as opposed to what we used to believe was our self, and we shall see that this is the necessary condition for peace of mind. If I can discover that the self I thought I was is not the self I am, then nothing can get to me.

Circumscribing the self

Marcus Aurelius speaks several times of the need for the self and for the guiding part of the soul to delimit and circumscribe themselves. On one occasion, he takes the trouble to describe this exercise in detail (XII, 3):

> There are three things of which you are composed: your body, your vital breath, and your intellect *(nous)*.
>
> The first two are yours only insofar as you must take care of them. Only the third is yours in the proper sense of the term.
>
> This is why, if you separate yourself from *yourself*,
>
> that is to say, from your thought *(dianoia)*,
>
> —everything that others may say or do;
>
> —or again, everything that you yourself have said and done (in the past), as well as the things which trouble you because they are still to come;
>
> —and everything that happens to you, independently of your will,

because of the body which surrounds you, or your innate vital
breath;
—and everything which stirs the waves of the violent sea which
bathes you,
   in order that
—raised above the interweavings of Fate,
—pure,
—free for itself,
   the living intellectual power
—*by doing what is right,*
—*by willing everything that happens,*
—*by telling the truth,*
———if, I say, you separate from this guiding principle *(hēgemonikon)*
the things which have become attached to it, because it has become
attached to them,
   and if you separate from time that which is beyond the present
and that which is past,
   and if you make yourself like the *Sphairos* of Empedocles, "a pure
orb, proud of its joyful uniqueness,"
   and if you strive to live only what you live—that is to say, the
present,
———then you will be able to live the time that is left to you, up
until your death, untroubled, benevolently and serenely with regard
to your inner *daimōn.*

The exercise designed to circumscribe and delimit the self, then, begins with the analysis of the components of human beings: the body; the
vital breath, or soul which animates the body; and the intellect. This last
is equivalent to our faculty of judgment and assent, our power of reflection *(dianoia)* or guiding principle *(hēgemonikon).* We encounter this description of the human being several times in Marcus (II, 2, 1–3; II, 17,
1–4; III, 16, 1; V, 33, 6; VII, 16, 3; VIII, 56, 1; XI, 20; XII, 14, 5; XII, 26,
2). At other times, the only things mentioned are the soul and the body,
with the soul being identified with the *hēgemonikon,* as is clear from a
passage like VI, 32, in which soul and *dianoia*—and therefore
hēgemonikon—are synonyms.

Traditional Stoic doctrine made a distinction between the body and
the soul, and further, within the soul, it distinguished a superior part: the
guiding part of the soul, in which the various psychic functions were

situated. Such a schema was purely dichotomous, in that it opposed soul and body. It is easy to understand, however, how the Stoic doctrine of the soul was able to evolve in the direction of the position we find taken by Marcus Aurelius. The meaning of this evolution is well explained by a passage from the Skeptic Sextus Empiricus:[10]

> Some Stoics say that the word "soul" is used in two ways: on the one hand, to designate that which holds together the entire mixture of the body [this is what Marcus calls the *pneuma,* or vital breath], and on the other, in a more proper sense, the guiding principle. . . . In the division of good things, when we say that some things are goods of the soul, others of the body, and others are exterior, we are not referring to the soul in its entirety, but to that part of the soul which is the guiding principle.

Although we encounter this splitting up of the soul into vital principle and thinking principle in Marcus Aurelius, it does not seem that there is any trace of the trichotomy proposed by Marcus in the sayings of Epictetus as recorded by Arrian. It is, however, perhaps worth noting that Epictetus (II, 1, 17) does use terminology analogous to that of Marcus when he contrasts the body (designated by the diminutive term *sōmation*) with the vital breath (designated by the diminutive *pneumation*).

The general principle which presides over the exercise of the delimitation of the self, which I am now describing, was formulated by Epictetus, and placed by Arrian at the beginning of his *Manual:* the difference between the things that depend on us and the things that do not depend on us. In other words, it is the difference between inner causality, or our faculty of choice—our inner freedom—and external causality, that is to say, Destiny and the universal course of Nature.

The first step in the delimitation of the ego consists in recognizing that, of the being which I am, neither the body, nor the vital breath which animates it, is mine in the proper sense of the term. I must, of course, take care of them: this is part of the doctrine of "duties" or "actions appropriate" to nature. It is both natural and in conformity with my instinct for self-preservation that I care for my body and the *pneuma* which makes it live; but it is precisely this decision which I make concerning these things which belong to me that belongs to a principle of choice, and this principle of choice *does* belong to me in the proper sense. The body and the vital *pneuma* are not completely mine, because they are imposed upon me by Destiny, independently of my will. It might be objected that the *hēgemonikon* is also "given," but it is given as a source of my initiative, or an "I" who decides.

In the passage quoted above, Marcus describes in a quite remarkable way the different circles which surround the ego or the "I," as well as the exercise which consists in rejecting them one by one, as something foreign to my self.

The first circle, and the most exterior, is *the others*. As Marcus says elsewhere (III, 4, 1):

> Don't waste the part of life that remains to you in representations *(phantasiai)* concerning other people, unless you relate them to something which benefits the common good. Why do you deprive yourself of the opportunity of accomplishing another task . . . imagining what so-and-so is doing, why he is doing it, what he thinks, what he is plotting and all those other questions which make you dizzy inside and turn you away from the attention which you should be paying toward your own guiding principle *(hēgemonikon)*?

The second circle is that of the past and the future. If we want to become aware of our true selves, we must concentrate upon the present. As Marcus puts it, we must "circumscribe the present," and separate ourselves from that which no longer belongs to us: our past words and actions, and our future words and actions. Seneca had already expressed this idea:[11]

> These two things must be cut away: fear of the future, and the memory of past sufferings. The latter no longer concern me, and the future does not concern me yet.

Thus, neither the past nor the future depend upon me, and only the present is within my power.

The third circle is constituted by the domain of involuntary emotions; these are caused by impressions received by the body, and by the soul considered as the principle of the body's animation, or "inborn vital breath." In order to understand these involuntary emotions, let us recall the passage alluded to earlier from the lost fifth book of Epictetus' *Discourses,* as recorded by Arrian. In his *Attic Nights,* Aulus Gellius reports that, during a sea voyage, he had seen a Stoic philosopher grow pale during a storm, and when they arrived in port he had asked the philosopher why he had experienced such a moment of weakness. At this, the philosopher had pulled Arrian's book out of his traveling bag, and pointed to the passage in which Epictetus explained that if the sage experienced a particularly strong and violent sensation, then he, too, despite his wisdom, would experience an involuntary emotion which would echo throughout the body and the rest of the soul. That, he explained, was why the color of the sage's face might change, but, as Epictetus had put it, "The sage does not give his assent to this emotion."

What this means is that when our rational consciousness or guiding principle translates such an emotion into its inner discourse, and announces that "This is terrible and appalling," then the guiding principle immediately refuses to give its assent to this value-judgment. Let us note in passing that this testimony is all the more interesting in that it lets us glimpse how Epictetus, in those books written by Arrian which have since become lost, spoke of themes very different from those which are dealt with in the first four books. In the *Discourses* which have come down to us, there does not seem to be any allusion to the sage's involuntary movements.

In any case, Marcus Aurelius returns in another passage to the relation between the guiding principle and involuntary movements (V, 26, 1):

> Let the sovereign and directing part of your soul remain unaltered in the presence of movements, whether gentle or violent, which are produced in the flesh. Let it not be mixed with them, but let it delimit itself and circumscribe these affections within the parts of the body.

The guiding principle draws a border, as it were, between sensitive emotions and its freedom of judgment, by refusing to consent or give its assent to judgments which would attribute a positive or negative value to the pleasures or pains that occur within the body. This border does not prevent the guiding principle from perceiving everything that goes on within the body, and thereby it ensures the unity of consciousness of the entire living being, just as, within the cosmic living being, everything goes back to the single consciousness of the guiding principle of the universe (IV, 40). From this new perspective, Marcus continues, we cannot prevent sensations from penetrating within the guiding principle, since they are natural phenomena; nevertheless, the guiding principle must not add its own value-judgments concerning them.

On one hand, the guiding principle ensures the unity of living beings, so that the sensations and emotions which I perceive are mine, since I perceive them from within. On the other hand, however, the guiding principle considers these sensations and emotions as somehow alien to itself, insofar as it refuses to acquiesce and participate in the disturbances which they introduce into the body. And yet, shouldn't the sage be completely impassive, and the complete master of his body and of his soul? This is how the Stoic sage is usually conceived. In fact, however, the Stoic sage, as Seneca points out,[12] is far from being insensitive:

> There are misfortunes which strike the sage—without incapacitating him, of course—such as physical pain, infirmity, the loss of friends or children, or the catastrophes of his country when it is devastated by war. I grant that he is sensitive to these things, for we do not impute to him the hardness of a rock or of iron. There is no virtue in putting up with that which one does not feel.

This initial shock of emotion is the same movement, independent of our will, of which Marcus Aurelius speaks. Seneca is quite familiar with it, too:[13]

> This is how passions are born, develop, and become excessive. First of all, there is an initial involuntary movement; a kind of preparation for and threat of passion. Then there is a second one, accompanied by a desire which we are still able to reject: to wit, the idea that "I have to get even because someone has done me wrong. . . ." Finally, there is a third movement which can no longer be mastered . . . we must have revenge at all costs. The first shock to the soul cannot be avoided with the help of reason, any more than other reflex movements which happen to the body, such as yawning . . . reason cannot vanquish them, but perhaps habit and constant attention may attenuate them. The second movement, which arises from a judgment, can be suppressed by a judgment.

According to the Stoics, then, even the sage himself cannot escape these first involuntary movements. As Seneca puts it,[14] he always feels appearances or "shadows of passions."

The fourth circle, a "rushing tide which bathes you with its waves," is that of the course of events; in other words, it is the course of Destiny and of the time in which Destiny unveils itself (IV, 43):

> A river of all events, a violent current: that is what eternity is. No sooner has each thing appeared than it has already passed; another comes along, and it too will be swept away.

Elsewhere, Marcus writes (V, 23):

> Think often of how quickly beings and events pass and disappear;
> for substance is like a river in perpetual flux.

If, Marcus adds, we can recognize that all this flux of things and events
is alien to us, then we will be "raised above the tangled web of Destiny."
To be sure, our body and our vital breath are swept along by this flux,
and both our representations of things which are received into the body
and our vital breath belong to this flux, because they are produced by
causes outside of us. Yet the self becomes aware of the fact that, thanks to
its freedom of judgment—which also implies freedom of desire and of
the will—it stands apart from this flux. The self, then, identical with the
guiding principle, is raised above the web of destiny.

When the self thus becomes aware of its freedom, it acts only by
making its reason coincide with the Reason of universal Nature. It *wants*
that which happens; in other words, it wants what universal Nature
wants. The self now tells the truth, both inwardly and outwardly: in
other words, whenever a representation presents itself to the guiding
principle in order to obtain its assent, the self restricts itself to what is. It
holds fast to the objective representation, without adding value-judgments to things which have no moral value. Finally, the self now does
what is right: that is, it acts in accordance with Reason, in the service of
the human community. Here (XIII, 3, 3) we recognize Epictetus' three
exercise themes *(topoi)*, which, as we have seen, were taken up again by
Marcus Aurelius. To circumscribe and delimit one's self thus means to
practice the following exercises:

(1) in the area of *assent,* it means not approving those value-judgments
which may be influenced by the body and the vital breath, which are
something other than myself;

(2) in the area of *desire,* it means recognizing that everything that does
not depend upon my moral choice is indifferent; and

(3) in the area of *action,* it means going beyond the egoistic concern for
my body and my vital breath, in order to rise up to the viewpoint of
Reason, which is common to all human beings; thus, it means willing
that which is beneficial to the common good.

After he has arrived at this culminating point, Marcus returns to the
theme of the delimitation of the self, in order to clarify certain aspects of
the process. The effort of concentration must make us aware of the fact
that things have become attached to us, and are no longer distinguishable

from us. Our self has become confused with such things, because we have attached ourselves to them. Epictetus is fond of this theme of our alienation toward things to which we attach ourselves (IV, 1, 112):

> Purify your judgments, so that nothing that is not "yours" may become attached to you or become connatural with you, so that you do not feel any suffering if it is snatched away from you.

Such objects are not "ours," Epictetus reminds us, not only because they are different from us, but above all because they belong to Destiny and to God, who are free to take them back after they have given them to us (III, 24, 84):

> When you become attached to something, do not do so as to an object that cannot be taken away from you, but as if it were something like a pot or a glass cup, so that, if it is broken, when you remember what it was, you will not be disturbed . . . Remember that what you love is mortal, and that nothing of what you love belongs to you in the proper sense of the term. It has been given to you for the time being, not forever or in such a way that it cannot be taken away from you, but, like a fig or a bunch of grapes, at a particular season of the year. If you get a craving for them during the winter, then you're stupid.

Marcus Aurelius then returns to the importance of concentrating upon the present moment. This indissoluble link between the delimitation of the self and the delimitation of the present moment is extremely significant. It is only when I am active, either within myself or upon the outside world, that I am truly myself and at liberty; and it is only in the present moment that I can be active. Only the present is mine, and the present is all that I live.

When the self has thus isolated and returned into itself, says Marcus, it can be compared to the *Sphairos* of Empedocles. For Empedocles, this term denoted that unified state of the universe when it is dominated by Love, as opposed to the state of division it is in when dominated by Hate. While in its state of unity, the universe is perfectly round, delighting in its joyful immobility. In the philosophical tradition, Empedocles' *Sphairos* had become the symbol of the sage, "completely within itself, well-rounded and spherical, so that nothing extraneous can adhere to it, because of its smooth and polished surface," in the words of Horace.[15]

Such an image corresponds to the ideal of the inner citadel, invincible and impenetrable (VIII, 48, 3), which represents the self that has delimited itself.

At the end of this passage, Marcus alludes to our inner *daimōn,* which, for him, is identical with the self, the guiding principle, or the faculty of reflection. I shall return below to this notion of the *daimōn.*

As we can see, this delimitation of the self is, in the last analysis, the fundamental exercise of Stoicism. It implies a complete transformation of our self-consciousness, of our relation toward our body and toward external goods, and of our attitude toward the past and the present. It calls for concentration on the present moment, an asceticism of detachment, the recognition of the universal causation of Destiny, in the midst of which we are plunged, and the discovery of the power we possess to judge freely, that is, to give things whatever value we *wish* to give them.

Thus, the process of the delimitation of the self brings about a distinction between two elements. On the one hand, there is what we believe to be our true self: our body, but also our soul—the vital principle— together with the emotions that it feels. On the other hand, there is our power to choose. That which we think is our true self is imposed upon us by Destiny, but in fact our genuine self is situated high above Destiny. This opposition between our two "selves" appears quite clearly in a passage where Marcus Aurelius confesses that he is slow-minded. This trait, he writes, is inborn in him; it belongs to his character and his physical constitution, and therefore does not depend upon him, any more than do his size or the color of his eyes. What *does* depend on him, by contrast, is his freedom to act in a moral way (V, 5):

> So it's not likely that they're going to admire your quick-wittedness. So be it! But there are many other matters about which you cannot say that you are not gifted; these are the things that you must display, because they are completely within your control: avoiding duplicity; being serious; putting up with suffering; having contempt for pleasure; not complaining about Destiny; having few needs; being free, benevolent, and simple; avoiding idle chatter; possessing greatness of soul. Can't you feel how many things there are which you are capable of displaying, and for which the absence of talent and natural capacities can no longer serve you as an excuse?

Two things are opposed in this passage: the awareness by means of which one discovers one's psychological self, with its qualities and its defects, and such as it is determined by Destiny. Over and against this, we see the awareness of one's self *qua* guiding principle, and therefore capable of acceding to the sphere of morality. We thus have to do with two aspects of the faculty of reasoning and thinking. Although reason is inherent in every human being, it is only *equally* present in all human beings in its role as a faculty of judgment and of moral decision-making. This, however, does not prevent the existence of qualitative differences in speculation and in expression, according to one's individual particularities.

Let us be clear: the self, whether envisaged as a principle of freedom capable of acceding to morality, or as a guiding principle, is not, by itself, either good or evil. It is indifferent. To be able to choose means being able to choose between good and evil; consequently, it means being able to *be* either good or evil. For Marcus, rationality is not good in and of itself, as it was for Plato. Reason can be utterly depraved (X, 13):

> Men commit [these evil actions] not with their hands or feet, but with the noblest part of themselves. If it so wishes, however, this same part may become faith, modesty, truth, law, or a good *daimōn*.

This delimitation of the self, as a potential for liberty which transcends Destiny, is equivalent to the delimitation of the faculty I possess to judge, and either to give or to withhold my assent from my value-judgments. I may be constrained by Destiny to have a body; to be sick or poor; to be hungry; or to die on such-and-such a day; but I can think whatever I please about such situations. I can refuse to consider them as misfortunes, and no one can tear this freedom of viewpoint away from me.

In the name of what, however, or in virtue of what shall I judge that the only good is moral good, and the only evil moral evil? This is where the mystery of freedom comes in. As Marcus says, the self, in its capacity as the power of judging and choosing, can also become "faith, modesty, truth, law, or a good *daimōn*," as well as the contrary of any of these. Thus the self, if it so desires, can identify itself with universal Reason, or the transcendent Norm which posits the absolute value of morality. This is precisely the level at which Marcus was situating himself when he wrote his spiritual exercises; in other words, he was identifying himself with this universal Reason or transcendent Norm. This is what Epictetus used to call "the Other" (I, 30, 1):

> When you go to see some important personage, remember that there is an Other, watching what happens from above, and that it is better to please this Other than that man.

Like an inner voice, this Other has a dialogue with the guiding principle in the discussion which Epictetus imagines following this passage. It is, moreover, this same transcendent Other with whom Marcus Aurelius carries on a dialogue in the *Meditations*.

It can thus be said—although Marcus does not make the distinction explicitly—that there is a difference between two kinds of freedom. On the one hand, there is *freedom of choice,* by virtue of which the guiding principle has the possibility of rendering itself either good or evil. On the other, there is *real freedom,* thanks to which the guiding principle chooses moral good and universal Reason, and thereby ensures that its judgments are true, its desires fulfilled, and its acts of will efficacious. Only real freedom is freedom in the full sense of the term.

Thus, the guiding principle is an "inner citadel," already impregnable in its guise as freedom of choice, which cannot be forced if it refuses. This citadel is still more impregnable, however, in its guise as real free- dom—that is, if it manages, thanks to its identification with universal Reason, to liberate itself from all that could possibly subjugate its judg- ments, desires, and its will (VIII, 48):

> Remember that the guiding principle becomes invincible when it turns itself toward itself, and is content with not doing that which it does not wish to do, even if its resistance is unreasonable.
>
> What shall happen, then, if it surrounds itself with circumspec- tion and reason when it emits a judgment? This is why the intellect, when freed from the passions, is a citadel; for mankind has no stronger fortress than this. If we take refuge within it, we will be in an impregnable position from now on.

When the guiding principle thus discovers that it is free in its judg- ments, that it can give whatever value it pleases to the events which happen to it, and that nothing can force it to commit moral evil, then it experiences a feeling of absolute security. From now on, it feels, nothing can invade it or disturb it. It is like a cliff against which the crashing surf breaks constantly, while it remains standing unmoveably as the waves come, bubbling, to die at its feet (IV, 49, 1).

In the passage from Marcus which I have discussed at length above, one can observe a complete equivalence between five terms:

1. the self;
2. intellect *(nous);*

3. the power of reflection *(dianoia);*
4. the guiding principle *(hēgemonikon);* and
5. the inner *daimōn.*

All this is in complete conformity with Stoic tradition, including the idea of the *daimōn,* which seems clearly to turn up in the writings of Chrysippus.[16] The definition of the happy life, according to Chrysippus, is that in which everything is done "in accordance with the harmony between the *daimōn* within each one of us and the will of the governor of the universe."

It is not difficult for modern readers to understand this identification of the self with the intellect, the power of reflection, or the guiding principle; but the idea of the *daimōn* may seem more obscure. It is a very old notion: in the Homeric poems, *daimōn* often evokes the idea of individual destiny, or more generally, a diffuse divine power. Everyone is familiar with Socrates' *daimōn,* which Plato presents as an inner voice; but we ought not to forget that Plato himself, when he speaks near the end of the *Timaeus* (90a) of the rational soul "which is the sovereign soul within us," asserts that "the god has given it to each one of us as a present, as if it were a *daimōn.*" A few lines later (90c), Plato adds that whoever has succeeded in touching true reality "renders ceaseless worship to the divinity, and keeps the *daimōn* which lives within him in good state." For Aristotle, the intellect within us is something divine.[17]

Might not this *daimōn* within us be a power which transcends the self, and which cannot therefore be identified with the self? And yet, even though for Plato we *are* the rational soul, he nevertheless tells us that we must keep this *daimōn* "in good state." This is probably a reference to the statue of a god, to which worship must be offered.

We find the same ambiguity in Marcus Aurelius. Sometimes he tells us that we must conserve this inner divinity and preserve it from all contamination, as if it could be stained (II, 13, 1; II, 17, 4; III, 12, 1; III, 16, 3). Elsewhere, however, Marcus asserts that we must carry out the will of the *daimōn* which God has given to us, as though we had to do with a reality which transcends us (III, 5, 2; V, 27).

In fact, however, such assertions do not mean that Marcus thinks of the *daimōn* as something different from the intellect or the power of reflection. For instance, he says of the power of reflection (III, 7, 4)—just as he says of the *daimōn*—that we must take care all our lives "to preserve it from a deformation which would not be fitting for a being which thinks and lives in community with other human beings."

Everything becomes clear if we replace the word *daimōn* by "reason."
On the one hand, reason for the Stoics is a part of universal divine
Reason; it was given to us by the latter, and we must do what reason
wishes. On the other hand, however, our reason may become corrupted,
and we must therefore take care to preserve it against every attack. This
celestial gift is a fragile one.

What, however, is the precise relationship between this *daimōn* and the
self? To be sure, it corresponds to the transcendent Norm, which, as we
have seen, was equivalent to Reason. It also corresponds to the "Other"
mentioned by Epictetus: a kind of inner voice which imposes itself upon
us. Here, however, we come face to face with the paradox of moral life,
for the self identifies itself with a transcendent Reason which is simultaneously above it and identical with it; it is a case of "Someone within me,
more myself than myself."[18] As Plotinus[19] said of the Intellect, by virtue
of which we lead a spiritual life: "It is a part of ourselves, and we ascend
toward it."

Although the self may thus raise itself to a transcendent level, it is very
difficult for it to keep itself there. The figure of the *daimōn* allows Marcus
Aurelius to express, in religious terms, the absolute value of moral intent
and the love of moral good. No value is superior to virtue and the inner
daimōn (III, 6, 1–2), and everything else, compared to the mysteries
which honor the eminent dignity of the inner *daimōn,* is worthless petty-
mindedness (III, 6, 3).

There is something quite remarkable in this Stoic affirmation of the
transcendence of the realm of moral intent, compared to all other reality.
It could be compared to the distinction between the three orders which
we find in Pascal: the order of the "flesh"; that of the "spirit"; and that of
the "will."[20] Above all, it can be compared to Pascal's distinction between the triad of "bodies," "spirits," and "charity." Each order transcends the others to an infinite degree:[21]

> One little thought could not be made to arise from all bodies taken
> together, for this is impossible and they are of different orders. One
> single movement of true charity could not be derived from all
> bodies and all spirits; for that is impossible. It is of another order,
> and is supernatural.

In Pascal, this idea is intended to allow us to understand that Jesus Christ
has neither the splendor of physical grandeur, nor that of intellectual
genius. There is nothing more simple than He, and yet more hidden. His

grandeur is of another order. Similarly, for the Stoics, the order of good will and moral intent infinitely transcends the order of thought and of theoretical discourse, as well as that of physical magnitude. What makes humankind equal to God is reason, when it chooses moral good.

"Everything is a matter of judgment"

The discipline of assent, then, orders us to consent only to comprehensive representations, and it represents logic as the latter is lived and put into practice. It might therefore appear that this discipline is exercised only in a limited and determinate area—the rectitude of our inner discourse—and that it does not interfere with the other areas of exercise, namely those of desire and of action.

In fact, however, this is by no means the case. In the first place, the discipline of assent is not exercised only with regard to inner discourse, but also with regard to outer discourse. In other words, part of it consists in not lying, either to oneself or to others. It is for this reason that Marcus calls the virtue which corresponds to this discipline "truth" (IX, 1, 2). Above all, however, as we have seen throughout this chapter, there is a sense in which the discipline of assent embraces all the other disciplines, which can only be practiced through the perpetual rectification of our inner discourse—that is, what we say to ourselves about things. On the one hand, the discipline of assent is the same thing as the criticism of our value-judgments, and to practice it presupposes that we accept a fundamental Stoic principle of action: that the only good is moral good, and the only evil is moral evil. On the other hand, practicing the disciplines of desire and of action consists essentially in rectifying the judgments which we bring to bear upon things. Leaving aside doctrinal refinements and quarrels within the school, we can say that for the Stoics in general, desire and impulses to action are essentially acts of assent.[22] It is no doubt true that their notion implies that of "movement-toward," but this movement is inseparable from our inner adherence to a specific judgment or discourse which is uttered about things.

Thus, we can say that, for Marcus, "everything is a matter of value-judgments." This does not imply any kind of subjectivism or skepticism, but is the simple application of what we could call Stoic "intellectualism." Inherited from Socratism, this doctrine proclaims that all virtue is a kind of knowledge,[23] and that all vice is ignorance. Whatever the precise meaning of this Socratic doctrine may have been, it is clear that it is not a question of theoretical or abstract knowledge and ignorance, but of a knowledge and a non-knowing which engage the individual. The kind of knowledge at issue does not have to do with judgments of existence, but with value-judgments, which bring into question one's entire way of living. This nuance is conveyed well by the term "realize." A person who commits a fault does not "realize" that his action is bad. He thinks it is good, by means of a false value-judgment. A good man, by contrast, "realizes" that moral good is the only good, which is the same as to say that he understands the kind of life to which his value-judgment commits him. There is implied within this doctrine the idea that every person has a natural desire for the good, and that he can only fail to achieve it by being mistaken about the nature of the good. As René Schaerer[24] has correctly observed, this is the postulate upon which Socratic and Platonic dialectics are based: "No discussion is possible if one's adversary refuses to admit that good—in one form or another—is better than evil."

It is from the viewpoint of this "intellectualism" that we can say that "no one is evil voluntarily"; for the apparently evil person, although he naturally desires the good, is simply mistaken by the value-judgment he brings to bear upon the nature of the good. As Epictetus and Marcus Aurelius both say, following Plato: "each soul is deprived of the truth involuntarily."

Epictetus elsewhere gives forceful expression to this doctrine (II, 26):

All errors imply a contradiction, for since he who errs does not wish to err, but to succeed, it is obvious that he is not doing what he wishes. What does the thief want to do? That which is profitable to him. If therefore, theft is a harmful thing for him, then he is not doing what he wishes. Now contradiction is, for every rational soul, naturally abhorrent. So long as the soul is not aware that it is involved in a contradiction, nothing prevents it from doing contradictory things. Once it has become aware, however, it is absolutely necessary that it desist from contradiction and flee, just as in the case of error. He who notices his error is obliged by harsh necessity to renounce it; but as long as the error does not appear, he adheres to it as if it were the truth. He who is able to show each person the contradiction which is the cause of his error, and to make clear to him in what sense he is not doing what he wants, and is doing what he does not want, is therefore a skilled talker, and knows how to refute and persuade at the same time. Indeed, if a person can be shown this, then he will retreat of his own accord. As long as you do not show this, however, do not be surprised if he persists in his error, for he does what he does because he believes it is a good action. Socrates was full of confidence in his ability to do this, and that is why he used to say: "I don't usually quote authorities to back up what I say, but am always satisfied with my interlocutor. It is he whose vote I take, and him I call forth as a witness, and he alone replaces all the others for me." For he knew that once the rational soul is set in motion, like a scale, it is going to tip whether people want it to or not. Point out a contradiction to the guiding principle, and it will give it up. If you do not, then it is yourself you should accuse, rather than the person you cannot persuade.

"Everything is a matter of value-judgment," says Marcus (II, 15; XII, 26, 2), whether the subject is the discipline of assent, the discipline of desire, or that of action. Can the last two, then, be reduced to the first? The descriptions given by Marcus Aurelius and Epictetus incline us to think that they apply to different domains, in accordance with the various relationships with reality into which we enter. My relationship to universal Nature and the cosmos is the subject of the discipline of desire; my relationship to human nature is that of the discipline of action; and my relationship with myself—insofar as I am a power of assent—is the domain of the discipline of assent. Nevertheless, it is the same method which is used in the three disciplines. It is always a matter of examining and criticizing the judgments which I bring to bear, either on the events which happen to me, or on the actions which I want to undertake. From this point of view, as Émile Bréhier has said, "logic penetrates the whole of our conduct."[25]

7

THE DISCIPLINE OF DESIRE,
OR *AMOR FATI*

❧

Discipline of desire and discipline of the impulses

The ancient Stoics distinguished two main functions of the guiding principle: assent, which is concerned with the areas of representation and knowledge, and active impulse *(hormē)* or the will, which is concerned with the area of the motor functions, or of the movement toward objects which is caused by our representations.[1] After them, Epictetus and Marcus Aurelius are the *only* Stoic thinkers who distinguish not two, but three functions: assent, desire, and active impulse, to which the three disciplines of assent, desire, and impulse correspond. It is interesting to note that we find in Marcus Aurelius a systematic description of reality, which justifies this opposition between desire and impulse in a way that is much more precise than anything to be found in the sayings of Epictetus as reported by Arrian.

Desire and active impulse represent a reduplication of the notion of the will. Desire is, as it were, an ineffective will, whereas active impulse or tendency is will which produces an action. Desire is related to affectivity, while tendency is related to the motor functions. Desire is situated in the area of what we feel—pleasure and pain—and of what we wish to feel: it is the domain of passion, in the double sense of a state of the soul and of passivity with regard to an external force which imposes itself upon us. Tendency, by contrast, is situated in the domain of what we want or do not want to do. It is the domain of action and initiative, and implies the idea of a force within us which wants to exercise itself.

For Marcus, desire and aversion presuppose passivity. They are provoked by external events, which are themselves the product of a cause which is *external* to us; the tendency to act or not to act, by contrast, is the effect of that cause which is *within* us (IX, 31). For Marcus, these two causes correspond respectively to *common and universal Nature,* on the one hand, and to *our nature,* on the other (XII, 32, 3):

Don't imagine that anything is important except that you act as *your own nature* leads you, and that you suffer as *common Nature* ordains.

Elsewhere, Marcus writes (V, 25):

At this moment, I have what *common Nature* wants me to have in this moment, and I'm doing what *my own nature* wants me to be doing at this moment.

And again (VI, 58):

No one is going to stop you from living according to the reason of *your own nature,* and nothing will happen to you contrary to the reason of *common Nature.*

By opposing external and internal causes, common Nature and one's own nature, Marcus provides an ontological foundation for the disciplines of desire and of impulse. The former's object is my relationship with the immense, inexorable, and imperturbable course of Nature, with its ceaseless flux of events. At every instant, I encounter the event which has been reserved for me by Destiny; that is, in the last analysis, the unique, universal, and common Cause of all things. The discipline of desire will therefore consist in refusing to desire anything other than what is willed by the Nature of the All.

The object of the second discipline—that of active impulses and the will—is the way in which my own minuscule causality inserts itself within the causality of the world. In other words, this discipline consists in wanting to do that which my own nature wants me to do.

We saw earlier that the discipline of assent constitutes, as it were, the fundamental method of the other two disciplines, since both desire and impulse depend on the assent which we either give to, or withhold from, our representations.

If this is the case, and the discipline of assent is somehow implied by the two others, then one can say that the practice of the philosophical life can be summed up in the two disciplines of desire and the active will (Marcus Aurelius, XI, 13, 4):

What evil can there be for you, if you *do* that which, in this present moment, is appropriate to *your nature;*
and if you *accept* that which, in this present moment, comes at the moment which is opportune for the *Nature of the All?*

What precisely is meant by these two natures? "My" nature is not my particular individual character, but my nature as a human being and my reason, which I have in common with all human beings. Thus, it corresponds to that transcendent self which we have seen in the context of the discipline of assent: that divine principle or *daimōn* which is within us (V, 10, 6):

> Nothing will happen to me which is not in accordance with the Nature of the Whole, and it is possible for me to *do* nothing which is contrary to *my god and my daimōn*.

"My" nature and the common Nature are not opposed, nor external to each other, for "my" nature and "my" reason are nothing other than an emanation from universal Reason and universal Nature, which are immanent in all things. Thus, these two natures are identical (VII, 55, 1):

> Keep looking straight ahead, in order to see where nature is leading you; both *the nature of the All,* by means of the *events* which happen to you, and *your own nature,* by means of that which you *must do*.

These ideas go back to the Old Stoa, and can be traced at least as far back as Chrysippus.[2] While defining the moral goal as life in conformity with nature, Chrysippus specified that he understood by this term both universal Nature and that nature which is peculiar to humankind. The identity between "nature" *(physis)* and "reason" *(logos)* is, moreover, attested throughout the Stoic tradition.[3] The fact that these two terms are identical means that the world, together with all beings, is produced by a process of growth (in a sense, this is the meaning of the word *physis*), which has within itself its own method, rational law of cause and effect, and organization (this is the meaning of the word *logos*). Human beings, as rational animals, live according to nature when they live according to that inner law which is reason.

We constantly return to the fundamental intuition of Stoicism: self-coherence, which is at the same time the law which generates reality and that which regulates human thought and conduct. The two disciplines of desire and impulse thus consist, in the last analysis, in remaining coherent with oneself; and this is the same thing as remaining coherent with the Whole of which we are only a part (IV, 29, 2):

> He who flees the reason of the human community is a fugitive. . . .
> He who separates and distances himself from the Reason of com-

mon Nature, and complains about what happens to him, is an abscess upon the world . . . He who splits off his own particular soul from the soul of other rational beings is like an amputated limb of the city, for the soul is one.

By means of the discipline of desire, we are to desire only that which is useful to the All constituted by the world, because that is what universal Reason wants. By means of the disciplines of the will and of our impulses, we must want only that which serves the Whole constituted by the human city, because that is what is wanted by right reason, which is common to all humankind.

Circumscribing the present

As the reader has perhaps already noticed, what characterizes the presentation of the three exercise-themes in Marcus Aurelius, and differentiates it considerably from the analogous expositions found in the sayings of Epictetus as written down by Arrian, is the insistence with which Marcus emphasizes that these exercises are concerned with the present. In the case of the discipline of assent, they are concerned with our *present* representations. In the discipline of desire, these exercises are directed toward the *present* event; and in the discipline of active impulse what counts are our *present* actions. We have already seen that the exercise intended to delimit and circumscribe the self was, simultaneously and indissolubly, an effort to concentrate upon the present.

This process of delimiting the present is entirely analogous to the process by means of which we hold fast to the facts and to reality in our objective and adequate representations, and refuse to add value-judgments to them. There is, after all, a sense in which the value-judgments which trouble us are always related either to the past or to the future. We become agitated about the consequences which a present event—or even something that happened long ago—may have for us in the future; or else we are afraid of some future event. In any case, instead of sticking exclusively to what is happening right here and now, our representations constantly overflow toward the past and the future—in other words, toward something which does not depend on us, and is therefore indifferent (VI, 32, 2):

Everything other than its own activity is indifferent to the faculty of reflection *(dianoia)*. Everything that *is* its own activity, however, is within its power. Moreover, even among these latter activities, the reflective faculty concerns itself only about the present; for even its past or future activities are now indifferent to it.

Only the present is within our power, simply because the only thing that we live is the present moment (II, 14; III, 10, 1; XII, 26, 2). Becoming aware of the present means becoming aware of our freedom.

For the present is real and has value only if we become aware of it; that is to say, if we delimit it by distinguishing the present action or event from the past and from the future. We must therefore recognize that our real lives are limited to a minuscule point which, by the intermediary of the present event or action, places us in constant contact—whether actively or passively—with the overall movement of the universe. "To circumscribe that which is lived in the present" means simultaneously to isolate oneself with regard to the past and to the future, and to recognize our puniness.

The delimitation of the present has two principal aspects. On the one hand, its goal is to make difficulties and hardships bearable, by reducing them to a succession of brief instants. On the other, it is a matter of increasing the attention we bring to bear upon our actions, as well as the consent which we grant to the events that happen to us. These two aspects can, moreover, be reduced to one fundamental attitude, which consists, as we can already glimpse, in transforming our way of seeing things, and our relationship to time.

The first of these aspects appears very clearly in the following passage (VIII, 36):

> Don't trouble yourself by representing to yourself the totality of life in advance. Don't try to go over in your mind all the painful hardships, in all their varying intensity and number, which might possibly happen. Rather, when each of them occurs, ask yourself: "What is there about this situation that is unbearable or intolerable?", for you will be ashamed if you answer affirmatively. In addition, remind yourself that it is not the present, nor the past, which weighs upon you, but always the present; and this present will seem smaller to you if you circumscribe it by defining and isolating it, and if you make your reflective faculty ashamed at the fact that it cannot put up with such a small, isolated little matter.

We always encounter the same method of the criticism of representations and value-judgments, which consists in tearing away from things their false appearance—which is what frightens us—and in defining them adequately, without mixing in any representations which are alien to the initial, objective representation we have of them. This is what I have called the method of physical definition. For Marcus, it consists not only in reducing a given reality to what it is, but also in decomposing it into its parts, in order to discover that it is only an assembly of its parts, and nothing else. No object can make us lose our mastery over ourselves, if we submit it to this method of division (XI, 2):

> A seductive melody . . . you can despise it if you divide it into each of its sounds, and if you ask yourself if you are lesser than each one of them taken separately; if you are, you would be filled with shame. The same thing will happen if you repeat this procedure in the case of the dance, by decomposing it into each movement or each figure. . . . In general, then, and with the exception of virtue and its effects, remember to head as quickly as you can for the parts of a process, in order, by dividing them, to get to the point where you have contempt for them. Transpose this method, moreover, to life in its entirety.

Either because of his reading of Marcus Aurelius, or as a result of a personal experience, Anatole France wrote something similar:[4]

> My mother used to say that when you went over them one by one, there was nothing extraordinary about Mme. Gance's features. Every time my mother expressed this opinion, however, my father used to shake his head in disbelief. No doubt, my worthy father was doing the same thing I was: he wasn't going over Mme. Gance's features one by one; and whatever they may have been like in detail, their total effect was charming.

In any case, the reader will not have failed to notice Marcus' concluding remark: "Transpose this method to life in its entirety." Here we recognize the methods of definition and delimitation of the present instant, which I have just discussed. We must not, says Marcus, lose our self-control because of a song or a dance, since these things can ultimately be resolved into a series of notes or movements which are nothing but so many successive instants. Similarly, we must not let ourselves become discouraged by the global representation of the whole of life— that is, of all the hardships and difficulties which await us. Like a song or a dance, our lives are divisible into smaller units, and consist only of such units. In order to execute a song or a dance step, we need to perform each one of these units in succession. Life, too, consists only of a series of such instants which we live in succession, and the better we are able to isolate each one and define it precisely, the better we shall be able to gain control over the entire series.

The other intention of the exercise of defining the present is to intensify the attention we bring to bear upon what we are doing or experiencing. Here, we are no longer concerned with diminishing hardships or suffering; on the contrary, our goal is to exalt the consciousness of our existence and our freedom. Marcus does not expand upon this theme, but we can sense it in the insistence with which he returns to the necessity of concentrating upon our *present* representations, our *present* actions, and the *present* event, as well as the necessity of avoiding worry about the past or the future (XII, 1, 1–2):

> All the happiness you are seeking by such long, roundabout ways: you can have it all right now. . . . I mean, if you leave all of the past behind you, if you abandon the future to providence, and if you arrange the present in accordance with piety and justice.

It should be pointed out here that, for Marcus, "piety" represents that discipline of desire which makes us consent "piously" to the divine will, as the latter is made manifest in events. Likewise, "justice" corresponds to the discipline of action, which makes us act in the service of the human community.

Marcus repeats the same exhortation elsewhere (XII, 3, 4):

> If you apply yourself to living only that which you are living—in other words, the present—then you can live the rest of your life until your death in peace, benevolence, and serenity.

What is required is that we dedicate ourselves, completely and wholeheartedly, to what we are in the process of doing at a given instant, without worrying about either the past or the future (VI, 7):

> Take joy and repose in one thing only: to pass from one action accomplished in the service of the community to another action accomplished in the service of the community; all this accompanied by the remembrance of God.

There is also a feeling of urgency about this attitude, for death can arrive at any moment (II, 5, 2):

Each of life's actions must be performed as if it were the last.

When we view things from the perspective of death, it is impossible to let a single one of life's instants pass by lightly. If, like Marcus and the Stoics, we believe that the only good thing is moral action and a perfectly good and pure intent, then we must transform our way of thinking and of acting in this very instant. The thought of death confers seriousness, infinite value, and splendor to every present instant of life. "To perform each of life's actions as if it were the last" means to live the present instant with such intensity and such love that, in a sense, an entire lifetime is contained and completed within it.

Most people are not alive, because they do not live in the present, but are always outside of themselves, alienated, and dragged backwards and forwards by the past and by the present. They do not know that the present is the only point at which they are truly themselves and free. The present is the only point which, thanks to our action and our consciousness, gives us access to the totality of the world.

In order to fully comprehend Marcus' attitude toward the present, we must recall the Stoic definition of the present, as it is given in a summary of Stoic philosophy:[5]

Just as the entire void is infinite in every direction, so all of time is infinite in both directions. Both the past and the future are infinite. He [i.e., Chrysippus] states very clearly that, in general, time is never present, for since that which is continuous is divisible *ad infinitum,* then in accordance with this division all of time is also divisible *ad infinitum.* Therefore, there is no present time, in the proper sense of the term; rather, it is spoken of in an extended sense *(kata platos).* Chrysippus says that only the present "actually belongs" *(hyparchein)* [to a subject]; whereas the past and the future are realized *(hyphestanai),* but "do not at all belong actually [to a subject]," just as it is said that only those predicates which really occur "actually belong." For instance, "walking" belongs to me actually when I am walking, but does not belong to me actually when I am lying or sitting down . . .

Here we are faced with two diametrically opposed conceptions of the present: the first considers the present as the limit between the past and the future, within a time which is continuous, and hence infinitely divisible. From this quasi-mathematical point of view, the present does not exist. According to the second conception, the present is defined in relation to the human consciousness which perceives it, as well as to the unity of the intention and attention which I bring to bear upon it. It is, on this analysis, that which I am currently doing, expressing, and feeling. From this point of view, the present does have a certain duration or "thickness" which admits of greater or lesser degrees *(kata platos)*. In this sense, the Stoic definition of the present is entirely analogous to that of Henri Bergson, who in *La Pensée et le mouvant* drew a distinction between the present as a mathematical instant, which is nothing but a pure abstraction, and that present which has a certain thickness or duration, which is more or less defined and delimited by my attention.[6]

In attempting to understand the opposition introduced by Chrysippus between, on the one hand, the present, and on the other the past and the future, the reader will no doubt have been willing to grant that the present is "that which currently belongs to me," but may have been quite astonished to read that the past and the future "are realized." Without entering into Chrysippus' technical refinements, which already seemed exaggerated to the writers of antiquity, one can say in response that what is important in the passage discussed above is not so much the opposition between the two Greek terms which Chrysippus chose to use—*hyparchein* and *hyphestanai,* elsewhere *hyphestēkēnai,* both of which mean "to exist," "to be real"—but rather their difference of tense. The word *hyparchein,* when used with relation to the present, means "to be real *qua* current process"; whereas the word *hyphestanai,* used with regard to the past and the future, means "to be real *qua* something determined and definitive." The former has an inchoative and durative force: it denotes that which is happening right at this moment. The latter, by contrast, has a definitive value. The reader may, moreover, be willing to grant that the past has a definitive value. But the future?

Here we must recall that, for the Stoics, the future was just as much determined as the past.[7] For Destiny, there is neither future nor past, but everything is determined and definite.[8] Chrysippus chose the verb *hyparchein* because it was a technical term of logic, which Aristotle frequently used to designate the inherence of an accident or an attribute in a subject; thus it is a word which denotes a relationship to a subject. Walking is "present"—that is, it belongs to me currently—when I am walking. The past and the future, by contrast, do not currently belong to me. Even if I think about them, they are independent of my initiative and do not depend on me. Therefore, the present has reality only in relation to my consciousness, thought, initiative, and freedom. It is these which give it a kind of thickness and duration, which in turn is linked to a series of unities: of the meaning of the discourse which I utter, of my moral intention, and of the intensity of my attention.

When Marcus speaks of the present, he is always talking about this durative present, which has a kind of thickness. Clearly, it is within this present that I situate the representation which I am having at this moment, the desire I am feeling at this moment, and the action which, at this moment, I am performing. It is also this "thick" present, however, which I can lessen by circumscribing and delimiting it, in order to make it more bearable. Such a "shrinkage" of the present does not imply, as Goldschmidt thought,[9] that the lived present would then be reduced to a mathematical, infinitely divisible instant. Goldschmidt thought he could percieve two attitudes toward the present in Marcus: one which denounced the unreality of the present instant, and another which bestowed reality upon the present instant via the initiative of a moral agent. On the contrary: we have seen how Marcus compared life to songs and to dance. Songs and dance are made up of units—notes and movements—which do have a certain thickness, however slight it may be. Now, a succession of unreal entities can never be put together so as to give rise to a dance, a song, or a life. Moreover, when Marcus speaks of the present in terms of a point within infinity, we can tell from the context that he is still talking about a lived present, which has a certain thickness (VI, 36, 1):

> Asia and Europe are corners of the world. The sea is a drop of the world. Athos is a lump of earth, and all present time is a point within infinity. Everything is tiny and unstable, and everything vanishes (in immensity).

Here, Marcus is not affirming the unreality of Asia, of the sea, or of Mount Athos, and hence not of the present, either. Rather, he is affirming—in a very scientific way, so to speak—their relative smallness within the immensity of the Whole, and not their nonexistence.[10] Once again, we are dealing with the method of "physical" definition.

Events, the present, and cosmic consciousness

According to Epictetus, the goal of the discipline of desire was that we not be frustrated in our desires, nor fall into that which we had been trying to avoid. In order to realize this goal, we had to desire only that which depends upon us—that is, the moral good—and flee only from that which depends on us: in this case, moral evil. That which does not depend on us is the realm of the indifferent: we must not desire it, but we must not flee from it either, for if we do we risk "falling into what we are trying to avoid." Epictetus, we noted, linked this attitude to our consent to Destiny.

Marcus Aurelius takes up this doctrine point for point, yet in his writings its implications and its consequences appear more clearly and explicitly. Above all, the discipline of desire in Marcus is related first and foremost to the way in which we are to greet the events which result from the overall movement of universal Nature, which are produced by what Marcus calls the "exterior cause" (VIII, 7):

> Rational nature (that is, the nature peculiar to human beings) follows the path which is appropriate to it . . . if it has desires and aversions only for that which depends upon us, and if it greets with joy all that common Nature allots to it.

What is thus allotted to human nature is nothing other than the events which happen to it (III, 16, 3):

> The proper characteristic of the good man is to love and to greet joyfully all those events which he encounters *(ta sumbainonta),* and which are linked to him by Destiny.

We have already seen that, for the Stoics, what is present for me is that which is currently happening to me: in other words, not merely my current actions, but also the present event with which I am confronted. Here again, as in the case of the present in general, it is my thought and my attention which singles out from the flux of things that which has meaning for me; at which point my inner discourse will declare that such-and-such an event is happening to me. Moreover—whether I know it or not—the overall movement of the universe, set in motion by divine Reason, has brought it about that I have been destined, from all eternity, to encounter such-and-such an event. This is why I have translated the word *sumbainon* (etymologically "that which goes together [with]"), which Marcus customarily uses to denote that which happens, by the phrase "the events which we encounter." To be still more precise, one would have to translate this as "the event which adjusts itself to us," but such an expression cannot always be used. This is, however, precisely the meaning which Marcus gives to the word *sumbainon* (V, 8, 3):

> We say that events are fitting to us *(sumbainein)*, just as masons say that the square stones they use in walls or in pyramids "fit each other" *(sumbainein)*, when they are well-adapted to each other in a given combination.

The imagery of the construction of the edifice of the universe is reinforced by that of weaving. The interweaving of the woof and the warp was a traditional, archaic image, linked to the figure of the Moirai, who, as early as Homer, spun the destiny of each human being.[11] The three Parcai, named Lachēsis, Clothō, and Atropos, appear—first in the Orphic Derveni papyrus,[12] and then in Plato[13] and the Stoics—as the mythical figures of the cosmic law which emanates from divine Reason. The following is a testimony to the Stoic doctrine:[14]

> The *Moirai* (or "Parts") are so named because of the process of separation *(diamerismos)* which they carry out: Clothō ("the spinner"), Lachēsis ("she who distributes the lots"), and Atropos ("the inflexible one"). Lachēsis is so called because she distributes the lots which individuals have received according to justice; Atropos [gets her name] because the division of the parts is unchangeable in any of its details, and is immutable since eternal time. Finally, Clothō is so named because the distribution takes place in accordance with Destiny, and that which occurs reaches its end in conformity with what she has spun.

Another testimony gives voice to approximately the same representations:[15]

> The *Moirai* get their name from the fact that they distribute and assign things to each one of us. . . . Chrysippus suggests that the number of the *Moirai* corresponds to the three times in which all things have their circular movement, and by means of which all things achieve their completion. Lachēsis is so called because she attributes to each human being his or her destiny; Atropos is so called because of the immutable and unchanging character of the distribution; and Clothō is so called because of the fact that all things

are woven and linked together, and that they can travel only one path, which is perfectly well-ordered.

The "events which I encounter," and which "adjust themselves to me" have been woven together with me by Clothō, the figure of Destiny or universal Reason (IV, 34):

Abandon yourself willingly to Clothō; let her weave you together with whatever event she pleases.

Marcus Aurelius is fond of mentioning this interweaving:

This event which you are encountering . . . it happened to you; it was coordinated with you; and was in relation to you, since it was woven together with you, from as far back as the most ancient of causes (V, 8, 12).

So something has happened to you? Good! Every event that you encounter has been linked to you by Destiny, and has, since the beginning, been woven together with you from the All (IV, 26).

Whatever happens to you has been prepared for you in advance from all eternity, and the interweaving of causes has, since forever, woven together your substance and your encounter with this event (X, 5).

While this motif is strongly emphasized by Marcus, it is not absent from Epictetus' sayings, as recorded by Arrian (I, 12, 25):

Will you be angry and unhappy with what Zeus has ordained? He defined and ordained these things together with the *Moirai,* who were present at your birth and wove your destiny.

For the Stoics, events were predicates, as we saw in the case of "walking," which is present to me when "I am walking." If, then, an event happens to me, this means that it has been produced by the universal totality of the causes which constitute the cosmos. The relationship between myself and such an event presupposes the entire universe, as well as the will of universal Reason. We shall have to examine later whether this will defines the event in all its details, or merely gives it an initial impulse. For the moment, it is sufficient to note that whether I am ill, or lose my child, or am the victim of an accident, it is the entire cosmos which is implicated in the event.

This interconnection or interweaving—the mutual implication of all things in all things—is one of Marcus' favorite themes. For him, as for the Stoics in general, the cosmos is but a single living entity, endowed with a unique consciousness and will (IV, 40):

> How all things cooperate to produce everything that is produced;
> how everything is linked and wound up together

in order to form a "sacred connection" (IV, 40; VI, 38; VII, 9).

Thus, each present moment, the event which I encounter within it, and my encounter with this event, imply and potentially contain all the movement of the universe. This notion is in agreement with the Stoic conception of reality as total mixture, or the interpenetration of all things within all things.[16] Chrysippus used to speak of a drop of wine which first becomes mixed with the entire sea, and thence is extended to the whole world.[17] Similar world-visions are not, moreover, out of date: Hubert Reeves, for example, speaks of E. Mach's notion according to which "the whole universe is mysteriously present in each place and at each instant of the world."[18] I am not trying to claim that such representations are based upon science; rather, they are based upon an original, funda-mental, existential experience, which can be expressed in poetic form, as it is in these verses by Francis Thompson:

> All things
> Near and far
> Are linked to each other
> In a hidden way
> By an immortal power
> So that you cannot pick a flower
> Without disturbing a star.[19]

Here again, we encounter the fundamental intuition of the cohesion and coherence of reality with itself, an intuition which led the Stoics to perceive love of self and accord with oneself in each movement of a living being as much as in the movement of the universe as a whole, or in the perfection of the sage. This is what Marcus expresses in passages like the following (X, 21):

The Earth loves! She *loves* the rain! And the venerable Ether? It *loves* too! The World, too, *loves* to produce that which must occur. And I say to the World: I, too, *love*—along with you. Don't we say: "such-and-such *loves* to happen"?

Everyday language, which could use the verb "to love" to signify "to be accustomed to," is here congruent with mythology, which gives us to understand, in its allegorical way, that it is characteristic of the All to love itself. What Marcus is alluding to here is the grandiose image of the *hieros gamos* between the sky (or Ether) and the earth, such as it is described by Euripides:

The Earth loves! She loves the rain, when the waterless field, sterile with dryness, needs moisture. The venerable Sky, too, when filled with rain, loves to fall upon the earth, by the power of Aphrodite.[20]

This myth allows us to glimpse that such self-love is not the solitary, egoistic love of the Whole for itself, but rather the mutual love, within the Whole, of the parts for each other, of the parts for the Whole, and of the Whole for the parts. Between the parts and the Whole, there is a "harmony" or "co-respiration," which puts them in accord with one another. Everything that happens to the part is useful for the Whole, and everything that is "prescribed" for each part is, almost in the medical sense of the term, "prescribed" (V, 8) for the health of the Whole, and consequently for all the other parts as well.

The discipline of desire therefore consists in replacing each event within the perspective of the Whole, and this is why it corresponds to the physical part of philosophy. To replace each event within the perspective of the Whole means to understand two things simultaneously: that I am encountering it, or that it is present to me, because it was destined for me by the Whole, but also that the Whole is present within it. Since such an event does not depend upon me, in itself it is indifferent, and we might therefore expect the Stoic to greet it with indifference. Indifference, however, does not mean coldness. On the contrary: since such an event is the expression of the love which the Whole has for itself, and since it is useful for and willed by the Whole, we too must want and love it. In this way, my will shall identify itself with the divine Will which has willed this event to happen. To be indifferent to indifferent things—that is, to things which do not depend on me—in fact means to make no difference between them: it means to love them equally, just as Nature or the Whole produces them with equal love. It is the Whole which, through and by me, loves itself, and it is up to me not to destroy the cohesion of the Whole, by refusing to accept such-and-such an event.

Marcus describes this feeling of loving consent to the will of the Whole and identification with the divine will in terms of the need to "find satisfaction" in the events which happen to us. He writes that we must "greet them joyfully," "accept them with pleasure," "love" them and "will" them. The *Manual* of Epictetus, as written by Arrian, expressed this same attitude in striking terms which encapsulate the entire discipline of desire (chap. 8):

> Do not seek for things to happen the way you want them to; rather, wish that what happens happen the way it happens: then you will be happy.

This entire attitude is admirably summed up in Marcus' prayer to the World (IV, 23):

> All that is in accord with you is in accord with me, O World! Nothing which occurs at the right time for you comes too soon or too late for me. All that your seasons produce, O Nature, is fruit for me. It is from you that all things come; all things are within you, and all things move toward you.

This brings us back to the theme of the present. A particular event is not predestined for me and accorded with me only because it is harmonized with the World; rather, it is so because it occurs in this particular moment and no other. It occurs in accordance with the *kairos* ("right moment"), which, as the Greeks had always known, is unique. Therefore, that which is happening to me at this moment is happening at the right moment, in accordance with the necessary, methodical, and harmonious unfolding of all events, all of which occur at their proper time and season.

To will the event that is happening at this moment, and in this present instant, is to will the entire universe which has brought it about.

Amor fati

I have entitled this section *"amor fati."* Marcus Aurelius, who wrote in Greek, obviously did not use these two Latin words; what is more, they are not, as far as I know, used by any Latin writer in antiquity. The phrase is Nietzsche's, and my intention in alluding to the love of Destiny of which Nietzsche speaks is to help us better to understand, by means of analogies and contrasts, the spiritual attitude which, in Marcus, corresponds to the discipline of desire. Nietzsche writes, for example:

> My formula for what is great in mankind is *amor fati:* not to wish for anything other than that which is; whether behind, ahead, or for all eternity. Not just to put up with the inevitable—much less to hide it from oneself, for all idealism is lying to oneself in the face of the necessary—but to *love* it.[21]

> Everything that is necessary, when seen from above and from the perspective of the vast economy of the whole, is in itself equally useful. We must not only put up with it, but *love* it. . . . *Amor fati:* that is my innermost nature.[22]

"To wish for nothing other than that which is": Marcus Aurelius could have said this, just as he could have concurred with the following:

> The main question is not at all whether or not we are satisfied with ourselves, but whether, more generally, there is anything at all with which we *are* satisfied. Let us suppose we said Yes to one single instant: we have thereby said Yes not only to ourselves, but to the whole of existence. For nothing is sufficient unto itself—neither in ourselves, nor among things—and if, just one single time, our soul has vibrated and resonated with happiness, like a stretched cord, then it has taken all of eternity to bring about that single event. And, at that unique instant of our Yes, all eternity was accepted, saved, justified, and affirmed.[23]

For Marcus, as for Epictetus, there is no link between this loving consent to the events which happen to us and the Stoic doctrine of the Eternal Return. This doctrine asserted that the world repeats itself eternally, for the rational Fire which spreads throughout the world is subject to a perpetual alternation of diastoles and systoles, which, in their succession, engender a series of periods all of which are unique, and during which the same events repeat themselves in a completely identical manner. For the Stoics, the ideas of Providence and Destiny, together with the concepts of the complete interpenetration of all the parts of the world, and of the loving accord between the Whole and all its parts, were enough to justify that attitude of loving acceptance in the face of all that comes from Nature which constitutes the discipline of desire. Nietzsche, by contrast, links the love of Destiny to the myth of the Eternal Return. To love Destiny thus means to want that what I am doing in this moment, as well as the way in which I live my life, should be eternally, identically repeated. It means to live any given instant in such a way that I want to relive again this instant I am now living, eternally. This is where Nietzsche's *amor fati* takes on a highly idiosyncratic meaning:

> The highest state which a philosopher can attain: to have a Dionysiac attitude toward existence. My formula for that is *amor fati*. . . .
>
>   For this, we must conceive of the heretofore denied aspects of existence not only as necessary, but as desirable: and not only desirable with regard to the aspects which have been approved up until now (as their complements, for example, or as their presuppositions), but in themselves, as the aspects of existence which are more powerful, more fertile, and more true, in which its will expresses itself most clearly.[24]

As we shall see, Marcus did indeed consider the repulsive aspects of existence as necessary complements or inevitable consequences of the initial will of Nature. Nietzsche, however, goes much further: in fact, an abyss appears between his views and those of Stoicism. Whereas the Stoic "yes" means a rational consent to the world, the Dionysiac affirmation of the world of which Nietzsche speaks is a "yes" given to irrationality, the blind cruelty of life, and the will to power which is beyond good and evil.

We have wandered far from Marcus; yet this detour has perhaps allowed us to arrive at a better definition of that consent to Destiny which is the essence of the discipline of desire.

As we have seen, the exercises of definition of the self and concentration on the present, together with our consent to the will of Nature as it is manifested in each event, raise our consciousness to a cosmic level. By consenting to the present event which is happening to me, in which the whole world is implied, I want that which universal Reason wants, and identify myself with it in my feeling of participation and of belonging to a Whole which transcends the limits of individuality. I feel a sensation of intimacy with the universe, and plunge myself into the immensity of the cosmos. One thinks of Blake's verses:[25]

> To see the World in a Grain of Sand
> And a Heaven in a Wild Flower
> Hold Infinity in the palm of your hand
> And Eternity in an hour.

Thus the self *qua* will or liberty coincides with the will of universal Reason, or the *logos* which extends throughout all things. The self as guiding principle coincides with the guiding principle of the universe.

If, then, the self's awareness is accompanied by a consent to events, it does not become isolated, like some tiny island, in the universe. On the contrary: it is opened up to the whole of cosmic becoming, to the extent that the self elevates itself from its limited situation and partial, restricted individual viewpoint, toward a universal perspective. Thus, my consciousness is dilated until it coincides with the dimensions of cosmic consciousness. In the presence of each event—no matter how banal—my vision now coincides with that of universal Reason.

When Marcus writes (IX, 6): "Your present inner disposition is enough for you, as long as it finds its joy within the present conjuncture of events," the expression "is enough for you" has two meanings. In the first place, as we have seen, it means that we possess the whole of reality within this present instant. As Seneca said,[26] at each present moment we can say, with God, "Everything belongs to me." This, however, means that if my moral intentions are good in this present moment, and I am consequently happy, neither all the duration of life nor all eternity could bring me one iota more of happiness. In the words of Chrysippus:[27] "If one has wisdom for one instant, he will be no less happy than he who possesses it for all eternity." Elsewhere, Seneca[28] writes: "The measure of the good is the same, although its duration may vary. Whether one draws a large circle or a small one does not depend on its shape, but on the surface which they enclose." A circle is a circle, whether it is large or small. Similarly, moral good, when it is lived within the present moment, is an absolute of infinite value, which neither duration nor any other external factor can affect. Once again, I can and I must live the present which I am living at this moment as if it were the last moment of my life; for even if it is not followed by any other instant, I will be able, because of the absolute value of moral intention and of the love of the good which I have lived in this instant, to say in that very instant: I have realized my life, and have gotten everything I could have expected out of it.[29] It is this that enables me to die. As Marcus says (XI, 1, 1):

> The rational soul . . . attains its proper end wherever it achieves the limit of its life. It is not like the dance or the theater or other arts of that kind, in which all the action is incomplete if they are interrupted. On the contrary: the action of the rational soul, in each of its parts, and at whatever point one considers it, carries out for itself what it was planning fully and without fault, so that it can say, "I have reached my fulfillment."

Whereas a dance or the reading of a poem reach their goal only when they are finished, moral activity reaches its goal in the very instant when it is accomplished. It is therefore entirely contained within the present moment, which is to say, within the unity of the moral intention which, in this very moment, animates my actions or my inner disposition. Once again, we note that the present instant can thus immediately open up the totality of being and of value. One thinks of the words of Wittgenstein: "If we understand by "eternity" not an infinite temporal duration, but a lack of temporality, then he who lives within the present lives eternally."[30]

Providence or atoms?

Marcus asks, rather enigmatically (IV, 3, 5):

> Are you unhappy with the part of the All which has been allotted to you? Then remember the disjunction: either providence or atoms.

In the first sentence, we recognize the problematic characteristic of the discipline of desire: we must accept, and even love, that part of the All which has been allotted to us. If, says Marcus, we are initially unhappy at and irritated by events, then we must remember the disjunctive dilemma: either providence or atoms. Marcus is here alluding to an argument, and it is enough for him to cite its first proposition—either providence or atoms—in order to remind his readers of the entire thing. This dilemma reappears throughout the *Meditations,* often accompanied by the argument, or by variations on the argument, which remains implicit in this first quotation.

Before we try to understand its meaning, it is necessary to spend some time clarifying this initial proposition, which opposes two factors: on the one hand, providence—elsewhere identified with Nature, the gods, or with Destiny—and on the other hand, atoms. These two opposing concepts correspond respectively to the models of the universe set forth by Stoic and by Epicurean physics. Marcus uses a variety of images to describe these alternatives: there is either a well-ordered world or a confused one; there is either union, order, and providence, or else a formless mess, the blind linking up of atoms, and dispersion (IV, 27, 1; VI, 10, 1; IX, 39, 1).

Marcus thus opposes two models of the universe: that of Stoicism and that of Epicureanism. His reason for doing so is to show that, on any hypothesis, and even if one were to accept, in the field of physics, the model most diametrically opposed to that of Stoicism, the Stoic moral attitude is still the only possible one. If one accepts Stoic physical theory—that is to say, the rationality of the universe—then the Stoic moral attitude—that is, the discipline of desire, or rational consent to the events brought about by universal Reason—does not raise any difficulties: one must simply live in accordance with reason. If, however, one accepts the Epicurean physical theory—a model where the universe is a dust of atoms produced by chance and lacking unity—then the grandeur of humankind consists in our introduction of reason into this chaos:

If the All is God, then all is well. But if it is ruled by chance, don't you, too, be ruled by chance (IX, 28, 3).

Consider yourself fortunate if, in the midst of such a whirlwind, you possess a guiding intelligence within yourself (XII, 14, 4).

On either hypothesis, then, we must maintain our serenity and accept events the way they are. It would be just as crazy to blame atoms as it would be to blame the gods (VI, 24).

This serenity must especially be maintained in the face of death. Whether one accepts the Stoic or the Epicurean model, death is a physical phenomenon (VI, 24):

After their deaths, Alexander of Macedon and his mule-driver wound up in the same state: either they were taken back up into the rational forces which are the seeds of the universe, or else, in the same way, they were dispersed among the atoms.

Our choice of a model of the universe thus changes nothing with regard to the fundamental Stoic disposition of consent to events, which is nothing other than the discipline of desire (X, 7, 4). If we reject the hypothesis of rational Nature, says Marcus, and choose to explain the transformations of the parts of the universe by saying that "that's just the way things are" (that is, that things occur by virtue of some kind of blind spontaneity), then it would be ridiculous to affirm, on the one hand, that the parts of the All can thus spontaneously transform themselves, and yet, at the same time, to be surprised and angry at these transformations, as if they were something contrary to nature.

Such arguments are obviously not Marcus' inventions. When he first speaks about them (IV, 3), he makes only a brief allusion to them, as if he were speaking of a well-known school-doctrine ("Remember the disjunction . . ."), without bothering to set forth the entire chain of reasoning.

There is nothing in Epictetus which coincides word-for-word with Marcus' formulations; yet we do find an argument of the same kind as that set forth by Marcus in Seneca. The latter says roughly: "Whichever hypothesis we accept—whether God or chance—we must philosophize; that is, we must either lovingly submit to the will of God, or proudly submit to the will of chance."[31]

Whatever modern historians may claim, the dilemma "either providence or chance," when used by Seneca or by Marcus Aurelius, does not signify either the renunciation of Stoic physical theories or an eclectic attitude which refuses to decide between Epicureanism and Stoicism.[32] In fact, we can see that Marcus has already made his choice between Epicureanism and Stoicism, by the very way in which he describes the Epicurean model with a variety of pejorative terms: "confused mixture" or "formless mess," for example. More important, Marcus refutes the "atoms" explicitly and repeatedly, notably in IV, 27:

> Should we accept the hypothesis of an ordered world, or that of a confused mixture? —Why, quite obviously, that of an ordered world.[33] If not, it would be possible for there to be order in you, and for disorder to reign over the All, even though all things are so distinguished from one another, and so deployed compared to one another, and so much in sympathy with one another.

A similar refutation occurs in Book XI, 18, 2 of the *Meditations,* where, in order to remind himself of his duty to love other human beings,

Marcus utilizes the Stoic principle which affirms the cohesion and accord with itself of Nature, all of whose parts are related to one another. Marcus arrives at this principle by rejecting the other branch of the dilemma—that is, the Epicurean model:

> Go back farther up from the following principle: if we reject the atoms, then it is Nature which governs the All. If this is so, then the inferior beings exist for the sake of the superior beings, and the latter exist for each other.

One the one hand, then, Epicurean physics is impossible to uphold, in the face of both inner and exterior experience. On the other hand, Epicurean ethics, which could follow from Epicurean physics, is impossible to defend from the viewpoint of inner moral demands. If all that exists are atoms, disorder, and dispersion, then (IX, 39, 2):

> What are you worried about? All you have to do is say to your guiding principle: "You are dead; you are destroyed. You've become a wild beast; you defecate, you mingle with the flocks, and you graze.

With caustic irony, Marcus thus implies that in a world without reason, human beings become irrational beasts.

When, in other passages, Marcus seems to imply that the Stoic moral attitude would be the same, whichever model of the universe one uses, and whichever physics one accepts, he is trying to demonstrate that, on all possible hypotheses, it is impossible *not* to be a Stoic. Aristotle affirmed that even when we say that we must not do philosophy, we are still doing philosophy.[34] Similarly, the arguments of Seneca and Marcus Aurelius run as follows: even if we agree with the Epicureans, and say that there is no universal Reason, and that therefore Stoicism is false, in the final analysis we must nevertheless live like Stoics; that is to say, in accordance with reason. "If everything is random, don't you, too, act at random" (IX, 28). This does not by any means signify the abandonment of Stoic physics, which Marcus elsewhere fully accepts and recognizes as the foundation of moral choice. What we have here is instead a kind of thought-experiment, which consists not in hesitating between Epicureanism and Stoicism, but rather in demonstrating the impossibility of not being a Stoic. Even if Epicurean physics were true, we would still have to renounce the Epicurean idea that pleasure is the only value. We would still have to live like Stoics; which means recognizing the absolute value of reason, and consequently the indifferent nature of those events which are independent of our will. In any event, we will still have to practice the discipline of desire, which, as we have seen, consists in making no distinction between indifferent things, which do not depend upon us.

Again and again, we find ourselves returning to the same central theme: the incommensurable value of moral good chosen by reason, and of true freedom, which are values compared to which nothing else has value. This affirmation of the virtually infinite value of autonomous moral reason does not, however, prevent the Stoic—precisely because he does attribute this value to reason—from concluding that it would be highly implausible for us to possess reason, and yet for the All of which we are only a part not to possess it. Either providence—in which we case we must live like Stoics—or else atoms—in which case we still have to live like Stoics. In the last analysis, however, the fact that we do live like Stoics proves that there are no atoms, but rather universal Nature. We must therefore always live like Stoics.

The disjunction I have just discussed, which was used to prove that, whatever our hypotheses, we have to live as Stoics, was a traditional part of a more vast and developed argument sketched by Seneca.[35] This argument took into account all possible hypotheses on the ways in which events may be brought about, in order to prove that, on all these hypotheses, the Stoic philosopher's moral attitude remained unchanged. The accompanying diagram presents these hypotheses schematically; in this regard, the following passage from the *Meditations* is highly significant (IX, 28, 2; numbers in parentheses refer to subdivisions of the diagram):

> Either the universe's thought exercises its impulse upon each individual (5). If this is so, then accept this impulse with benevolence.
>
> Alternatively, it gave its impulse once and for all (4) and everything else occurs as a necessary consequence (3). Why, then, should you worry?
>
> Finally, if the all is God (2), then all is well. If it is random (1), don't you, too, act at random.

As we can see, each of the hypotheses presented brings us back to the fundamental attitude of the discipline of desire.

In the diagram, we note that the disjunction—a fundamental and absolute opposition—is situated between the affirmation of chance

(= Epicureanism), and the negation of chance (= Stoicism), which implies the affirmation of providence. All of the subdisjunctions, by contrast, are compatible with the Stoic system. This schema, however, which makes explicit the logical structure of Marcus' text, shows us that the affirmation of providence contains a great many nuances, and that the events which result from the action of providence can have widely varying relationships with this providence. The initial opposition between chance and non-chance, or chance and providence, is, as Marcus himself affirms, a disjunction, which is to say that one of the alternatives completely excludes the other. They are absolutely incompatible.

The remaining oppositions, however, are not true disjunctions, but are what historians of logic call "subdisjunctions."[36] In this case, exclusion is not absolute, but relative: this means that, according to Marcus, in the same world, *some things* may be brought about by the direct action of providence (= hypothesis 2), while *others* may be produced in a way which is merely indirect and derivative (= hypothesis 3). Alternatively, we could say that, in the same world, some things may be brought about *either* by a one-time general impulse on the part of providence (= hypothesis 4), *or* by a specific impulse which relates to rational beings (= hypothesis 5).

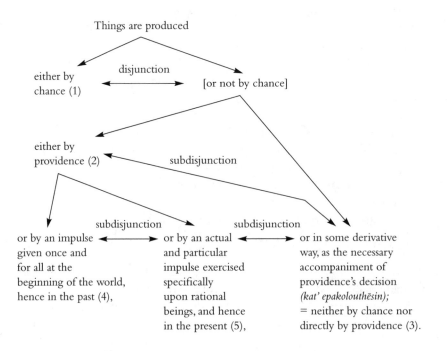

Things are produced

either by chance (1) — disjunction — [or not by chance]

either by providence (2) — subdisjunction

or by an impulse given once and for all at the beginning of the world, hence in the past (4), — subdisjunction — or by an actual and particular impulse exercised specifically upon rational beings, and hence in the present (5), — subdisjunction — or in some derivative way, as the necessary accompaniment of providence's decision (kat' epakolouthēsin); = neither by chance nor directly by providence (3).

The distinction between hypotheses 2 and 3 is of capital importance as far as the discipline of desire is concerned (VI, 36, 2):

> Everything comes from above, either under the impulse of the common guiding principle (2), or else as a consequence (3) *(kat' epakolouthēsin)*. Thus, the gaping jaws of a lion, poison, and everything which is unpleasant, such as thorns or mud, are only the accidental consequences *(epigennēmata)* of these things from above, which are venerable and beautiful. Therefore, do not represent to yourself these things which happen as a consequence (3) as alien to that which you venerate; rather, rise up in your thought to the source of everything (2).

All things and events, therefore, are the results of universal Reason, but in two different ways: either directly, in accordance with the will of universal Reason, or else indirectly, as consequences which have not been willed by universal Reason.

This distinction goes back to Chrysippus[37] himself:

> The same Chrysippus, in the fourth book of his *On Providence,* treats and examines a question which he thinks worthy of being asked: "Whether human illnesses come about in accordance with Nature." In other words, did that very Nature of things, or providence, which has produced the system of this world as well as the human race, also produce the illnesses, sicknesses, infirmities, and bodily suffering which people endure? He thinks that it was not Nature's primary intention to arrange things so that people should be exposed to illnesses, for such a goal has never been compatible with Nature, the creatrix and mother of all good things. However, he says, while Nature was engendering and bringing into the world a large number of great, appropriate, and useful things, other inconvenient things which were linked to these great things she was accomplishing came to be added accessorily. Thus, he says that these obstacles were not produced by Nature, but as a result of certain necessary consequences which he calls *kata parakolouthēsin*. For example, the construction of the human body required that the head be formed of very small and thin bones. Thus, an inconvenient side-effect—the weakness of the head—came about as a result of the interest of the principal task.

This theory of accessory consequences plays a very important role in Marcus' discipline of desire, since it is intended to justify our love for things and events which may seem painful or repulsive to us. If universal Reason has laid down the laws of Nature which ensure the health and the conservation of the entire universe, then

> I must therefore joyfully accept and love that which happens to me as a consequence of them *(kat' epakolouthēsin)* (VI, 44, 3).

That which could be called an accidental and blind consequence of Nature's initial will is the fact that a given natural phenomenon—a plague, for example, or an earthquake—should happen to strike *me* in particular; it is also the fact that certain natural phenomena—such as lions, thorns, or dirt—seem to me to be terrifying or repulsive. The notion of "accidental consequence" is, then, intimately linked to subjectivity. The reason I think that an accident cannot be the work of a benevolent Providence is because it is happening to *me,* is present to *me,* and is perceived by *me,* or because *I represent to it to myself* as repulsive or terrifying. I may then rebel, criticize Reason and universal Nature, and refuse to accept it. Consequently, the discipline of desire consists in rectifying this false judgment, by discovering that the event in question is indeed the result of the benevolence of Nature, although without having been willed directly by her. This has two implications: on the one hand, the initial will of Nature was not to harm me. In the words of Cicero,[38] "If drought or hail do harm to a landowner, that is no business of Jupiter's." In other words, "natural" phenomena do not pick and choose among individuals.

Second, Nature's initial will was not to produce something catastrophic, repulsive, dangerous, or ugly. Everything is natural, but it is an accidental consequence of Nature's will that such natural phenomena as lions, poison, and thorns may possibly represent a danger for human beings, or at least *appear* to be a threat to them.

Here again, the discipline of desire is based upon a physical definition: that which, setting aside all-too-human value-judgments, restricts itself to the objective, adequate representation of its object. Such a definition sees reality as if human beings were not a part of it.

Precisely because Stoic providence is rational, it is not omnipotent. Chrysippus told us that providence was constrained, in its construction of the human body, to give the bones of the head a dangerous thinness. Stoic Nature, like its Aristotelian counterpart, acts like a good administrator or craftsman, who gets the best she can from the available materials. This has less to do with any defect of matter than with the very nature of Reason. Reason demands a determinate, and therefore finite, object. The possibilities open to it are limited, and it must choose between quite determinate contrary solutions, each of which have their drawbacks and advantages. The result is not only a determinate universe which cannot be other than the way it is—this is but another aspect of the doctrine of Destiny—but also "such-and-such"[39] a universe, which unfolds "such-and-such" an evolution from beginning to end, and repeats itself eternally.

When universal Reason produces the world, it engraves certain laws into the coming-into-being of things. It is a law, for instance, that the elements are in constant transformation, and yet that the beings brought about by the transformation of the elements tend to preserve themselves. The result of these fundamental laws, however, can be phenomena which, on a subjective level, seem to us to be repulsive, terrifying, or dangerous. The law of the perpetual metamorphosis of the elements, for example, has among its results death, dust, and mud; while the law of self-preservation results in such defensive elements as a rose's thorns or a lion's teeth. All these are incidental consequences of Nature's initial decision.

The notion of necessary and incidental consequences is thus intimately linked to the idea of a Providence which gives a one-time, originary impulse (see hypothesis 4 above). Everything then happens by way of a necessary chain of events *(kat' epakolouthēsin),* of which the effects that are painful to humankind were not willed by the original impulse (hypothesis 3). The two notions of originary impulse and consequential linkage, then, strictly imply each other.

At the origin of everything is a single, universal impulse, which is the work of Nature/Reason. We must not, however, imagine this impulse as a "fillip," to use Pascal's term[40] when he said that the God of Descartes does nothing more than snap his fingers in order to set the universe in motion. We are not talking about an impulse imposed from outside by some being different from the world, which then allows the world to roll along like a billiard ball. On the contrary: the impulse Marcus speaks of is imposed by a force which is within the world: the soul or mind of the world. This must not be imagined in accordance with a model which is mechanical, but rather according to an organic one; for the Stoics see the development of the universe as like that of a living being, developing from a seed. A seed has two aspects: on the one hand, it contains within itself a force which exerts pressure or an impulse. On the other, it contains programmed within itself all the stages of the living being's development. Since this program proceeds methodically, it is "rational," and this is why the Stoics call the forces which bring forth living beings "seminal reasons."[41] God, who is identical with Reason and Nature, is the source of all beings; but he is himself a seminal reason containing within himself all other seminal reasons.[42] This is why Marcus Aurelius (IX, 1, 10) can speak of

> . . . the ancient impulse of providence, by means of which, starting from a particular beginning, it gave the impulse so that this arrange-ment of the world might be brought about. Prior to this, it had gathered together some productive reasons of things which are to come, and determined the forces which would engender births, transformations, and successions of such-and-such a kind.

We are to picture this originary impulse as the effect of a force which, from within, sets in motion the process of the expansion and deployment of the universe. More exactly, what Marcus has in mind is a movement of relaxation and expansion, which somehow causes the original energy to explode. Thus, this universe contains within itself its rational laws of development and organization. In this evolutionary process, as in the growth of a living being, everything contributes to the welfare of the entire organism, and everything is brought about as a necessary conse-quence *(kat' epakolouthēsin)* of the initial impulse, and the rational pro-gram which the latter sets in motion. As we have seen, however, it may be that these necessary consequences appear as evils to any given part of the Whole, and it may seem that they have been "willed" by this devel-opmental law.

This theory of the originary impulse thus corresponds to the idea of an impersonal, immanent providence, within the development of the uni-verse as a whole. The fact that the world is rational does not mean that it is the result of the deliberation, choice, or calculation of some craftsman exterior to his work. Rather, it means that the world possesses its own internal law.

This image of an impersonal providence (hypothesis 4 above) seems utterly opposed to that of a particular providence taking care of the human race, and of some specific human beings in particular (hypothesis 5). We now find the physical model of an impersonal law of nature, which runs the risk of crushing individuals, replaced by the images of

gods who care for human beings, who can be prayed to, who are susceptible to pity, and who concern themselves with the smallest details of life.

These two representations appear to be completely incompatible, and
one might think that Marcus brings up the idea of a providence susceptible to pity in the same way as he brought up the dilemma "providence or
atoms": in order, that is, to show that we must maintain the same Stoic
attitude, no matter which hypothesis is true (XII, 14):

> Either the necessity of Destiny and unbreakable order, or else provi-
> dence capable of pity, or else directionless chaos.
>
> If it is inflexible necessity, why do you resist?
>
> Is it providence susceptible to pity? Then make yourself worthy
> of divine assistance.
>
> Directionless chaos? Then consider yourself fortunate that, in
> midst of such a whirlwind, you possess within yourself a guiding
> intelligence.

The very idea of a providence capable of pity does not seem compatible with the principles of Stoicism, insofar as it seems to imply that
universal Reason could deviate from its initial movement. Seneca emphasizes this point: "If divine majesty had done something which it later
had to modify, it would be an affront and the admission of an error."[43]
God himself cannot change the course of destiny, because it is the necessity and the law which he has imposed upon himself. God is his own
necessity unto himself.

Nevertheless, the opposition between the unique initial impulse and
individual providence is not as radical as it appears at first glance. In order
to discover the true meaning of this opposition, we must simply take into
account religious attitudes, as well as the mythical language which ac-
companies them.

It is certain that the theory of an individual providence is a response to
the need to personalize our relationship with the world and with Nature,
as well as to the need to sense God's presence, his goodness, and his
paternity. Such a need had been felt since the very beginnings of Stoicism; the famous Hymn to Zeus by the Stoic Cleanthes is a striking
testimony to it, since it requests the god's spiritual assistance: "O Zeus,
giver of all good things . . . save men from sorry ignorance. Chase it, O
Father, far from our hearts . . ."[44] Generally speaking, the figure of Zeus
is intended to provide a face for the impersonal force of the *logos,* Nature,
or the first Cause. Such an identification is clearly apparent in Seneca:

"The Ancients did not believe that the Jupiter [= Zeus] we adore on the Capitol and in the other temples sent bolts of lightning with his own hand."[45] On the contrary: by "Jupiter," they meant the soul and mind of the world.

All names are appropriate to him.

Do you want to call him *Destiny?* You won't be wrong, for it is from him that all things are suspended; he is the cause of causes.

Do you want to call him *Providence?* You will speak rightly, for it is by his counsel that the needs of the world are provided for, in order that it may reach its appointed term without impediment, and that it may unfold all its movements.

Nature? You will not be in error, for it is from him that all things are born, and thanks to whose breath we live.

The *World?* You will not be wrong, for he is all that you see; he is present in all of his parts and he conserves both himself and his parts.[46]

The rest of this passage applies the theory of the unique initial impulse to Zeus-Jupiter:

Lightning-bolts are not hurled by Jupiter, but all things have been so disposed that even those things which are not done by him do not happen without that Reason which belongs to Jupiter . . . For even if Jupiter does not now do these things himself, yet he *has* caused these things to happen.[47]

For the Stoics, the figures of the other gods correspond to the elements which make up the world, and they represent the phases of the general movement of the universe. Epictetus (III, 13, 4–8) mythically depicts Zeus—that is to say, Reason or Nature—at the moment when the universe, after a phase of expansion (diastole) followed by concentration (systole), is returned via a general conflagration to its seminal state: in other words, the moment when Reason is alone with itself. Will Zeus cry out: "Oh unhappy me! I have neither Hera, nor Athena, nor Apollo . . ."? "No," says Epictetus: "Zeus then keeps company with himself, and rests within himself . . . he entertains himself with thoughts worthy of himself."

All this corresponds, then, to a religious need: the need to personalize that power, to the will of which the discipline of desire instructs us complacently to consent. This is why Marcus Aurelius, like Epictetus, often employs the expressions "follow the gods" or "obey the gods"[48] to describe this attitude of consent.

Marcus also feels the need to perceive the attention which the gods pay to him. In the first book of his *Meditations* (I, 17), he thanks them and enumerates all the benefits they have accorded to him. In particular, he mentions the dreams they have sent to him about his health, or the communications, support, and inspiration which he has received from them in his philosophical life. We may say that this corresponds to what Christian theology calls "present graces." Thus, not only do the gods help humankind in the realization of their moral life, but they also take the trouble to help them to obtain those indifferent things (such as health, wealth, and glory) which human beings seek (IX, 11, 2; 27, 3).

I have spoken of a religious need; but the problem is just as much sociopolitical, since the daily life of people in antiquity was punctuated by religious ceremonies. Moreover, prayers and sacrifices would have no meaning if there were no current and individual providence (VI, 44, 4):

> If the gods do not deliberate about anything—to believe this would be impious; or else let us make no more sacrifices, prayers, oaths, nor let us carry out any of the other rites which we practice, as if the gods were present and lived with us . . .

This religious need thus corresponds to the desire to have a relationship with some personal being who can, as it were, enter into a dialogue with humankind. Another response to this same aspiration is the conception of the *daimōn,* which is, moreover, traditionally nothing more than a particular element of the more general theory of providence.[49] In this regard, the following words of Epictetus are significant (I, 14, 12):

> God has placed next to each person, as a guardian, his own *daimōn,* and he has entrusted each person to its protection. . . . When you close your doors . . . remember never to say to yourselves that you are alone . . . for God is within you.

In fact, however, such conceptions of gods mixing with human beings and of the inner *daimōn* do not fundamentally alter Stoicism's rational demands. What I mean by this is that the figures of the gods deliberating over the fate of an individual, or the figure of the *daimōn,* are nothing but mythical, imaginative expressions, intended to render the Stoic conceptions of Reason and Destiny more alive and personal. We can observe this process at work, for example, in the following passage from Marcus Aurelius (V, 27):

> He lives with the gods who constantly shows them a soul which greets that which has been allotted to it with joy; it does everything that is willed by the *daimōn* which Zeus has given each person as an overseer and a guide, and which is a small parcel of Zeus. It is nothing other than each person's intellect and reason.

Here, then, the *daimōn* is straightforwardly identified with humankind's inner reason or the proper nature of humankind, which is a part of universal Nature and Reason.

Once we disengage the hypothesis of special and individual providence from its mythical formulation, it can perfectly well be integrated within the overall scheme of the Stoic theory of providence. The Stoics not only thought that universal Reason had, by means of its initial impulse, set in motion a law of the development of the universe which has as its goal the good of the Whole; but they also admitted that this fundamental law of the universe has as its primary goal the good of rational beings (V, 16, 5):

> Inferior beings are made for the purposes of superior ones, and superior beings are made for one another.

Providence, then, is exercised directly, especially upon reasonable beings, and by way of consequence it is also exercised upon other beings (VII, 75):

> The Nature of the All gave the impulse in the past [= hypothesis 4], so that the creation of the world might come about. Now, however, either everything that happens happens as a consequence *(kat' epakolouthēsin)* of that [= hypothesis 3], or else there is a tiny number of things *(oligista)*—and these include the most important ones— which are the object of a particular act of will [= hypothesis 5] on the part of the world's guiding principle.

This "tiny number of most important things" refers to rational beings. There is thus a general providence for the entire universe, which corresponds to the "initial impulse" which Marcus mentions here. There is also a special providence for rational beings: it is a particular act of will, which "exercises its impulse upon each individual," as Marcus had said elsewhere (IX, 28, 2). These two notions are not, however, mutually exclusive, for the general law, which is immanent within the universe and results from the initial impulse, wants rational life to be the end that justifies the universe. Origen[50] attributes this doctrine explicitly to the Stoics:

> Providence made all things primarily for the good of rational beings. Rational beings, since they are the most important, play the part of children who have been brought into the world. Non-rational and inanimate beings play the part of the placenta which is produced at the same time as the child. . . . Providence looks primarily to the needs of rational beings, but non-rational beings also profit, by way of accessory consequence, from what is made for human beings.

This text should not, however, be opposed to that in which Cicero states that Jupiter does not care about the damage caused by hail in some landowner's garden; for what counts from the Stoics' point of view is not such morally indifferent things as harvests. For them, the only important thing is humankind's moral elevation and its quest for wisdom. Divine providence, creative and nurturing toward inferior creatures, becomes the educator of human beings. Henri Bergson used to call the world "a machine for making gods";[51] but the Stoics would gladly have called it a machine for making sages.

Indeed, sages seem to be the privileged objects of this individual providence. Note, for example, the following passage from Epictetus (III, 26, 28):

> Could God become so disinterested in his masterpieces, his servants, and his witnesses: those he places as examples before people without any moral training?

There is also this text from Cicero:[52]

> The immortal gods do not only cherish the human race, but also particular men . . . who could not have been what they were without divine assistance.

For Marcus Aurelius, the main interest of this theory of providence's various modes of action is that it specifies the way in which we should practice the discipline of desire. We can look at events from two different and yet convergent viewpoints, according to whether we place ourselves in the perspective of the initial impulse, or in that of individual providence.

On the one hand, from the perspective of universal Nature and general providence, things which can seem repulsive, unpleasant, ugly, or terrifying, such as the thorns of a rose, the jaws of ferocious beasts, mud, or earthquakes, will seem to be physical phenomena which are completely natural: they are not directly programmed by the initial impulse, but are the accessory and necessary consequences thereof. If these inevitable consequences of the order of the world personally affect the unfortunate vineyard-owner of whom Cicero speaks, and he considers this to be a misfortune for him, then it does not follow that "Jupiter" has willed him to consider this phenomenon as a misfortune. The vineyard-owner is free to represent events to himself as he pleases; in fact, however, such events are only the accessory consequence of physical laws which result from the initial impulse. If Cicero's vineyard-owner is a Stoic, he will say "Yes!" to this universal order. He will say "Yes!" to the world, and will love everything that happens. He will consider that the loss of his property is morally neither good nor bad, but pertains to the order of indifferent things. Indifferent things do not concern Jupiter, and have no meaning within a universal perspective. They correspond only to a subjective and partial point of view.

Nevertheless, from the perspective of particular providence, the events that happen to me *are* individually destined for me. Clothō—that is, the course of the universe, which has issued from the original impulse—has woven them together with me since the origin of the world (IV, 34; V, 8, 12; IV, 26; X, 5). Everything that happens to me is destined for me, in order to give me the opportunity to consent to what God wants for me, in precisely this moment, and in precisely this form. I am to accept "my" own particular destiny, which the entire universe has reserved for me alone (V, 8):

A phrase like "Asclepius ordered him to practice horseback-riding, or cold baths, or walking barefoot" is analogous to this one: "The Nature of the All ordered for him an illness, a deformity, a loss or something else of the sort." For in the first phrase, "ordered" means "he prescribed that for him, since it corresponded to the state of his health." In the second phrase, the event which comes to each person has been assigned to him because it corresponded to his destiny. . . . Let us therefore accept these events, just as we accept the "orders" of Asclepius.

On the one hand, says Marcus, this event has happened especially for you; it was "ordered" for you, was related to you, and was woven together with you by the most ancient of causes. On the other hand, that which was "ordered" for you in this way was the condition for the efficient working and the very existence of the universe.[53]

These two outlooks are not mutually exclusive, since each event is at the same time the result of the general law of the universe, taken by itself, and of this same general law of the universe, when applied to the good of rational creatures.

Depending on which perspective one adopts, however, the practice of the discipline of desire can take on different tonalities. One may be more impersonal, tending as it does to eliminate all subjectivity in the admiring contemplation of the ineluctable laws of a majestic but indifferent Nature (IX, 1). The other may be more personal, since it gives the individual the feeling of contributing to the general good of the All, as he fulfills the task, role, and destiny for which Nature has chosen him (VI, 42):

We are all contributing to the accomplishment of a single result. Some of us know this and cooperate consciously, whereas others do so unconsciously. I think it was Heraclitus who said that those who sleep are the workers and collaborators of what happens in the world. . . .He who governs the universe will, in any case, know perfectly well how to use you; he will know how to make you a collaborator.

Pessimism?

"His joyless, disillusioned *Meditations* are penetrated by a profound pessimism . . . they are an authentic testimony to the solitude of an intellectual." These extracts from the catalogue[54] of an exposition dedicated to Marcus Aurelius in 1988 provide a good summary of the idea most historians since Renan have had of our philosopher-emperor. It is true that there is no lack of seemingly pessimistic declarations throughout the pages of his book (VIII, 24):

> Just as your bath appears to you—oil, sweat, filth, sticky water, and all kinds of disgusting things—such is each part of life, and every object.

Or again (IX, 36):

> The decomposition of matter which underlies each one of us: water, dust, bones, stench.

Sometimes, this disgust seems to be accompanied by a feeling of boredom which reaches the point of nausea (VI, 46):

> What you see in the amphitheater and similar places makes you sick: it's always the same thing, and such uniformity makes the spectacle tedious; you feel the same way about the totality of life. From top to bottom, it is always the same thing, made up of the same things. Where will it all end?

Nevertheless, we must not rush into thinking that Marcus is here giving us his personal impressions, or the expression of some incurable sadness. We know, in fact, that he is embroidering upon a canvas already prepared for him. His meditations are exercises which he practices in accordance with a quite determinate method, while following pre-existing models. Our task, therefore, is to try to understand the true meaning and range of such traditional formulas.

In the first place, in many of these declarations we can recognize the method of physical definition which we have encountered earlier. We recall that this method is intended to make us rely upon our objective representations, thereby avoiding the false and conventional value-judgments which people tend to emit about objects. This method, says Marcus (III, 11, 2), must be applied to all objects which present themselves to us in life, so that we may "see everything that happens in life with exactness and from the perspective of Nature" (X, 31, 5). Such a method of physical definition will strip things naked (VI, 13, 2; III, 11, 1); it will "make it clear how little value they have, and will strip from them that appearance of which they are so proud" (VI, 13, 3). When speaking of the method which defines things by reducing them to their parts (XI, 2, 2), Marcus gives the following advice:

> Except for virtue and that which relates to virtue, remember to get right down to the parts which you've divided, and get to the point where, by means of this division, you despise them. Then, transpose this method to the whole of life.

Marcus' goal is thus to denounce false values, and to see things in their naked, "physical" reality. Fancy foods are only cadavers; purple vestments are only sheep's hair; sexual union is only two bellies rubbing together (VI, 13, 1). The war Marcus is waging, he says, is a hunt analogous to that of the spider and the fly (X, 10, 1), while social and political life are not worth much (V, 33, 2):

> Everything by which people set so much store in life is emptiness, putrefaction, pettiness; little dogs nipping at one another; little children who laugh as they fight, and then suddenly burst into tears.

The same method is to be applied to people who think themselves important (IX, 9):

> Imagine them as they are when they are eating, when they are sleeping, when they are making love, or going to the bathroom. Then imagine them when they are putting on airs; when they make those haughty gestures, or when they get angry and upbraid people with such a superior air.

We must always look to the "physical" reality; this also holds true for fame, and the name which one leaves to posterity (V, 33):

> It is nothing but a simple sound, as weak as an echo.

Likewise, by the method of dividing a whole into its parts, we may strip life of its false appearances and reduce it to one of its moments:

> Just as your bath appears to you—oil, sweat, filth, sticky water, and all kinds of disgusting things—such is each part of life, and every object (VIII, 24).

Always consider human affairs as ephemeral and without any value: yesterday, you were a bit of phlegm; tomorrow, you will be ashes or a mummy (IV, 48, 3).

In the midst of a series of "physical" definitions, Marcus' definition of death reveals once more the lack of value of our physical existence (IX, 36):

The decomposition of the matter which forms the foundation of the being of each one of us: water, dust, bones, stench. Or consider marble: it is only a concretion of the earth. Gold and silver? They are the dregs of the earth. Clothing? Mere animal hair. The purple? Just some blood; and so forth . . .

Here we can catch Marcus as he trains himself to give physical definitions of the most diverse objects, and we can legitimately suppose that the definition of the decomposition of matter is no more charged with emotional and personal power than are those of marble or of gold. Instead, we are dealing with a (slightly artificial) method for finding striking formulas. The goal of the whole exercise, however, is to denounce false values, and this is the task of the discipline of desires.

Some historians[55] have thought they could discern in these passages a genuine attitude of repulsion on Marcus' part toward matter and physical objects. According to them, Marcus thereby abandoned the Stoic doctrine of Reason's immanence in matter, and the admiration which Chrysippus had felt for the sensible world can no longer be found in Marcus. This seems to me quite incorrect.

In the first place, when Marcus speaks about the "decomposition of matter," he does not mean that matter itself is putrefaction, but that the transformation of matter—which corresponds to death—is a natural process necessarily accompanied by phenomena of decomposition which, though they may appear to us to be repulsive, should nevertheless be exactly and physically defined.

Marcus does not by any means abandon the Stoic doctrine of the immanence of Reason in matter. He speaks of the Reason which governs substance (ousia)—that is to say passive matter—as well as of that Reason which spreads throughout all substance (VI, 1), and molds all beings with the help of substance (VII, 23). He also speaks of the constructive force within natural creatures (VI, 40), which is to be revered. To be sure, Marcus also speaks of the "weakness of matter" (XII, 7), but this "weakness" is nothing other than its "fluid" nature—that is, its constant susceptibility to passive change and inability to act by itself, which characterize Stoic matter.

It is also true that Marcus sometimes speaks of the body in terms of a corpse (IX, 24; X, 33, 6); but he himself tells us that he has learned this from Epictetus (IV, 27):

> "You are nothing but a little soul carrying a cadaver," as Epictetus said.

A glance at the *Discourses* as collected by Arrian does indeed reveal that Epictetus used this expression several times (II, 19, 27; III, 10, 15; 22, 41); especially when he wonders if his corpse is his "self" (IV, 7, 31). Elsewhere, Epictetus sometimes adds, as does Marcus, that the body is made only of earth (III, 22, 41). These expressions, then, which could be classified as pejorative, are not Marcus' original invention.

Finally, when Marcus compares life to bath-water, together with the oily dirt which it contains, he is doing nothing other than practicing the method of physical definition of which I have spoken. If we want to see things for what they are, we must also learn to see as they are the realities which are indissolubly linked to everyday life, such as the physical and physiological aspects of our bodily functions. We must also become accustomed to the constant transformation of things within and around us, including dust, filth, bad odors, and stenches. Such a realistic view will enable us to face life as it really is. One is reminded of the words of Seneca:

> It is no less ridiculous to be shocked by these things than it is to complain because you get splashed in the baths, or get shoved around in a public place, or that you get dirty in muddy places. What happens in life is exactly like what happens in the baths, in a crowd, or on a muddy road . . . Life is not made for delicate souls.[56]

Such a pitiless vision will strip life's objects of all the false values in which our judgments wrap them up. The true reason for this alleged pessimism is, then, that Marcus considers everything vile and petty in comparison to that unique Value constituted by the purity of our moral intention and the splendor of virtue. From this perspective, life is a "stain" (VII, 47). At the same time, however, such a way of looking at life invites us to reflect on the relative and subjective character of our ideas of "stain" and of "repulsive things." What is *really* repulsive is not certain aspects of matter, but the passions and the vices.

In fact, the reason we consider certain aspects of physical reality "repulsive" is that we are the victims of a prejudice, and we therefore do not know how to resituate such aspects within the vast perspective of universal Nature. All these aspects are, in fact, the necessary but accessory consequences of the original impulse which Nature once gave to the origin of things (VI, 36, 3):

> The gaping jaws of a lion, poison, and everything unpleasant—mud, thorns, and so forth—are accessory consequences of these sacred and venerable things on high. Don't imagine, then, that these things are foreign to the principle which you venerate, but rather rise up by your rational power to the source of all things.

Mud, dust, and dirty bath-water—all phenomena which we judge to be repugnant—are in fact intimately linked to the processes, course, and development of the world, which in turn can be traced back to universal Reason. Marcus goes farther still (III, 2):

> We must also bear in mind things like the following: even the accessory consequences of natural phenomena have something graceful and attractive about them. For instance: when bread is baked, some parts of it develop cracks in their surface. Now, it is precisely these small openings which, although they seem somehow to have escaped the intentions which presided over the making of the bread, somehow please us and stimulate our appetite in a quite particular way. Or take figs as an example: when they are perfectly ripe, they split open. In the case of ripe olives, it is precisely the proximity of rot which adds a unique beauty to the fruit. Ears of corn which bend toward the earth; the lion's wrinkled brow; the foam trailing from the mouth of boars: these things, and many others like them, would be far from beautiful to look at, if we considered them only in themselves. And yet, because these secondary aspects accompany natural processes, they add a new adornment to the beauty of these processes, and they make our hearts glad. Thus, if one possesses experience and a thorough knowledge of the workings of the universe, there will be scarcely a single one of those phenomena which accompany natural processes as a consequence which will not appear to him, under some aspect at least, as

pleasant. Such a person will derive no less pleasure from contemplating the actual gaping jaws of wild beasts than he does from all the imitations which painters and sculptors provide thereof. His pure eyes will be able to see a kind of flourishing maturity in aged men and women, as well as a kind of amiable charm in children. Many such cases will occur, and it is not just anyone who can derive pleasure from them. Rather, only that person who has become truly familiar with Nature and her works will do so.

It is worthwhile to compare these lines with Aristotle's preface to his *Parts of Animals* (644b31ff.):

In fact, some of the creatures in this world do not have a pleasant appearance. Nature, however, who has created them, provides whoever contemplates her with marvelous enjoyments, as long as one is able to recognize the principles of natural phenomena, and is of a philosophical nature. It would, moreover, be illogical and absurd if we took pleasure in contemplating reproductions of such creatures—since, as we contemplate them, we simultaneously admire the talent of the artist, be he painter or sculptor—and yet did not feel still more joy while contemplating the very beings which Nature has created—at least when we are able to discern their principles. This is why we must not yield to any kind of childish repugnance when we are examining some of the less noble animals, for there is something wonderful in all that is natural.

It is the creatures themselves, as produced by Nature, which interest Aristotle. According to the Stagirite, even if these creatures have a terrifying or repulsive appearance, the philosopher, insofar as he recognizes the creative power of Nature within them, can discover their beauty. For Marcus, by contrast, as we have seen, such creatures are to be explained as the consequences, both necessary and accessory, of the natural phenomena which result from the initial decision, yet seem to humankind to be contrary to Nature's intentions—snake venom, for instance, or the thorns on roses. In the final analysis, however, Marcus also recognizes in these consequences the creative power of Nature. Even though such consequences do not fit within the classical canon of beauty, they nevertheless, insofar precisely as they are the consequences of natural phenomena, "have something charming and attractive about them."

Our baker would like to have given his bread a perfectly regular form.

When it is baked, however, the bread takes on unforseeable forms, and cracks in unexpected ways. Likewise, the general movement of the universe should be completely rational, and yet, when this movement occurs, there also occur concomitant, accessory phenomena which go above and beyond Nature's intentions, and the impulse which she gave at the beginning. Just as in the case of the bread, however, it is precisely such anomalies and irregularities—these cracks in the crust, if you will—which make us sense that the bread is crusty, and stimulate our appetite.

For Aristotle, only the philosopher could perceive the beauty of the products of Nature, for it was he who could discover Nature's plan: a force which ensured the growth of beings from within. Marcus, too, holds that only the philosopher or the sage—someone who possesses experience and a deep understanding of the processes of the universe—can feel the beauty and grace of the phenomena which accompany natural processes. This is because only he can perceive the link between these natural processes and their necessary accompaniments.

In the place of an idealistic aesthetics, which considered beautiful only that which manifested the ideal form and the canons of proportion, Aristotle, Marcus, and the entire Hellenistic period substituted a realistic aesthetics. For them, living reality, in its nudity and even in its horror, is more beautiful than beautiful imitations. "An ugly man," as Plotinus[57] was to say, "if he is alive, is more beautiful than a man represented in a statue, however beautiful he may be."

Here the perspective has been utterly transformed. Things which used to appear repulsive, disgusting, or terrifying now become beautiful to the eyes of the person familiar with Nature, precisely because they exist, are natural, and are part of the natural processes which flow indirectly from Nature's intentions.

Like Nature (IX, 1, 9), we must not make any distinctions between indifferent things, which depend not upon us, but on universal Nature. Dirt, mud, thorns, and poison come from the same source and are just as natural as roses, the sea, or spring. In the eyes of Nature, and of people familiar with Nature, there is no difference to be made between bathwater and the rest of life: everything is equally "natural." We are fairly close to Nietzsche here: "Everything which is necessary, when seen from above and from the point of view of the vast economy of the whole, is in itself equally useful. We must not only put up with it, but *love* it."[58]

Familiarity with Nature is one of the fundamental attitudes of one who practices the discipline of desire. Being familiar with Nature means recognizing things and events as familiar, and realizing that they belong to the same world, and come from the same source, as we do. It thus means "doing physics" in the sense of becoming aware of the unity of Nature and its accord with itself. He who is familiar with Nature associates himself with Nature's self-accordance; in Marcus' words, he is "no longer a stranger in his homeland," and is "a man worthy of the world which has engendered him" (XII, 1, 5).

It is only when one considers the things in life from a cosmic perspective that they can appear both beautiful and valueless: beautiful, because they exist, and yet valueless because they cannot accede to the realm of freedom and morality. Instead, they vanish rapidly into the infinity of space and time, and the uninterrupted flux of becoming (VI, 15, 2):

> In the midst of this river, in which one cannot stand still, who could attach any value to any of the things which flow past?

Marcus never tires of contemplating the great laws of Nature. He is particularly fascinated by the perpetual metamorphoses of all things, and this is what he is constantly trying to contemplate:

> Acquire a method for contemplating how all things are transformed into each other: concentrate your attention on this ceaselessly and exercise yourself on this point (X, 11).

> When you regard each substance, imagine that it is already being dissolved, is in the midst of transformation, in the process of rotting and being destroyed (X, 18).

Thus, Marcus tries to perceive the process of dissolution already at work in the people and objects which surround him. He would certainly have approved of Princess Bibesco, who, in order to meditate upon death, had only to contemplate a bouquet of violets.[59] Marcus recalls the imperial courts of the past—that of Augustus, for example—in order to realize that all these people who have, for an instant, come back to life in his memory are in fact long dead. This is no more a case of obsession with death or morbid complacency than when, in the film *The Dead Poets' Society,* Robin Williams, who plays a teacher of literature, makes his students carefully study a picture of the school's old boys. In order that his students appreciate the value of life, the teacher wants them to become aware that all the boys in the picture—apparently so alive—are now dead. He hopes they will thereby discover life's preciousness, as he

instills in them Horace's saying *Carpe diem* ("Seize the day!"). The only
difference in these two outlooks is that for Marcus the only value is not
just life itself, but *moral* life.

Marcus' vision of universal metamorphosis teaches us not to fear
death, which is only a particular instance of such metamorphosis (II, 12,
3), and not to attribute any value to transitory things (IX, 28, 5). At the
same time, however, it sweeps the soul along toward the contemplation
of the grandiose spectacle of Nature, which constantly transforms all
things "so that the world may always be new" (VII, 25).

In the immensity of the universe, and the infinity of time and space,
Marcus annihilates himself in a kind of intoxicated vertigo, as many
others had done before him.

Such a vision of the totality of substance and of time can be obtained
by a view from above:[60] that is, the soul's flight above all things, in the
immensity of the universe (IX, 32):

> You will open up a vast field for yourself as you embrace the totality
> of the cosmos in your thought, conceive everlasting eternity, and
> consider the rapid metamorphosis of each individual thing.

Marcus allows himself to be swept along by the revolutions of the
stars, and the torrential metamorphosis of the elements (VII, 47):

> For such images purify us from the stains of terrestrial life.

Marcus plunges in thought into a universe which conforms to the
Stoic model: a universe, that is, which is finite within the immensity of
the surrounding void, and which ceaselessly repeats itself within the
infinity of time (XI, 1, 3):

> The soul traverses the entire world and the void which surrounds it,
> as well as its form; it extends itself throughout the infinity of eter-
> nity, and it embraces and conceives the periodic rebirth of the
> universe.

Human beings are made for infinity, and their true city and fatherland
is the immensity of the whole world. In the words of Seneca:[61]

> How natural it is for man to extend his spirit throughout all immen-
> sity . . . The only limits which the human soul allows are those

which it shares with God himself . . . Its fatherland is everything which the sky and the world contain.

One of the things, says Marcus, which is peculiar to mankind, and which fills him with joy, is to contemplate the Nature of the All, as well as everything which happens in conformity with what Nature has willed (VIII, 26).

The first result of this spiritual exercise of the view from above or cosmic flight of the soul is to reveal to people both the splendor of the universe and the splendor of the spirit. Another of its effects, however, is that it furnishes powerful instigations for practicing the discipline of desire. Human affairs, when seen from above, seem very tiny and puny; they are not worthy of being desired, nor does death appear as something to be feared.

From such a perspective, Asia and Europe are nothing but a tiny corner of the world; the sea is a drop of water; Mt. Athos is a mound of earth; and the present moment nothing more than a point (VI, 36). Mankind's place and role are minuscule amidst such immensity (XII, 32). And what of the minuscule swarms of human beings crawling all over the earth?

Crowds, armies, farmers; weddings, divorces, births, deaths; the hubbub of the courts; deserted places; the diversity of the customs of barbarous peoples; celebrations, lamentations; marketplaces: what a hodgepodge! And yet, there is the harmony of contraries (VII, 48).

This effort to look at things from above thus allows us to contemplate the entire panorama of human reality in all its aspects—social, geographical, and emotional—and to resituate them within the immensity of the cosmos and the human species, swarming anonymously over the earth. When we look at things from the perspective of universal Nature, those things which do not depend on us, and which the Stoics called "indifferent"—health, glory, wealth, and death, for example—are brought back to their true proportions.

When this theme of the view from above assumes this specific form of observing people on earth, it seems particularly to belong to the Cynic tradition. We find it used abundantly by the satirist Lucian, a contemporary of Marcus Aurelius, who was strongly influenced by Cynicism. In Lucian's dialogue *Icaromenippus,* or "The Man Who Rose Above the

Clouds,"[62] the Cynic Menippus tells a friend how, discouraged by the disagreement among philosophers about the ultimate principles of the universe, he decided to go up to the heavens himself, in order to see how things really were. In order to fly, Menippus fixed himself up with wings: the right wing was that of an eagle, and the left that of a vulture. He then took off in the direction of the moon. Once there, he could see the entire earth from above, and just like Homer's Zeus, he says, he could observe now the land of the Thracians, now that of the Mysians—even, if he wished, the lands of Greece, Persia, and India. Such variety fills him with pleasure, but he also observes the people:

> The whole of human life appeared to me; not only the nations and the cities, but every individual: some were sailing ships, others waging war, and others on trial.

Menippus observes not only what is going on out in the open, but also what is happening behind closed doors, where everyone thought they were perfectly well hidden.[63] After a lengthy enumeration of the crimes and adulteries which he sees being committed inside the houses, Menippus resumes his remarks, calling everything a hodge-podge, a cacophony, and a ridiculous spectacle. In his view, the most ridiculous thing of all is to see people quarreling over the borders of a nation, since the earth appears minuscule to him. The rich, says Menippus, have darned little to be proud about. Their lands are no bigger than one of Epicurus' atoms, and when people gather together they resemble a swarm of ants. Menippus finally leaves the moon and travels among the stars until he reaches Zeus, where he is amused at the ridiculously contradictory nature of the prayers which human beings send up to this god.

In another of Lucian's dialogues, entitled *Charon or The Overseers*, we find Charon, ferryman of the dead, asking for a day off in order to go up to the surface of the earth and see what life is like—this life which the dead miss so much when they arrive in Hell. With the help of Hermes, Charon piles several mountains on top of each other and climbs up on them in order to observe human life. We then have the same kind of description which we have already encountered in the *Icaromenippus* or in Marcus Aurelius: an enumeration of sailing ships, armies at war, trials, farmers working their fields—a wide variety of activities, but everywhere life is full of torments. As Charon remarks, "If people realized from the beginning that they are mortal, and that, after a brief sojourn in life, they must leave it as they would a dream, and leave everything upon this

earth, then they would live more wisely and die with fewer regrets."
But, continues Charon, people are unaware of their condition, like the
bubbles produced by a raging stream, which vanish as soon as they are
formed.

This look from above at man's earthly life takes on a form peculiar to
Cynicism. One sign of this is the fact that the dialogue *Charon* bears the
Greek title *Episkopountes,* or "Those who watch." The Cynic philosopher, for his part, believes that his role is to watch over people's actions.
He is a kind of spy, lying in wait for mankind's defects in order to
denounce them, as Lucian himself says.[64] It is the Cynic's job to watch
over other men; he is their censor, and he observes their behavior as if
from the heights of an observatory. The Greek words *episkopos* ("over-
seer") and *kataskopos* ("spy"), moreover, traditionally designate the Cynics in the ancient world.[65] For them, the view from above was meant to
denounce the senseless way in which people led their lives. It is no
accident that, in this dialogue, it is precisely Charon, ferryman of the
dead, who thus looks at human affairs from above; for looking at things
from above means looking at human affairs from the point of view of
death. Only this point of view can give us the detachment, elevation, and
distance which are indispensable in order for us to see things as they
really are.

The Cynics denounced that form of human madness which attaches
itself so passionately to things, such as luxury and power, which people
will inevitably have to abandon. This is why they urge them to reject
superfluous desires, social conventions, and artificial civilization—all of
which are the source of their worries, cares, and sufferings—and encour-
age them to return to a simple, purely natural style of life.

Thus, our philosopher-emperor coincides with Lucian, the ancient
equivalent of Voltaire, in this imaginative exercise of the view from
above, which is also a view of things from the point of view of death. It
is, moreover, a merciless view, which strips false values naked.

Among these false values is fame. Marcus came up with remarkable
formulas to denounce our desire to be known, either by our contemporaries or by posterity:

Short is the time which each of us lives; puny the little corner of
earth on which we live; how puny, finally, is even the lengthiest
posthumous glory. Even this glory, moreover, is transmitted by little
men who'll soon be dead, without even having known themselves,
much less him who has long since been dead (III, 10, 2).

Are you obsessed with a little bit of glory? Turn your eyes to the rapidity with which everything is forgotten. Think about the abyss of eternity, infinite in both directions; and about the vanity of the echo which reaches us. Think about how quickly those who now seem to be applauding change their minds, and have no judgment; think also about the narrowness of the space by which your fame is circumscribed. The whole earth is no more than a point, and of this point only the tiniest part is inhabited. From such an origin, how many people will there be to sing your praises, and of what character? (IV, 3, 7–8).

Soon, you will have forgotten everything; soon, everyone will have forgotten you . . . (VII, 21).

In a short time, you will no longer be anything or anywhere . . . (VI, 37).

While the view from above reveals that human affairs are only an infinitesimal point within the immensity of reality, it also allows us to discover what Marcus calls *to homoeides,* which we could render as both the identity and the homogeneity of all things. This is an ambiguous notion: it can mean, for example, that in the eyes of one who plunges his gaze into the cosmic immensity, everything is within everything else. Everything holds itself together, and the entire universe is present in each instant of time, as well as in each part of reality (VI, 37):

> He who has seen the present has seen everything: all that has oc-
> curred from all eternity, and all that will occur throughout infinity,
> for everything is homogeneous and identical in form.

Death, then, will not deprive me of anything, since I have already, within each instant, had everything. At any moment at which the limits of its life cease, the soul attains its end. Within each present moment, I possess everything I can expect from life: the presence of the entire universe and presence of universal Reason, which is the presence of one and the same thing. At each moment, I possess all of Being, present in the least of things.

If, however, we are afraid to die, because we would like to continue enjoying life, honors, pleasures, and all other false human values, then *to homoeides,* or homogeneity, takes on a different meaning. For one who has discovered true value—that of Reason, which rules within us and within the entire universe—these elements of life, which endlessly repeat their pettiness and banality, are just as disgusting as the games in the arena (VI, 46).

When human affairs are viewed from above, we are able to imagine the past as well as the future, and this view reveals that even if individuals disappear, the same scenes are repeated throughout the centuries. The soul which extends itself throughout the immensity of space and time

> sees that those who will come after us will see nothing new, and that those who came before us saw nothing more than we did. Rather, there is a sense in which a man of forty, if he has some slight measure of intelligence, has seen everything there has been, and everything that will be, because of the uniformity of things (XI, 1, 3).

Marcus returns to this idea frequently and insistently (XII, 24, 3):

> Each time you are elevated in this way, looking at human affairs from above, you would see the same things: uniformity and brevity. And to think that this is what men brag about!

Marcus imagines the imperial courts of his predecessors: Hadrian and Antoninus Pius, for example; or those of former times: Philip, Alexander, or Croesus:

> All these uniform scenes and dramas, whether you have come to know them through personal experience or through ancient history . . . All these spectacles were the same, and only the actors were different (X, 27, 1–2).

For the ancients, history always repeats itself. This, moreover, is the reason why historians of that time wrote history. As Thucydides declared in his *Histories* (I, 22, 4): "For all those who wish to have a clear idea both of past events and of those in the future which, because of their human character, will bear similarities or analogies to them, this exposition will be useful, and shall suffice." From this point of view, it must be admitted that Thucydides' work was an extraordinary success, for his description of the hypocrisy of the victorious and the strong remains appallingly relevant.

Marcus, for his part, would no doubt have approved of Schopenhauer's views on history:

> From beginning to end, it is the repetition of the same drama, with different costumes and names . . . This identical element, which persists throughout all changes, consists in the basic qualities of the human heart and head—many of them are bad; a few of them good. History's overall motto ought to be *Eadem, sed aliter.* One who has read Herodotus has, from a philosophical point of view, already studied enough history, for his work already contains everything which constitutes the subsequent history of the world.[66]

When Marcus mentions this uniformity, by contrast, he has not the slightest intention of elaborating a philosophy of history. On the contrary, we ought rather to say that the view from above which he takes of human affairs leads him to evaluate them: in other words, to denounce their pseudo-value, especially when considered from the point of view of death.

These spectacles which repeat themselves identically throughout one's life and throughout the ages are almost always scenes of human evil, hypocrisy, and futility. It makes no difference whether one sees them for forty years, or for ten thousand (VII, 49, 2). Death will deliver us from this spectacle, as tiring as the games of the amphitheater (VI, 46); or at least it will not make us miss anything, since it is impossible for anything new to happen.

The Epicurean Lucretius had already placed a similar argument in the mouth of Nature, as she tried to console mankind with regard to the inevitability of his death: "I cannot think up some new invention to please you, for things are eternally the same . . . you must always expect the same things, even if you were never to die."[67]

Once again, we can see that the declarations contained in the *Meditations,* which modern historians have classified as pessimistic, do not correspond to Marcus Aurelius' impressions or experiences. The only personal experience which seems to be expressed in his work is that of disappointment with regard to his entourage, but I shall return to this point later. When Marcus says that human affairs are as nothing within the immensity; that they are vile and petty; or that they repeat themselves until one is sick of them, he is not expressing some negative experience of his own. Instead, he is engaging in exercises, both spiritual and literary. Sometimes, we feel that some of his wonderfully striking formulas are even a bit artificial, since all they do is reproduce traditional themes of ancient philosophy. In the final analysis, however, what inspires all this is the love and fascination which Marcus feels in the depths of his being for that unique Value, which is the only thing necessary. Does human life, he asks, contain "anything more valuable than Justice, Truth, Temperance, and Bravery" (III, 6, 1)? The good worth more than anything else is the feeling of inner joy which occurs when the guiding principle or thought "is content with itself (in those things in which it is possible to act in accordance with right reason), and is content with Destiny (in those things which are allotted to us, independently of our will) . . . Choose this greatest of all goods, and never let it go" (III, 6, 6).

This superior good is, in the last analysis, the inner God, which must be "preferred to everything" (III, 7, 2), and revered, since it is of the same substance as the guiding principle which governs the world (V, 21).

> Your only joy, and your only rest: let it be to pass from one action performed in the service of the community to another action performed for the service of the community, together with the remembrance of God (VI, 7).

It is this unique Value that brings joy, serenity, and rest to Marcus' soul.

Compared to this unique, transcendent Value, human affairs are petty indeed; they are like a point within the immensity of the universe. In fact, the only thing which is great compared to the latter is the purity of moral intent. As Pascal would agree, moral good is infinitely greater than physical size.

To anyone who has contemplated the immensity of the universe, human affairs—to which we attach so much importance—seem petty, unimportant child's play. As Marcus likes to repeat: "Everything is vile and petty." Yet since human affairs are almost always alien to the moral good, dominated as they are by passions, hatred, and hypocrisy, they seem not only puny, vile, and petty, but also disgusting in their monotonous baseness. The only greatness in earthly life—but also the only joy—is therefore the purity of moral intent.

The Levels of Cosmic Consciousness

Earlier I spoke of the stages of consciousness of the self as a faculty of freedom and moral choice. We can now return to this theme, in order to see how the various levels of self-consciousness correspond to different levels of cosmic consciousness.

As long as the self has not yet gained awareness of its potential freedom, and has not yet carried out the delimitation or circumscription of this potential freedom in which the guiding principle consists, it believes itself to be autonomous and independent of the world. In fact it is, as Marcus says, a "stranger to the world" (IV, 29), and it is swept along against its will by Destiny. In the course of the movement by which it becomes aware of the fact that it is not identical with the body, the vital breath, or involuntary emotions, however, the self discovers that, up until then, it had been unconsciously and passively determined by Destiny: it had been nothing but a tiny point in the immensity of space, or a little wave in the immense tide of time. The moment freedom becomes aware of itself, however, it becomes aware of the fact that that self which is determined by Destiny is only an infinitesimally tiny part of the world (XII, 32):

> What a tiny part of the gaping abyss of infinite time is assigned to each one of us! For it disappears so quickly into the everlasting. What a tiny portion of universal substance, what a tiny part of the universal soul! On how tiny a part of the entire earth do you crawl!

Our perspective is changed once again when the self, as a principle of freedom, recognizes that there is nothing greater than the moral good, and therefore accepts what has been willed by Destiny, that is to say, universal Reason. If the self accepts itself as a principle of freedom and of choice, it also accepts the portion which Destiny has allotted to it, as the ego which has been determined by Destiny. As the Stoics used to say, the self accepts the role which the divine director has reserved for it in the drama of the universe;[68] in Marcus' case, for instance, this role was that of emperor. As the self accepts this role, however, it becomes transfigured: for what the free self wills is all of Destiny, the entire history of the world, and the entire world, as if the self were that universal Reason which is at the origin of the world, or universal Nature. At this point, the self as will and as freedom coincides with the will of universal Reason and of the *logos* dispersed throughout all things.

The realization of one's self as identical with universal Reason, then, as long as it is accompanied by consent to this will, does not isolate the self like some minuscule island in the universe. On the contrary, it can open the self to all cosmic becoming, insofar as the self raises itself from its limited situation and partial, restricted, and individualistic point of view to a universal and cosmic perspective. At this point, self-consciousness becomes consciousness of the world, and consciousness of the divine Reason which guides the world. Finally, we may say that the self, by means of this process of realization, discovers both its limitation and its transcendence. It discovers the limitation of its individuality within the immensity of the universe—this is a theme which recurs frequently in Pascal's *Pensées:* "I am nothing but an unimportant thing in the abyss of time and space"—and this is the limitation of the self as determined by Destiny. At the same time, however, it discovers the transcendence of the self as moral conscience, whose value is somehow infinite with regard to the merely physical domain.

We find this opposition between the self caught up in the web of the universe and of Destiny and the self which identifies itself with universal Reason already in Epictetus (I, 12, 26):

> Don't you know how tiny a part you are, compared to the All? With regard to your body, that is; for with regard to your reason, you are not worse nor lesser than the gods. The size of reason cannot be measured by length or height, but by the value of judgments (*dogma;* or "of principles of action").

Perhaps I may be allowed here to refer to a similar opposition, between the puniness of the empirical self, plunged in the immensity of the world, and the incommensurable grandeur of the moral self as the legislative power of reason, which we find in the last pages of Kant's *Critique of Practical Reason:*

> Two things fill the soul with ever-new and ever-growing admiration and awe, the more frequently and constantly one applies one's reflection to them: *the starry sky above me and the moral law within me.* These are two things which I have neither to search for, nor simply to presuppose, as if they were shrouded in darkness or plunged within a transcendent region, beyond my horizon: I can see them in front of me and I attach them immediately to the consciousness of my existence. The former begins at that place *which I occupy within the sensible world,* and extends my connection to that which is immensely large, with its worlds upon worlds and its systems of systems, in addition to the unlimited times of their periodic movement, their beginning and their duration. The latter begins at my

invisible self, or *personality,* and it represents me within a world which possesses a genuine infinity, but which can be detected only by the understanding, and with which (and thereby also with all these visible worlds) I realize that I am in a relationship of . . . universal and necessary linkage. The first spectacle, that of an innumerable multitude of worlds, somehow *annihilates* my importance *qua* that of a bestial creature which must return to the planet—a mere point in the universe—the matter out of which it was formed, after having been—one knows not how—provided with vital force for a brief span of time. The second spectacle, by contrast, *increases my value infinitely, qua* that of an intelligence, thanks to my personality within which the moral law displays to me a life independent with regard to animality, and even with regard to the entire sensible world.[69]

Obviously, Marcus Aurelius would not have accepted this Kantian distinction between a sensible and an intelligible world. For him, as for all the Stoics, there is one single world, just as, he says, there is one single law which is that reason common to all intelligent beings (VII, 9). For Marcus and the Stoics, however, it is the self's awareness of itself which transforms it, making it pass in succession from the domain of necessity to the domain of freedom, and from the domain of freedom to the domain of morality. The self—that infinitesimal point within the immensity—is thereby transformed, and made equal to universal Reason.

8

THE DISCIPLINE OF ACTION, OR
ACTION IN THE SERVICE OF MANKIND

※❉※

The discipline of action

The result of the discipline of desire, as we saw, was to bring people inner serenity and peace of mind, since it consisted in the joyful consent to everything that happens to us through the agency of universal Nature and Reason. *Amor fati,* or the love of fate, thus led us to want that which the cosmos wants, to want what happens, and to want what happens *to us.*

This fine serenity risks being disturbed by the discipline of active impulse and action, since in this case it is a matter of acting, not accepting. We now must engage our responsibility, not just consent; and we must enter into relations with beings—our fellow creatures—who provoke our passions precisely because they are our fellow creatures: beings whom we must love, although they are often hateful.

Here again, the norm will be found to be conformity with Nature: not, this time, that universal Nature which we know in general to be rational, but one of the more specific and determinate aspects of this universal Nature: human Nature, the Nature of the human race, or that Reason which all people have in common. This is a particular norm, which is the basis of precise obligations: insofar as we are parts of the human race, we must

(1) act in the service of the whole;
(2) in our actions, respect the hierarchy of values which may exist between different types of action; and
(3) love all human beings, since we are all the members of one single body.

Another way of putting it would be to say that humankind is ruled by the laws of four natures. In the first place, people, as parts of the All, are ruled by universal Nature. They must consent to the great laws of this Nature—in other words, to Destiny and to the events willed by this universal Nature. For the Stoics, however, who had developed an entire theory of the lower levels of Nature, the Greek word *physis* which we translate as "nature" can also, when used without a qualifier, mean the faculty of growth which is peculiar to each organism. Plants possess nothing but this faculty of growth, while human beings have it within them, alongside other faculties. It is this faculty, for instance, which forces people to feed themselves and to reproduce. We must, says Marcus (X, 2) also observe the demands of this law of vegetative "nature." For instance, we have the "duty"—I shall return to the meaning of this term—to conserve ourselves by nourishing ourselves, as long as the satisfaction of this demand has no negative effects upon the other internal faculties which we have within us. For human beings are not only a "faculty of growth" *(physis),* but also a "faculty of sensation": this is a higher level, which also goes into the constitution of humankind. Marcus (X, 2) calls it a "force" or "nature" of the animal. This law of animality also has its own demands with regard to humankind: in this case, self-conservation is achieved through the vigilance of the senses. Here again, we have the duty to carry out our functions as animals provided with sensation, as long as the higher inner faculties are not thereby damaged. To exaggerate the role of sensation would mean compromising the workings of Nature, that faculty higher than sensation which is also called reason.

All this, then, corresponds to the discipline of action, which implies all the acts and movements which respond to the requirements of integral human nature. As we have seen, this nature is, at the same time, the faculty of growth, of sensation, and of reason. Marcus is then quick to add (X, 2): "The rational faculty is simultaneously the faculty of social life"; in other words, the law of human and social reason demands that we place ourselves entirely in the service of the human community.

In many of his *Meditations,* Marcus emphasizes the symmetrical opposition which arises between the discipline of action and the discipline of desire. For example:

Act as *your own nature* commands you; put up with whatever *common Nature* brings to you (XII, 32, 3).

Am I really carrying out an *action?* I am carrying it out, when I relate it to the good of humankind. Is something *happening* to me? I greet it by relating what happens to me to the gods and to the source of all things, whence the web of all events has its origin (VIII, 23).

Impassivity (ataraxia) with regard to the *events,* brought about by the exterior cause. *Justice (dikaiosynē)* in the *actions* brought about by the cause that is within you. In other words, let your impulse to act and your action have as their goal the service of the human community, because that, for you, is in conformity with your nature (IX, 31).

He gave himself over entirely to *justice,* insofar as the *actions* which he carried out are concerned, and to *universal Nature* with regard to everything which *happens* to him (X, 11, 2).

For Marcus Aurelius, then, as for Epictetus, the goal of our actions must be the good of the human community, and the discipline of action will therefore have as its domain our relations with other people. In turn, these relations will be ruled by laws and the duties imposed by human, rational nature and reason, which are fundamentally identical to universal Nature and Reason.

The seriousness of action

The discipline of action, like the other disciplines in the domains in which they are exercised, will therefore begin by imposing the norms of reason and reflection upon human activity:

In the first place: nothing at random, and nothing that is not related to some goal. Second: do not relate your actions to anything other than a goal which may serve the human community (XII, 20).

The human soul dishonors itself when it does not direct its actions and impulses, as much as possible, toward some goal, but instead, whatever it does, it does inconsiderately and without reflection, whereas the least of our actions ought to be accomplished by being related to its goal. And the goal of rational beings is to obey the Reason and the Law of the most venerable of Cities and Republics (II, 16, 6).

In all that you do, make sure that you do not act at random, or otherwise than Justice herself would act (XII, 24, 1).

The vice which is opposed to the discipline of action is thus frivolity (*eikaiotēs*). It is the opposite to that seriousness or gravity with which all human actions should be accomplished. This human frivolity or lack of reflection does not know how to submit to the discipline of action; it is the agitation of a jumping jack, a puppet, or a top:

> Stop letting the guiding principle within you be tugged around like a marionette by the strings of selfish impulses (II, 2, 4).

> Cease this puppet-like agitation (VII, 29, 2).

> Stop spinning around like a top; instead, on the occasion of every impulse to act, accomplish what is just, and whenever a representation presents itself, confine yourself to what corresponds exactly to reality (IV, 22).

Acting seriously means, in the first instance, acting with all one's heart and soul (XII, 29, 2):

> With all your soul, do what is just.

Marcus is here alluding to Epictetus, who reproached his apprentice philosophers with failing to engage themselves seriously in the philosophical life; like children, he says,

> . . . one minute you are an athlete, then a gladiator; the next a philosopher, then a rhetor; but you are nothing with all your soul . . . because you haven't undertaken anything after having examined it, looked at the matter from all angles, and thoroughly tested it; instead, you've engaged yourself casually and with a desire that has no warmth in it (III, 15, 6).

Marcus wanted to bring this warmth of the heart to his consent to the will of universal Nature (III, 4, 4) as well as to his love of the Good (III, 6, 1), or his practice of justice (XII, 29, 2).

To act seriously is also to become aware of the infinite value of each instant, when one thinks of the possible imminence of death (II, 5, 2):

> Carry out each action of your life as if it were the last, and keep yourself far from all frivolity.

And again (VII, 69):

> What brings perfection to one's way of life is to spend each day as if it were the last; without agitation, without indolence, and without role-playing.

The idea of death strips actions of their banality, and uproots them from the routine of daily life. From this perspective, it is impossible to accomplish any action without reflection or attention, for one's being must be fully engaged in what may perhaps be the last opportunity it has to express itself. One can no longer wait or postpone purifying one's intentions, in order to act "with all one's soul." Even if the action which we are carrying out were in fact interrupted by death, this would not make it incomplete; for what gives an action its completeness is precisely the moral intention by which it is inspired, not the subject matter on which it is exercised.

Acting seriously also means not dispersing oneself in feverish agitation. In *Meditations,* IV, 24, Marcus quotes an aphorism by Democritus: "Act little, if you want to maintain serenity." But Marcus immediately corrects this statement, as follows:

> Wouldn't it be better to say: Do what is indispensable, and do what you are ordered to do by the reason of a naturally political animal, and do it in the way you are ordered to do it? For that is what brings serenity: not only because one acts well, but because one acts little. For since the majority of our words and actions are not necessary, if we cut them off, we will have more leisure and peace of mind. Concerning each action, therefore, we must remind ourselves of this question: Is this action not one of those which are not indispensable? It is not only unnecessary actions which have to be eliminated, however, but also unnecessary representations; if we eliminate these, the actions to which they would give rise will not follow either.

It is not, as Democritus seems to say, the mere fact of reducing the number of one's actions which brings serenity, or the fact of not getting involved in many things, but the fact of limiting one's activities to that which serves the common good. This is the only thing necessary, and it alone brings joy, because everything else causes only troubles and worries.

When he adds that this principle of action allows us to find leisure, however, Marcus is not taking his own experience into account. Fronto, Marcus' friend and rhetoric teacher, when urging him to take a rest at Alsium on the seashore, speaks of the days and nights without interruption which Marcus used to spend at his judicial responsibilities, and of the scruples which tormented him: "If you condemn someone, you say: 'it looks as though he wasn't given enough guarantees.'"[1]

I will have more to say about the worries and uncertainties brought about by action. In any event, Marcus repeats throughout the *Meditations* that we can save a great deal of time by eliminating useless activities, such as trying to find out what other people have done, said, or thought (IV, 18):

> Do not spend any more time than is necessary on insignificant matters (IV, 32, 5).

In a sense, becoming aware of the seriousness which we must bring to every action is precisely the same thing as becoming aware of the infinite value of each instant, from the perspective of death (VIII, 2):

> On the occasion of each action, ask yourself this question: What is it to me? Will I not regret it? In a short time, I will be dead, and everything will disappear! If I now act as an intelligent living being, who places himself in the service of the human community and who is equal to God, then what more can I ask?

If we become aware of the value of the slightest instant, and if we consider our present actions as the last ones of our life, how could we waste our time in useless and futile acts?

"Appropriate actions" *(ta kathēkonta)*

Epictetus often repeats that the exercise-theme whose object is active impulses and actions corresponds to the domain of what the Stoics called the *kathēkonta,* usually translated as "the duties." Marcus Aurelius is not explicit on this point, but when, in the context of this exercise-theme, he speaks of actions performed "in the service of the human community" (IX, 6; XI, 37), he is using Epictetus' terminology, and thereby shows his familiarity with the latter's doctrine. Within the Stoic system, moreover, human actions necessarily belong to the domain of the *kathēkonta*.

Let me briefly resituate this notion within the totality of Stoic teaching. Its fundamental principle, as we have seen, is that there is no good
but the moral good. What is it, however, that makes a good a moral
good? In the first place, the fact that it is located within humankind, and
the things which depend on us: thought, active impulses, and desire.
Second, our thought, active impulse, and desires must wish to conform
to the law of Reason. There must be an effective will, wholly oriented
toward doing the good. Everything else, therefore, is indifferent, which
means it is without intrinsic value. As examples of indifferent things, the
Stoics enumerated life, health, pleasure, beauty, strength, renown, and
noble birth—as well as their opposites: death, sickness, pain, ugliness,
weakness, poverty, obscurity, and humble birth. All these things do not,
in the last analysis, depend on us, but on Destiny, and they do not
provide us either with happiness or with unhappiness, since happiness is
located only in our moral intentions. Here, however, a twofold problem
arises: on the one hand, it is not enough to *want* to do good; we must also
know what concrete acts to undertake. On the other hand, how should
we live and orient ourselves in life, if everything that does not depend on
us is neither good nor bad? This is where the theory of "duties" or
"appropriate actions"[2] *(kathēkonta),* or of "suitable things,"[3] comes in. It is
intended to provide a field for exercising our good will, and to provide
us with a practical code of conduct which would, in the last analysis,
allow us to make distinctions between indifferent things, and to accord a
relative value to things which are, in principle, without any value.

Here, we can glimpse the "physical" roots of Stoic ethics. In order to
determine what concrete actions must be performed, the Stoics take as
their starting-point a fundamental animal instinct, which expresses the
will of Nature. By virtue of a natural impulse which impels animals to
love themselves and to accord preference to themselves, they tend to
preserve themselves and to reject whatever threatens their integrity. It is
in this way that what is "appropriate" to nature is revealed to natural
instinct. With the appearance of reason in human beings, natural instinct
becomes reflective choice.[4] At this stage, we recognize *rationally* which
things have "value," since they correspond to the innate tendencies
which nature has placed within us. Thus, it is "natural" for us to love life,
for parents to love their children, and that human beings, like ants and
bees, should have an instinct of sociability: that is, that they should be
prepared by nature to form groups, assemblies, and cities. Getting married, engaging in a political activity, serving one's country, are all "appropriate" to human nature and therefore have a "value." Nevertheless,

from the point of view of the fundamental principles of Stoicism, all these things are indifferent—nether good nor bad—since they do not depend entirely upon us.

Thus, we can see what the Stoics meant by "appropriate actions"—appropriate, that is, to Nature—and "duties" *(kathēkonta)*. They are actions, hence something which depends upon us; and they presuppose an intention, either good or evil. They cannot, therefore, be accomplished indifferently. These actions are related to a subject matter which is, in theory, indifferent, since it does not depend exclusively upon us, but also on other people and on circumstances, external events, and, in the last analysis, on Destiny. This indifferent subject matter can, however, reasonably and with some probability be judged to be in conformity with the will of Nature, and thereby to acquire a certain value, either by virtue of its content, or by virtue of its circumstances.

Such "appropriate actions" are also "duties"; more precisely, they are social and political obligations linked to human life in a city. As we have seen, they include the duty not to do anything which is not in the service of human groups, be they one's city or family; the duty to participate in political activity and in the responsibilities of a citizen; to defend one's country; to procreate and raise children; and to respect the bonds of marriage. Epictetus enumerates some of these "duties" when he reviews the actions which permit us to recognize the true philosopher (III, 21, 4–6):

> A carpenter doesn't come to you and say, "Listen to me discourse on the art of carpentry"; but he draws up a contract to build a house, builds it, and thereby shows that he possesses the carpenter's art. Do as he does: eat like a human being, drink like a human being, get spruced up, get married, have children, lead the life of a citizen, learn how to put up with insults, tolerate an unreasonable brother, father, son, neighbor, or traveling companion. Show us these things, so that we can see if you really have learned anything from the philosophers.

Uncertainty and worry

In the context of the discipline of action, along with such "duties," "appropriate actions," and "suitable things," uncertainty and worry are liable to creep into the philosopher's soul. In the first place, the result of such actions—the initiative for which depends on us, but the result of which does not—is far from being a sure thing. To the question, "Ought we to do good to someone who may be ungrateful?" Seneca[5] replies as follows:

> When it comes to action, we can never wait until we have an absolutely certain understanding of the entire situation. We only take the path down which we are led by probability. Every "duty" (officium) must follow this path; for this is how we sow, sail, make war, get married, and have children. In all these things, the result is uncertain, but we nevertheless decide to undertake those actions which we think have some hope of succeeding. . . . We go where reason—and not the absolute truth—leads us.

According to Epictetus (II, 6, 9):

> Chrysippus was quite right to say, "so long as the consequences remain hidden from me, I remain attached to the things which are best able to permit me to obtain that which is in conformity with nature, for God himself has made me able to choose between things of this kind. If, however, I knew for a fact that Destiny had reserved sickness as my fate, then I would head toward it; for if the foot had any intelligence, it would head toward the mud."

Thus, the Stoics do not only say "I don't know whether my action will succeed." Rather, they also say: "Since I don't know in advance what the results of my actions will be, and what Destiny has in store for me, I have to make such-and-such a decision in accordance with probability and a rational estimate, without any absolute certainty that I am making the right choice or doing the right thing."

One of the most dramatic choices which a Stoic could face was that of suicide. Stoicism considered that suicide—in specific circumstances and for good reasons; in other words, according to rational probability—was a choice open to the philosopher. Thus, even though life would seem to be more in conformity with nature, circumstances can bring us to choose death. Similarly, as we have just seen, Chrysippus used to say that the sage would choose sickness rather than health, if he knew with certainty that such was the will of Destiny.

In the area of rational and probabilistic choice, the Stoics tried to define what ought to be done in various possible situations. Their treatises entitled On Duties were, at least in part, manuals of casuistry, and one can see from the differences in the judgment of particular cases that existed between the leaders of the various schools that their "rationally justified" choices could only be based upon probability. Here are some examples, preserved by Cicero in his treatise *On Duties*,[6] of the cases which were discussed in the schools, and of the divergent responses to them. Is a man who sells his house obligated to disclose all of its defects to a potential buyer? Yes, said Antipater of Tarsus; no, said Diogenes of Babylon. During a food shortage, a businessman had bought wheat in Alexandria, and was transporting it by boat to Rhodes. He knew that other boats were following him, and that the price of grain would soon go down. Should he say so? Yes, said Antipater; no, said Diogenes of Babylon. Obviously, the position of Antipater is closer to the fundamental principles of Stoicism, and the arguments he uses to justify his position are the same ones used by Marcus Aurelius to found the discipline of action:

> You must care for the salvation of all human beings, and serve the human community. Nature has fixed as a principle that your particular usefulness should be the common usefulness; and, reciprocally, that the common usefulness should be your particular usefulness . . . You must remember that there is a community between human beings, which has been formed by Nature herself.[7]

It seems as though Epictetus—and therefore, in all probability, Marcus Aurelius, who follows him—pictured himself as representing the more orthodox tradition which, starting with Chrysippus, went on through Antipater of Tarsus and Archedemus. Still, the fact that different Stoics, while remaining faithful to the fundamental principles of the school, could nevertheless propose completely different ethical choices in the cases we just observed is a good indicator of the fact that there existed some degree of uncertainty concerning the relationship between the moral end—which was unanimously agreed upon—and the "appropriate actions" which ought to be undertaken in order to attain it.

Stoicism is often regarded as a philosophy of certainty and intellectual self-confidence. In fact, however, it was only to the sage—that is, to an extremely rare being who represented more an inaccessible ideal than a concrete reality—that the Stoics attributed infallibility and perfect soundness of judgment. Most people, including philosophers—who, in their own view, are precisely *not* sages—must painfully orient themselves within the uncertainty of everyday life, making choices which seem to be justified reasonably—in other words, probabilistically.[8]

Moral intent, or the fire fed by all matter

Action thus risks introducing worry and care into the Stoic's life, to the same extent to which he does good, and where he intends to do good. By means of a remarkable reversal, however, it is precisely by becoming aware of the transcendent value of doing good that the Stoic can regain peace of mind and serenity, which will enable him to act effectively. There is nothing surprising about this, for it is precisely within the moral good—that is to say, the intention of doing good—that the good is situated for the Stoics.

For the Stoics, intentions bear within themselves a value which infinitely transcends all the objects and "matters" to which they are applied, for these objects and matters are in themselves indifferent, and only assume a value to the extent that they provide an opportunity for intentions to be applied and become concrete. In sum, there is only one will, profound, constant, and unshakable, and it manifests itself in the most diverse actions, on the most diverse occasions and objects, all the while remaining free and transcendent with regard to the subject matters upon which it is exercised.

In Marcus Aurelius, but also in Epictetus and in Seneca,[9] the vocabulary of the discipline of action includes a technical term meaning "to act 'with a reserve clause'" (Greek *hypexairesis;* Latin *exceptio*), which implies the transcendence of intention with regard to its objects. The idea of a "reserve clause" reminds us that, for the Stoics, act and intention to act are fused into an inner discourse which enunciates, as it were, the plans of the agent. According to Seneca,[10] the sage undertakes everything "with a reserve clause," insofar as he says to himself:

> "I want to do thus and so, as long as nothing happens which may present an obstacle to my action."

> "I will sail the across the ocean, if nothing prevents me."

Putting matters this way may seem banal and useless; from the Stoic point of view, however, it is full of meaning. In the first place, it reveals to us the seriousness of Stoic "intention." To be sure, Seneca's formula could be reduced to the following: "I want to do x, if I can"; and it would be easy to joke about such a "good intention," which quickly gives up its goal at the first difficulty that arises. In fact, however, the contrary is true. Stoic intentions are not "good intentions" but "intentions that are *good*"—in other words, firm, determined, and resolved to overcome all obstacles. It is precisely because the Stoic refuses to give up easily on his decision that he formulates a reserve clause, in quasi-judiciary terms. In the words of Seneca:[11]

> The sage does not change his decision, if everything remains entirely what it was when he took it. . . . Elsewhere, however, he undertakes everything "with a reserve clause" . . . in his most steadfast decisions, he allows for uncertain events.

Our intention to perform a certain action, therefore, after we have weighed and pondered it at length, is firm and stable. This is one of the examples that Marcus Aurelius had retained from his adoptive father, Antoninus Pius (I, 16, 1): "Firm perseverance in decisions which are taken after mature reflection." The "reserve clause" means that this firm decision and intention always remain integral, even if an obstacle should arise which prevents their realization. Such an obstacle is a part of what the sage has foreseen, and it does not prevent him from willing what he wants to do. In the words of Seneca:[12]

> Everything succeeds for him, and nothing unexpected happens to him, for he foresees that something may intervene which prevents that which he has planned to carry out.

This Stoic attitude reminds one of the saying embedded in popular wisdom: "Do what you must; let happen what may." We must undertake what we think is good, even if we foresee the failure of our undertaking, because we must do what we must do. Stoicism, however, also contains the idea that carrying out a certain action is not an end in itself.

Here we see the emergence of an extremely important distinction: that which opposes goal (*skopos*) and end *(telos)*. Whoever has the firm, fixed moral intention to carry out a given action is like an archer aiming at a target *(skopos)*. It does not depend entirely on him whether he hits the target or not; likewise, he can only wish for the "goal" *(skopos)* with a "reserve clause": namely, on the condition than Destiny also wills it. In the words of Cicero:[13]

The shooter must do everything he can to hit the target *(skopos)*, and yet it is this act of doing everything in order to hit the target and realize his plan, which is, if I may say, the end *(telos)* that the shooter is seeking. It is this that corresponds to what we call the sovereign good in life, whereas hitting the target is only something that can be wished for, but is not something worthy of being sought after for its own sake.

We encounter the same fundamental principle again and again: the only absolute value is moral intention, and it alone depends entirely upon us. It is not the result that counts—for this does not depend on us, but on Destiny—but rather the intention one has when seeking this result. We find this theme in Epictetus (II, 16, 5):

> Show me a man who is anxious to know *how* he does something, and is not worried about getting something, but about his act itself . . . who, when he deliberates, worries about the deliberation itself, and not about obtaining what the deliberation was about.

If our activity is animated by the perfectly pure intention of wishing only for the good, it attains its goal at every instant, and has no need to wait for its achievement and result to come from the future. Insofar as the very exercise of action is an end in itself, one could compare moral action to dance. In dance, however, the action remains incomplete if it is interrupted. Moral action, by contrast, is perfect and complete at every instant, as Marcus Aurelius remarks (XI, 1, 1–2):

> The rational soul achieves its proper end, wherever the limit of its life may be. It is not as in dance or the theater or other such arts, in which, if something comes along to interrupt them, the entire action is incomplete. The action of the rational soul, by contrast— in all of its parts, and wherever it is considered—carries out its projects fully and without fail, so that it can say: "I have achieved my completion."

Elsewhere, Marcus writes (VIII, 32):

> You must set your life in order by accomplishing your actions one by one; and if each of them achieves its completion, insofar as is

possible, then that is enough for you. What is more, no one can prevent you from achieving its completion.

Here we can grasp—in the flesh, as it were—the fundamental Stoic attitude. In the first place, the Stoic "composes" his life, by accomplishing his actions one by one. In other words, he concentrates upon the present instant and the action he is accomplishing right now, without allowing himself to be troubled by the past or the future. As Marcus says (VII, 68, 3):

> For me, the present is constantly the matter on which rational and social virtue exercises itself.

Second, this concentration on the present introduces order into one's life, allowing problems to be arranged in a series, so that "one is not troubled by the representations of an entire life" and by the difficulties which one may encounter (VIII, 36, 1). It gives a harmonious form to life, just as, as in a dance movement, one passes from one graceful movement to another (VI, 7):

> Your only joy, and your only rest, is to pass from one action performed in the service of the human community to another action performed in the service of the human community, together with the remembrance of God.

Third, each action upon which good intentions and good will are focused finds its completion and its plenitude within itself, and no one can prevent us from completing it and succeeding in it. This is the paradox mentioned by Seneca, to the effect that even if the sage fails, he succeeds. Marcus takes up this theme, by saying that no one can prevent him from giving his own actions their completion and plenitude (VIII, 32):

> No one can stop you from having it attain its completion.
>   —But surely something external will prevent it from being completed!
>   —Be that as it may, no one can stop you from acting with justice, temperance, and prudence.
>   —But perhaps some other one of the action's effects will be prevented?

—Perhaps, but if you adopt an attitude of serenity with regard to such an obstacle, and if you know how to return prudently to that which you are able to do, then another action will instantly take the place of the first one, and it will fit in with the harmony we are talking about.

No one—that is, no power in the world—can prevent us from the following actions: in the first place, from wishing to act with justice and prudence, and therefore from practicing the virtue which we intend to practice by making the decision to perform such an action. Yet Marcus objects: what if the result of the action which we wished to perform cannot be realized? Then the action will fail. Reason then replies: but this will just provide the opportunity to practice another virtue: that of the consent to Destiny, and perhaps also of choosing another action, more appropriate to the situation. In turn, this new action will insert itself into the ordered series of actions which embellishes our life.

With the mention of serene consent to Destiny, we return to the discipline of desire. When we can no longer act as we wished, we must not allow ourselves to be troubled by vain desires to do the impossible. Instead, we must willingly accept the will of Destiny. Then we shall have to return to action and the discipline of action, prudently taking all new information into consideration. In the last analysis, then, a good person can always find completion and plenitude, even if his action is interrupted or impeded by some external cause, because it is perfect at each instant, and in the very act of its exercise. Even if an obstacle should arise, action makes of it a new source of exercises. This is what Marcus calls "turning an obstacle upside down" (V, 20, 2):

People can perfectly well prevent me from carrying out such-and-such an action. Thanks, however, to action "with a reserve clause" and to "turning obstacles upside down," there can be no obstacle to my intention *(hormē)*, nor to my disposition. For my thought *(dianoia)* can "turn upside down" everything that presents an obstacle to my action, and transform the obstacle into an object toward which my impulse to act ought preferably to tend. That which impeded action thus becomes profitable to action, and that which blocked the road allows me to advance along the road.

When he speaks of "turning obstacles upside down," Marcus means that if something becomes an obstacle to what I was doing, and thereby to the exercise of a certain virtue that I was practicing, I can find in that very obstacle the opportunity to practice another virtue. For example, if someone were to devote himself to the service of the human community, and thereby devoted himself to exercising the virtue of justice, then a sudden illness would constitute an obstacle to this virtue, but it would also provide the opportunity to exercise oneself in consenting to the will of Destiny. At each instant, the good person tries to do what seems to him in reasonable conformity with that which Reason wants. If, however, Destiny reveals its will, then he accepts it wholeheartedly (VI, 50):

> First try to persuade them, but act against their will, if the reasonable order *(logos)* of justice leads you that way. If, however, someone violently stands in your way, then shift over to that disposition which greets that which does not depend on us serenely and without regrets, and use this obstacle to practice another virtue. And remember that your impulse to act was always "with a reserve clause," for you did not desire the impossible. What, then, *did* you desire? Nothing other than to have such an impulse; and *that* you have achieved.

Thus, we always come back to the fundamental will and intention to be in conformity with reason. It is thanks to them that we have complete inner liberty with regard to the objects of our action. The failure of a given action does not trouble our serenity, for such a failure does not prevent the action from being perfect in its essence and intention, and it gives us the opportunity either to undertake a new action, better adapted to circumstances, or else to discipline our desire by accepting the will of Destiny. Thus, our basic intention and will find new fields for exercise (IV, 1):

> If the principle which commands within us is in conformity with Nature, it is always ready, when anything happens, to adapt itself without difficulty to what is possible and what has been granted to it. It does not like to restrict itself to one subject matter. No doubt it directs its intention—"with a reserve clause"—toward objects worthy of being preferred; but if something else is substituted for these objects, then it turns it into matter for itself, just like fire, which triumphs over everything thrown upon it, by which a feeble flame could easily be extinguished. A quick and violent fire, by contrast,

quickly assimilates and consumes all that is brought to it, and it is thanks to these very objects that it rises to such great heights.

The paradox of fire, which grows stronger the more things are brought to it which could smother it, or at least present an obstacle to it, is the same as the paradox of the good will. The latter is not content with one field of exercise, but assimilates all objects, including the most diverse goals, communicating its goodness and perfection to all the events to which it consents. Fire and the good will are thus utterly free with regard to the matter they use; their matter is indifferent to them, and the obstacles which are set in their way do nothing but feed them. In other words, nothing is an obstacle for them (X, 31, 5):

> What kind of matter or exercise-theme are you fleeing! What is all that, after all, if not exercises for your reason, which has seen, with precision and an exact knowledge of Nature, the phenomena of life? Hold fast, then, until you have assimilated these things as well, as a robust stomach assimilates everything to itself, or as a bright fire transforms everything thrown into it into flames and light.

Seneca, using a different metaphor, had already said:

> A good person dyes events with his own color . . . and turns whatever happens to his own benefit.[14]

The paradox of fire is also that of divine Reason or universal Nature, which the Stoics conceived as a spiritual fire (VIII, 35):

> Just as universal Nature has communicated to each rational being its other powers, so we have received from her the following power: just as she takes everything which bars her route and resists her, and turns it around in her favor, reinserts it within the order of Nature, and transforms it into a part of herself, in the same way rational beings can turn everything which presents an obstacle to them into their own matter, and use it, no matter what goal their intention was first directed toward.

Let us note one thing from this comparison between divine action and the sage's action: the idea of one unique intention, which transcends all the subject matters to which it is applied. The unique intention of God, which is at the origin of the world, wants the good of the All; in particular, it wants the good of that summit of the All constituted by rational beings. With a view to this end, God's good intention makes everything—even obstacles and resistances—turn out for the best. The unique intention of the sage comes to identify itself with this divine intention, by wanting only what divine goodness wants: primarily, the good of other rational beings. It, too, transforms every obstacle which opposes the realization of a given action or a specific goal into good, insofar as it utilizes such obstacles in order to consent to the will of God or of universal Nature. Thus, for the good will, everything is good.

Inner freedom with regard to actions: the purity and simplicity of intentions

Ancient philosophy had long reflected on how to do good to others, and in particular on the psychological problems caused by the relation between benefactor and beneficiary. It was traditional to tell the story of the Academic philosopher Arcesilaus, who had a friend who was poor, but tried to conceal his poverty. One day when his friend was sick, Arcesilaus slipped a small purse, which would allow him to provide for his needs, under his pillow.[15] For the Stoics, benevolence was a part of the "duties" or actions which were "appropriate" to our human nature. Seneca used a work by the Stoic Hecaton to compose his treatise *On Benefits,* in which he repeatedly affirmed that the benefactor should not consider that the person receiving his benefits was in his debt.[16]

Marcus Aurelius also returns to this theme several times. For him, however, it represents the opportunity to insist forcefully upon the purity of intention which must inspire our actions (VII, 73–74; XI, 4):

> When you have done something good, and thus, from another point of view, you have thus been benefited, why do you look for a third thing besides these, as idiots do; I mean, besides appearing to have done good or getting paid back in return?

> Nobody gets tired of being benefited. It is beneficial to act in conformity with nature. Therefore, do not tire of being benefited, by being beneficial to others.

> I did something in the service of the human community; therefore, I have been beneficial to myself.

The first reason why we must do good unto others, without asking for anything in return, is that, by virtue of the principle "what is good for the whole is good for the part," doing good unto others is the same as doing good to oneself. To this we can add the fact that performing such an action brings joy: the joy of doing one's duty, but also, and more important, the joy of feeling that human beings are not only the parts of one single whole, but the limbs of one single body. If, as Marcus says, you have not yet understood that you are a member of the body made up of rational beings (VII, 13, 3),

> . . . then you do not yet love human beings from the bottom of your heart; you do not yet rejoice purely and simply in doing good, and, moreover, you only do good for appearance's sake, not yet because you do good to yourself in this way.

Up until this point, it might justifiably be thought that the motivation of actions performed in the service of the human community is not entirely pure, for one still expects some usefulness out of it for oneself. In other words, one still hopes to gain from such actions some kind of happiness, however disinterested it may be. This is the noble Stoic principle that "virtue is its own reward," which would later be taken up by Spinoza.[17] Nevertheless, one does still speak of a "recompense," and one is conscious of doing good. Therefore, one runs the risk of watching oneself do good.

Marcus goes farther in his demands for purity, when, in order to provide a foundation for the disinterested nature of good actions, he introduces the notion of natural functions (IX, 42, 12):

> What more do you want when you have benefited some human being? Isn't it enough for you to have done something in conformity with your nature? Do you want to get paid for that? It's as if an eye were to ask for compensation because it sees, or the feet because they walk . . .

Elsewhere, Marcus tells us that there are three types of benefactor: he who openly considers the recipient of his benefits as his debtor; he who only thinks this, and knows that, nevertheless, he did good for the other's sake; and finally, he who does not know what he has done (V, 6, 3):

> He is like a vine which bears grapes and does not seek anything more, once it has given its own fruit; or like a horse which runs, a

dog which hunts; or a bee which makes its honey. Thus, the person who does good does not know it, but he moves on to another action, as the vine will give its grapes again when the proper season comes. We must therefore be like those who, in a way, do good unconsciously.

Here we can see the Stoic notion of "action in conformity with nature" taking on a new meaning. Each species has an inborn instinct, given to it by nature, which impels it to act in accordance with its structure and its constitution: thus it impels the vine to produce grapes, the horse to run, and the bee to make honey. Thus, every species acts in accordance with its nature. That which corresponds to instinct within the human species is the impulse to act *(hormē);* that is, the will and intention to act in accordance with reason, which defines the human constitution. Acting in accordance with reason means preferring the common interest—that of humanity—to one's own interests. Thus, acting in accordance with reason means acting in conformity with nature. Just as bees and vines do the work which is proper to bees and vines, so human beings must do the work which is proper to human beings. Precisely because doing good is the same thing as acting naturally, however, good actions must be accomplished spontaneously, purely, and almost unconsciously. Animal instinct, like a force which never exhausts itself in its manifestations, somehow transcends all the actions which it accomplishes, as it passes spontaneously from one action to another; it does not linger to take pleasure in any specific action. In the same way, moral intention transcends all the actions which it inspires, and passes "from one action to the next,"[18] without considering these actions as ends in themselves, without claiming ownership of them, and without wanting to derive any benefit from them. It therefore remains completely free with regard to its actions, and it accomplishes them naturally—that is to say spontaneously, and in a way unconsciously. As Christ had said: "When you give alms, let your left hand not know what your right hand is doing."[19]

Later, Plotinus[20] would affirm that

it is not at all necessary for a brave person to be conscious of the fact that he is acting courageously and in conformity with the virtue of courage . . . One could even say that consciousness seems to trouble and weaken the activities and acts of which it is conscious. If these acts are not accompanied by consciousness, it is then that they are pure, and that they are as intense and as alive as they can be.

Marcus Aurelius' reflections already point in this direction. A genuinely good action, he says, must be spontaneous and unconsidered, like animal instinct. It must come without effort, and from one's very being, for consciousness disturbs the purity of the act. Being conscious of doing good means to assume an attitude—to take pleasure in such affectation, and not to devote all one's energy to the act itself.

There is a most profound idea behind this criticism of the consciousness of doing good: goodness cannot be anything other than complete generosity, without any return upon or complacency in itself. It must be wholly directed toward others. It is perfectly disinterested, inwardly free, and is not attached to what it is accomplishing.

Marcus, however, is quite aware that such an attitude seems to go against the Stoic's fundamental disposition of attention to oneself and acute consciousness of what one is doing. Thus, he introduces an objector to remind him of this (V, 6, 6):

> It is characteristic of a person acting in the service of the community to be aware of the fact that he is acting in the service of the community, and, by God, to want his neighbor to know it too.

Marcus does not, moreover, attempt to resolve the contradiction. "That is true," he replies, "but you don't understand what I mean." What Marcus "means" here, in all probability, is that moral life is the art of reconciling such opposing attitudes as, on the one hand, attention to oneself and the awareness of duty, and, on the other, spontaneity and complete disinterestedness.

The freedom of moral intention with regard to the actions it undertakes is also manifested on the occasion of another problem which crops up in the discipline of action. We have seen that this discipline requires that decisions be carefully considered, so that, in theory, nothing could cause a person to change his mind once he has made his decision. Here too, however, the agent must not attach himself blindly to his decision to undertake a given action: he must be able to change his mind, if someone gives him valid reasons to do so (VIII, 16):

> Remember that changing your mind and following one who can lead you back onto the right track is another sign of inner freedom.

For such an action is still yours, since it is accomplished in conformity with your will, your judgment, and, finally, with your intellect.

To reiterate: what matters is not the fact of performing a specific action, and then to appropriate it as something belonging to us. Rather, what matters is to conform our intentions to reason and to reasonable nature. This is equally true when we listen to the advice of a counselor whose reasons seem to us to be well founded (IV, 12, 2). The same holds true if we are not able to accomplish an action by ourselves (VII, 5, 3):

> Whatever I do, whether alone or with some other, I must aim at one single goal: that which is useful to the human community and is in accord with it.

The "reserve clause" and exercices to prepare oneself to encounter difficulties

As we have seen, when Marcus discusses the discipline of action, he often brings up the idea of a "reserve clause." This is particularly true when he quotes this text from Epictetus (XI, 37) which defines the three exercise-themes:

> In the exercise-theme which deals with the impulses which lead us to action, we must never relax our attention, so that these impulses may be accompanied by a reserve clause, that they may have as their goal the service of the community, and that they may be proportionate to value.

This "reserve clause" corresponds to the formula "if nothing prevents me." That which can prevent an action from being carried out is Destiny, and therefore the will of universal Nature and Reason, and hence the will of God or of the gods. The exercise-theme which deals with impulses and intentions to act thus becomes confused with the exercise-theme which deals with the desires, since when an obstacle comes up which prevents an action, the only thing left for us to do is to wish—in vain—for the act to succeed in spite of everything. Therefore, we must desire nothing other than what is willed by the All, or universal Nature. This joyful consent which Marcus demands of us, however, is not easy.

We must practice it and prepare ourselves for it; in particular, we must foresee the difficulties and the setbacks which we will have to confront.

Acting "with a reserve clause" means precisely to prepare oneself for such setbacks. In the words of Seneca:[21]

> Nothing happens to the sage contrary to his expectations, for he foresees that something may intervene to prevent what he has planned from being carried out.

> All things happen to him, not according to his wish, but according to what he has thought. What he thinks above all is that something can always oppose his plans. But the pain caused by an unsatisfied desire must be lighter for one who has not promised success to himself beforehand.

This last sentence shows us that we can distinguish two aspects in the exercise intended to prepare us for encountering hardships. In the first place, there is a psychological aspect: blows that are not unexpected, but foreseen, strike us less hard, and wound us less deeply, than those which strike unexpectedly. Greek wisdom had long since made this observation.[22] The Stoics had made it a part of their system, and we probably have an echo of this Stoic theme in the following passage from Philo of Alexandria:[23]

> They do not bend under the blows of fate, because they have calculated its attacks in advance. For of the things that happen against our will, even the most painful are alleviated by foresight. Then, thought no longer encounters anything unexpected in events, but the perception of them is dulled, as if it were dealing with old and worn-out things.

In his ninety-first letter to Lucilius, Seneca imagines in a somewhat grandiloquent fashion all the wars, earthquakes, fires, mud slides, tidal waves, volcanic eruptions—in a word, every catastrophe that could possibly occur. If we leave such rhetoric out of consideration, what Seneca means is essentially that we must always be ready for everything.

Marcus does not give us such lengthy descriptions of every possible calamity. He does, however, constantly remind himself of the great law of nature called universal metamorphosis, or the swift course of the movement of things. He practices seeing beings and things concretely, in their perpetual movement and transformation. Once, he evokes the vanished cities of Helice, Pompeii, and Herculanum. Above all, he tries to place himself within the fundamental disposition of constant vigilance and readiness for anything that is characteristic of such Stoics as Epictetus (see III, 24, 86). Marcus sums up Epictetus' thought in the following terms (XI, 34):

> When you kiss your child, you must say to yourself in your mind: "Perhaps you will be dead tomorrow."

It must be admitted, however, that this kind of exercise is not easy to practice. Do we not run the risk of being troubled, overwhelmed, and discouraged by imagining everything that might happen in this way? Is there not a criticism of this exercise in the following passage?

> Don't let yourself be troubled by the representation of your entire life. Don't try to add up in your mind all the painful difficulties that are likely to happen, in all their intensity and numbers (VIII, 36).

The way to avoid this, Marcus continues, is to concentrate on the present and the present action, as well as on present difficulties, which are easier to bear if they are isolated. Is there not a contradiction between the exercise of concentration on the present, which Marcus is talking about here, and the exercise which consists in imagining future difficulties?

In fact, what Marcus is criticizing here is the same thing that Seneca attacks in several of his letters: the "anguished imagination of the future";[24] that is to say, imagination when it is not controlled by reason. As Seneca says, "A soul obsessed with the future is miserable indeed; it is unhappy even before any mishaps."[25]

The exercise of preparing oneself for hardships is intended to help us avoid not only being unhappy during mishaps, but also being "unhappy before any mishaps." It does this in two ways: in the first place, it makes us understand that future misfortunes—misfortunes, that is, which are merely *possible*—are not misfortunes *for us*. Second, it reminds us that, according to Stoic principles, misfortune itself—which may perhaps occur—is not really a misfortune.

Future misfortunes are not misfortunes. When Marcus writes, "Don't let yourself be troubled by the representation of your entire life," he is practicing not only the exercise of concentration on the present, but also the exercise of foreseeing misfortunes, such as it ought to be practiced.

He thinks about future misfortunes, but only in order to add right away that it does no good to worry about them in advance. This implies that misfortunes which exist only in the future are not genuine misfortunes:

> It is not the past or the future which weigh upon you, but only the present.

Besides, Marcus knows that if one concentrates on the present, and circumscribes misfortunes at the moment when they occur, it will be easier to put up with them one instant at a time. The exercises of concentration on the present and of preparation for misfortune are thus intimately linked and mutually complementary.

The evils that we fear are, moreover, not really "evils" in the Stoic sense of the term. The preparation for difficulties and hardships consists essentially in recollecting the fundamental principles of Stoicism, while still thinking about the future. The first principle we must recall is that what we consider an evil is really an event willed by Destiny. Consequently, it must be resituated within the overall movement of the Whole, and be given the "physical" definition of which I have spoken. In other words, apparent evils must not be considered anthropomorphically, but as natural phenomena.

It is from this perspective that we may interpret the exercise of foreseeing misfortunes, as we found it in the passage from Epictetus which Marcus cites: "When you kiss your child, you must say to yourself in your mind: 'Perhaps you will be dead tomorrow.'" Epictetus continues by imagining the following dialogue (III, 24, 86–87 = Marcus Aurelius, XI, 34):

> "Those are words of ill omen."
> —"They are not ill-omened at all; rather, they are words which mean nothing other than a natural process. Or would it be 'ill-omened' to say that grain will be harvested?"

Marcus himself often returns to this theme; as we have seen, he affirms that the things which seem unpleasant and painful to us are only the necessary consequences of natural laws.

Finally, the exercise of preparation consists in remembering the Stoic dogma that will enable us to understand that whatever difficulties, obstacles, trials, and sufferings may happen to us are not evils, since they do not depend upon us and fall outside the realm of morality.

The recollection of Stoic principles is not just for dramatic circumstances, but is also effective against the difficulties of everyday life (II, 1):

> At the break of dawn, say to yourself, "I am going to encounter a busybody, an ingrate, an insolent person, a crook, an envious person, and an egotist. All this happens to them from their ignorance of the distinction between goods and evils."

Marcus then continues by recalling the principles which define good and evil, but which also define the community among human beings. Since people participate in the same intellect, and belong to the same divine race, says Marcus, I cannot suffer any damage at their hands and I cannot get angry with them.

Here we can see that the exercise of preparation for difficulties—a kind of examination of conscience in advance—does not concern only the discipline of desire and the acceptance of the will of Destiny. Rather, it is an integral part of the discipline of the will and of action. In this latter case, its function is to motivate a specific type of conduct toward other human beings. Throughout the *Meditations,* Marcus Aurelius returns several times to this exercise, which consists, on the one hand, in expecting to encounter resistance and ill will on the part of his collaborators and subjects, and, on the other, in preparing to assume an attitude which is firm but benevolent, indulgent, and even loving, toward those who oppose him.

The exercise of rational foresight will not only prevent us from being "unhappy before mishaps"—that is, victims of a false representation of future evils—but it will also allow us not to be unhappy in misfortunes, by means of a twofold process of psychological preparation. First, as we have seen, we will practice confronting in our minds the future trials which may happen to us, so that they do not take us by surprise. Second, we will accustom ourselves to remain inwardly free with regard to what may be beyond our control in our daily lives. As Epictetus says (IV, 1, 112):

> Begin with the little things: a pot, a cup, and then continue in the same way as far as a little tunic . . . as far as a piece of land. From there, move on to yourself, your body, the parts of your body, your children, your wife, and your brothers. . . . Purify your judgments so that nothing which does not belong to you becomes attached to

you or becomes as one with you, so that it causes you suffering if it is torn away from you . . . for this is true freedom.

Resignation?

As we have seen, when our action fails or encounters an obstacle, the Stoics—and Marcus Aurelius the Stoic—seem to tell themselves: "My intentions were good, and that's what really counts. Destiny has decided otherwise. I must accept its will and resign myself; the virtue I must practice now is not justice but the virtue of consent. I must switch from the exercise of the discipline of action to that of the discipline of desire."

This posed a problem for the Stoics. Marcus does not articulate it explicitly, but it was very real for him; it might even be called the drama of his life.

How can we avoid having our consent to the will of universal Nature—that will which is preventing our action from being accomplished—transformed into fatalistic resignation and nonchalance? How can we not be overcome by worry and even by anger, when our collaborators impede our action or when Destiny—by means of plagues, wars, earthquakes, or floods—prevents us from achieving the happiness of the Empire? Above all, what should we concretely do, when the obstacles, difficulties, and trials which Destiny has willed turn up?

Epictetus had devoted one of his *Discourses* (II, 5) to the problem: "How can concern coexist with greatness of soul?" By "greatness of soul," Epictetus meant "serenity," while by "concern" he meant "being concerned about acting well." This is the same problem that we are facing now.

In order to reply to it, Epictetus used a comparison taken from dice games. It does not depend upon me, he reasoned, that a particular die should fall. Likewise, the fact that I am in a certain situation, or that circumstances present an obstacle to my action, does not depend upon me, but upon Destiny. I must accept my situation with *serenity,* and consent to it. In a dice game, however, it *does* depend on me to play the die that does fall with concern, care, and skill. Similarly in life: it *does* depend on me to use the die which *has* fallen—that is, the circumstances of my action such as they have been willed by Destiny—with *care,* attention, and skill.

We find this conception of action—at least implicitly—in a passage by Marcus which has the merit of recapitulating the various situations in which the Stoic may find himself when he undertakes an action (X, 12):

What good is it to suppose, when you can clearly see what must be done? If you see this, you must travel that path, benevolently, but without turning around.

Marcus emphasizes that such an energetic, firm, and unshakable decision must not impede our benevolent dispositions. He repeats this motif in another passage (VIII, 5, 2):

Do what the nature of man demands, without turning aside from the path you have entered upon, in accordance with what seems most just to you. Only do it with benevolence and discretion, without any posing.

One can, of course, have doubts about what one ought to do (X, 12, 1):

If you cannot see what must be done, then suspend your judgment and use your best advisers.

Obstacles—willed by Destiny—can also arise:

If other things oppose your plan, then keep advancing, and, after having considered things at length, use whatever resources are available to you, while holding firmly to that which seems just to you.

The "resources" which we can find in any given situation are the possibilities which we must be able to exploit in our dice game. They must, however, be exploited in a rational and thoughtful way, so that two apparent opposites may be reconciled: the serenity of the sage, who is not troubled by dramatic situations, but accepts reality for what it is; and the concern of the man of action, who pursues whatever action he has undertaken, in spite of all obstacles and difficulties, modifying it in accordance with circumstances, yet always remaining aware of the goal which must be his: justice and the service of the human community. After all, isn't inner peace the surest guarantee of effective action?

Altruism

As we have seen, the discipline of action consists essentially in acting for the good of the community. Once again, divine action is the model for human action (V, 30):

The Intellect of the All cares about the common good of the All
(koinōnikos). This is why it has done the lower things for the sake of
the higher, and has set the higher things in harmony with one
another. See how it has introduced subordination and coordination;
how it has distributed to each thing its portion, in accordance with
its value; and how it has brought the most excellent things together
into a state of mutual concord.

Here the Intellect of the All appears like a good king who watches
over the health of the City. He cares about the well-being of his subjects,
the other rational beings, and places inferior things—that is, animals,
plants, and inanimate things—in their service. He institutes community,
harmony, and concord among rational beings, and distributes goods with
justice. Such an anthropomorphic and "political" representation of the
City of the World should not, however, make us forget that the relationship between the Intellect and intelligent beings is based upon Nature
herself. The City of the World is first and foremost the common City of
rational beings—gods and men—ruled by that law which is at the same
time common and particular to each of these beings. It is also simultaneously Reason and Nature, since their nature is reasonable. The very
definition of "man" is "rational animal" (VII, 11):

For rational animals, action in conformity with nature is at the same
time in conformity with reason.

The goal of rational animals is to obey Reason and the Law of the
most venerable city (II, 16, 6).

This most venerable City is the City on high, of which man is the
citizen and "of which the other cities are mere houses" (III, 11, 2).
"What is a man?" Epictetus had asked (II, 5, 26).

A part of a city. Of the first city, that is, which is made up of gods
and men; then of that which is so called in order to come as close as
possible to it, and which is a tiny image of the whole.

As Emperor, Marcus could not fail to be attentive to such a doctrine,
which placed his entire life in question, as we can see in the following
Meditation, which forms, as it were, his motto or his rule of life (VI,
44, 6):

My City and my Fatherland, insofar as I am an Antonine, is
Rome.

My City and my Fatherland, insofar as I am a man, is the world.

Everything that is useful to these two Cities is, for me, the only
good.

It is, says Marcus (IV, 4, 2), from the City of the World, or the City on
high, which is the City of reasonable beings, that we receive intelligence,
reason, and law. This equation is not without significance. Intelligence
and reason are common to all reasonable beings; hence they are universal. This is why they are that common and universal law which is within
all rational beings, for by virtue of their universality which transcends
individuals, they allow us to shift from the egocentric viewpoint of the
individual to the universal perspective of the All. This is why intelligence
and reason tend naturally to envisage the good and the interests of the
Whole. *Logikon* ("rational") and *koinōnikon* ("caring about the common
welfare") are inseparable (VII, 55):

Each being must act in conformity with its constitution. By their
constitution, the other beings are made for rational beings . . . and
rational beings are made for one another. The primary constituent
in the makeup of human beings is therefore the tendency to act for
the common good.

It has often been held that Stoicism was fundamentally a philosophy of
self-love, since the point of departure both for its physics and for its ethics
is the tendency to self-preservation, and to remain in a state of coherence
with oneself. In fact, however, the fundamental tonality of Stoicism is to
a much greater extent the love of the All, for self-preservation and
self-coherence are possible only by virtue of complete adherence to the
Whole of which one is a part. To be a Stoic means to become aware of
the fact that no being is alone, but that we are part of a Whole made up
of the totality of rational beings and that totality which is the Cosmos.

The reason the divine Intellect cares about the common welfare of the
All is that it unfolds itself within this All. It is at the same time itself and
all things, by virtue of a dynamic identity. If it has set in harmony the
beings which participate in the Intellect, this is because all such beings are
parts of it, and all have communion within it. It communicates its intention to realize the common good of the Whole to all beings, insofar as it
is present within them. Like the Intellect, all rational beings are *koi-*

nōnikoi: that is, they tend naturally to place themselves in the service of the All, and to ensure the unity of the All.

In a particularly beautiful *Meditation,* Marcus evokes the great "unities" which reveal to us the fundamental unity of all things (XII, 30): "The light of the sun is one," even if walls present an obstacle to it. "One is the common substance, even if it is divided among thousands of bodies which possess individual qualities." "One is the intelligent soul," even if it seems to divide itself. If there is a force of unity in all things, albeit an unconscious one, then, by contrast, in the unity constituted by the intelligent soul—constituted, that is, by all the intelligent souls which participate in it and which are one with it—there is this particular privilege to tend consciously "to join that which is akin to it and to unite with it." "This passion for community knows no obstacles."

Here we can glimpse, beyond the unifying forces which cause bodies to be held together, a universe of transparency and innerness where minds tend toward one another in reciprocal community and intimacy. Rational beings are linked together, insofar as their intention, like that of the divine Intellect, wills the good of the All; and hence to the extent that their intentions coincide with the end willed by the divine Intellect. Such a spiritual universe is thus one of concordant wills. From this point of view, moral intention becomes an absolute value and a goal in itself, which transcends all the particular goals to which it may be applied, and each rational being, insofar as it is free to have this moral intention, becomes in turn an end for itself and for others. Marcus never tires of repeating this (see, for example, IX, 1):

Universal Nature has made rational beings for the sake of one another.

In a sense, then, it could be said that this community of rational beings which the divine Intellect unites around itself reminds one of the "kingdom of ends" discussed by Kant. For Kant, this "kingdom of ends" corresponds to the community of rational beings, insofar as it is linked together by the law which each person postulates and accepts for himself. This law prescribes that each rational being must be an end in itself, both for itself and for others, by virtue of the moral freedom within it.[26] It is because rational beings postulate the moral end for themselves as a law that they are themselves an end in themselves. As Marcus said, such an end is to be preferred above all else (XI, 1, 4):

It is the property of the rational soul to love its neighbor . . . and to prefer nothing to itself, *which is also the property of the law.*

Most people, however, are unaware of this City of the World, and of Reason. They live in egotism, which is just as pernicious to the City of the World as it is to the city here below (IX, 23, 2):

Each of your actions which is not related either distantly or imme- diately to an end which serves the common good tears life apart, and prevents it from being one. It is a seditious act, as when, within a nation, someone separates his party from the concordant union of all citizens.

Egotism is harmful not only to the State, but also to the individual. Egotism isolates him, and as Epictetus had said (II, 5, 26):

When he is isolated, man will no longer be a man, any more that a foot would be a genuine foot. For what is man? A part of the state . . .

Marcus Aurelius takes up the same metaphor (VIII, 34):

Have you ever seen a lopped-off hand, foot, or head, lying sepa- rated from the rest of the body? That is what one does when he does not accept what happens, and thereby separates himself from the All, or who commits any act inspired by egotism. You yourself have excluded yourself from the unity of Nature, for you had grown within the Whole like a part, and now you have cut yourself off from it.

The two disciplines are brought up here: that of desire, implying that one must accept everything that happens, and that of action, which prescribes that we act for the common good. It is clear from the passages quoted above that they both correspond to one and the same attitude: that of becoming aware that we are only a part of the Whole, and that we live only by and for the Whole. What other beings do "naturally," man must do "rationally"; yet in the last analysis this is the same for him as acting "naturally," since his nature is reason and freedom. Mankind therefore has the strange power (VIII, 34, 3–5) to be able, by means of his intentions, his freedom, and his reason, to separate himself from the

Whole by refusing his consent to what happens, and by acting egotisti-
cally. He thus has the uncanny power, in a sense, to annihilate himself
spiritually. And yet, says Marcus, by means of an even more marvelous
power, mankind can return to the Whole after having cut himself off
from it. He can convert and transform himself, and change from egotism
to altruism.

Action and value; justice and impartiality

In his definition of the discipline of action which is cited by Marcus
Aurelius (XI, 37), Epictetus enumerates three characteristics which distinguish active impulses *(hormai)*, if they are good. First, they must be
accompanied by a "reserve clause," and their goal must be the service of
the common welfare. I have already discussed these first two points.
They must also, says Epictetus, be in accordance with value *(kat' axian)*.

This terminology seems vague and imprecise; are we talking about the
value of the objects upon which our action is exercised, or about the
people affected by such action? Marcus himself often uses the term *kat'
axian;* in fact it is a *terminus technicus,* current in the Stoic schools of
Marcus' time. Its meaning was obvious to contemporary initiates, but
today we must try to explain it.

The Stoics had long since developed a rather elaborate theory of
"value."[27] To summarize this doctrine—albeit in simplified form—we
may say that they distinguished three degrees of value. First came those
things which are an integral part of "life according to nature"—that is, of
virtue—for instance, the exercises consisting in the examination of conscience and in attention to oneself, which contribute to the practice of
moral life. The value of these things was considered to be absolute. In
second place came those things which could help the practice of virtue in
a secondary way. Taken by themselves, these things are neither good nor
bad, but are indifferent with regard to moral good. Possessing them and
exercising them, however, allows us to practice better the virtuous life.
Examples would include health, which makes it possible for us to do our
duty; and wealth, if it allows us to come to the aid of our fellow man.
These second-rank values do not have the absolute value which pertains
only to the moral good, but they can be ranked in hierarchical order
according to the closeness of their relationship to the moral good. Finally,
in last place came those things which, under certain circumstances, could
be useful to virtue. Such things have no value in and of themselves, but
can be exchanged for some good.

To recognize the exact value of a thing was thus a very important exercise, and a part of the discipline of judgment. Not only must we always try to see each object as it appears in its naked reality, says Marcus (III, 11, 1–2), but we must also become aware of its place within the universe, and of

> the value it has in relation to the Whole and in relation to mankind, insofar as mankind is a citizen of the highest City, of which the other cities are like mere households.

As we have seen, the discipline of judgment is intimately linked to the discipline of action. Once we have seen the value of things in this way, we must act in consequence (VIII, 29):

> I see all things as they are, and I use each of them in accordance with its value *(kat' axian)*.

What Marcus means by this is that, when faced with each event and each situation, he tries to recognize the benefit he can derive therefrom for his moral life, and thus to use it in the best possible way (VIII, 43):

> What brings me joy is to keep the guiding principle within me healthy, so that it has no aversion for any human being, nor for anything that can happen to them, but can look at all things with benevolent eyes, and know how to receive and to utilize each thing in accordance with its value.

The discipline of actions thus demands that we be able to recognize the value of objects, and be able to distribute the intensity of our acts proportionately. Seneca[28] had defined the discipline of action as follows: in the first place, judge the value of the matter in question; then adjust our active impulses to this value; finally, bring active impulse and action into harmony, so that we may always remain in accord with ourselves.

This, then, is the first meaning that can be given to Epictetus' phrase *kat' axian*. Yet the consideration of value is not situated only on the level of individual conduct, but also at the level of social life.

It is here, moreover, that a grave problem arises for the Stoic, for he does not have the same scale of values as other people. Others attribute an absolute value to things which, to the Stoics, are indifferent, and therefore can only have a relative value. Conversely, the Stoic attributes an absolute value to moral good, which is of no interest to most people. Marcus seems to allude to this conflict when he writes, à propos of the topic of helping others (V, 36):

> Don't let yourself be completely carried away by their representation.[29] Instead, help them as far as possible, and in accordance with the value of the matter at hand. If they incur a loss in the domain of indifferent things, do not say to yourself that they have suffered harm, for that is a bad habit.

What is needed is to help others, and therefore also to help them in the domain of indifferent things, which seem so important to them. Yet we must still bear in mind the real value of things—their moral finality—without sharing other people's judgments about the value of things. Nor must we pity them, as if what happens to them were a genuine misfortune.

This is the problem that Marcus faced as Emperor: he had to seek the happiness of his subjects in the domain of indifferent things, which had no value in his eyes. Yet by so doing, he would be imitating the divine example:

> The gods help mankind in every possible way: through dreams and through oracles; and yet it is in order to obtain things which have value only in the eyes of mankind (IX, 27, 3).

> The gods themselves wish the best for mankind, for such is their goodness that they often help them to obtain health, wealth, and glory (IX, 11, 2).

Thus, the gods place themselves within mankind's reach, and provide them with that which, in itself, has only a very relative value. The same thing must therefore apply to the Emperor. When defining his attitude to his fellow human beings—whom Marcus declares to be his relatives and his associates, even if they do not practice virtue—Marcus declares (III, 11, 5):

> I behave with benevolence and justice toward them, in conformity with the natural law which founds the human community. At the same time, however, I share their quest for what has value among indifferent things.

In addition to one's inner dispositions of benevolence, then, we here have concrete action, which obliges the Emperor to occupy himself with things which people consider to be values. In his eyes, too, they can have a certain value: insofar as they allow for eventual moral progress.

Such, then, is the second meaning we can attribute to the allusion to *axia,* or value in Epictetus' definition of the discipline of action.

There is, however, another meaning of the word "value." Here, the word no longer designates the value of an object, but that of a person, and it is synonymous with his or her merit. For Marcus, as for the Stoics in general, justice consists in giving to all people what they deserve according to their value or merit.[30] We cannot, however, assert that this new sense of the word "value" could also be reconciled with Epictetus' definition of the discipline of action, as discussed above. Curiously enough, we find very few allusions to the virtue of justice in the discourses of Epictetus as recorded by Arrian, and no definition of it. In Marcus, by contrast, the virtue of justice is so important that it is sometimes sufficient to define the discipline of action, as for instance in VII, 54: "To conduct oneself with justice with regard to the people present."

Is it because Marcus was conscious of his responsibilities as Emperor that he attributed such importance to justice? In any event, he alludes to the definition of this virtue when, speaking about the emperor Antoninus Pius, his adoptive father, Marcus says (I, 16, 5) that "he distributed goods to each person, without letting himself be influenced." This means in particular that he distributed duties and responsibilities without favoritism, taking into consideration only the individual's merits and value, as well as his ability to carry out the tasks in question. It certainly also means that he rendered justice with impartiality.

"Value" and "merit," moreover, do not necessarily mean Stoic moral value, but can mean either the ability to carry out a specific task, or else, in judicial matters, guilt or innocence. According to the historian Cassius Dio, Marcus did not demand perfection of those to whom he entrusted a mission:

> If someone did something good, he praised him for it, and he used him in the task in which he excelled; but he did not take the rest of his conduct into consideration. He used to say that it was impossible to create men the way one would like them to be, but that it was fitting to use men such as they are for the tasks in which they are useful.[31]

The people who have value are those who carry out their "duties" conscientiously. They are those who, in the domain of political and everyday life—which is also the domain of indifferent things—do what needs to be done, even if they do not do it in a Stoic spirit (that is, considering that the only absolute value is the moral good).

The model of this justice which distributes goods as a function of personal merit, without favoritism, and in all impartiality, is divine action. There is nothing surprising about this, for mankind's moral action proceeds from his rational nature, which is a part of or an emanation from divine rational nature. Marcus says of this divine nature (VIII, 7, 2):

> It has no obstacle; it is intelligent and just, since it carries out a distribution—equal and in accordance with value *(kat' axian)*—of time, of substance, of causality, of activity, and of the conjunctions of events.

One might think that an "equal" distribution cannot be "in accordance with value"; but we must recall that, since Plato and Aristotle,[32] political equality had been a geometrical equality—in other words, it had been a proportion in which it was fitting to attribute a superior good to a superior value, and an inferior good to an inferior value. Distribution was proportionate to *aretē,* which once designated aristocratic nobility, but which for the Stoics meant nobility of the soul, or virtue. Stoic justice, then, was aristocratic: not in the sense that it consisted in giving wealth and power—that is, indifferent things—to the aristocratic class, but in the sense that it made the consideration of value and of moral responsibility enter into every decision of political and private life. The historian Herodian relates that when it came time for Marcus Aurelius to marry off his daughters, he did not choose patricians or rich personages for them, but men of virtue. Wealth of the soul, Herodian continues, was, in Marcus' eyes, the only genuine, proper, and inalienable wealth.[33]

Divine action, then, is "without obstacle" and "just" because it is supremely rational, which means that it imposes an order upon itself. In the first instance, such an order subordinates particular goals to one unique end: the intention to ensure the good of the Whole. This is why divine action has no obstacles: because it aims at one thing only throughout all the particular goals, and knows how to make all the obstacles which seem to oppose it cooperate toward this unique end. Divine action also introduces an order and a hierarchy of values among the particular goals it assigns to itself. Inferior beings—minerals, plants, and

animals—are at the service of rational beings, and rational beings themselves are ends for one another. From the perspective of such a hierarchy
of values, then, divine action distributes time, matter, and causality as a
function of the value of each thing. That is why it is just.

The justice of rational Nature is at the same time the justice of the
Intellect of the Whole (V, 30), "which has introduced subordination and
coordination into the Whole," and which "distributes to each its portion, in accordance with its value." It is, moreover, the justice of the
Nature of the Whole (IX, 1, 1), "which has fashioned rational beings for
each other's sake, so that they may help each other mutually, in accordance with their value and their merit."

Everyday experience could, of course, inspire doubts about such a
divine justice. Indeed, experience seems (IX, 1, 6)

> to carry out a distribution which is contrary to merit *(par' axian)* in
> the case of good and of evil men, for evil men often live in pleas-
> ures, and obtain the means to do so, while the good encounter only
> misery, and that which causes misery.

This, however, is the judgment of people who consider pleasures to be
good, and who do not understand that life and death, pleasure and pain,
glory and obscurity, are neither good nor bad, when what one is search-
ing for is the moral good. On the contrary, says Marcus (IV, 10):

> Everything that happens, happens in a just way. If you examine this
> attentively, you will see that it is true. I am not just saying that "that
> happens by way of necessary consequence," but that "that happens
> in accordance with justice," just as if it was brought about by some-
> one who distributed to each his portion, in accordance with his
> merit.

In the context of the discipline of desire, we have already caught a
glimpse of the problems posed by the mode of action of Nature or
universal Reason. Did the latter start the cosmic process in motion by
one unique initial impulse, with all things then happening by way of
"necessary consequence"? Or rather, did Nature or Reason pay attention
to each individual, "distributing to each his portion, in accordance with
his merit" (IV, 10)? We saw that, in the final analysis, these two hypotheses did not exclude each other, since the general law of the universe
somehow assigned to each person the role he or she had to play within

the universe. Divine action is a unique action, which seems to adapt itself marvelously to each particular case. It is, then, as if "it was brought about by someone who distributed to each his portion, in accordance with his merit" (IV, 10). This holds true for the lower beings, which, as Marcus said (VIII, 7, 2), receive their portion of duration, substance, and causality in accordance with their value in the hierarchy of beings. Yet it is still more true in the case of rational beings. Destiny distributes to each person that which corresponds to his or her being and value. Each event is in perfect conformity with the person to whom it happens:

> Love only the event which happens to us, and which is linked to us by Destiny. After all, what could be better suited to us? (VII, 57).

> Such-and-such an event happened to you, was coordinated with you, was set in relation to you, was woven together with you, from the beginning, starting from the most ancient of causes (V, 8, 12).

> Has something happened to you? Good! Every event that comes your way has been linked to you by Destiny, and has been woven together with you, starting from the Whole, since the beginning (IV, 26, 4).

> Whatever happens to you was prepared for you in advance from all eternity, and the network of causes has woven together your substance and the occurrence of this event for all time (X, 5).

Everything that happens, then, happens in a just way, because everything that happens to us brings us that which belongs to us and was owed to us—in other words, that which suits our personal value—and therefore also contributes to our moral progress. Divine justice is an educator. The end it aims for is the good of the Whole, as ensured by the wisdom of reasonable beings.

The Stoic Diogenes of Babylon[34] said that, in the definition of justice as that virtue which gives to each person the portion corresponding to his or her value, the word "value" *(axia)* meant "the portion due to each person" *(to epiballon)*. The mystery of divine justice shows itself in such nuances of vocabulary. Marcus Aurelius, for instance, speaks (X, 25) of "He who administers all things," that is to say, he adds, "who is the Law *(nomos)* which distributes *(nemōn)* to each person that which is due to him *(to epiballon)*." "What is distributed according to the laws is equal for all"

(XII, 36, 1). When, therefore, the divine Law gives to each person the portion which corresponds to his value, this means at the same time the portion which is due to that person as a function of his merit and of what he is, and the portion which falls to his lot or is given to him by fate or Destiny. It is thus at the same time what *people choose* to be their own moral decision, and what the *Law,* by means of its initial decision, *chooses* that they should be. In the same way, the *daimōn* (that is, individual destiny), which according to Plato is attached to each soul, is assigned to it by fate, and yet is chosen by it.[35]

Such, then, was the ideal of justice which his Stoic faith proposed to Marcus, and if he could, he would certainly have realized on earth such a justice which takes only moral value into consideration, which has no other objective than human moral progress, and for which "indifferent" things have value only as a function of the assistance they may provide for moral progress. We shall see that Marcus did not have many illusions about the possibility of what he ironically called "the realization of Plato's Republic."

Such an ideal of justice could, however, inspire an overall inner disposition, which imitated both the impartiality of universal Reason, which imposes the same law upon all, and the attentive solicitude of providence, which seems to adapt itself to each particular case and take care of each individual, taking into consideration the individual's particular strengths and weaknesses.

In order to describe this attitude, one might quote a passage from Louis Lavelle,[36] who, without wishing to give an account of Stoic doctrine, gives quite exact expression to the spirit of justice according to the Stoics:

> There is a sacred indifference: it is that which consists in according no preference to any of the beings upon our path, but in giving them our entire presence, and responding with precise faithfulness to the call they utter to us. This is positive indifference, which is the converse of negative indifference, with which it is often confused. Positive indifference only requires us to reserve for all the same luminous greeting. We must keep the balance between them equal: may there be in us neither prejudice, nor predilection to cause the beam to sway. It is then that, in our conduct toward them, we become capable of introducing the most subtle differences; all the while giving to each person what he expects, requires, and is fitting

for him. Here, the most perfect justice becomes one with the purest love, and we cannot tell whether it abolishes all choice, or whether it is everywhere the same loving choice.

We all know that "not making any distinction" is the same thing as being just; it means applying the same rule to all, without introducing any exception or favor into our judgment. It is to place ourselves in the point of view of God, who embraces all beings in the simplicity of one single glance. Yet this glance is the opposite of an insensitive glance; it is a loving glance which distinguishes, within each individual being, precisely what he or she needs: the words that touch him, and the treatment that he deserves.

Pity, gentleness, and benevolence

In the context of the discipline of judgment, we have seen that although the Stoics held that the majority of humanity was in an evil state, they were in this state against their will, simply out of ignorance of the definition of true good and true evil. This is the great Socratic tradition, which thus extends, through Plato and Aristotle, as far as Stoicism. "No one is voluntarily evil."[37] Such Platonic assertions are based upon the Socratic idea that virtue is a "science"; in other words, that it consists essentially in knowing, with all one's soul, where the good is and what the true good is. After all, the human soul naturally desires the good, and spontaneously tends toward that which seems to it to be good. If it seems to become evil, this is because it allows itself to be deceived by the appearance of the good; but it never desires evil for evil's sake. It was all the more easy for the Stoics to take up this doctrine, in that for them, "everything is a matter of judgment," and the passions themselves are judgments. In his treatise *On Becoming Aware of Psychic Defects,*[38] the physician Galen gives excellent expression to this Stoic doctrine: "The principle of many defects is the false judgment which is brought to bear upon the goal which ought to be assigned to one's own life."

The great Socratic tradition which runs from Platonism and Stoicism through Neoplatonism is united by its faith in the eminent dignity of human nature, which is based on the natural and unconscious desire for the good which every human being possesses.

Epictetus also fits within this tradition, as he makes an explicit allusion (I, 28, 4–9) to the teachings of Plato:

> When someone gives his assent to error, know that it was not done on purpose, for "every soul is deprived of the truth against its will," as Plato says. Rather, what was false seemed to him to be the truth.

Epictetus goes on to remark that what corresponds to truth and error in the area of action is duty and its contrary, as well as the advantageous and its contrary. We cannot *not* choose what we think is duty, or what is advantageous. The mistake is therefore an error, and as long as the soul has not been shown the error of its ways, it cannot behave otherwise. Why, then, should we be angry at it?

> Shouldn't you rather have pity for those who are blind and mutilated with regard to what is most important, as we have pity for the blind and the lame?

This gives Epictetus the opportunity to describe the ideal attitude which the Stoic must exhibit toward his fellow man (II, 22, 36):

> With regard to those who are different from him [by the principles of their life], he will be patient, gentle, delicate, and forgiving, as he would toward someone in a state of ignorance, who missed the mark when it came to the most important things. He will not be harsh to anyone, for he will have perfectly understood Plato's words: "Every soul is deprived of the truth against its will."

Following Epictetus, Marcus Aurelius also felt tremendous respect for the unconscious desire for the truth and the good, which constitutes the most profound wellspring for mankind's rational nature. Marcus takes pity on the illness of those souls which, against their will, are deprived of what they obscurely desire:

> "Every soul," says Plato, "is deprived of the truth against its will." And the same holds true of justice, temperance, benevolence, and all such virtues. It is therefore absolutely necessary to remind yourself of this constantly. Thus, you will be more gentle with others (VII, 63).

> If they do not act rightly, it is obviously against their will and out of ignorance. For "every soul is deprived, against its will, of truth" just

as much as of the possibility of behaving toward others in an appropriate way (XI, 18, 4–5).

Here, Marcus reveals himself as a faithful student of Epictetus. As he quotes Plato, he does not follow the text of Plato, but instead he repeats the literal form of the quotation in the deformed state in which it is to be found in Epictetus. Above all, he draws the same moral consequences from it.

This ignorance of genuine values in which people are submerged, says Marcus, is "in a sense, worthy of pity" (II, 13, 3). We will feel this if we attempt to understand the error in judgment which explains their misdeeds (VII, 26, 1). "*In a sense,* worthy of pity": this qualification is an allusion to the traditional Stoic critique of pity, which the Stoics considered a passion. "Pity," said Seneca,[39] "is an illness of the soul produced by the sight of the suffering of others, or a state of sadness caused by the misfortunes of others. But no illness affects the soul of the sage, who always remains serene."

Marcus Aurelius and Epictetus remain faithful to Stoic doctrine, insofar as what they call "pity" is not a passion or an illness of the soul, but is instead defined negatively as the lack of anger and hatred toward those who are ignorant of genuine values. It is not enough, however, to have pity on people or to be indulgent with them. We must above all try to help them, by informing them about their error, and teaching them genuine values (IX, 42, 6):

> In general, it is within your power to instruct the mistaken person so as to make him change his mind, for whoever commits a misdeed is a person who misses what he was aiming at, and goes astray.

We must, then, try to reason with the mistaken person (V, 28, 3; VI, 27, 3; VI, 50, 1; IX, 11). If we fail in our efforts, then it will be time to practice patience, forgiveness, and benevolence. Marcus likes to present our duty toward our fellow men in the form of a dilemma:

> People were made for one another; so either instruct them or put up with them (VIII, 59).

> If he is wrong, instruct him to that effect with benevolence, and show him what he has overlooked. If you do not succeed, then be mad at yourself; or rather not even at yourself (X, 4).

Epictetus (II, 12, 4; II, 26, 7) had said that we must, like good guides, set those who have gone astray back on the right track again, without mocking them or insulting them. If we do not succeed, we must not make fun of the person who has gone astray, but rather must become aware of our own inability and accuse ourselves, rather than the person whom we cannot persuade. As we have just seen, Marcus adds to this that we must not even be upset with ourselves, for it could be that some people are incorrigible, and "it is necessary that there be some such people in the world" (IX, 42, 2).

Be that as it may, we must try to convert those who go astray and are ignorant of genuine values. Above all, however, we must do this without getting angry (VI, 27, 3; V, 28, 3). What is more, we must display an infinite delicacy. It seems as though Marcus was extremely sensitive to the tact and gentleness with which souls must be treated, and with which we must try to change their way of perceiving the world and the things within it. I must address others

> without humiliating them, and without making them feel that I am merely putting up with them, but with genuineness and goodness (XI, 13, 2).

> . . . without irony, without humiliation, but with affection, and a heart free from bitterness; not as one would act in school, nor in order to be admired by some bystander, but truly one on one, even if others are present (XI, 18, 18).

There is a great wealth of psychological observation in these remarks, and a remarkable sense of the purity of intention. The paradox of gentleness is that it ceases to be gentleness if we make an effort to be gentle: any artifice, affectation, or feeling of superiority will destroy it. Delicacy only acts insofar as it does not seek to act, with an infinite respect for beings, and without any shadow of violence, be it only spiritual. Above all, we must not do violence to ourselves in our attempt to be gentle. Gentleness must possess an almost physiological spontaneity and sincerity. Marcus expresses this in a striking way (XI, 15), as he satirizes those people who begin their conversation by saying, "I've decided to be frank with you." What good are these words? asks Marcus:

> If you are sincere, it must be written on your forehead, ring out instantly in your voice, and shine from your eyes, just as a beloved person immediately sees his lovers' feelings in their eyes . . . The

person who is good, without duplicity, and gentle, has these qualities in his eyes, and everybody can see them.

Even more strikingly, Marcus states that goodness can be sensed when
one approaches a good person, just as, whether one likes it or not, one
immediately smells the odor of someone who smells bad. This pure
gentleness and delicacy have the power to change people's minds, to
convert them, and to make those who are unaware of genuine values
discover them:

> Goodness is invincible, if it is sincere, without a phony smile, and
> without affectation (XI, 18, 15).

Far from being a weakness, goodness is a strength:

> It is not anger that is manly, but gentleness and delicacy. It is because
> they are more human that they are more manly; they possess more
> strength, more nerve, and more virility, and this is precisely what is
> lacking in the person who gets angry and loses his temper (XI, 18,
> 21).

What underlies its strength is the fact that gentleness is the expression
of a profound urge of human nature, which seeks harmony between
people. In addition, its strength resides in the fact that it corresponds to
the domination of reason, whereas anger and ill-temper are mere illnesses
of the soul.

In the words of Louis Lavelle,

> Gentleness is so far removed from weakness that it alone possesses
> genuine strength. . . . All wills become tense when one tries to
> defeat or break them; but gentleness can persuade them. Only it can
> triumph without a combat, and transform an enemy into a friend.[40]

One might say that only gentleness has the power to reveal to people
the good of which they are unaware, although they desire it with all their
being. It acts both by its persuasive force and by the unexpected experience that encountering it represents for those who know only egotism
and violence. It brings with it a complete reversal of values, by making
those who are its object discover their dignity as human beings, since
they feel themselves to be deeply respected as beings who are ends in
themselves. At the same time, gentleness reveals to them the existence of

a disinterested love of the good, which inspires gentleness and which addresses itself to them.

Despite this, gentleness toward others must not be allowed to exclude firmness (VI, 50, 1):

> Try to persuade them, but act even against their will; when that is required by the rational order of justice.

Here, then, we finally discover a whole new aspect of the discipline of action: our duty to help our neighbor spiritually, by revealing genuine values to him, calling attention to his defects, and correcting his false opinions. To what extent did Marcus really fulfill this role? We do not know. We can, however, suppose that he attempted to promulgate around him a Stoic vision of life and of the world. There must be an allusion to this in the following passage, in which Marcus imagines what will happen after his death. Someone will say (X, 36, 2):

> Now that that schoolteacher is gone, we can breathe freely. Granted, he wasn't hard on any of us; but I could feel that he was criticizing us in silence.

Until now, we have looked only at the first part of the dilemma which Marcus formulated: "Instruct them." We can now understand this as follows: "Instruct them with gentleness, and by means of gentleness."

Now we are in a position to complete the second part of the dilemma as well: "Put up with them gently." For gentleness is not reserved for those whom we want to convert, but is also intended for those whose minds we have not succeeded in changing:

> If you can, make them change their minds. If not, remember that it is precisely for such situations as these that benevolence was given to you. Besides, the gods themselves are good to such people (IX, 11, 1).

> There is one thing in this world which is of great value: to spend our life in truth and in justice, all the while remaining benevolent to liars and to the unjust (VI, 47, 6).

> Do not let those who present an obstacle to you in your progress in right reason turn you away from healthy action, nor let them succeed in making you lose your gentleness toward them (XI, 9, 1).

Liars, unjust people, and all those who persist in error nevertheless retain—at least in their essence—their rational nature and the unconscious desire for the good which is inscribed in it. They must therefore be treated with respect and gentleness:

> I cannot be angry with one who is related to me, nor hate him, for we were made to cooperate (II, 1, 3).

> Imagine that they are akin to you, that they sin out of ignorance and against their will (VII, 22, 2).

> It is just as much a sign of weakness to get angry at them as it is to give up an undertaking you have begun . . . both the man who allows himself to be frightened, and he who denies the person whom nature has given him to be a friend and a kinsman, are equally deserters (XI, 9, 2).

Such an attitude, based on the idea of the community between rational beings, finally leads to the doctrine of the love of one's neighbor, which extends even to those who commit injustices against us.

Loving our neighbors

> A *proprium* of humankind is to love even those who make mistakes. This will happen if you realize that they are akin to you and that they sin out of ignorance and against their will (VII, 22, 1–2).

This transcendence of justice, not only in the direction of pity or indulgence, but in that of love, was implied by the arguments which invited the Stoic to reflect, on the one hand, on the indestructible urge which moves each person toward the good, and, on the other, on the solidarity which unites all rational creatures together.

Thus, the discipline of action attains its culminating point in the love of one's neighbor. All the logic of human action tends to reveal that the prime motive of our activity must be the love of other people, since this love becomes fused with the deepest urges of human nature (XI, 1, 4):

> It is a *proprium* of the soul, if it is rational, to love its neighbor, which corresponds both to truth and to respect.

The reason for this is that human beings, if they live in accordance with reason, become keenly aware that they belong to one great body: that of all rational beings. Insofar as he is part of this All, man *is* everybody else, as much as he is himself (VII, 13):

> As are the limbs of the body in organic unities, such is the relationship between rational beings, who, although they exist within separate bodies, are nevertheless constituted in order to realize one single and harmonious activity.
>
> This concept will impress itself better within you if you often repeat to yourself: I am a limb *(melos)* of the organism *(sustēma)* formed by rational beings. But if you only use the letter *rhō,* saying that you are a part *(meros),* then you do not yet love mankind from the bottom of your heart. You do not yet find your joy, without seeking anything else, in the simple fact of doing good to others. Moreover, you are acting for the sake of mere appearance, not yet because when you do good, you are doing good to yourself.

This feeling of belonging, and of identification with a kind of "mystical body" which Kant was to call the kingdom of ends, joins the almost mystical feeling of belonging to the cosmic Whole. The unity of the latter, like that of the "body of rational beings," is ensured by the universal presence of Reason—that is to say, of God himself.

The Stoic's fundamental attitude is thus the love of those realities in whose presence he is constantly placed by the All, which are intimately linked to him, and with which he somehow identifies himself (VI, 39):

> Harmonize yourself with the things to which you are linked by Destiny.
>
> As for the people to whom you are linked by Destiny: love them, but genuinely.

For the basis of reality is love. In order to express this idea, Marcus appeals to the grandiose mythical image of the marriage of Heaven and Earth (X, 21):

> The Earth loves! She *loves* the rain! And the venerable Ether? It *loves* too! The World, too, *loves* to produce that which must occur. And I say to the World: I, too, *love*—along with you. Don't we say: "such-and-such *loves* to happen?"

What fascinates Marcus here is that this mythical image means that natural processes are, in the last analysis, processes of union and of love. He notes that language itself seems to express this vision, since in ancient Greek, in order to designate a thing which habitually occurs or tends to happen, one says that it "loves" to happen. If things love to happen, we too must love *that* they happen.

Thus, the ancient image of the *hieros gamos* allows us, in a mythic way, to glimpse the grandiose perspective of the universal love which the parts of the Whole feel for one another, as well as the comic vision of a universal attraction which becomes more intense the higher one climbs on the scale of beings, and the more conscious they become (IX, 9). The closer people get to the state of wisdom—in other words, the closer they approach to God—the more the love which they feel for one another— for all other human beings, as well as for all beings, even the most humble—grows in depth and in lucidity.

It cannot, then, be said that "loving one's neighbor as oneself" is a specifically Christian invention. Rather, it could be maintained that the motivation of Stoic love is the same as that of Christian love. Both recognize the *logos* or Reason within each person. Even the love of one's enemies is not lacking in Stoicism:

> When he is beaten, the Cynic [for Epictetus,[41] the Cynic is a kind of heroic Stoic] must love those who beat him.

We have seen Marcus assert that it is proper, and therefore essential, to human beings to love those who make mistakes. One could say, how- ever, that the tonality of Christian love is more personalized, since this love is based on Christ's saying: "What you have done to the least of my brethren, you have done to me."[42] In the Christian view, the *logos* is incarnate in Jesus, and it is Jesus that the Christian sees in his fellow man. No doubt it was this reference to Jesus which gave Christian love its strength and its expansion. Nevertheless, Stoicism was also a doctrine of love. As Seneca[43] had said:

> No school has more goodness and gentleness; none has more love for human beings, nor more attention to the common good. The goal which it assigns to us is to be useful, to help others, and to take care, not only of ourselves, but of everyone in general and of each one in particular.

9

VIRTUE AND JOY

The three virtues and the three disciplines

The *Meditations* as a whole are thus organized in accordance with a threefold structure—one could even call it a system—which was developed, and perhaps invented, by Epictetus. This threefold structure or system has an internal necessity, in the sense that there can be neither more nor fewer than three exercise-themes for the philosopher, because there can be neither more nor fewer than three acts of the soul. The exercise-themes which correspond to them are related to three forms of reality: Destiny, the community of rational beings, and the individual's faculties of judgment and assent. These forms, too, cannot be either more or fewer in number, and they are respectively the subjects of the three parts of the system formed by philosophy: physics, ethics, and logic.

What is quite remarkable is that in Marcus Aurelius, we can see another structure, which had been traditional since at least the time of Plato, that of the four virtues—prudence, justice, strength, and temperance—take on, under the influence of this systematic structure, a threefold structure as well, insofar as Marcus makes the virtues correspond to each of the disciplines I have mentioned.

The scheme of the four virtues was very ancient. We should recall that the Greek word *aretē,* which we translate as "virtue," originally had a quite different meaning from our word "virtue." The term went back to the aristocratic ethic of archaic Greece, and consequently did not at all signify a good habit or a principle which leads us to behave well. Rather, it meant nobility itself, excellence, value, and distinction. We may suppose that this ideal of excellence and value always remained present in the mind of the philosophers. For the Stoics, *aretē* is absolute value, based no longer on warrior nobility, but on the nobility of soul represented by the purity of our intentions.

Since very early times, it seems that there existed a model or a canon of the four fundamental virtues. In the fifth century B.C., Aeschylus, in his tragedy *The Seven Against Thebes* (verse 610), enumerates four basic values when discussing Amphiaraos: he is wise *(sōphrōn)*, just *(dikaios)*, brave *(agathos)*, and pious *(eusebēs)*. Wisdom consists in knowing, with reserve *(aidōs)*, one's place in society and in the world—in other words, in having a sense of mankind's limits. Justice consists in behaving well in social life. Bravery, of course, is courage in the face of difficulties, and especially in combat. Piety, in the case of Amphiaraos, who is a seer, corresponds to the knowledge of things divine and also human. In the fourth book of Plato's *Republic* (427e ff.), there appears a systematization and justification of this enumeration of the four virtues. Plato distinguishes three parts of the soul: "reason," "anger" *(to thumoeides)*, which means that part which urges people on to fight, and "desire" *(epithumia)*. Three virtues correspond to these three parts of the soul: prudence or wisdom to reason, courage to anger, and temperance to desire. It is up to justice to ensure that each part of the soul carries out its function: that reason is prudent, anger courageous, and desire temperate. The three parts of the soul, moreover, correspond to the three social classes of the *Republic:* reason is the distinctive feature of the philosophers, anger of the guardians, and desire of the workers. In the State as in the individual, then, justice will be realized if each class and each part of the soul fulfills its function perfectly. This systematization, which is linked to a specific political model, and which makes justice the virtue which contains the three others, is not to be found in the rest of Plato's dialogues, where the four virtues are enumerated in various contexts, and without any particular theorization.[1]

In their description of moral life, the Stoics also allude to the four virtues.[2] Here, however, they are not subordinate to one another, but are all on the same level. They mutually imply one another, as do the parts of philosophy. It is enough to practice one in order to practice them all. Nevertheless, it is difficult to find in our surviving summaries of Stoic doctrine the real reason why it is necessary that there be only four fundamental virtues. The definitions of the various virtues are rather divergent, but we may note the following: prudence is the science of what ought and ought not to be done; courage is the science of what ought and ought not to be tolerated; temperance is the science of what ought and ought not to be chosen; and justice is the science of what ought and ought not to be distributed. Unlike Plato, the Stoics do not appear to link the four virtues to the parts of the soul.

From this perspective, it is of great interest to observe the transformations which the system of three disciplines caused the classification of
virtues in Marcus' *Meditations* to undergo. Let us begin by noting that the
philosopher-emperor often summarizes the three disciplines—of assent,
of desire, and of action—by making the names of virtues correspond to
them. Thus the discipline of assent takes on the name of the virtue of
"truth"; the discipline of desire acquires the name of the virtue of "temperance"; and the discipline of action, that of the virtue of "justice." In
itself, the substitution of the notion of "truth" for that of "prudence"
should not surprise us, for Plato had already once (*Republic,* 487a5) given
the four virtues the names of "truth," "justice," "courage," and "temperance."

The substitution of "truth" for "prudence" can, however, be perfectly
well justified from the perspective of Marcus Aurelius. This is shown by
the following lengthy passage (IX, 1), which must be cited for two
reasons: first, we can see in it the establishment of an exact correspondence between the discipline of action and justice, the discipline of assent
and truth, and the discipline of desire and temperance. Second, it offers
an admirable summary of the three exercise-themes.

Justice and the discipline of action

He who commits an *injustice* commits an impiety. For since *universal
Nature* has constituted rational animals for the sake of each other, so
that they might help each other in accordance with their respective
merit and never harm each other, he who transgresses the will of
Nature most obviously commits an impiety against the most venerable of gods.

Truth and the discipline of assent

He who *lies,* moreover, also commits an impiety toward the same
Goddess. For *Universal Nature* is the nature of beings; now beings
have a relationship of affinity with true attributes [that is, with what
can be truly said of them]. Moreover, this Goddess is also named
truth, and she is the first cause of all that is true. Therefore, he who
willingly lies commits an impiety, in so far as he commits an injustice by deceiving. And he who lies involuntarily also commits an
impiety, insofar as he is in disaccord with universal Nature, and he

disturbs order insofar as he is in a state of incompatibility with the Nature of the world. For that person is in a state of incompatibility who, of his own free will, tends toward that which is contrary to the truth. He has received from Nature dispositions to know the truth, but since he has neglected them, he is now no longer capable of distinguishing the true from the false.

Temperance and the discipline of desire

Finally, the person who pursues pleasures as *goods* and who flees pains as *evils* also commits an impiety. For such a person must necessarily often reproach *universal Nature,* for Nature attributes a particular lot to the bad and to the good, contrary to their merit; for the bad often live in pleasures and possess that by which they may procure them, while good people encounter only pain and that which is its cause. What is more, he who fears pain will one day come to fear one of the things which must happen in the world, and this is already impious. Nor will he who pursues pleasures be able to keep away from injustice; and this is clearly impious. Concerning things with regard to which universal Nature is equally disposed (for she would not produce both, if she were not disposed toward them in an equal way): with regard to these things, those who wish to follow Nature, and be in perfect community of sentiments with her, must also be in a disposition of "equality." Therefore, as far as pain and pleasure are concerned, death and life, glory and obscurity, which universal Nature treats in an "equal" manner, he who does not behave in an "equal" manner obviously commits an impiety.

Here it is easy to recognize the three disciplines: that of action, which ordains that people should help one another; that of assent, which consists in distinguishing the true from the false; and that of desire, which consists in accepting the lot which universal Nature has reserved for us. To these three disciplines correspond three virtues. In the discipline of action, we must respect the value hierarchy of people and of things, and thus act in accordance with *justice*. According to the discipline of assent, our discourse must be true, and the virtue particular to this discipline is *truth*. He who knowingly lies commits a twofold sin: in the area of assent, since his discourse is not true, and in the area of action, since he is committing an injustice with regard to other people. As for the person

who lies involuntarily—in other words, who deceives himself—it is because he has not succeeded in criticizing his judgments and in becoming
the master of his assent that he is no longer capable of distinguishing the
true from the false. Finally, in the discipline of desire, we must desire
only that which universal Nature wants, and we must not desire pleasures
or flee sufferings. This discipline is characterized by *temperance*.

Here, then, Nature appears to us in three aspects. She is the principle
of attraction which urges human beings to help one another and to
practice justice, and is therefore the basis of *justice*. She is also the basis of
truth; that is to say, the principle which founds the order of discourse, and
the necessary relationship which must exist between beings and the true
attributes which are said about them. To speak falsely, whether voluntarily or involuntarily, is therefore to be in disaccord with the order of the
world. Finally, universal Nature, since she is indifferent to indifferent
things, is the basis of *temperance,* in other words of that virtue which,
instead of desiring pleasure, wants to consent to the will of universal
Nature.

Marcus here portrays universal Nature as the most ancient and august
of goddesses, in such a way that any lapse with regard to the virtues—
justice, truth, and temperance—of which this goddess is the model and
the principle, is an impiety. The Stoics traditionally identified God, Nature, Truth, Destiny, and Zeus. In Marcus' time, there were hymns
which presented Nature as the most ancient of goddesses. For example,
an Orphic hymn[3] invokes her in the following terms:

> Goddess, mother of all things, celestial mother, very ancient *(pres-
> beira)* mother.

A hymn by Mesomedes, one of Hadrian's freedmen, which also dates
from the second century A.D., begins:

> Principle and origin of all, very ancient Mother of the world,
> Night, Light, and Silence.[4]

In our long passage from Marcus, we can note a certain tendency to
privilege the importance of justice as compared to the other virtues.
Impiety toward Nature consists in injustice, not only if one refuses to
practice justice toward other human beings, but also if one lies to them,
and even if, involuntarily, one cannot distinguish the true from the false.
For then one destroys the order of Nature, and introduces a discordant

note into universal harmony. Likewise, if we accuse Nature of injustice in her distribution of lots among good and evil people, then we ourselves are committing an injustice. We find a similar idea expressed in XI, 10, 4:

> Justice cannot be preserved if we attribute importance to unimportant things, or if we are easily deceived; if we give our assent too rapidly, or if we change our mind too often.

To give importance to unimportant things is not to practice the discipline of desire, and hence to sin against temperance; whereas to be easily deceived, or to be too rapid or changeable in our judgments, means not to practice the discipline of assent, and hence to sin against truth.

Truth, justice, and temperance can thus designate the three disciplines, as in XII, 15:

> Whereas the flame of a lamp shines until it goes out, and does not lose its luster, will the truth, justice, and temperance which are within you be extinguished before their time?

Elsewhere (XII, 3, 3), the soul's guiding principle, when it frees itself of everything foreign to it,

> does what is just, wills the events which happen, and tells the truth.

Nothing, says Marcus (VIII, 32, 2), can prevent us from acting

> in accordance with justice, temperance, and prudence.

Sometimes, as in this last example and the following one, we find some variations in the names of the virtues; yet the tripartite scheme is retained (III, 9, 2):

> Absence of hurry in judgment, a feeling of kinship toward other human beings, and obedient consent to the gods.

Alongside this triad of virtues, we sometimes find the traditional quaternium, adapted and brought into line with the tripartite structure (III, 6, 1):

If you find something in human life better than justice, truth, temperance, and bravery . . .

In fact, the continuation of this passage reduces these four virtues to the disciplines of desire and of action (III, 6, 1), when it becomes apparent that they consist

in thought which is content with itself (in those things in which it is possible to *act* in accordance with right reason), and which is content with Destiny (in those things which are allotted to us, independently of our will).

The virtues are linked to the functions of the soul: truth and the intellectual virtues are linked to reason; justice to active impulses; and temperance to desire. Where, then, can we find a place for courage? It seems to be shared between temperance, *qua* strength in adversity and suffering, and justice, *qua* active force.

We find no trace of this theory of the virtues in the *Discourses* of Epictetus, as reported by Arrian. This does not prove, however, that it did not exist. As I have said, it was impossible for Arrian to have transmitted all of the teachings of Epictetus; moreover, the discourses which he did note down do not correspond to a systematic exposition of the whole of philosophy.

Be that as it may, a first sketch of this doctrine may be glimpsed well before Epictetus. In Cicero's treatise *On Duties*,[5] which in its first book reproduces the teachings of Panaetius, the ancient virtue of prudence becomes "the knowledge of truth"; justice is based on the social links between human beings; strength becomes greatness of soul, linked to scorn for the things which do not depend on us; and temperance submits our desires to reason. In a way, then, Panaetian strength and temperance correspond to the discipline of desire in Marcus Aurelius. In the last analysis such comparisons are rather tenuous, but they do allow us to glimpse an evolution of the Stoic doctrine of the virtues, which culminates in the synthesis attested in Marcus.

Joy

In Marcus' view, these three disciplines and virtues bring to the soul the only true joy which exists in the world, since they place the soul in the possession of all that is necessary: the one absolute value.

Living beings experience joy when they fulfill the function for which they are made, and act in accordance with their nature. As we have seen, man fulfills his function *qua* man, and follows his nature as well as universal Nature, when he consents to order: the order of the universe as fixed by Destiny; the order of the City of the World and of human beings, based as it is upon the mutual attraction of rational beings, and hence on the proper nature of mankind; and finally to the order of discourse, which reproduces the relation which Nature has established between substances and attributes, and above all between events which necessarily follow upon one another. It is therefore by practicing the three disciplines that man follows Nature, and finds his joy:

> Philosophy wants only that which your nature wants. You, however, wanted something else, which was not in accordance with nature. And yet, what is more attractive than what is in conformity with nature? Is this not how pleasure leads us astray?[6] Look and see, however, if there is anything more attractive than greatness of soul, freedom, simplicity, benevolence, and piety; for what is more attractive than wisdom itself? (V, 9, 3–5).

> You must consider the activity which it is possible for you to carry out in conformity with your own nature as a delight—and that is always possible for you (X, 33, 2).

For the person who strives at every moment to live, act, will, and desire in conformity with his rational nature and with universal Nature, life is constantly renewed happiness. In the words of Seneca:[7] "The effect of wisdom is a continuous joy . . . and only the strong, the just, and the temperate can possess this joy." Marcus Aurelius often returns to this theme:

> To do what is just with all one's soul, and to tell the truth. What remains for you to do but enjoy life, linking each good thing to the next, without leaving the slightest interval between them? (XII, 29, 3).

> Enjoy and take your rest in one thing only: to pass from one action carried out in the service of the human community to another action accomplished in the service of the human community, together with the remembrance of God (VI, 7).

For man, joy consists in doing what is proper to man. What is proper to man is benevolence toward other human beings, who are his relatives; disdain for movements based on sense-perception; criticism of deceptive representations; and the contemplation of universal Nature, and of that which happens in conformity with its will (VIII, 26).

Joy, then, is the sign of an action's perfection. It is only when we love human beings from the bottom of our hearts, and not merely out of duty, that we feel pleasure in benefiting them (VII, 13, 3), just because we then have the feeling of belonging to the same living organism, and of being the limbs of the body of rational beings.

Unlike Epicurean pleasure, Stoic joy is not the motive and the end of moral action: rather, virtue is its own reward. Virtue seeks nothing above and beyond itself; instead, for the Stoics, joy, like Aristotelian pleasure, comes along as an extra surplus in addition to action in conformity with nature, "like beauty for those in the flower of youth."[8] In the words of Seneca:[9]

Pleasure is not a reward for virtue, nor its cause, but is something added on to it. Virtue is not chosen because it causes pleasure; but if it *is* chosen, it *does* cause pleasure.

The joy which arises from virtue . . . like happiness and tranquillity . . . are consequences of the greatest good, but they do not constitute it.[10]

Such joy is not, moreover, an irrational passion, because it is in conformity with reason. According to the Stoics, it is rather a "good emotion" or a "good affection."[11]

The joy produced by action accomplished in accordance with Nature is a participation in Nature's love for the All that she has produced, and in the mutual love of the parts of the Whole.

For mankind, to be happy means feeling the sentiment of participating in an ineluctable movement, issuing from the impulse given to the All by original Reason, in order to realize the good of the All. In the word *physis,* which we translate as "nature," the Greeks perceived the idea of a movement of growth, of unfolding, and, as the Stoics used to say, of "swelling"[12] *(emphysēsis).* To be happy meant to embrace this expansive movement, and thus to go in the same direction as Nature, and to feel, as it were, the joy which she herself feels in her creative movement.

This is why Marcus, when he describes joy, uses images which evoke progress on the right path and in the right direction, and the accord of our desires, wills, and thoughts with the path of Nature. It is then that "rational nature follows the path that is proper to it" (VIII, 7, 1). The Stoics[13] defined happiness as *euroia biou,* "the good flowing of life." Marcus likes to link this image (II, 5, 3; V, 9, 5; X, 6, 6) to that of "progress in the right direction"—that is, in the direction of Nature (V, 34, 1). While the material elements move up, move down, or turn in a circle,

> the movement of virtue does not resemble any of these physical motions, but is something divine, and it proceeds along the right path, which it is hard for us to imagine (VI, 17).

This right path is the "straight line" or "right road"—that of Nature herself, whose way is always straight ahead (X, 11, 4). Her way is short and direct (IV, 51):

> Get to the end of your race in a straight line, following your own nature and universal Nature, for both of these follow the same way (V, 3, 2).

Here, Marcus is reviving an ancient image which had been used by Plato:[14]

> The God who, as ancient tradition will have it, holds the beginning, end, and middle of all things, *gets to the end of his race in a straight line,* in accordance with the order of nature.

Already in Plato, then, the order of nature appears as a triumphant movement which reaches its end without ever allowing itself to be distracted from the rectitude of its decision and its intention. According to Marcus, the movement of the governing part of the soul—the movement of the intellect—also proceeds in a straight line, like the sun, which illuminates that which is in its way, and in a sense assimilates it to itself (VIII, 57). For the Stoics, all moral action reaches its goal straightaway, insofar as it is its own end, and insofar as it finds its perfection in its very activity. A propos of this topic, Marcus recalls the technical expression *katorthōsis,* which the Stoics used to designate such actions: it means that they follow a straight way (V, 14).

Joy has its roots in that profound tendency of living beings which impels them to love that which makes them exist, and this means not only their own structure and unity, but the All, without which they would be nothing, and of which they are integral parts. It also means Nature and her irresistible movement, of which they are but a tiny moment, but with which they identify themselves wholly, by means of their moral will.

Finally, and most important, joy is based on the recognition of the unique value of the one necessary thing that can exist in this human world: the purity of moral intention. We cannot find

> in human life, a good superior to justice, truth, temperance, and strength (III, 6, 1),

and this, therefore, is the good which we must enjoy (VI, 47, 6):

> Only one thing has value down here: to spend one's life in truth and justice, all the while remaining benevolent to liars and to the unjust.

10

MARCUS AURELIUS IN
HIS *MEDITATIONS*

The author and his work

In interpreting the writings of antiquity, and particularly those of Marcus Aurelius, we must be on our guard against two errors which are diametrically opposed, but equally anachronistic. One of these, inherited from Romanticism but still very much alive, consists in believing that an author expresses himself totally and adequately in the work which he produces, and that the work is therefore completely in the image and resemblance of its creator. The other, which is very fashionable today, holds that the idea of an "author" is passé; the work has its own autonomy and its own life, and it can be explained without our having to find out what the author wanted to do or say.

In fact, ancient authors were subject to strict rules, which were not of their choice. Some of these rules regulated the way in which one should write; these include the rules of literary genres as defined by rhetoric, which prescribed in advance the plan of exposition, style, and the various figures of thought and elocution which must be used. Other rules regulated the subject matter itself: what was written, the themes with which the author must deal (which, in the case of the theater, were supplied to him by mythical or historical tradition). Philosophers were also situated within a school-tradition, which imposed upon them a list of questions and problems to be discussed in a specific order, a method of argumentation which had to be followed scrupulously, and principles which had to be adopted.

In the case of Marcus Aurelius, we have seen that the spiritual exercises which he wrote down were prescribed by the Stoic tradition, and in particular by the form of Stoicism defined by Epictetus. Canvas, themes, arguments, and images were provided for him in advance. For Marcus, the essential thing was not to invent or to compose, but to influence himself and produce an effect upon himself. Even if this effect was efficacious at one moment, however, it would soon lose its strength, and the exercise would have to be begun again in order constantly to revive the certitude derived from the striking formulations of the principles and rules of life.

This state of affairs will thus lead us to question the attempts of psychological history, on the basis of the text of the *Meditations,* to arrive at conclusions about "the Marcus Aurelius case"—for instance, about his stomach ailments or his opium addiction.

This does not mean, however, that Marcus is totally absent from the *Meditations,* or that any Stoic who happened to be in Marcus' situation could have written approximately the same work. It is true that the *Meditations* attempt, as it were, to eliminate the point of view of individuality, in order to rise up to the level of universal and impersonal Reason; yet Marcus the individual still shines through, in this ever-renewed and never finished effort to assimilate the principles of Reason, in order to apply them to his particular circumstances. In the last analysis, this apparently impersonal work is highly personalized. Marcus has a favorite style and themes; he sometimes has obsessions and lacerating preoccupations, which arise from his carrying out the business of an emperor. We know very well what Marcus wanted to accomplish by writing this work: to act upon himself, place himself in a certain state of mind, and respond to the concrete problems which the various situations of daily life posed for him.

The limits of psychological history

The Marcus Aurelius case

What I have said about the "impersonal" nature of ancient works in general and of Marcus Aurelius' spiritual exercises in particular must incite us to the greatest prudence in any effort we might be tempted to make to reconstruct the psychology of the philosopher-emperor. As far as I know, it was Ernest Renan who was the first to attempt to sketch a portrait of Marcus. He ended up, moreover, with a portrait that is rather incoherent. Sometimes, he insists on the emperor's disillusioned serenity:[1]

> The most solid goodness is that which is based on perfect boredom, and the clear view of the fact that this whole world is frivolous and

lacking any true substance . . . The goodness of the Skeptic is the most certain, and the pious emperor was more than skeptical. The movement of life in this soul was almost as quiet as the tiny noises in the intimate atmosphere of a coffin. He had attained Buddhist nirvana, or the peace of Christ. Like Jesus, Shakya-Muni, Socrates, St. Francis of Assisi, and three or four other sages, he had utterly conquered death. He could smile at it, because it truly had no more meaning for him.

Elsewhere, by contrast, Renan discovers in Marcus a tormented soul:[2]

The desperate effort which was the essence of his philosophy, this frenzied renunciation, sometimes pushed as far as sophism, finally conceals an immense wound. One must have said farewell to happiness to arrive at such excesses! We shall never understand all that this poor withered heart had suffered, and how much bitterness lay hidden by his pale visage, always calm and almost smiling.

Here, far from having attained Buddhist nirvana or the peace of Christ, Renan's Marcus seems "consumed" by an inner sickness:

This strange sickness, this worried study of himself, this demonic scrupulousness, this feverish perfectionism, are the signs of a nature less strong than it is distinguished.[3]

What he lacked was the kiss of a fairy at his birth, which is, in its way, a very philosophical thing. What I mean is the art of yielding to nature: that gaiety which learns that *abstine et sustine* is not everything, and that life must also be able to be summed up by the formula "smile and enjoy."[4]

This portrait of Marcus by Renan gave rise to what must be called the obstinate and tenacious myth which turns Marcus into a disillusioned pessimist. In the twentieth century—the century of psychology, psychoanalysis, and suspicion—the Renanian representation of the philosopher-emperor has had a tremendous influence. P. Wendland[5] speaks of Marcus' "mournful resignation." More recently, J. M. Rist[6] has spoken of the philosopher-emperor's "extreme Skepticism," and of his "penchant for doubt." Paul Petit[7] speaks of a "rather negative despair." What I have said about the alleged pessimism of the *Mediations* ought, I think, to be sufficient to refute such affirmations.

According to E. R. Dodds,[8] the emperor considered human activity to be not only unimportant, but in a way almost unreal. It seems very difficult to reconcile such an interpretation with what Marcus says about the discipline of action. Dodds insists on the perpetual self-criticism to which Marcus subjects himself, and on the need which the emperor feels to be "another." Dodds relates this tendency to a dream which, according to Cassius Dio and the *Historia Augusta,* Marcus had at the age of seventeen, on the night of his adoption by the emperor Antoninus. Marcus dreamed that he had ivory shoulders, and this suggests to Dodds that Marcus suffered from an acute form of what modern psychologists would call an identity crisis.

Here we have a typical example of the dangers of historical psychology. Dodds gives a poor definition of what it means to "desire to be something other than one is." It is true that Marcus aspired to be another man and to begin another life (X, 8, 3). But as the context shows, what he means by this is that he wants to acquire truth, prudence, and nobility of soul (X, 8, 1). I think that every normal person also desires to be someone else in that sense, and if that is an identity crisis, then every person has an identity crisis. I cannot, moreover, see how "so much self-reproach" presents a "morbid" aspect, as Dodds maintains.[9] On this theme, Dodds attributes to Marcus the formula "It is difficult for a man to put up with himself," which, we are to believe, lets us infer either that Marcus was unbearable to himself, or that, more generally, human nature taken in itself is unbearable to itself. In fact, however, Dodds completely deforms the meaning of Marcus' text (V, 10, 4; not V, 10, 1 as is incorrectly indicated in Dodds's note). Marcus' actual tone is the following:

> Also consider the ways of life of the men who live with you; the most pleasant of them is difficult to put up with, not to say that he can scarcely put up with himself.

Thus, the issue is not at all Marcus' relationship with his own self, but a wholly other problem, to which I shall return. Neither is this Marcus' personal experience; rather, it is a description, traditional within Stoicism and even within the other schools, of the misery of a person who does not live as a philosopher, does not devote himself to the unique value of the moral good, and who is therefore in contradiction and at war with himself. To live philosophically—that is to say, to live "according to nature"—is to be coherent with oneself. In all this, no "identity crisis" on the part of Marcus can be discerned.

Moreover, when discussing Marcus' dream, Dodds does not give a complete report of what the ancient historians had to say. The *Historia Augusta,*[10] for example, tells us that not only did the young man dream that he had ivory shoulders, but that he wondered if they would be able to support a burden, whereupon he discovered that they were extraordinarily stronger. Cassius Dio,[11] writing shortly after Marcus' death, specifies that in his dream, Marcus could use these shoulders just as easily as the other parts of his body. In fact, however, the question is not what such a dream might represent to a person of modern times, but what it may have meant to a person of antiquity. The mistake made by some kinds of psychological history is to project back onto the past our modern-day representations, according to which shoulders which are "other" must correspond to "another" man. What we must try to understand is what the images which appeared to the people of antiquity in their dreams could represent within their collective mentality. As Pierre Grimal[12] has shown, for them ivory shoulders immediately brought to mind the story of Pelops. Pelops' body, torn to pieces by his father Tantalus, had been served to the gods for dinner. Demeter, still grieving over the death of her daughter Persephone, was the only one not to recognize the dish, and she ate Pelops' shoulder. Clothō, goddess of Fate, replaced it with an ivory shoulder and revived the young Pelops. According to the *Images* by Philostratus, who wrote a few decades after the death of Marcus, Poseidon was dazzled by the sight of this ivory shoulder, and he fell in love with Pelops. "When the night covered the earth, the young man was illuminated by his shoulder, which shone like the evening star in the midst of the darkness."[13]

To have ivory shoulders was thus to be the object of divine solicitude and grace; it was to be protected by Fate, as personified by Clothō. In the situation of increased responsibility announced by his adoption, the ivory shoulders announce the help from the gods and from Fate which will make Marcus strong enough to assume his task. This, for a man of antiquity, is the true meaning of Marcus' dream.

The psychosomaticist R. Dailly and H. van Effenterre have undertaken collaborative research in order to diagnose what they call "the Marcus Aurelius Case."[14] In particular, they sought to know the reason why, in a kind of contradiction with his principles, this emperor surrounded himself with highly dubious characters. He chose as co-ruler his adoptive brother, Lucius Verus; he entrusted the position of Commander in Chief over the entire East to Avidius Cassius, the general who later took up arms against him; and finally, he chose as his successor in the imperial dignity his son Commodus, who was to become a tyrant comparable to Nero. "These were three fine male specimens," write the authors of this article, "who had a definite ability to enchant the crowds; and we are entitled to wonder whether they did not also exert a kind of unconscious fascination upon Marcus Aurelius." Thus, right at the beginning of the article, we encounter the thesis which the two authors mean to defend: the philosopher-emperor was a weak man, lacking in virility, who felt the need to compensate for his doubts and hesitations by surrounding himself with strong, self-confident men. Here we can glimpse the inner workings of this kind of psychological explanation: people believe they have uncovered a highly characteristic symptom, which is not in fact the symptom of anything, since it is not even a symptom. Nothing proves that Marcus chose these individuals out of attraction toward their virile force. The elections of Lucius Verus, Avidius Cassius, and Commodus were dictated by complex political reasons, which historians have analyzed thoroughly. Nor is there anything to prove that these "fine male specimens" (were they indeed so fine?) were really so sure of themselves. Since, however, the subject of this book is the *Meditations,* I do not wish to allow myself to be dragged into the domain of history. I wish simply to affirm, most firmly, that the *Meditations* do not, either in their goal or in their content, permit us either to affirm or to deny that Marcus was a weak man, that he lacked virility, or, as our two authors would have it, that he had a stomach ulcer. They arrive at this last diagnosis on the basis of the following passage from the historian Cassius Dio:[15]

> [During the Danubian campaign], he became physically very weak, to the point that, at the beginning, he could not stand the cold, and after the soldiers had been assembled on his order, he had to retire before having spoken to them. . . . For it was not his custom to eat anything during the day, with the exception of the medicine called theriac. He took this not because he was afraid of anything, but because his stomach and his chest were in poor shape. And it is said that it was because of this medicine that he was able to resist this illness, and others as well.

This text makes no mention of any chronic illness, but rather refers to Marcus' state during the Danubian campaign. Elsewhere, Cassius Dio bears witness to the fact that the Emperor was vigorous in his youth, and that he took part in violent sports like hunting.[16] According to Dio, it was the worries of his office and his ascetic ways that weakened his body. Be that as it may, our two authors, after having diagnosed a gastric ulcer, move on to the psychological correlates of this illness:

> The ulcerous man . . . is he who is essentially withdrawn into himself, worried and preoccupied . . . His neighbors are masked from him by a kind of hypertrophy of the self: it is himself, in the last analysis, that he seeks in others . . . Conscientious to the point of minutiae, he is more interested in the technical perfection of administration than in those human relations of which administration should be only the sum total. If he is a thinking man, he will incline to seek for justifications, to compose superior personalities, and to adopt Stoic or Pharisaic attitudes. In the area of ethics, he will be virtuous by effort, good by application, and a believer by force of will.[17]

I am not qualified to debate the scientific value of the psychological portrait which these two authors trace of these "gastropaths," although it would be interesting to ask them if they recognized themselves in this dark portrait. What I question is the possibility of deriving from the *Meditations* even the slightest hint which might confirm or invalidate this description of Marcus Aurelius' psychology. The authors are completely mistaken as to the nature of this work when, to justify their diagnosis, they claim that the *Meditations* respond to a need for "justification in his own eyes," and constitute "a long series of exhortations to persist in the path chosen beforehand." As we have seen, the *Meditations* do not represent an exceptional phenomenon, proper to Marcus. Such written meditation was highly recommended by Stoic masters, and is, moreover, still practiced today by people who do not have a stomach ulcer, but who are simply trying to live in a somewhat human way. And this is not a case of self-justification, but rather of an attempt at self-criticism and self-transformation. These variations on themes supplied by Epictetus cannot inform us about the Emperor's gastric ulcer, and can tell us nothing decisive about the Marcus Aurelius "case." Here we have a good example of the dangers of psychological history when applied to ancient texts. Before we present the interpretation of a text, we should first begin to distinguish between, on the one hand, the traditional—one might almost say "prefabricated"—elements used by the author, and, on the other, what he or she wishes to do with them. If we do not make this distinction, we will consider as symptomatic formulas or attitudes which are not at all such, because they do not emanate from the author's personality but are imposed upon him by tradition. We must try to find out what the author wants to say, but also what he can or cannot say, and what he must or must not say, as a function of the traditions and the circumstances imposed upon him.

Was Marcus an opium addict?

This is what T. W. Africa should have investigated, before he claimed to discover the symptoms of Marcus' alleged opium addiction in the *Meditations*.

Africa bases his claim on three pieces of evidence. He takes up the passage from Cassius Dio discussed above, which, while describing the Emperor's state of health during the winter campaigns on the Danube, told us that he did not consume anything during the day except an antidote called theriac. He did this not because he was afraid of being poisoned, as we saw, but in order to calm his chest and stomach. Elsewhere, Africa mentions a work by Galen entitled *On Antidotes,* which describes the different ways of preparing theriac, the usefulness of this medicine, and the way in which Marcus used it. Finally, Africa thinks he can discover visions and psychic states produced by opium abuse within the *Meditations*.

Here is how Africa summarizes the evidence of Galen[18] on Marcus' theriac consumption:

> When he found himself getting drowsy at his duties, he had the poppy juice removed [from the mixture] . . . But, then, he was unable to sleep at night. . . . So he was obliged once again to have recourse to the compound which contained poppy juice, since this was now habitual with him.

If we read Galen's text[19] through to the end, however, we find that it says precisely the opposite of what Africa wants to make it say. In the continuation of his text, Galen specifies two things. In the first place, when Marcus took up the mixture containing poppy juice again, his personal physician, Demetrius, made sure that it contained aged poppy juice, which did not have the same soporific effect. Second, after the death of Demetrius, Galen himself was responsible for preparing the

Emperor's theriac, and he is quite proud to be able to say that Marcus was completely satisfied with the way he composed the antidote in accordance with the recipe that was traditional among the physicians to the emperors. Thus, according to Galen, the Emperor's sleepiness was only a temporary accident which happened during the Danubian campaigns, and which did not happen again after aged poppy juice was used, and especially after Galen intervened. That is what the latter's text actually says.

In fact, the question is exceedingly complex, and we have no way of determining the exact quantity and quality of the opium juice that went into the theriac which the Emperor consumed. On the one hand, his doctors took care to see that the opium juice was aged and weakened. On the other hand, Galen, in the course of his treatise, speaks of three kinds of antidotes which he had prepared for Marcus Aurelius: *galene* (the antidote of Andromachus), which contained sixty-four ingredients, one of which was poppy juice; theriac of Hera, which contained no poppy juice, but had equal parts of bituminous clover, *Aristolochia rotunda,* mountain rue *(Ruta halepensis),* and ground vetch *(Vicia Ervilia).* Finally, there was an antidote consisting of one hundred ingredients, which contained very little poppy juice. Thus, the quantity of poppy juice was highly variable.[20]

For his part, Galen saw a proof of Marcus' wisdom in this custom of his:

> Some people use this medicine every day, for the good of their body, as we know personally from the case of the divine Marcus who once ruled in respect of the laws, and who, thanks to the consciousness he had of himself, observed the mixture of his body with very precise attention. He used this medicine copiously, as if it were nourishment. It was from him that theriac began to be famous, and that its powerful effectiveness appeared among men. Indeed, thanks to the fact that the Emperor's health improved because of it, people's confidence in the usefulness of this medicine increased considerably.[21]

Thus, we can see from this body of evidence, taken from Cassius Dio and from Galen, that nothing in any way allows us to infer that Marcus was an opium addict.

This, moreover, is the conclusion which T. W. Africa himself reaches,[22] in a footnote to his article: "Admittedly the amounts of opium could vary, and, on the basis of the antidote of the younger Antimachus (Galen XIV 42), a *kyamos* (Marcus' daily dose) would contain about 0.033 gram of opium, hardly sufficient for addiction."

In that case, however, can we still speak of an opium addiction? Yes, says Africa, because Marcus displays two symptoms: his "odd detachment from domestic realities," and the "bizarre visions" which we find in the *Meditations*. The strange detachment mentioned by Africa is probably— for he never clarifies the point—what historians have always censured Marcus for: his apparent indifference to the infidelities of his wife Faustina and to the extravagances of his colleague Lucius Verus, as well as the unfortunate choice he made of Commodus as his successor. As we have already seen, however, the question with regard to Lucius Verus and Commodus is very complex, and political motives must have played a large role in determining Marcus' attitude. As for Faustina: she bore Marcus thirteen children, and he mentions her briefly but very emotion- ally in the first book of the *Meditations*. Everything leads us to believe that she was the victim of court gossip. Be that as it may, it is difficult to see why Marcus' attitude was any more a symptom of opium addiction, as Africa maintains, than it was of a stomach ulcer, as Dailly and van Effen- terre had thought.

There remain the "bizarre visions." Here, bad historical psychology reaches one of its summits; this is a piece worthy of an anthology. I quote T. W. Africa:[23]

Marcus' vision of time as a raging river carrying all before it into the abyss of the future was no school doctrine of life viewed from the Porch, but an attempt to express the extended perspectives of time and space which opium had opened up to him. Temporal and spatial dimensions were accelerated until Europe was but a speck and the present a point and men insects crawling on a clod. History was no longer a reference but an actual pageant of the past. Marcus shared the exacerbated sensations of his fellow opium-addict De Quincey:[24] "The sense of space, and, in the end, the sense of time, were both powerfully affected. Buildings, landscapes, etc., were exhibited in proportions so vast as the bodily eye is not fitted to receive them. Space swelled and was amplified, to an extent of unutterable infinity. This, however, did not disturb me so much as the vast expansion of time; I sometimes seemed to have lived for 70 or 100 years in one night; nay, sometimes had feelings representative of a millennium passed in that time, or, however, of a duration far beyond the limits of any human experience."

Let us now examine the passages from Marcus Aurelius to which Africa refers in a footnote:

A river of events, a violent current: that is what eternity is. No sooner has one thing been seen than it has already passed; another one passes, and will, in its turn, be swept away (IV, 43).

Think often about the rapidity with which beings and events pass and disappear: for substance is like a river in perpetual flux; activities are in constant transformation; and causes are in a myriad of modes. Almost nothing is stable, even that which is close to you. Think also of the infinite abyss of the past and of the future, into which everything is swallowed up (V, 23).

Pace Mr. Africa, this theme is well attested in Stoicism, for instance in Seneca:[25]

Represent to yourself *(propone)* the vastness of time and embrace the universe, and then compare what we call human life to this immensity.

Time passes with infinite speed. . . . Everything falls into the same abyss. . . . Our existence is a point, or less; but nature, by dividing this minimal thing, has given it the appearance of a longer duration.

We find this ancient image in the following fine verses by Leonidas of Tarentum:[26]

Infinite, O man, is the time before you came to the dawn; infinite is that which awaits you in Hades. What portion of existence remains to you, if it is not barely the value of a point, or still less?

Marcus' river is no doubt the Stoic river of substance, "which flows ceaselessly,"[27] but in the last analysis it is the river of Heraclitus—that Heraclitus who Plato said compared beings to the flow of a river.[28] It is also the river of the Platonists, mentioned by Plutarch: "Everything appears and disappears in one unique moment; be it actions, words, or feelings; like a river, time sweeps everything away."[29] Finally, we also encounter this river in Ovid: "Time flows in perpetual movement; like a river, wave is pressed by wave."[30]

When Seneca uses the expression *propone,* which means "represent to yourself" or "place before your eyes the bottomless chasm of time," he emphasizes that he is speaking of an exercise of the imagination, which the Stoic must practice. We find an exercise of the same kind in those *Meditations* in which Marcus seeks to embrace the dimensions of the universe by his imagination, or to see things from on high, in order to reduce them to their true value:

Remember the totality of substance, of which you participate in only the smallest portion; remember also the whole of eternity, of which you have been assigned but a brief, tiny interval. Finally, remember destiny, of which you are a part: but how tiny! (V, 24)

If you suddenly found yourself transported into the air, and contemplated human affairs and their variety from above, you would have contempt for them, as you saw, in the same glance, how vast is the domain of the inhabitants of the air and of the ether (XII, 24, 3).

You can cut off many of the superfluous things which present obstacles to you, and which rest entirely on your value-judgment. Thus you will clear for yourself a vast open field, by embracing the entire universe in your mind; you will comprehend perpetual eternity, as you consider the rapid transformation of each individual thing. How short is the time from birth to dissolution; how gaping is the infinity before birth, and similarly the infinity after dissolution (IX, 32).

The soul traverses the entire world and the void which surrounds it; it examines the form of the world; extends itself into the infinity of eternity, and embraces and conceives the periodic rebirth of the universe (XI, 1, 3).

Asia and Europe are corners of the world; the entire sea is a drop of the world; Athos is a lump of earth in the world; all of present time is a point in eternity; everything is tiny, fragile, and evanescent (VI, 36, 1).

We can immediately see the difference between these passages and those by De Quincey. For the latter, the distention of duration and space is an impression imposed upon the addict from outside, and he is in a sense its passive victim. For Marcus, by contrast, the consideration of the infinity of time and space is an active maneuver, as we can see from his frequent admonitions to "represent to himself" or to "think" the totality. Here again, we are in the presence of a traditional spiritual exercise, which utilizes the faculties of the imagination. Moreover, De Quincey speaks of a distention of the instant, which takes on outlandish proportions; whereas Marcus speaks of an effort to imagine the Infinite in its totality, in order subsequently to see the instant, or the place, reduced to infinitesimal proportions. This voluntary exercise of the imagination presupposes that Marcus adhered to the classical representation of the Stoic universe: the universe is situated within an infinite void, and its duration within an infinite time, within which the periodic rebirths of the universe repeat themselves eternally. This exercise is intended to obtain a vision of human affairs which resituates them within the perspective of universal Nature.

A procedure such as this is the very essence of philosophy. Thus we find it, always identical beneath the diversity of vocabularies, in all the philosophical schools of antiquity. Plato defined the philosophical nature by its ability to contemplate the totality of time and of being, and therefore to hold human affairs in contempt.[31] We find this theme again among such Platonists as Philo[32] or Maximus of Tyre,[33] in Neopythagoreanism,[34] among the Stoics,[35] and even among the Epicureans. Representative of the last-named is the following saying by Metrodorus:

> Remember that, although you were born mortal and with a limited life, you have nevertheless, by means of discussions about nature, risen up to the eternity and infinity of things. You have also seen the future and the past.[36]

In Cicero's famous *Dream of Scipio*,[37] the grandson of Scipio Africanus contemplates the world from the heights of the Milky Way. He sees the earth so small that the Roman Empire seems imperceptible to him; the inhabited portion of the world seems like a tiny island in the middle of Ocean; and life seems to be less than a point. This theme was to remain very much alive throughout the Western tradition. We have an echo of it in Pascal's "two infinites":[38] "Let the earth appear to him as a point, compared to the vast circle described by this star . . ." Was Pascal, then, also an opium addict?

Marcus also transports this view from above onto the past (X, 27):

> Think constantly about this: how all events which are similar to those which are happening now, have also happened in the past; and think that they will happen again. Place entire dramas, and homogeneous scenes, which you know through your personal experience or through ancient history, before your eyes: for instance, all of Hadrian's court; or that of Antoninus; the whole courts of Philip, Alexander, or Croesus. For all of that was similar; only the actors were different.

T. W. Africa has read De Quincey, and has noticed the fine page in which the latter evokes the reveries in which there appeared to him the luminous spectacle of the ladies of the court of King Charles I, or Paulus Aemilius, surrounded by centurions, striding in front of the Roman legions. Africa believes he finds an analogous phenomenon in Marcus Aurelius. Once again, however, it is enough to read Marcus attentively to recognize the difference. De Quincey's description is purely oneiric: the dream is told for its own sake, as a strange and marvelous spectacle. For Marcus, however, it is not a dream: the Emperor demands an imaginative effort from himself, in order to try to represent to himself the courts of the past. As Paul Rabbow has shown,[39] this practice is carried out in accordance with the rules which rhetoric prescribed when one had to depict a scene or a circumstance in an expressive way. Moreover, the picture was not there for its own sake, but only in order to provide a highly austere conviction in the soul of the person practicing the exercise; namely, that human affairs are banal and ephemeral (VII, 49):

> Behold the past. So many changes of regime; and the future can be predicted equally well. Things will be entirely homogeneous, and we cannot escape the rhythm of what is happening now. That is why there is no difference between studying human life for forty years, or ten thousand years, or more: what more could one possibly see?

I believe I have sufficiently demonstrated the workings of a certain type of historical psychology. Generally speaking, it is based upon ignorance of the modes of thought and composition of ancient authors, and it anachronistically projects modern representations back upon ancient texts. It would, moreover, be interesting to psychologize some historical psychologists; I believe we could discover in them two tendencies. One is iconoclastic: it takes pleasure in attacking such figures as Plotinus or Marcus Aurelius, for example, who are naively respected by right-thinking people. The other is reductionist: it considers that all elevation of the soul or of thought, all moral heroism, and all grandiose views of the universe can only be morbid and abnormal. Everything has to be explained by sex or drugs.

Stylistic elegance

From everything that has just been said, we must not conclude that Marcus is absent from his *Meditations*. Rather, he is present in them in many ways, and the work has an autobiographical value which is limited, but very real.

First and foremost, Marcus is present by virtue of his stylistic elegance. We have already seen that the Emperor, who was writing for himself, usually makes an effort to write with the greatest care, certainly because he is aware of the psychological power of a well-turned phrase. The procedures Marcus uses have been well analyzed by J. Dalfen,[40] Monique Alexandre,[41] and R. B. Rutherford,[42] who have also pointed out the felicitous expressions in which they result. As Monique Alexandre has shown, Marcus here reveals himself to be a true student of Fronto. It appears that Fronto required his student to compose a saying *(gnōmē)* every day, and above all to formulate it in different ways. As Fronto writes,[43] "Each time you conceive of a paradoxical thought, turn it over within yourself, vary it with diverse figures and nuances, make trial of it, and dress it in splendid words." Throughout this book, we have been able to admire Marcus' skill at developing multiple variations on the same theme. Fronto also advised his student to make collections of sayings for himself.[44]

It is difficult to add anything new to the remarkable studies that have been carried out on Marcus' style. I think, however, that it may be useful to cite some examples of the quest for stylistic elegance which appears in some passages from his work.

The quest for conciseness often gives such passages a remarkable vigor, and an almost enigmatic character:

Correct, not corrected! (VII, 12).

Grow on the same trunk, but don't profess the same doctrines! (XI, 8, 6: the opposition is between *homothamnein* and *homodogmatein*).

Neither an actor nor a whore! (V, 28, 4).

For the stone thrown up in the air, it is neither bad to fall back down, nor good to rise up (IX, 17).

Receive without pride, let go without attachment (VIII, 33).

Men have come into being for one another; so either teach them or put up with them (VIII, 59).

Leave the fault of another right where it is (IX, 20).

A bitter cucumber? Throw it away! Brambles on the road? Avoid them! (VIII, 50).

We have already frequently encountered the brutal, explosive formulas which Marcus uses to describe the ugliness of life when it is bereft of moral value:

A mime *(mimos)* and a war *(polemos)*; excitement *(ptoia)* and numbness *(narka)*; the slavery *(douleia)* of every day! (X, 9).

Note the assonances in this last passage, which are indicative of Marcus' search for literary effect.

In how short a time, ashes or a skeleton! A mere name, or no longer even a name. But a name is nothing but meaningless noise, or an echo.
    And everything to which people attach so much importance in this life is empty, rotten, and petty: little dogs that nip at one another; kids who fight, laugh, and then suddenly burst into tears. Faith, however, and Modesty, Justice, and Truth "have taken flight toward Olympus, fleeing the road-furrowed earth" (V, 33).[45]

The most striking formulas deal with the brevity of life, death, and the vanity of fame:

Soon, you will have forgotten everything! Soon, everyone will have forgotten you! (VII, 21).

Everything is ephemeral; both that which remembers, and that which is remembered (IV, 35).

Soon you too will close your eyes, and someone else will have wept for the person who laid you to rest (X, 34, 6).

Yesterday, a bit of phlegm; tomorrow, ashes or a mummy (IV, 48, 3).

Marcus not only had a knack for turning concise phrases, but he also knew how to tell of the beauty of things in few words, as in a passage from the *Meditations* (III, 2) cited earlier. There, Marcus evoked crusty bread and ripe figs which split, and maturity, which is already almost rottenness, which gives its beauty to the color of olives, and which also gives a kind of flourishing to elderly men and women, and makes heavy-laden ears of corn lean toward the earth. The "lion's wrinkled brow," the "foam dripping from the boar's muzzle," and the "gaping jaws of wild beasts" also have their own savage beauty.

Fronto had taught his imperial student to introduce images and comparisons into his sayings and discourses, and Marcus learned his lesson well:

On the same altar, there are many grains of incense. One falls before the others, another later. What difference does it make? (IV, 15).

Dig within. That's where you'll find the source of the good, and it can always burst forth anew, if you keep digging (VII, 59).

A spider hunts down a fly, and thinks he is pretty hot stuff. One man hunts down a little hare; another catches a sardine in his net; another hunts boars, another bears, another Sarmatians. Aren't they all thieves, if you examine the motives of their actions? (X, 10).

Have you ever seen a hand which has been cut off, or a foot, or a severed head lying somewhere apart from the rest of the body? That is what a person does to himself . . . who does not wish for what happens, and who separates himself from the All . . . (VIII, 34).

In certain *Meditations,* we also notice a striving after rhythm and the harmonious balance of phrases, as for instance in the following prayer to the World:

> Everything which is in accord with you is in accord with me, O World! Nothing of what comes in an opportune way for you comes either too soon or too late for me! All that your seasons produce, O Nature, is fruit for me (IV, 23).

Elsewhere, a thought is developed in parallel and ascending formulas, as in the following passage, of which I will cite only the beginning:

> One is the light of the sun, even if it is divided by walls, mountains, or a thousand other things.
> One is the common substance, even if it is divided into thousands of bodies, each with its own individual qualities.
> One is the soul, even if it be divided into thousands of faculties of growth and individual differences.
> One is the thinking soul, even if it seems divided . . . (XII, 30).

In these stylistic exercises, to which Marcus accorded all his attention, one may, I believe, glimpse two characteristic features of his personality: a great aesthetic sensitivity and an intense search for perfection.

It may be of interest to point out that W. Williams[46] has carried out a study of the style of Marcus' constitutions, and therefore of the juridical texts which he wrote. According to this author, we can note in these writings a meticulousness highly concentrated upon details, and an almost exaggerated insistence on explaining points that are self-evident. This seems to indicate a certain lack of confidence in the moral and intellectual qualities of his subordinates, and a quest for purity in the use of Greek and of Latin. Finally, it shows the scrupulous attention that Marcus devoted to finding the most equitable, humane, and just solutions possible.

Chronological signposts

The reader of a literary work always likes to know at what moment of the author's life it was written, and in what atmosphere. To be sure, there is something atemporal about the *Meditations,* and it must be admitted that the attempts made by various historians to attach certain passages to specific moments of the Emperor's life have been disappointing. As we have seen, the *Meditations* are spiritual exercises, carried out upon a canvas prefabricated by the Stoic tradition, which did not leave any room for personal anecdotes. In order to suggest a date for their composition, we possess only two pieces of objective evidence. Between what is now Book I and what is now Book II of the *Meditations,* the *editio princeps* contains a sentence which can be translated as follows: "Written in the land of the Quadi, on the banks of the Gran, I." Between what is now Book II and what is now Book III, it contains the indication "Written in Carnutum." It may have been the Emperor himself who added these two specifications, as he made for himself a classification of the notes he had written.

Carnutum was a military base which the Romans had established starting at the beginning of the first century B.C. on the Danube, not far from Vienna, and it was home for several thousand legionnaires. A small town had sprung up near the camp, with an amphitheater which was built in the second century. It was there that Marcus established his headquarters during his wars against the Quadi and the Marcomanni, from 170 to 173.

The river Gran is still called either by this name or by that of the Hron; it flows from north to south through Slovakia, and joins the Danube in Hungary. Marcus' allusion to this river is invaluable: it reveals to us that the Emperor was not content to direct operations from the fortified camp at Carnutum, but that he had crossed the Danube and had penetrated the territory of the Quadi—a Germanic people who, together with the Marcomanni, had invaded the Empire in 169—to a distance of more than 60 miles.

To what books of the *Meditations* do these two notations refer? The allusion to the Quadi is placed between Books I and II, whereas the mention of Carnutum comes between Books II and III. In antiquity, indications of this kind could appear either at the beginning or at the end of a book. If these two notes were placed at the end, then the first one refers to Book I, and the second to Book II. If they were placed at the beginning, then the first one refers to Book II, and the second to Book III. Historians have adopted both views, without ever furnishing decisive proof. I am inclined to follow G. Breithaupt[47] and W. Theiler[48] in thinking that these indications were placed at the beginnings of Books II and III respectively.

It is most interesting, and even moving, to note that at least a part of the *Meditations* was written during the Roman operations carried out on the Danube in 170–173—not only in the relative calm of a military headquarters, but amidst the discomfort of an expedition into the land of the Quadi. This situation may explain the distinctive tone of Books II and III: the haunting presence of the theme of death. There is no more time to read; it's not the moment to wander. I find it easy to believe that this warlike atmosphere explains the decision Marcus seems to make in Book II to concentrate on the practice of those spiritual exercises which would help him finally to live the philosophical life which he should have lived, and would have liked to live, all throughout his life.

Although I have no proof, I suspect that the manuscript which was copied by the *editio princeps* contained other indications of this kind, which were omitted by the editor. Thus, we do not know where the other books were composed. Are we to suppose, with Breithaupt,[49] that the books which deal with the court and with speeches to the Senate were written between November 176 and August 178, after Marcus had returned to Rome? But already at Carnutum, Marcus could very well have thought in a general way about his life as an emperor. It is very likely that Books IV to XII were written between 173 and 180, when Marcus died.

Let us return to the indication placed between Books I and II: "Written in the land of the Quadi, on the banks of the Gran, I." How can we explain the number I, if this indication refers to Book II? What is now Book I, in which Marcus, in a style wholly different from that of the *Meditations* properly so called (Books II–XII) evokes all that he has received from men and from the gods, seems to be a text in its own right, which has its own unity, and which was placed at the beginning of the *Meditations,* if not by Marcus himself, then at least by an ancient editor. Thus, what is now Book II was in fact the first book of the *Meditations* properly so called.[50] This would explain the number I after the indication "Written in the land of the Quadi"; it must have been introduced by an editor or a secretary who had numbered the various groups of notes which Marcus had written.

Moreover, it is legitimate to suppose—although it cannot be proved with certainty—that what is now Book I was written very late in the Emperor's life. This book gives the impression that it speaks only of people who have died. Since the Empress Faustina, who is mentioned in these pages,[51] died in 176, it seems that this book was written between 176 and 180. Perhaps it was written at Rome between 176 and 178, after the revolt of Avidius Cassius, when Marcus returned from his great eastern voyage; or perhaps it was at Sirmium, Marcus' headquarters from

178 to 180, when war with the Germans broke out again. It was probably at Sirmium that Marcus died, on March 17, 180. The present-day Book I, which has a marked unity with regard both to its style and to its overall structure, seems alien to the literary project of the *Meditations* properly so called (Books II–XII). It is now located at the beginning like a kind of introduction, but it is really more of a parallel work; it is obviously related to the *Meditations* (in Book VI, 30, for example, we can discern an initial sketch of the portrait of Antoninus Pius), but it represents a wholly different psychic disposition. Book I is a prayer of thanksgiving, whereas Books II to XII are a meditation on the Stoic dogmas and rule of life. These latter books were composed on a day-to-day basis, with each thought following without any connection to the previous thought; whereas Book I was written at a precise moment, and in accordance with a precise plan.

Books II–XII

As discussed previously, it is not certain whether the twelve books as we have them today corresponded to twelve groups of meditations which, in the eyes of their author, had their own unity, defined by one or more dominant themes. In that case, they would allow us to glimpse something of Marcus' personal preoccupations, or of what he happened to be reading. Or is this grouping into twelve books purely accidental, perhaps a result of the form and dimensions of the writing materials that were used? Book I obviously represents a coherent whole in itself; it responds to a very particular intention and is independent from the eleven other books. What can we say about Books II–XII?

At first glance, the divisions between these groups of meditations seem purely arbitrary. The same themes and expressions are repeated throughout them. The tripartite structure of the disciplines which I have described has no influence on the work's literary form; instead, it is repeated in the most varied forms. A precise plan cannot be discerned in any of these books, with the possible exception of Book III, which turns out to be a kind of series of essays on the theme of the good man.

Nevertheless, a close examination allows us to discover some characteristics which are peculiar to each of these books: favorite themes, special vocabularies, the greater or lesser frequency of the literary forms that are used—whether they are sayings, for example, or rather short dissertations. We are justified in supposing that if Marcus wrote his *Meditations* on a day-to-day basis, and probably during the last years of his life, then certain spiritual preoccupations or readings may have influenced him in different ways at different moments in the process of composition.

The preferred themes in a given book often appear by means of a process that I would call "interwoven composition." Marcus does not gather together one after the other those meditations which deal with the same subject; instead—probably on a day-to-day basis—he interweaves them with other thoughts which deal with entirely different subjects. In other words, after an interruption, which may be very brief, he returns to the theme which, for the time being, has retained his attention. Throughout a given book, then, one or more precise themes reappear intermittently, like a leitmotif.

Books II and III are very close to each other. Within them, death is sensed as imminent (II, 2; II, 5; II, 6; II, 11; II, 12; II, 14; II, 17), and there is no more time to distract oneself by reading (II, 2; 3). Marcus decides not to write anything more which does not contribute to the transformation of his moral life and to his meditation on Stoic doctrines (III, 14). It is urgent that he change his life, especially since he has received so many reprieves from the gods (II, 14). Only one thing counts: philosophy (II, 17, 3), which consists of the three disciplines. First, it means keeping the guiding principle of the soul (hēgemonikon; II, 2, 4), or—another way of expressing the same thing—the soul (II, 6) or else the inner daimōn (II, 17, 4; II, 13, 2), free from the slavery of false thoughts (II, 2, 4). This is the discipline of thought or judgment. Second, the soul must be kept pure of all irritation against events, and accept the portion which has been attributed to it by destiny (II, 2, 4; II, 16, 1–2; II, 17, 4); this is the discipline of desire. Finally, it must be kept pure of all egoistic action, or actions which are undertaken lightly or without a goal (II, 2, 4; II, 17; 4); this is the discipline of action.

Book III takes up exactly the same themes. We find in it the same atmosphere of the imminence of death, and Marcus' decision to devote himself exclusively to spiritual exercises intended to transform moral life:

Cease your wandering. Don't read your little notebooks any more (III, 14).

We also re-encounter the description of the one thing necessary, and the only thing that counts in such an urgent situation: to maintain the purity of one's daimōn or guiding principle, in the areas of thought, desire, and action.

It is very interesting, however, to observe how Book III attempts to present these themes from Book II in a much more developed and elaborate way, so that Book III is essentially made up of a series of short dissertations which are all on the same topic: the description of the "good man" as an ideal for life, and the enumeration of those precepts which permit the realization of such an ideal (III, 9–11). An initial attempt is presented in III, 4 (in about forty lines), then briefly taken up again in III, 5 (for about ten lines), and then finally set forth abundantly once again in III, 6–8 (in about forty lines). The "good man," who has preferred his inner *daimōn* in every circumstance, and is in some way its priest and its servant, attains the supreme level of human happiness, which consists in acting in accordance with right reason (III, 7, 2).

Books IV–XII are rather different from the two preceding books. First of all, even if we do sometimes find short dissertations of the same kind as those in Book III, especially in Books V, X, and XI, the majority of meditations in these books appear in the form of short, striking sayings. Marcus himself seems to theorize about this literary genre when he mentions the "spiritual retreat into himself," which consists precisely in the act of concentrating on "short and fundamental" sayings which can dissipate all grief and irritation (IV, 3, 1–3).

Some themes from Books II–III are still present in Book IV: for instance, the theme of the imminence of death and the ideal of the "good man" (IV, 17; cf. IV, 25; 37):

> Don't live as if you were going to live for ten thousand years. The inevitable is hanging over you. As long as you are still alive, and as long at it is still possible, become a good man.

As in the previous books, this sense of urgency does not allow Marcus to waste his time by concerning himself with what others do or say (IV, 18); rather, one must hasten toward the goal by the shortest path possible (IV, 18; 51).

The notion of the *daimōn* disappears almost completely in the later books, and reappears in the *Meditations* only sporadically (V, 10, 6; V, 27; VIII, 45, 1; X, 13, 2; XII, 3, 4). By contrast, new themes, which will be found throughout all the following books, make their appearance. For example, we find the dilemma "Providence or atoms" (IV, 3, 6), which I have already discussed at some length.

In Book V, the themes which had dominated Books II and III disappear or become blurred once and for all. In particular, although death is sometimes still mentioned as a possibility which might compromise our efforts toward perfection, it is now also present as a liberation for which we must wait with patience and confidence; for it will deliver us from a human world in which moral life—the only thing that counts, and the only value—is constantly frustrated (V, 10, 6; V, 33, 5).

In another new theme, Marcus exhorts himself to examine his conscience (V, 11):

> Toward which goal am I using my soul in this moment? Ask myself this question in every circumstance . . .

Similarly, he wonders (V, 31) how he has behaved with regard to the gods, his family, his teachers, his friends, and his slaves. Here we recognize the domain of "duties" *(kathēkonta),* which are the subject of the discipline of action. Marcus continues by sketching a kind of balance sheet of his life (V, 31, 2), which, as in V, 10, 6 and V, 33, 5, gives us to understand that he can wait for death with serenity, since he has had everything he could expect from life.

One particular notion, to which Book II had made only a brief allusion (II, 9), is amply and frequently developed in Book V: the distinction between universal Nature and "my" own nature. As we have seen, this distinction is the basis of the opposition between the discipline of desire, which consists in consenting to the fact that I "suffer" owing to the action of universal Nature, and the discipline of action, which consists in "acting" by virtue of my own rational nature (V, 3, 2; V, 10, 6; V, 25, 2; V, 27):

> In this very moment, I have what common Nature wants me to have at this moment, and at this moment I am doing what my own nature wants me to do at this moment (V, 25, 2).

As Marcus says, the road that these two natures follow is, in fact, the same (V, 3, 2); it is the straightest and shortest road. It is here, moreover, that the notion of the *daimōn* briefly reappears, and it is extremely interesting to observe an identification and an opposition between the "outer" god, who is universal Nature or Reason, and the "inner" god— the *daimōn* or *hēgemonikon*—who emanates from it (V, 10, 6):

> Nothing will happen to me which is not in conformity with the Nature of the All. It depends on me to do nothing which is contrary to my god and my *daimōn*.

This is why moral life can be defined as "a life with the gods" (V, 27):

> He lives with the gods who constantly shows them a soul which
> greets what has been allotted to it with joy, and, at the same time,
> does everything wanted by that *daimōn* which Zeus [i.e., universal
> Nature] has given to each person as a watchman and a guide, and
> which is a parcel detached from himself. This is nothing other than
> the intellect and reason of each of us.

This theme of the two natures is found in other books (VI, 58; VII, 55, 1;
XI, 13, 4; XII, 32, 3), but never as frequently as in Book V.

Other themes also seem to be characteristic of Book V. For example, it
contains two allusions to a Stoic cosmological doctrine which Marcus
mentions very rarely: that of the eternal return. Usually, Marcus imagines
the metamorphoses of things and the destiny of souls within the "period"
of the world in which we are now living, without worrying about the
eternal return of this period. This is what he does first, in V, 13, where he
begins by affirming that each part of the universe, as it is born and dies, is
transformed into another part of the universe. Yet he remarks:

> There is nothing to prevent one from talking like this, even if the
> world is administered in accordance with determinate periods.

In this case, he means, all the parts of the universe will be reabsorbed at
the end of each period into the original Fire-Reason, before they are
reborn from this same Fire in the following period. Elsewhere, in V, 32,
we get a glimpse of the immensity of the space that opens up before the
soul which "knows"—that is, which accepts Stoic doctrine:

> It knows the beginning and the end, and the Reason which tra-
> verses universal substance, and which administers the All through-
> out eternity, in accordance with determinate periods.

We do not find another allusion to the eternal return until XI, 1, 3.

Finally, an important autobiographical theme also makes its appearance in Book V: the opposition, which constitutes a serious personal
problem for Marcus, between the court at which he is obliged to live,
and philosophy, to which he would like to devote himself entirely (V, 16,
2). This theme will be taken up again in Book VI (12, 2), and in Book
VIII (9).

The first meditations of Book VI present a good example of the "interwoven composition" of which I have been speaking. Chapter 1 deals with the Stoic doctrine that explains the constitution of reality by the opposition between the matter of the world—which is docile and ready for any and all transformations, and in which there is therefore no evil—and the "Reason which guides it," in which there is similarly no place for evil. After three very short meditations, which have no connection with this problem, Marcus returns (VI, 5) to the theme of the beginning: the action which the "Reason which guides" exerts upon matter. The expression "Reason which guides/governs" *(dioikōn logos)*, which is attested in VI, 1 and 5, is not found elsewhere in the *Meditations,* with the exception of a quotation from Heraclitus in IV, 46, 3. One could say that it is as if this book's first meditations were inspired by a reading which dealt with the goodness of that Reason which governs matter.

Some personal features also appear in Book VI. For instance, Marcus mentions (VI, 26) his own name, Antoninus, which he received after having been adopted by Antoninus Pius. He also makes a distinction within himself, as it were, between "Antoninus," the Emperor whose city is Rome, and the "man," whose city is the World (VI, 44, 6). Marcus takes up this distinction between Emperor and man again in VI, 30, and he advises himself not to "become Caesarized," or let the imperial purple rub off on the man. He then turns to the model which Antoninus Pius, his adoptive father, had represented for him. Advising himself to "Do everything as a disciple of Antoninus," Marcus describes some of the qualities he admired in Antoninus, which may guide him in his way of governing and living.

Even more than Book VI, Book VII gives a number of examples of "interwoven composition." Marcus returns to a few favorite, recurrent themes, which, although they are present in other books as well, reappear with regularity from one end of Book VII to the other, separated from each other only by a few meditations which deal with other subjects. Thus, he repeats several times that we have the power to criticize and to modify the value-judgments which we apply to things (VII, 2, 2; VII, 14; VII, 16; VII, 17, 2; VII, 68); that things are subject to rapid and universal metamorphosis (VII, 10; VII, 18; VII, 19; VII, 23; VII, 25); that it is vain to seek for fame and glory (VII, 6; VII, 10; VII, 21; VII, 62). Marcus also speaks of how we are to behave and the principles we must recall when someone has committed a fault against us (VII, 22; VII, 26); and finally, he exalts the excellence and the supremacy of moral life (that is to say, of the three disciplines), by comparison with all other qualities (VII, 52; VII, 66–67; VII, 72).

Chapters 31 to 51 are extremely interesting because they seem to have preserved for us traces of the notebooks Marcus wrote for himself. These quotations from various authors—Democritus (VII, 31, 4), Plato (VII, 35; VII, 44–46), Antisthenes, and Euripides (VII, 38–42; VII, 50–51)— are probably secondhand. For example, Marcus probably read the following quote from Antisthenes, "To do good and yet to have a bad reputation is something which kings can expect," in the *Discourses* of Epictetus as recorded by Arrian (see IV, 6, 20). It was all the more likely to attract Marcus' attention in that it may have seemed to him to reflect his own experience. The quotations from Euripides, for their part, frequently appeared in collections of sayings. In another book (XI, 6), Marcus composes a brief history of the dramatic art, alluding successively to tragedy, old comedy, and new comedy. In the context of tragedy, Marcus notes that tragedians gave useful moral lessons, and he quotes the same three texts from Euripides—in which the Stoics recognized their own doctrine—which we find in chapters 38, 40, and 41 of Book VII:

If the gods have abandoned me, as well as my children, there is a reason for that as well.

We must not become angry with things, for it is not their fault.

To harvest life like a swollen ear of grain; one exists; the other is no more.

"Interwoven composition" is also used quite abundantly in Book VIII; I shall give only one very typical example. Book VIII marks the reappearance of a theme that we have already encountered: the short, straight path which is proper to nature. Rational human nature follows its path and heads straight for its goal if it practices the three disciplines (VIII, 7). In this book, however, the theme takes on a nuance which it did not have in the others: now Marcus speaks of the rectilinear movement not only of nature, but also of the intellect. Moreover, instead of describing the movement proper to the intellect on one occasion, Marcus returns to it three times in different chapters, and these occurrences are separated by meditations which are unrelated to this subject. He first touches on the theme in chapter 54, where he urges himself to breathe the intellect which embraces all things as if it were the surrounding air: for the power of the intellect, he writes, *is diffused everywhere,* like the air which beings breathe. Then come two chapters—55 and 56—which are unrelated to this theme. The theme reappears in chapter 57, where the movement of the intellect is no longer compared to that of the air, but to that of the light of the sun, which, says Marcus, *is diffused everywhere* and extends *in a straight line* as it illuminates the objects it encounters, thus somehow assimilating them to itself. Then come two other chapters, which deal with entirely different themes. In chapter 60, we return to our familiar theme: here the movement of the intellect is compared to that of an arrow. Like an arrow, the intellect moves *in a straight line* toward its goal when it advances prudently and takes the trouble to examine things attentively. Chapter 54 spoke only of the divine intellect in which we participate, whereas chapters 57 and 60 describe the movement of our intellect as it imitates the divine intellect. It is hard to imagine that Marcus would have thus returned three times to a very specific theme unless he had been under the influence of a particular reading, or at least of a momentary preoccupation. Be that as it may, chapters 54, 57, and 60 are intimately linked to one another.

In Book VIII, the theme of universal metamorphosis takes on a very particular form. Here, Nature has the power to use the detritus which results from its vital activity to create new beings (VIII, 50). Since it has no space outside itself where it can throw this detritus, it transforms it within itself and makes it into its matter once again (VIII, 18). Intellectual or rational nature, for its part, transforms the obstacles that oppose its activity into a subject for exercises, which thereby permits it to attain its goal by using that which resists it (VIII, 7, 2; VIII, 32; VIII, 35; VIII, 41; VIII, 47; VIII, 54; VIII, 57).

We can note a few autobiographical allusions in Book VIII, such as life at court (VIII, 9) and speeches before the Senate (VIII, 30). Figures of the dead who were close to Marcus are evoked: his mother (VIII, 25) and his adoptive brother (VIII, 37). Encouragements to examine his conscience, which had already occurred in Book V, reappear several times (VIII, 1–2) and are linked to the theme of the imminence of death (VIII, 1; VIII, 8; VIII, 22, 2).

Although Book IX, like Books IV, VI, VII, and VIII, is composed for the most part of brief sayings, it does contain five rather long expositions, which vary in length from about thirty to forty lines, and which have either no parallels in the rest of Marcus' works, or at the very least few parallels. In IX, 1, Marcus demonstrates rigorously that the lapses one commits in the three disciplines of action, thought, and desire constitute faults of impiety and injustice with regard to Nature, the most venerable of deities. In IX, 3, we find an exposition on the theme of death: not only does Marcus expect and wait for the dissolution of the body, but, as in Book V, this dissolution is perceived as a liberation. When Marcus speaks of the fatigue produced by discord in communal life (IX, 3, 8), and prays for death to come as soon as possible, we can perhaps detect an autobiographical trait; I shall return to this point later. In IX, 9, reason establishes that the higher up one rises in the hierarchy of beings, the more mutual attraction is increased. In IX, 40, the problem of prayer is examined. Finally, in IX, 42, we find a collection of considerations intended as a remedy for the temptation of anger.

Book IX may also contain some further autobiographical allusions: for example, the rapid evocation of Marcus' childhood (IX, 21); a possible allusion to the plague which was then ravaging the Empire (IX, 2, 4); and above all a highly important reflection on the art of governing (IX, 29).

Book IX also has its own peculiarities of vocabulary. Nowhere else, for instance, does Marcus use the expression *ektos aitia* ("outer cause") to designate the causality of Fate and of universal Nature (IX, 6; IX, 31).

In the entirely different context of the relations between oneself and others, Book IX is the only one to mention the paradigm of the gods, who, despite the faults of mankind, maintain their benevolence toward humans and help them in the area of things which, to the Stoics, are indifferent and have no moral value, such as health and glory, for example (IX, 11; IX, 27). The Emperor, too, will consequently also have to be attentive to those human desires which are not in conformity with philosophy.

Book IX likes to insist upon the necessity of "penetrating into the guiding principle of other people's souls," in order to understand the motives which make them act in a certain way, and therefore excuse them (IX, 18; IX, 22; IX, 27; IX, 34).

In Book X, the number of longer expositions (from thirty to one hundred lines) clearly increases, and we find far fewer examples of "interwoven composition." One should note, however, the recurrence of the theme of a realistic vision of other people (X, 13; 19). In order to judge people in accordance with their true value, we must observe them or imagine them when they eat, sleep, make love, and relieve themselves.

When Marcus evokes the picture of people whispering around a sickbed—which could be his own—we get the impression that the Emperor is sharing a confidence with us when he makes them say: "At last that schoolmaster is going to let us breathe!"

Book X is the only one to use the word *theōrētikon*. It occurs in X, 9, 2, where the importance of the *theoretic* foundations of action is affirmed;

and again in X, 11, 1, where Marcus exhorts himself to acquire a *theoretic* method, in order to practice the spiritual exercise which consists in recognizing the universal metamorphosis of all things; in other words, this exercise must be based upon solid, well-assimilated dogmas. It is also only in Book X that reason and the intellect, which take all events as food for their moral life, are compared to a healthy stomach, which assimilates to itself all kinds of food (X, 31, 6; X, 35, 3).

Book XI can be divided into two parts: there are the first twenty-one chapters, and then there are the final eighteen, which are a collection of quotations and notes jotted down in the course of Marcus' readings, comparable to the similar group which we encountered in the middle of Book VII. Why is it here? It is impossible to say. At least eight of these passages come from the *Discourses* of Epictetus, as collected by Arrian. The rest consists of quotations from Homer and Hesiod, fragments from the tragic poets, and other reminiscences from Marcus' readings.

In the first part of Book XI, long expositions (of which there are fourteen) are much more frequent than short sayings (seven). The phenomenon of "interwoven composition" scarcely appears, and there are few recurrent themes, with the exception of the theme of the freedom which we possess to criticize and to suspend our judgments on events and things. We find this theme in two passages, almost identical in form (XI, 11; XI, 16, 2):

Things do not reach us, but they remain immobile outside of us.

Several of the longer expositions have no parallel in the rest of Marcus' work: the detailed description of the properties of the rational soul (XI, 1), for instance, or the method of division of objects and events (XI, 2); the history of tragedy and comedy (XI, 6), which I mentioned above; the description of the luminous sphere of the soul (XI, 12), as well as that of true sincerity which one cannot help discerning immediately, like a man's bad odor (XI, 15). Finally, there is the long enumeration of the dogmas which can cure us of anger (XI, 18). By its content and its form, then, Book XI is rather different from the other books of the *Meditations*.

Book XII also has its characteristic expressions. "Stripped of their bark" *(gumna tōn phloiōn),* for instance, recurs twice in it. On the one hand, divine vision sees the guiding principles of souls "stripped of their bark" (XII, 2); on the other, we must exercise ourselves in order to be able to see the elements of those beings which have causal force—in other words, none other than the guiding principles of souls—"stripped of their bark" (XII, 8). The theme of the separation of the center of the soul from all its envelopes is, moreover, one of the major motifs of the *Meditations.* We find it sketched as early as the first chapter, where we are urged not to recognize anything but the *hēgemonikon,* or guiding principle of the soul, as the sole thing of value. The theme is developed in chapter 2 (like God himself, see nothing but the *hēgemonikon*), and in chapter 3 (separate everything foreign from the intellect, the faculty of thought, and the guiding principle of the soul). We find it again in chapter 8 (see those elements which have causal value—that is, the guiding principles of souls—stripped of their bark); in chapter 19 (become aware of what is most noble and divine within us); and finally, in chapter 33, where the Emperor asks himself about the use he is making of the guiding part of his soul, for "Everything depends upon that."

We have just encountered the notion of an "element having a causal value" *(aitiōdes).* For Marcus, this concept is opposed to the notion of a material element *(hulikon).* As we have seen, this is one of the fundamental oppositions of Stoic physics. For Marcus, however, it serves above all to formulate a spiritual exercise which is described again and again in Book XII: it consists in the intellect or guiding part of the soul becoming aware of itself as a causal, guiding, determining element, so that it may distinguish and separate itself from the material element. In other words, it must separate itself not only from the body, but from everything that does not depend upon us. This is why the theme of the opposition between the "causal" and the "material" also recurs constantly in Book XII (XII, 8; XII, 10; XII, 18; XII, 29).

The preceding brief analyses—no doubt somewhat tedious—should allow the reader to glimpse the fact that in almost all the books of the *Meditations,* a characteristic vocabulary and recurrent themes can be discovered. This leads us to suspect that each chapter forms a comparatively autonomous unity. Although it is true that there are many literal repetitions throughout the *Meditations,* it is nevertheless also true that particularities can be observed that are proper to each chapter.

The final three chapters of Book XII, which are also those of the entire work, are concerned with death. The last chapter, which is in the form of a dialogue, thus seems particularly moving (XII, 36):

O man, you have played your part as a citizen in this great City! What does it matter to you whether you have played it for five, or for one hundred years? For that which is distributed in accordance with the law is equal for all. What is there that is terrible if you are sent away from this City, not by a tyrant or an unjust judge, but by that Nature who had put you on stage in the first place, as a praetor dismisses an actor he has hired?

—But I acted only three acts, and not five!

—You are right; but in life three acts make up a complete play; for what makes the play complete is determined by He who is the cause both of constitution and of dissolution. You, by contrast, are cause neither of the one nor of the other. Leave, then, in peace; for He who dismisses you does so in peace.

It has been claimed[52] that the *Meditations* deliberately end with the word "peace." Perhaps; but who placed it there? Was it Marcus, foreseeing his imminent death? Was it the person who edited his meditations, and removed one from its place to put it there? These words are, moreover, an echo of the first pages of Book II (3, 3): "Don't die murmuring, but truly in peace, thanking the gods from the bottom of your heart."

We can thus see—in an entirely hypothetical way—that some kind of order and specific correspondences have perhaps been introduced among these eleven books (II–XII), which are groups of meditations written on a daily basis. It could no doubt be objected that in a work in which the thought of death plays so considerable a role, it is not surprising to encounter it—whether in the first or the last lines—without this indicating any kind of stylistic composition. One might also wonder, however, why at the beginnings of Books III, VIII, X, and XII, we find examinations of conscience which are all analogously inspired by the imminence of death. They are situated in a rather privileged position, as if the author or editor had wanted to provide a kind of introduction to the following meditations. In these examinations, Marcus exhorts himself to immediate conversion, for he is afraid that even before death, his intellectual capacities may be weakened to the point where they no longer allow him to live a moral life. He is still far from having succeeded in becoming a philosopher, and he recognizes that, in the last analysis, what he should fear the most is not ceasing to live, but failing to begin to live (XII, 1, 5). This is the source of Marcus' melancholy question at the beginning of Book X:

O my soul; will you ever be good and simple; one and naked; more luminous than the body which surrounds you? Will you ever be fulfilled, without need, neither regretting nor desiring anything . . .

Will you ever be happy with what is happening to you at the present moment?

Generally speaking, a short saying is never placed at the beginning of a book. Books II–XII always open with a relatively lengthy exposition, which can vary from five to thirty-five lines. Books II and V both begin with an exercise which is to be practiced in the morning: "At dawn . . ."; "In the morning, when you have trouble getting up . . ." The comparatively long dissertations on the rational soul (XI, 1) and on impiety with regard to nature (IX, 1) also seem to have been placed at the beginning of these books because of the importance of the subject matter with which they deal.

As I have said, the frequent repetitions which can be observed in the *Meditations* allow us to suppose that they were composed on a day-to-day basis. The slight indications which I have just enumerated, however, perhaps allow us to glimpse some of Marcus' habits—for instance, that of beginning a new notebook with a specific type of exhortation. In any event, I have thought it worthwhile to point out such details in the hope that they may inspire more in-depth research.

Remembering the dead

As we have seen, the *Meditations* are dominated, from one end to the other, by the thought of death. Within the work, death appears successively as an imminence which may prevent Marcus from finally raising himself up to the level of the philosophical life; or as a phenomenon of nature which is no more extraordinary than any other; and finally as a liberation, which will deliver Marcus from a world where people are ignorant of the sole value: that of virtue and the moral good.

From beginning to end, the *Meditations* are also an exercise of preparation for death, which involves, among other things, evoking famous figures of bygone times, who, in spite of their power, knowledge, and renown, died like everybody else. Just like François Villon, Marcus thus composes his *Ballad of the Lords of Former Times*. To be sure, it was too early for Marcus to wonder: "But where is the knight Charlemagne?"[53] Yet he does mention Alexander—as well as his mule-driver—Archimedes, Augustus, Caesar, Chrysippus, Croesus, Democritus, Epictetus, Eudoxus, Heraclitus, Hipparchus, Hippocrates, Menippus, Philip, Pompey, Pythagoras, Socrates, Tiberius, Trajan, and all those

who are now no more than legendary names (VIII, 25, 3) or are mentioned only rarely: Caeso, Volesus, Dentatus, Scipio, and Cato. He also
speaks of people who are less noble, but did have their moment of fame,
like the mimographers Philistion, Phoebus, and Origanion (VI, 47, 1).
Marcus also thinks of the whole crowd of anonymous people: doctors,
astrologers, philosophers, princes, and tyrants of bygone days; as well as
the people of Pompeii (IV, 48, 1; VIII, 1, 2) and Herculaneum. Finally,
he thinks of all the people who lived in the time of Vespasian or Trajan:
they have all been swept away by death.

Marcus also thinks of the people he knew during his life. His adoptive
brother Lucius Verus, who reigned together with Marcus, died comparatively young. He had married Lucilla, one of Marcus' daughters; but
before this marriage, when he was staying at Antioch, he had a mistress
named Pantheia. Pantheia was from Smyrna, and she was delightfully
portrayed by the satirist Lucian in 163–164. She figures in two of his
works: *Images* and the *Defense of Images*. Was she really as beautiful,
cultivated, good-hearted, simple, sweet, and benevolent as Lucian says?
And yet, unless he was mocking her, Lucian could scarcely have made up
such details as that she sang while accompanying herself on the cithara;
that she spoke Ionic Greek; that she behaved modestly and simply to
those who approached her; and that she knew how to laugh at Lucian's
praise. What happened to Pantheia after the marriage of Lucilla? Did she
remain in the entourage of Lucius, who, if we can believe the gossip of
the *Historia Augusta,* seems not to have had any qualms about bringing
back from Antioch to Rome a band of freed slaves, with whom he
caroused?[54]

In any event, it is rather touching to encounter the figure of Pantheia
in the *Meditations*. This allows us to suppose that she had remained close
to Lucius Verus until his death, and that she herself had died a few years
after her lover (VIII, 37):

> Are Pantheia and Pergamos [perhaps a male lover of Lucius Verus?]
> still sitting near the ashes of Verus?
>   Or Chabrias and Diotimos near those of Hadrian?
>   How ridiculous! [probably because they too were dead].
> And even if they were still sitting there, would the dead notice
> them? And if the dead noticed them, would they derive pleasure
> from their presence? And if the dead did derive some pleasure,
> would those who were sitting there be immortal? Has it not been
> fixed by Destiny that those who were sitting there should first

become old women and men, and finally die? What will happen to the dead, when those who had been sitting near their ashes are dead too?

This same Book VIII describes analogous situations, in which living people weep for the dead, and are themselves wept over shortly afterwards (VIII, 25): Marcus' mother Lucilla, who lost her husband Verus, and then died in turn; Secunda, the wife of Maximus, one of Marcus' friends and teachers, who died after having buried Maximus; Antoninus, Marcus' adoptive father, who decreed the apotheosis of his wife Faustina, and then did not survive her for long. Marcus also evokes Caninius Celer,[55] one of his rhetoric teachers, who had been secretary to the emperor Hadrian, and who had perhaps delivered the latter's funeral oration. He too was dead by the time Marcus was writing. In this context we also find a certain Diotimos, no doubt a freedman of Hadrian, and the same person whom Marcus had pictured sitting near Hadrian's funeral urn in the description cited above (VIII, 37).

Elsewhere, Marcus again causes all kinds of characters whom he has known to come to life before our eyes; but it is difficult for us to identify them.

It is especially in Book I that Marcus evokes the dead who had been close to him: his parents, his teachers, Antoninus Pius, his adoptive brother Lucius Verus, and the Empress Faustina. There is no melancholy in these pages, which retain only the virtues of the beings whom the Emperor has known and loved. Yet we cannot help feeling that the Emperor is thinking nostalgically of those whom he has loved, and whose departure has left him profoundly alone.

The "Confessions" of Marcus Aurelius

There is a sense in which Book I represents Marcus' "Confessions," in the way that there are "Confessions" of Saint Augustine: not the more or less indecent confessions of a Jean-Jacques Rousseau, but an act of thanks for the benefits one has received from gods and men.[56] The book ends with the following formula:

All this requires the help of the gods and of Good Fortune.

This remark refers especially to chapter 17, which enumerates all the special favors which the gods have granted; but it also applies to the entire book, for it is thanks to the "help of the gods and of Good Fortune" that Marcus thinks he has been lucky enough to have the parents, teachers, and friends that he has had.

Book I has a most peculiar structure. In sixteen chapters of unequal length, the Emperor evokes sixteen people to whom Destiny has related him. They have each been the example for him of specific virtues, either generally or in a given circumstance; or else they have given him a piece of advice which has had a strong influence upon him. The seventeenth chapter enumerates the benefits which the gods have showered upon him throughout his life, by making him meet a certain person or experience a particular event. There is thus often an echo between the first sixteen chapters and the seventeenth.

The first chapters provide a sketch, as it were, of the history of a life which has been a spiritual itinerary. First comes childhood, surrounded by the tutelary figures of Marcus' grandfather, Annius Verus; his father, who died so young; his mother; his great-grandfather, Catilius Severus; his tutor; and a certain Diognetus.

Then we have the discovery of philosophy, with Junius Rusticus, and Marcus' teachers Apollonius and Sextus. This part of his life is so important to Marcus that he inverts chronological order, by placing his grammar teacher, Alexander of Cotiaeum, and his rhetoric teacher, Fronto, after the philosophers. Then Marcus moves on to his friends and loved ones, whom he evokes because they have either been models for him, or philosophy teachers: there was Alexander the Platonist, who was his secretary for Greek correspondence; the Stoic Cinna Catulus; Claudius Severus, of whom Marcus remembers especially what he learned from him about the heroes of Republican Rome; and another statesman, the Stoic Claudius Maximus. Chapter 16 contains a lengthy portrait of the emperor Antoninus Pius. By living with him for twenty-three years— from the age of seventeen until he became emperor at the age of forty— Marcus had been able to observe his adoptive father at length, and to be profoundly influenced by him.

In the course of the enumeration in chapter 17 of the favors which the gods have granted Marcus, some of these characters reappear, especially Antoninus Pius, Marcus' relatives, his mother, and three philosopher-friends: Apollonius, Rusticus, and Maximus. He also evokes his grandfather's concubine, and two "temptations" named Benedicta and Theodotus; as well as his adoptive brother Lucius Verus, and Marcus' wife, the Empress Faustina.

In all likelihood, other people had also played a crucial role in Marcus'

life. One thinks, for example, of Herodes Atticus, the "ancient billion-
aire."[57] This renowned rhetor, such a powerful figure in Athens, had
been Marcus' rhetoric teacher; but he does not appear in Book I. In this
particular case, there could be two reasons for such silence. In the first
place, Herodes was a shady character. Marcus had a great deal of affection
for him, and guided him through the two trials in which Herodes was
implicated, particularly in 174, when Herodes was summoned to the
Emperor's headquarters at Sirmium on charges brought against him by
the Athenians.[58] Nevertheless, Marcus could hardly fail to recognize that
Herodes was scarcely a model for the philosophical life. Another reason
for Marcus' silence could possibly be that the Emperor seems to talk only
about the dead in Book I, whereas Herodes did not die until 179. We
might thus suppose that Book I was written between 176 and 179,
perhaps at Rome in 177 or 178.

To understand the way Marcus wrote Book I, it will perhaps be
sufficient to examine how he evokes the figure of Fronto, his Latin
rhetoric teacher. When we read the correspondence exchanged between
Fronto and Marcus, we get the impression of an intimate friendship, with
a perpetual exchange of ideas, advice, and favors. Thus, one would
expect Book I to contain a lengthy couplet on Marcus' venerated
teacher. Yet the Emperor devotes only three lines to him, whereas he
uses thirteen lines to speak of his debt toward Rusticus. What has Marcus
retained from all those years of working intimacy with Fronto? Only two
things, which have nothing to do with rhetoric (I, 11):

> To have learned how tyranny leads to envious evil, to caprices, and
> to dissimulation; and how, on the whole, those whom we call
> "patricians" are somehow lacking in affectionateness.

Marcus' remark about the patricians is indeed attested in his correspondence with Fronto; and this allows us to glimpse that behind each
one of Marcus' notes, there is certainly a precise matter of fact. For
instance, Fronto writes to the emperor Lucius Verus, in order to recommend to him one of his students, Gavius Clarus. He praises Gavius'
conscientiousness, modesty, reserve, generosity, simplicity, continence,
truthfulness, and entirely Roman uprightness:

> . . . I don't know if his affectionateness *(philostorgia)* is Roman, for in
> all my life at Rome, there is nothing I have found less often than a
> man having sincere affectionateness. I would not be surprised if,

since there is really no one to be found at Rome who has affection-
ateness, there is no Latin word to designate this virtue.[59]

When he writes to the proconsul Lollianus Avitus to recommend
Licinius Montanus to him, Fronto uses an analogous enumeration: "He
is sober, honest, tender in his affections *(philostorgus)* . . ." And he notes
once again that there is no Latin word for that quality.[60] When Marcus
writes to his teacher in Latin, he addresses him in Greek as *philostorge
anthrōpe,* as if there were indeed no Latin equivalent for this Greek
word.[61] We may wonder whether this remark does not contain a hint of
resentment on the part of the provincial *homo novus* Fronto with regard
to the old Roman aristocracy. In any case, Fronto's remark struck Marcus, and we may suppose that he too sensed a lack of tenderness of the
heart in the ruling class. In the *Meditations,* Marcus exhorts himself several times to be affectionate (VI, 30, 2; II, 5, 1; XI, 18, 18), while in Book
I he notes the *philostorgia* of his teacher Sextus.

With regard to Marcus' remarks on tyranny as a corruption of monarchy which consists in profiting from power for one's own pleasure: we
possess no text by Fronto that might shed light on this allusion. It may
have come from a conversation they had, or from a Latin literary text
relative to this theme which Marcus had studied together with his
teacher. At any rate, the Emperor retained the idea that the egotistical
exercise of power leads to evil, inconstancy, and dissimulation. As R. B.
Rutherford has rightly pointed out,[62] Marcus was particularly affected by
this idea because, as Emperor, he was the precisely the one who could
easily become a tyrant. Marcus was a "potential tyrant," and on several
occasions the *Meditations* ask him to question himself in order to see
whether he does not have a tyrannical soul. This is particularly the case in
IV, 28, which may be understood as a kind of description of the tyrannical character:

A dark character: effeminate, harsh, savage, bestial, puerile, cow-
ardly, false, foolish, mercenary, and tyrannical.

Elsewhere, such tyrants as Phalaris and Nero appear as yanked about by
their disorderly tendencies, like wild, androgynous beasts (III, 16).

From his long familiarity with Fronto, then, Marcus either can or will
retain no more than two items of moral instruction. He evokes no virtue
or character trait of Fronto's worthy of being mentioned.

This means that Book I is not a collection of recollections in which the Emperor causes those he has known to live again just as they were. Rather, it is a kind of precise record of those who have played a role in his life. The very style of the book makes it resemble the inventory of an inheritance, or an acknowledgement of debt.[63] At the beginning of each chapter, we first have a kind of label: "From my grandfather Verus . . .," "From my mother . . .," "From Sextus . . .," "From Fronto . . ." Then the qualities Marcus admires are enumerated, as are the teachings he has received and the exemplary actions performed. Grammatically, all this is expressed by neuter adjectives used substantively, or by an infinitive proposition; there are hardly any personally inflected verbs. Marcus does not say, "From my grandfather, I admired . . .," or "I retained," or "I learned"; but rather "From my grandfather Verus: good character and lack of anger." Thus, this balance-sheet concerns the virtues which Marcus saw practiced, the advice he heard, specific actions and significant examples which made an impression on him, and finally the benefits which he received.

In the case of some of the figures Marcus evokes, their personality disappears completely behind the advice they have given to the Emperor. Marcus mentions no particular virtue in the case of his tutor, or of Diognetus, or of Rusticus, or of Fronto. This does not mean that they did not possess any moral qualities, but that it was not by means of such qualities that they influenced Marcus. What "made" Marcus Aurelius were, for instance, the reprimands about his character addressed to him by Rusticus, or the fact that he communicated to him Epictetus' *Discourses*.

In the case of some other figures, such as that of his mother, the Emperor evokes only those virtues which were obviously exemplary for him (I, 3):

From my mother: piety; a disposition to give generously; and a horror not only of doing evil, but even of thinking about doing evil. In addition, frugality in my daily routine, far removed from the life-style of the rich.

The same holds true for Claudius Maximus, whose entire personality was exemplary for Marcus: self-mastery; peace of mind in adversity; gentleness and dignity; reflection in the carrying out of a project; harmony between words, actions, and moral conscience; the quality of not being surprised by anything, of fearing nothing, and of remaining self-identical; beneficence; indulgence; veracity; spontaneity in action; and the art of joking.

Finally, there are those of whom Marcus has remembered both the teachings and the virtues, such as Severus, who was beneficent, liberal, and free-speaking, but who also caused Marcus to discover the entire philosophical tradition of resistance to tyranny.

Through this catalogue of virtues and of teachings, an outline of Marcus' life itself is traced. Thus, thanks to his great-grandfather, he benefited from instruction at home; thanks to his tutor, he learned not to get caught up in the partisan battles of fans of the Greens and the Whites—factions of the circus games—and not to get excited about any particular group of gladiators. Diognetus turned him away from futilities, superstitions, and playing with quails, and instilled in him a taste for a Spartan life-style. Rusticus showed him the need to correct his character: as he taught him philosophy, he also prevented Marcus from getting carried away by enthusiasm for writing theoretical or hortatory philo-sophical tracts, and from falling into ostentatious asceticism. Rusticus made him give up rhetoric and poetry, and taught him simplicity of style, particularly by the example of a letter he had written to Marcus' mother. He taught Marcus how to read philosophical texts, and, most important, passed on to him some notes taken at the classes of Epictetus. More than any precise teachings, the Emperor retained the examples of how to live given him by his other philosophy teachers, Apollonius and Sextus.

From Alexander the grammarian, Marcus learned the art of repri-manding people without annoying them, and of making them aware of their faults indirectly. By frequenting Alexander "the Platonist," his sec-retary for Greek correspondence, the Emperor learned not to try to get out of his duties toward other people by claiming that one has no time to reply to letters. In the case of Marcus' three friends Catulus, Severus, and Maximus, it was especially their virtues which were exemplary; but Marcus owed Severus the discovery of an entire political attitude: the monarchy's respect for the freedom of its subjects. I shall return to this point.

Finally, there was the encounter with Antoninus, who, in his entire behavior, revealed to the future Emperor the features of the ideal ruler.

Chapter 17, which celebrates the benefits which the gods have show-ered upon him, gives Marcus the opportunity to go over the stages of his life once again. After the death of his father, the young Marcus lived briefly in the house of his grandfather, Annius Verus. It seems that this was a time of temptations for Marcus, and he thanks the gods for not having been brought up for too long with my grandfather's concubine; for having been able to maintain the bloom of my youth; for not having reached manhood too soon, but having even gone past the time for that.

Then comes youth, the time of Marcus' adoption by the emperor Antoninus Pius, at the age of seventeen (in 138). Once again, the main discovery which Marcus made then was that of simplicity (I, 17, 5):

to have been subject to a ruler who was to take away from me every trace of pride, and give me the idea that it was possible to live at court without any bodyguards, nor conspicuous dress, nor the lamps and statues which go along with it; nor in general with any of this kind of pomp; but that one may very well restrict oneself to a kind of life very close to that of a private citizen, without thereby becoming base or indifferent toward devoting oneself like a sovereign to what must be done for the public good.

His adoption would give Marcus an adoptive brother, Lucius Verus (I, 17, 6); and Marcus thanks the gods for having made him meet

such a brother, who, by his character, could awaken me to take care of myself, and who, at the same time, made me happy by his deference and his affection.

Soon would come Marcus' marriage to Faustina (in 145), which Marcus mentions further on. At the moment, he thinks of his children, "who were neither ungifted nor misshapen."

This was also the time of his rhetorical studies with Fronto and Herodes Atticus, but Marcus makes no allusion to them in this chapter. Too much success in this field would have taken him away from philosophy, but here again the gods were watchful (I, 17, 8):

Not to have made too much progress in rhetoric, poetry, and the other occupations, by which I might have been caught up, if I had felt that I was making good progress in them.

In any case, Marcus has, thanks to the gods, done everything to repay his teachers (I, 17, 9):

To have hurried to establish my teachers in the honorific positions which it seemed to me they wanted, and not to have left them in the mere hope that I would do it later, since they were still young.

Finally comes the main point: philosophy and its practice (I, 17, 10):

To have known Apollonius, Rusticus, and Maximus. To have had clear and frequent representations of the "life according to nature," so that, insofar as it depends on the gods and on the communications, assistance, and inspirations which come from above, nothing now prevents me from living "according to nature"; but I am far from that point by my own fault, because I pay no attention to the reminders, or rather to the teachings, which come from the gods.

Thus, divine graces helped Marcus to practice philosophy, and also to resist the temptations of luxuriousness and anger, as well as the fatigue of the imperial life (I, 17, 12):

That my body has resisted such a life for so long.

This brief remark perhaps allows us to glimpse the hardships which Marcus endured while on the Danubian campaign.

Not to have touched Benedicta or Theodotus; and later on, when I did fall prey to erotic passions, that I was cured.

Marcus was not the impassive Stoic that many have imagined. There were, of course, his youthful infatuations with Benedicta and Theodotus, about whom we know nothing; perhaps Marcus met them while living with his grandfather. But there were also more mature passions, from which he was able to be cured. We should recall, moreover, that after the death of Faustina, Marcus took in a concubine, with whom he lived for the last three years of his life.[64]

Although I often got angry with Rusticus, that I did not do anything extreme, which I would later have regretted.

There were thus stormy relations between the disciple and his director of conscience; but Marcus does not say whether they were limited to the period of his youth and philosophical education, or whether they continued after he became Emperor, when Rusticus became a highly influential counselor to Marcus.

It was also a blessing from the gods that his mother, who died young, was able to live with him for the last years of her life, at the court of Antoninus. Another was that he was always able to help the needy. It was another blessing for Marcus to have had such a wife, in the person of the Empress Faustina, "so sweet, so affectionate, so lacking in artifice." Finally, it was a blessing that he was able to provide his children with a good education.

Marcus then evokes the remedies against spitting blood and dizziness, which were revealed to him in dreams.

Finally, Marcus returns to a theme he has already mentioned when speaking of Rusticus: not the least of the gods' blessings was the fact that he did not become interested in abstract philosophical discourse, either logical or concerning the study of nature. Rather, we are to understand that Marcus learned, above all, to live in a philosophical way. "All this," Marcus concludes, "requires the help of the gods and of Fortune." In the last analysis, "all this" is the entire content of the *Meditations:* all those relatives, teachers, and friends who showered him with examples and advice; but also the divine inspirations which helped him in his physical and spiritual life. I have spoken earlier of the two viewpoints of the Stoic conception of providence, and I have said that these two viewpoints—a general law of the universe, indifferent to individual beings, and a particular action on the part of the gods, which takes care of individuals—were not mutually exclusive. Book I can obviously be classified under the second perspective: that of particular providence. In this book, Marcus sees his entire life in the peaceful light of the gods' solicitude for him.

The reader may be surprised that the author of the *Meditations,* reigning over an immense empire, overwhelmed with worries, but also used to elevating himself to grandiose visions which embraced the immensity of space and time, would thank the gods for things which may seem mundane or even trivial, such as the fact that he did not make progress in rhetoric. Other subjects for thanks do not rise above the level of the aspirations of an ordinary man: to raise his children well; to be in good health; to have good parents and a loving wife.

Perhaps we are touching here upon a particular aspect of Marcus' psychology. Thanks to his study of Epictetus and the Stoics, Marcus is quite capable of meditating, in a remarkable style, upon highly elevated themes. From his mother, however, as well as from Rusticus and Antoninus, he learned to live at court the life of an ordinary man; for instance, as we know from his correspondence with Fronto, he helped the farm workers with the grape harvest. We do not find in Marcus an aristocratic or rhetorical search for "great feelings" or geopolitical perspectives; instead, we find a highly characteristic attention paid to the realities of daily life. This was, moreover, also the lesson taught by Epictetus. In order to show that you are a human being, the latter used to say, "eat like a human being; drink like a human being; get married; have children" (III, 21, 4–6). In Marcus' case, we may add to the equation a certain candor, naiveté, and simplicity, which made him search, in the pitiless world of the Roman aristocracy, for tenderness, affection, and warmth of feelings, and the authenticity of simple human relations.

In the remaining books of the *Meditations,* we find only a very small number of autobiographical references. There are a few allusions to Marcus' name and his position as Emperor, and to his adoptive father, Antoninus Pius, of whom Marcus traces a brief portrait (VI, 30) which seems to be a sketch for the one that can now be read in Book I. There are also a few words on Marcus' old age (II, 2, 4; II, 6); on his difficulty in getting up in the morning (V, 1; VIII, 12); and on the repugnance he feels for life at court (VIII, 9) and for the games of the circus (VI, 46).

What is completely remarkable, both in Book I and throughout the *Meditations,* is Marcus' consciousness of his own fallibility[65]—to the point that his "Confessions" are also a kind of confession of his faults. This is an eminently Stoic attitude (Epictetus, II, 11, 1):

The starting-point of philosophy is our consciousness of our weakness and our incapacity with regard to necessary things.

For Marcus, however, this attitude perhaps comes naturally. In the first place, he admits that he has not really succeeded so far in living like a philosopher (VII, 1); that his soul is not yet in the dispositions of peace and love in which it should be (X, 1); that, despite reprieves and warnings from the gods, it is his fault that he does not yet live "according to Nature," that is, according to Reason (I, 17, 11). What is more, he perceives within himself a disposition to commit errors (I, 17, 2; XI, 18, 7); and if he does not commit a given error, it is only out of fear and of what others will say. Basically, however, he is no different from those whom he criticizes (XI, 18, 7). He also admits that he can be wrong, and he accepts that his errors must be corrected (VI, 21; VIII, 16). He knows that he runs the risk of seeing defects where there are in fact none (IX,

38; XII, 16); and he willingly accepts assistance, like a lame soldier incapable of climbing up a wall (VII, 7; VII, 5).

Marcus is, moreover, perfectly aware of the limits of his intelligence (V, 5, 1):

> They can hardly admire your quickness of mind. So be it! But there are many other things about which you cannot say, "I am not gifted." Show us, then, all these things that depend entirely on you: being without duplicity, being serious . . . being free . . .

To be sure, we do not find in Marcus the fondness for self-accusation which we find in Augustine, who is persuaded *a priori* of the corruption of human nature. It does seem, however, that Marcus was gifted by nature with an acute self-consciousness, and a considerable capacity for self-criticism; or rather with the ability of examining himself with objectivity, in which he recognized his faults, but also his qualities. The following brief remark is noteworthy (VIII, 42):

> I don't deserve to be ashamed of myself, for I have never voluntarily harmed anyone.

Near to death, Marcus makes a summation of his life which is, in the last analysis, confident and positive (V, 31, 2):

> Remind yourself of what kinds of things you have gone through, and what you have been able to bear. The story of your life is full, and your service is complete. Remember all the fine things you have seen; all the pleasures and sufferings you have overcome; all the motives for glory which you have despised; all the ingrates to whom you have been benevolent.

Renan[66] was critical of Marcus' "Confessions," especially as they appear in Book I:

> He could see the baseness of humanity, but he did not admit it to himself. This way of voluntarily blinding oneself is the defect of elite hearts. Since the world is not the way they would like it to be, they lie to themselves, in order to see it as other than it is. The result of this is a certain conventionality of judgment. In Marcus, this conventionality is sometimes annoying: if we were to believe him,

his teachers—several of whom were fairly mediocre men—would all, without exception, have been superior beings.

This judgment is far off the mark. In the first place, Marcus tried to render to each person exactly what he or she was owed, and no more; we have seen this in the case of Fronto. Let us also note what he says about his adoptive brother, Lucius Verus—who, although his exact personality is difficult to determine, can at least be said to have been extremely different from Marcus. Marcus does not say that Verus was perfect; on the contrary, when he saw Verus' life-style, Marcus was led to watch himself so as not to imitate him. In the end, Verus' bad example was a blessing from the gods; and all Marcus adds is that his brother showed deference and affection for him. It also seems as though Marcus made a careful choice of whom to mention and whom, since they had not contributed anything to him, he could ignore.

Book I is simultaneously an act of thanksgiving and a confession; a balance sheet of divine action and of Marcus' own resistance to divine action. For Marcus, this action took place in the only important area: that of moral value and virtue. He does not thank the gods for having elevated him to the Empire, nor for having granted him victory over the Germans, but for having guided him toward the philosophical life, with the help of a few men who were sent to him providentially.

Verus or fictus: "sincere" or "affected"

A passage from the *Life of Marcus Aurelius* contained in the *Historia Augusta* shows us that the Emperor's contemporaries wondered what his real personality was:

> Some also complained that he was affected *(fictus)* and not so simple *(simplex)* as he seemed, or as Antoninus Pius and Verus had been.[67]

A play on words is involved here: Marcus' original name was Annius Verus, and the word *verus* evokes sincerity. The emperor Hadrian, who had known Marcus in his childhood, had even given him the nickname *Verissimus,* "the very sincere." Some of Marcus' detractors, then, apparently said that he should have been called not *Verus* but *Fictus*—that is, not "Sincere" but "Affected." This criticism probably came from the historian Marius Maximus,[68] who had begun his political career in the last years of Marcus' reign. Maximus collected all the current gossip about the imperial family, and the *Historia Augusta* often echoes him.

Cassius Dio, a historian who was more or less contemporary with Marius Maximus, maintains a position that is diametrically opposed:

> He obviously did nothing out of affectation *(prospoiētōs)*, but every-
> thing out of virtue . . . he remained the same through everything,
> and did not change on any point. To such an extent was he a truly
> good man, and there was nothing affected about him.[69]

To reproach Marcus with affectation was in fact to reproach him with being a philosopher. The philosophical life he led caused him to have a strange attitude, which was different from that of other people, and therefore "affected," in their view.

Cassius Dio, for instance, who recognized the Emperor's sincerity, was astonished at the extraordinary clemency which he showed on the occasion of the rebellion by Avidius Cassius: "Nothing could force him to do anything alien to his own character: not the idea of making an example of someone, nor the magnitude of the crime."[70]

In fact, however, we must go further, and recognize the genuine difficulty of moral life. Whoever tries to control himself, to practice spiritual exercises, to transform himself, and to act with conscientiousness and reflection gives the impression of lacking spontaneity and of being calculating. Here we confront the eternal problem of moral effort, and of work by oneself upon oneself. We know, for example, that Marcus, in order to correct his own conduct, had investigations made concerning what the public was saying about him; when the criticisms were justified, he modified his behavior.[71]

The Emperor was quite conscious of this danger, which may be insurmountable. In Book I, he expresses his admiration for Claudius Maximus, because he gave the impression of being a man who was naturally "straight" and not one who has corrected or "straightened" himself (I, 15, 8). The same theme is present in other books of the *Meditations*:

> One must be straight, and not straightened (III, 5, 4; VII, 12).

When Marcus praises sincerity (XI, 15), he criticizes people who begin by saying "I shall speak frankly to you," and then obviously do nothing of the kind. Frankness, says Marcus, is written on one's face; it resonates in the voice and shines in the eyes. It is perceived immediately, as the beloved perceives love in the eyes of his lover. Good, simple, and benevolent people have their qualities in their eyes: they do not remain hidden. Marcus demanded that moral action be perfectly natural, as if it were unconscious, without any return upon itself.

It is possible that the gods, to whom Marcus addresses his thanks at the end of Book I, did not bestow upon him the supreme blessing, in the sense of supreme ease and beauty: the ability to make others believe that one does good deeds by nature. I think, however, that no one can deny the good will and scrupulous conscientiousness with which Marcus attempted to do good. In this point, at least, he was scrupulously sincere.

The solitude of the emperor and of the philosopher

In the famous portrait of the philosopher which he sketches in the *Theaetetus* (174e), Plato did not forget to mention what the philosopher thinks of kings and tyrants. What is a king? What is a tyrant? A shepherd or a cowherd, who is happy if he can squeeze lots of milk from his herd. In fact, however, he is not as fortunate as he seems, for the beasts he must milk and pasture are much more unpleasant, difficult, sneaky, and treacherous than those of a simple shepherd. Moreover, absorbed by the cares of governing these disagreeable beasts called men, he has no more mental freedom, and he is just as rough and uncultivated as the shepherds, "once he has surrounded himself with an enclosure around his animal pen in the mountains."

This is precisely what Marcus the philosopher tells Marcus the emperor: wherever he goes, he will be enclosed in the prison of power—alone, without any leisure, and confronted by the sneaky beasts mentioned by Plato (X, 23):

> Let it always be clear to you that your countryside is the place where you are living at this moment, and that everything here is identical to what is on a high mountain or on the seashore, or wherever you like; you'll immediately find there what Plato talks about: "Surrounding himself with a pen in the mountains," he says, and "milking his flocks."

What Marcus means is the following: wherever you go, you will find the prison of power and the solitude in which you are enclosed by your position as shepherd of men. Wherever you go, however, it will be within you and only within you that you will find that countryside, seashore, or mountain which can liberate you from the prison you find everywhere (cf. IV, 3, 1). In other words, it is the emperor's inner dispositions that will decide if he is imprisoned within his mountain enclosure, like Plato's king, or if he will find pleasure and relaxation in the mountains or the countryside, as he would like. No matter where we go, we find—according to our wishes—servitude or freedom.

"Mountain" here has two meanings: it is the symbol of the enclosure within which the tyrant/king lives as a prisoner together with the flock of animals he exploits; but it is also the symbol of retreat within ourselves and the inner freedom which we can find anywhere, as long as we want it (X, 15, 2):

> Live as if you were on a mountain. It doesn't matter whether one lives in one place or another, as long as one lives everywhere as within one's own City, which is the World.

And yet the philosopher's inner retreat, which is his philosophical life in conformity with Stoicism, will provoke another solitude and rupture between the flock and its shepherd: a serious disparity between the values of both parties.

This uneasiness explains Marcus' repugnance with regard to life at court, which he compares to a stepmother (VI, 12), whereas his true mother is philosophy, which allows him to put up with the court, and to make himself bearable to those who live at court. Yet he blames himself for this attitude (VIII, 9):

> Let no one hear you blame the life people lead at court any longer!
> Let not you yourself hear yourself doing it!

Here we encounter once again what we could call the theme of life on a mountain: wherever one can live, one can live well; that is to say, philosophically. But it is possible to live at court; therefore, it is possible to live well there (V, 16, 2). Marcus gives this argument as an example of the way in which the soul can suffuse itself with specific representations.

Marcus' repugnance for life at court was not, however, mere superficial annoyance: rather, the discord ran extremely deep. As he continues this meditation on life "on a mountain"—that is to say, within the City of the World—Marcus allows us to glimpse just how deep this discord and this rupture go (X, 15, 3):

> Let people see and discover what a man who truly lives in accord-
> ance with nature is like! If they can't put up with you, then let them
> kill you! That would be better than to live like them!

The conflict is situated in the profound difference between the two
parties' principles of life, and it is summarized by Marcus in a lapidary
formula which opposes the two Greek words *homothamnein* and *homodogmatein* (XI, 8, 6):

> Grow on the same trunk, but don't profess the same principles.

These two duties are hard to reconcile: on the one hand, our duty to
love other human beings, with whom we form one single body, tree, or
city; on the other, our duty not to let ourselves be cajoled into adopting
their false values and maxims of life.

This is the drama of Marcus' life. He loves mankind, and wants to love
them; but he hates what they love. Only one thing counts for him: the
search for virtue and the purity of moral intention. This human world—
from which this unique value is absent—provokes in Marcus an intense
reprobation and lassitude; yet he gets hold of himself, and attempts to
reintroduce gentleness and indulgence within himself.

This disgust and lassitude make Marcus long for death, and he knows
that this is wrong. We know how important a part is played in the
Meditations by the "helps," or arguments for preparing oneself for death.
Some are entirely philosophical, as for instance those which teach us to
consider death as a particular case of universal metamorphosis, or a mystery of nature (II, 12, 3; IV, 5; IX, 3, 1–4). Some of them, however, are
not philosophical, but are coarse *(idiōtika)* and vulgar, although highly
effective: for instance, those which consist in making a list of people who
hung on desperately to life, unwilling to let go, and who nevertheless
died (IV, 50). A similar consideration, which Marcus admits (IX, 3, 5) is
also completely unphilosophical *(idiōtikon),* but which touches the heart,
consists in telling oneself that, in the last analysis, what one is leaving is
not really worth much. This method consists in

> carefully examining the kinds of objects from which you are about
> to separate yourself, and with what bad characters your soul will no
> longer be mixed. To be sure, you must by no means be disgusted by
> them; on the contrary, you must be filled with solicitude for them,
> and put up with them gently. Nevertheless, you must also remem-

ber that you must take leave of people who do not share your principles. If it were possible, the only thing which could push you back in the other direction and maintain you in life, would be if it were possible for you to live in a society of people who had adopted the same principles as you.

As things are, however, you can see how much you are filled with lassitude at the discords of social life; to the point where you say: "Hurry up, O Death, lest I too forget myself."

One thinks of Baudelaire's cry, so expressive of fatigue with terrestrial life and an aspiration for the infinite: "O Death, old captain . . . this land is boring! Let us cast off!" Yet if Marcus calls on Death to come quickly, it is less out of lassitude than out of fear of becoming similar to those who forget themselves and live in a state of unconsciousness.

The disgust which Marcus feels for his entourage is certainly surprising. Did he not surround himself with friends and counselors who were also philosophers, like his beloved Rusticus and all those whom we were able to glimpse thanks to the testimony of Galen? It could be supposed that, by these last years of Marcus' life, his friends had disappeared, and that he now misses the beginning of his reign. And yet we know from Cassius Dio[72] that Marcus admitted that no one could be perfect:

He used to say that it is impossible to create people as one would like them to be, but that each one had to be utilized in the task which he was capable of accomplishing.

He used to praise them for the service they had rendered, and he paid no attention to the rest of their behavior.

Are we to suppose that he had become more intransigent in his old age? Alternatively, can we perceive in these lines the disappointment Marcus felt as he saw the development of the character of Commodus? This was the view of Renan, especially à propos of another passage (X, 36), which is also very striking in its expression of lassitude and disappointment:

No one is so well-favored by Destiny that, at the moment of his death, he is not surrounded by people who will rejoice at this sad event. The dead man was conscientious and well-behaved; yet someone will finally turn up to say, "This schoolteacher *(paidagōgos)* will now finally let us breathe. To be sure, he was not harsh with any of us; but I could feel that he was condemning us in silence."

Later on in the text, Marcus opposes the case of this good man to his own situation. In a sense, however, when he speaks of this good man, he is already thinking about himself; for he is well aware of the fact that not only those around him, but also the entire Empire, knew that he was trying to be a philosopher. An apocryphal letter from Lucius Verus to his adoptive brother, preserved by the *Historia Augusta,* may reflect an opinion widespread in Marcus' time: it warns Marcus that Avidius Cassius, who was to revolt against him near the end of Marcus' reign, spoke of him as an "old woman who plays at being a philosopher."[73] Many people must have had similar views of the Emperor; perhaps they had even nicknamed him "the pedagogue." In any case, Marcus uses this description of the death of a good man as an *a fortiori* argument: if such a man must expect such an end, then all the more must Marcus himself expect similar reactions at the moment of his own death:

> This is what people will say about a good man. In my case, however, how many more reasons there are for there to be many people to want to get rid of me. You'll have to think of that when you die. You will leave life more easily, if you think: the life that I am leaving is one in which my associates *(koinōnoi),* for whom I have fought so hard and prayed so much, for whom I have had so much concern, want me to go away. Perhaps they hope for some relief from my disappearance.

Who were these associates or companions *(koinōnoi)?* They could have been the Emperor's counselors, who made up the imperial council and who, in the words of the Emperor's contemporary Aelius Aristides, were participants in power. Yet the expressions "I have fought so hard" and "I have prayed so much" imply a very special relationship between the Emperor and these "associates." It is hard not to think, with Renan, of Commodus, Marcus' young son, who had been given imperial power in 177, three years before the Emperor's death, and who was probably already manifesting the disastrous tendencies that would develop during his reign.

Be that as it may, Marcus transforms his meditation on the ingratitude of others into a preparation for death. Unlike the preparation mentioned above, this one is not philosophical, since it sins against the discipline of action, which requires us to love our fellow human beings. Nevertheless, it is powerfully effective, since it diminishes the anguish and suffering caused by the loss of life:

> Why should we try to prolong our stay in this place?

Yet Marcus corrects himself immediately (X, 36, 6):

> And yet, don't go away for that reason less well-disposed toward them. Rather, you must remain faithful to your own character, and be friendly, benevolent, and merciful toward them.

This is the disposition in which we should always remain. Yet lassitude and disappointment sometimes win the day, and Marcus implicitly recognizes that they are not philosophical, but are a weakness, and perhaps even a passion.

Such a complex sentiment appears to consist of several elements. In the first place, we find in it a view of human frailty that is free of illusion. Marcus had a sharp and highly realistic sense of both his own fallibility and that of others, which sometimes went so far as to consider these others incorrigible (VIII, 4):

> They'll still do the same things, even if it kills you!

As W. Williams has shown, this is why Marcus was always careful to dot the i's and cross the t's of the official documents which expressed his decisions. He seems to have feared that his subordinates might fail to understand his orders, or refuse to carry them out in the way he wanted. For instance, in one case a slave was set free by a will, but this might have been contested because of the form of the will. Marcus, however, was in favor of the "cause of freedom," and always tended to make enfranchisement easier; thus he took the trouble to specify that his decision should be not left as a dead letter, by bringing up some other motive, such as the fact that the Treasury might claim the property left by the testator. As Marcus writes,

> Those who have our interests at heart must know that the cause of freedom is to be placed before all financial advantage.[74]

One the one hand, we can perceive here the importance of the human, moral point of view for Marcus. On the other hand, we can also glimpse a certain lack of confidence in the intellectual and moral qualities of his subordinates. These difficulties with his entourage, moreover, took on greater proportions as a result of Marcus' undeniable propensity toward anger, which the Emperor made no attempt to conceal; he was aware that becoming angry constituted a weakness (XI, 9, 2).

The main cause of Marcus' lassitude, however, was his passionate love for moral good. A world in which this absolute value was not recognized seemed to him an empty world, in which life no longer had any meaning. As he grew old in such an enormous empire, in the huge crowds which surrounded and acclaimed him, in the atrocious Danubian war as well as in the triumphal parades of the city of Rome, he felt himself alone. Marcus felt a void around himself, since he could not realize his ideal (IX, 3, 7): to live in community with others, in search of the only thing necessary.

Political models

Marcus does not propose any specific governmental program in the *Meditations*. This should not surprise us, for he is less concerned with what must be done than with *how* it must be done. Nevertheless, Book I does contain some allusions to political practice. Through Claudius Severus, Marcus writes (I, 14), he has come to know Thrasea, Helvidius, Cato, Dio, and Brutus. This list of names has a quite precise meaning.[75]

Paetus Thrasea was the famous senator who, in the year 66, was forced to commit suicide because of his outspoken opposition to the emperor Nero. Helvidius Priscus, Thrasea's son-in-law, was assassinated in the reign of Vespasian, probably in the year 75. Both were opponents of the emperors, and this attitude was a kind of family tradition, in which the women also often took part. The portraits of these martyrs were kept within the great aristocratic families, and their biographies were written. Under some emperors, however, writing such works also meant risking death. At the beginning of his *Life of Agricola,* Tacitus evokes the happiness which the emperor Nerva brought to Rome by establishing a reign which, says Tacitus, reconciled monarchy and freedom. Under Nerva's predecessor Domitian, by contrast, it had been forbidden to write the biographies of opponents of the emperor.

> Arulenus Rusticus wrote a panegyric of Paetus Thrasea, and Herennius Senecion wrote one of Helvidius Priscus: both paid with their lives . . . It was thought that the voice of the Roman people, the

free speech *(libertas)* of the Senate, and the conscience of the human race could be stifled.

It was almost fifty years after these events that Marcus Aurelius, through the intermediary of Claudius Severus, discovered this tradition of opposition. In turn, however, these opponents of the Empire had maintained the cult of other, older martyrs, who had lived in the last stages of the Republic, under Caesar. When Juvenal, a contemporary of Tacitus, speaks in his *Satires* (V, 36) of the high quality of a wine, he writes that it is similar to that which Paetus Thrasea and Helvidius Priscus drank on the birthdays of Brutus and Cassius, the murderers of Caesar.

According to Marcus, Claudius Severus had also told him about the figure of Brutus, who lived in the first century B.C. (85–42), and about Cato. The figure in question is obviously Cato of Utica (95–46), who, as an opponent of Caesar, committed suicide upon the approach of the latter's troops.

Did Claudius Severus provide Marcus with the biographies of Thrasea, Helvidius Priscus, Brutus, and Cato? Thrasea had written a life of Cato, and Helvidius a life of Thrasea, while Herennius Senecion had composed a life of Helvidius. Did Claudius also have Marcus read the parallel lives of Brutus and Dio of Syracuse, written by Plutarch, who had also composed the parallel lives of Phocion and Cato of Utica? It is in any case surprising to see, in the list of Romans enumerated by Claudius Severus, a Greek, who lived from about 409 to 354 B.C.: namely Dio, who deposed the Syracusan tyrant Dionysius, but who was in turn himself assassinated.[76] It is highly unlikely that the Dio mentioned here could be Dio Chrysostom, the rhetor and philosopher who was exiled under Domitian but later recovered imperial favor. The rest of the list consists of only statesmen, so that Dio Chrysostom would be an exception, and he was not really a "martyr" of opposition to the Empire.

Claudius Severus may very well have spoken of these figures in a conversation in which he emphasized the common element that linked them all together: the link between philosophy and a specific conception of politics; that is to say, the hatred of tyranny. Dio had been a disciple of Plato, and according to Plutarch,[77] he practiced the philosophical virtues of frankness of speech, greatness of soul, gravity, clemency toward his enemies, and frugality. By deposing Dionysius, Dio brought freedom back to Syracuse and abolished the tyranny, but he supported a middle path between tyranny and democracy: a monarchy subject to laws, which is the governmental program set forth in the *Eighth Letter,* attributed to Plato.

Brutus, a Roman, was also a Platonist. He followed the tendency which was fashionable in his time: that of Antiochus of Ascalon, strongly tinged with Stoicism. Brutus had written treatises entitled "On Duty," "On Patience," and "On Virtue." He was both the assassin of Caesar and the man who killed himself after having been defeated in the civil war which followed Caesar's assassination. Like Dio, Brutus was an enemy of tyranny, and he fought for public liberty.

In the eyes of Seneca, Cato was one of the rare incarnations of the ideal of the Stoic Sage.[78] Before his suicide, Cato discussed the Stoic paradox according to which only the Sage is free. Then, he read Plato's *Phaedo.*[79] His whole way of life was that of a philosopher, who tried at the same time to revive the rigorous life of the ancient Romans. He trained himself for physical endurance, traveled on foot, went against current fashions, affected disdain for money, and refused any form of connivery or complicity with the exactions carried out by powerful Romans.

Brutus and Cato were republicans. Freedom, for them, was above all that of the Senate: in other words, the right to govern of a ruling class which opposed the arbitrariness of the tyranny of one man. Cato also wished to introduce moral or philosophical rigor into the senatorial class.

Under the Empire, Thrasea and Helvidius dreamed of a return to the ancient institutions of the Roman Republic; in other words, they wished to restore political authority to the Senate. Both were Stoics, and within the Stoic tradition—particularly in Epictetus[80]—they would remain as examples of constancy, mental firmness, and indifference to indifferent things. Epictetus himself knew this opposition to imperial power well, thanks to his teacher Musonius Rufus, who had been closely linked to Thrasea.

All these memories were awakened by the reign and the persecutions of Domitian, as we can see from the numerous allusions to this somber period which can be found in the letters of Pliny the Younger. With the total change of atmosphere brought about by the accession of the emperor Nerva, which was prolonged under his successors Trajan, Hadrian, and Antoninus, both Senators and philosophers had the impression that the Empire had somehow become reconciled with the spirit of these supporters of the republican ideal and of Stoicism. This is certainly the meaning of the remarks by Claudius Severus on the martyrs who gave their lives in the fight against tyranny.[81]

By evoking these almost legendary figures, Claudius Severus gave

Marcus a glimpse of the principles of political conduct (I, 14, 2). It is to Claudius, writes Marcus, that he owes the

> fact of having had a representation of a State *(politeia)* in which the laws are equal for all, administered on the basis of equality and freedom of speech, and of a monarchy which respects the freedom of its subjects above all else.

The idea of a law that is equal for all goes back to the *Eighth Letter,* attributed to Plato. The equality in question is geometrical, and it distributes benefits to each person in accordance with his or her merit. This is precisely the Aristotelian and Stoic definition of justice: it accords advantages in proportion to merit.

The ideas of equal rights, of equal rights to speech, and of freedom had been extremely closely linked since the most ancient period of Greek democracy. However, when Tacitus, writing under the Empire, spoke of the reconciliation between monarchy and freedom brought about by Nerva, the idea of freedom had lost much of its content. It no longer meant the citizen's possibility to participate unhindered in political life. Rather, it included such notions as the protection and safety of individuals, and individual freedom (the right to express oneself, for example, or to move freely). For the cities, it meant the possibility of preserving their traditions and a certain degree of municipal autonomy; but above all, for the Senate, it meant the ability to influence the Emperor's decisions to a greater or lesser extent.

Claudius Severus taught the future sovereign that freedom is compatible with monarchy, if one understands by "monarchy" a regime that respects the laws and the citizens. In fact, since he was so close to the Emperor Antoninus, who exercised this kind of moderate power himself, Marcus could not fail to be familiar with this way of governing. Claudius Severus thus did not cause Marcus to discover it; instead, he probably revealed to him the historical roots of this conception of monarchy: the opposition to tyranny of the philosopher-martyrs.

Claudius thus made Marcus aware of the principles of conduct that must guide an enlightened monarch: respect for the law, recognition of the rights of the Senate, attendance at its sessions, participation in its deliberations, and recognition of the right to speak, not only for the prince's council or the Senate, but also for simple citizens, when they addressed the Emperor.

The ancient historians have given us some examples of the way Marcus applied these principles. In order to finance the Danubian war, he took the trouble to ask the public treasury for funds. It was not, as Cassius Dio notes,[82] as if these funds were not at the Emperor's disposition; yet Marcus insisted on acknowledging that they belonged to the Senate and the Roman People. Speaking to the Senate, Marcus said:

> We possess nothing of our own, and it is in your house that we live.

According to the *Historia Augusta*,[83] Marcus always deliberated with his council before undertaking anything, whether in war or in peace; for his motto was:

> It is more just for me to follow the advice of my friends, than that the multitude of my friends should follow my will alone.

Marcus was extremely careful to take the Senate's opinion into consideration. He let the mime-writers criticize him openly. The historian Herodian specifies that Marcus entertained all requests, and forbade his guards to bar the way to people who wished to approach him.[84] The *Historia Augusta* sums up Marcus' entire attitude in the following terms:

> Toward the people, he behaved exactly as if he were acting in a free State.[85]

The portrait of Antoninus Pius which Marcus gives in Book I serves in part to illustrate these principles of government. In a sense, it sketches the features of the ideal prince, with whom the Emperor would like to identify himself. We find a trace of this portrait in the *Meditations* (VI, 30), where Marcus exhorts himself not to become "Caesarized" and not to let the imperial purple rub off on him: instead, he is to become a true disciple of Antoninus. Marcus takes particular care to describe the moral qualities that Antoninus showed in his way of governing, which Marcus intended to imitate. When, after due reflection, Antoninus had made a decision, he held firmly to it: he was identical in every circumstance. He never abandoned a question without having examined it thoroughly. He put up with people who reproached him unjustly. He never hurried, did not listen to calumnies, and could fathom people's morals and actions with penetrating acuity. He did not seek to humiliate; neither did he fear nor scorn anyone. Nor was he a sophist: he led a simple life, and was content with little with regard to his lodging, his clothing, his food, and his household servants. He was patient and hardworking, loyal and constant in his friendships. He tolerated being contradicted with great frankness, and he was happy to hear a better solution proposed. He was pious, but not superstitious.

In this initial portrait of the ideal prince, which was to be partially taken up again in Book I, we note some forms of behavior that Marcus often exhorts himself to practice throughout the *Meditations:* for instance, to allow his counselors to have different opinions from his, and to agree to their opinion if it is better (IV, 12; VIII, 16); not to humiliate people (XI, 13, 2; XI, 18, 18); and to remain identical with himself throughout his entire life (XI, 21).

In the middle of the *Meditations,* this portrait of Antoninus appears like a foreign body; it is surprising that Marcus should have taken the time to produce such a sketch, apparently so distant from the exhortations with which he showers himself elsewhere. Yet its presence confirms an impression we may already have received while reading the work: the *Meditations* are addressed not only to Marcus the man, but to Marcus the man who exercises the imperial function. Hence, the model of Antoninus acquires a capital importance.

The features of Antoninus which are sketched in Book I (chapter 16) are more numerous and more precise: they are both memories and examples, and they often correspond to the canon of the ideal prince, which philosophical reflection, in accordance with an immemorial tradition, had attempted to formulate.[86]

Let us leave aside for the moment Marcus' remarks on his adoptive father's moral qualities, and concentrate on some of the characteristic political attitudes in this portrait.

First, as far as the relations between sovereign and people are concerned, we find the rejection of all demagogy; a total lack of currying popular favor or gratitude; disdain for vain glory; and the refusal of acclamations. Antoninus knew when to keep a tight rein, and when to slacken it; and he practiced rigorous justice, which meant "inflexibly distributing to each person what was due to his or her merit."

More broadly, he was constantly attentive to the general needs of the Empire, and he was extremely thrifty when it came to public expenditures. People made fun of him for this, but he was very tolerant with regard to such criticisms. In particular, he thought long and hard before offering spectacles to the public, building monuments, or distributing gifts. Above all, he thought about what it was right to do, and not about the glory he could derive from his acts. He thus tried—without making a show of it—to remain faithful to his ancestral customs.

Antoninus showed a great deal of gentleness in his way of governing;

there was nothing hard, inexorable, or violent about him. He used meticulous care in resolving the most minor affairs, and in using foresight with the utmost detail. Once he made a decision, he stuck to it, and would not allow himself to be moved. He had few secrets. He listened attentively to his counselors—traditionally called the "Emperor's friends"—and he accorded them a great deal of freedom; yet he enjoyed their company.

We can detect an implicit criticism of Antoninus' predecessors in this portrait, and in particular of Hadrian.[87] If the Emperor took the trouble to emphasize that his adoptive father put an end to "the love of young boys," this was certainly an allusion to what went on in the courts of Trajan and Hadrian. If he insisted on the fact that Antoninus liked to stay in the same place, this was probably in order to criticize Hadrian's many trips to every corner of the Empire. When Marcus spoke of Antoninus' prudent frugality with regard to expenditures incurred by organizing spectacles and building monuments, he probably had in mind Hadrian's prodigality and love of fine construction. Finally, Marcus probably intended to contrast Antoninus' conservatism, and his wish to remain close to ancestral customs—in other words, to old Roman traditions—with Hadrian's innovations.

Marcus saw in Antoninus a true philosopher, comparable to Socrates, who knew how to enjoy good things when they were present, and to abstain from them when they were absent (I, 16, 30). He evokes Antoninus' perfect and invincible soul (I, 16, 31), as well as the tranquil conscience he displayed in his final hour (VI, 30, 15). We do not know if Antoninus considered himself to be a philosopher, but it is quite remarkable that at the moment of his death, he gave the following password to the tribune of the praetorian cohort: *Aequanimitas,* or "Serenity"—a word which lets us glimpse an entire philosophical attitude.[88] In any event, we have every reason to suppose that when it came to sketching the portrait of his adoptive father, Marcus did not simply collect a few edifying features. Rather, he expressed his adherence to a quite specific way of governing: that of Antoninus. The *Historia Augusta*[89] summarizes this continuity as follows:

From the beginning of their reign, Marcus Aurelius and Lucius Verus behaved in a manner which was so benevolent and close to the people *(civiliter),* that no one had cause to miss the gentleness of Antoninus.

"Don't wait for Plato's republic"

How ridiculous are these little men who play at being politicians, and, as they think, deal with affairs of State like philosophers! Snotty little men! Man, what must you do? Do what Nature asks you to do in this very moment. Direct your will in this direction, if it is granted you to do so, and don't look around to see whether anyone will know about it. Don't wait for Plato's Republic! Rather, be content if one tiny thing makes some progress, and reflect on the fact that what results from this tiny thing is no tiny thing at all!

Indeed, who will change the principles upon which they guide their lives? And yet, without a change in these principles, what else is there but the slavery of people who moan as they pretend to obey?

Go on, now, quote me some Alexander, some Philip, or some Demetrius! Let *them* worry about whether they knew what Universal Nature wanted, and if they educated themselves. But if they were only acting, no one has condemned me to imitate them. Don't push me into acting solemn (IX, 29).

Who were these "ridiculous" and "snotty little men"? It is hard to say. Perhaps they were people who considered themselves philosophers, and criticized Marcus because he was not carrying out "great politics." The continuation of the passage allows us to suppose that he was accused of two things: first, he had not realized Plato's Republic. As the philosopher-emperor, should he not reform the State completely, in accordance with the principles of philosophy? Second, he had not, unlike Alexander, Philip of Macedonia, or Demetrius Poliorcetes,[90] the "taker of cities," carried out a politics of conquest, which would be glorious for him and for the Empire.

No, replies Marcus: what is essential is to concentrate on present political and moral action, however modest it may be. Do what Nature (that is to say, reason) asks you to do in this very moment, and don't let yourself be carried away by vast utopian views, to the point where you believe you are in "Plato's Republic."

"Plato's Republic" was a proverbial expression, which had a very precise meaning. It did not, properly speaking, designate the political program set forth in the great philosopher's dialogue. Rather, more generally, it referred to a state in which all the citizens would have become philosophers, and therefore perfect. It was in this sense that

Cicero[91] told how the Stoic Mucius Scaevola had pleaded the cause of Rutilius Rufus "as it could have been pleaded in Plato's Republic"—in other words, as if he were addressing only philosophers. Elsewhere, Cicero says[92] of Cato of Utica that he used to act as if he were living in Plato's Republic, and not in the mud of Romulus. This is precisely what Marcus means. It is extremely difficult to transform the human masses; to change the values which fascinate them, and the opinions which cause them to act; or to make philosophers of them. Unless one transforms their way of looking at things, completely changing the moral life of each individual, any reform imposed without their consent would plunge them into the slavery "of people who moan as they pretend to obey." This is the eternal drama of humanity in general and of politics in particular. Unless it transforms people completely, politics can never be anything other than a compromise with evil.

Marcus wants to be lucid and realistic: he has no illusions about the general conversion of humanity, or the possibility of imposing upon people some ideal state. Yet this does not mean that nothing can be done. Just as Stoic philosophers knew that they would never be sages, but nevertheless attempted gradually to progress toward this ideal, so the statesman knows that humanity will never be perfect; yet he must be happy if, from time to time, he manages to achieve some slight progress. After all, even slight progress is no minor achievement: moral progress, however minimal, takes a lot of effort and, above all, has a great deal of value; for no moral progress is ever slight.

We can perhaps find an example of Marcus' political practice in his attitude toward gladiatorial combats. Stoic philosophy was hostile to such spectacles, because they went against the personal human dignity of the combatants. As Seneca wrote,[93]

It is a sacrilege to teach men how to inflict and receive wounds.

Man, a sacred thing for man, is nowadays killed out of sport and by way of pastime.

It is therefore false, I might add, to maintain as does G. Ville[94] that the Stoics were hostile to such spectacles only because they were degrading for the spectators, but that these philosophers completely ignored the drama of the victims. This is another example of the prejudice of certain historians, who persist in attempting to minimize the importance of the reversal of values represented by Stoic philosophy. Unfortunately for them, however, the texts are there and they cannot be avoided: as Seneca says, *Homo sacra res homini.*

It would have been utopian to suppress the games, which were an essential part of the people's life. Thus, when Marcus enrolled the gladiators to fight on the Danube, and the spectacles at Rome were interrupted, the people already began to murmur that the Emperor wanted to convert them to philosophy by taking away their pleasures.[95] Be that as it may, Marcus must have considered it a small but not negligible progress to have achieved what we are told by the historian Cassius Dio:[96]

> Marcus Aurelius was so averse to the killing that, at Rome, he attended combats in which the gladiators fought like athletes, without danger. For he did not allow them to be given sharp weapons, but they had to fight with blunt ones, with buttons on the point.

No utopia, then, but a realistic view of the possibilities and limits of human nature, and a political policy that had only precise and limited objectives as its goal. Moreover, the philosopher-emperor rejected any form of prestige politics: he had to do what was ordered by reason "at that very moment," and "not look around to see whether anyone will know about it" (IX, 29, 4).

It goes without saying that Marcus could be crushed by a comparison with Alexander, Philip, or Demetrius (the person in question is Demetrius Poliorcetes, the "taker of cities"). They were certainly great conquerors, but Marcus could reply that they were also people dominated by their passions. Stoic tradition—for instance, Epictetus (II, 13, 24)—opposed to their brute material power the spiritual and moral power of Diogenes, who did not hesitate to speak frankly to them. This is, moreover, the meaning of one of Marcus' *Meditations,* which expresses an analogous idea (VIII, 3):

> Alexander, Caesar, and Pompey: what are they compared to Diogenes, Heraclitus, or Socrates? The latter saw realities, causes, and matter; and the guiding principles of their souls were sufficient unto themselves. As for the others: so much pillage![97] so many people reduced to slavery!

Alexander, Philip, and Demetrius may have been great conquerors; but did they know what Nature or universal Reason wanted? Were they masters, not only of the world, but also of themselves? Or were they, instead, nothing but "tragic actors"? In other words, were they people who, by means of their conquests, were the cause of atrocious events, worthy of being represented in a tragedy, and were they themselves actors who took up false and solemn poses? *Pace* the "snotty little men" to whom Marcus alludes, nothing can make him imitate them. He will continue to do his job as an emperor and a true philosopher: that is to say, by conforming at every instant to the will of Reason and Nature, not with turgid solemnity but with simplicity.

For Marcus, philosophy does not propose a political program. Rather, he expects that philosophy will form him and prepare him, by means of the spiritual exercises which he performs, to carry out his political action in a specific spirit and style. What one does matters less than the way in which one does it. In the last analysis, the only true politics is ethics. It consists, above all, in the discipline of action, which, as we have seen, consists essentially in service to the human community, devotion to others, and justice. Like the discipline of action, politics cannot be separated from the great human and cosmic perspectives that are opened up for us by our recognition of a transcendent universality—Reason or Nature—which, by means of its harmony with itself, founds both people's love for one another and their love for that Whole of which they are the parts. It is hard not to think of the recent comments of Vaclav Havel,[98] as he discusses what he calls the "moral State" or the "spiritual State":

> True politics—the only thing worthy of the name, and the only thing I will consent to practice—is politics in the service of our fellow man, and in the service of the community. . . . Its basis is ethical, insofar as it is only the realization of the responsibility of all toward all. . . . [It] is nourished by the certainty, conscious or unconscious, that . . . everything is inscribed forever; that everything is evaluated elsewhere, somewhere "above us," in what I have called "the memory of Being": it is that part which is indissociable from the cosmos, from nature and from life which believers call God, and to whose judgment all things are submitted. . . . To try to remain, in all circumstances, courteous, just, tolerant, understanding; and at the same time uncorruptible and infallible. In sum, to try and remain in harmony with my conscience and with my better self.

CONCLUSION

At the beginning of this book I alluded to the extraordinary success which Marcus Aurelius' *Meditations* have enjoyed throughout the centuries, beginning with the first edition in the sixteenth century. How can we explain this phenomenon? Why does this work continue, even today, to fascinate us to such an extent? Perhaps one reason is the consummate art with which the Emperor chiseled out his aphorisms. In the words of Nietzsche:

> A good saying is too hard for the teeth of time, and all the millennia are not enough to consume it, although it serves as food for every epoch. It is thus the great paradox of literature: the imperishable in the midst of the changing, the food which always is appreciated, like salt, and again like salt, it never becomes insipid.[1]

Yet the nutritive substance which we find in this work is, as we have seen, the Stoic system, as it was set forth by Epictetus. Is it possible that it could still serve as spiritual nourishment for us, people of the modern era?

Ernest Renan,[2] for one, did not think so. For him, the *Meditations* went beyond Epictetus, Stoicism, and all definitive doctrines:

> Fortunately, the little box which contained the *Meditations* on the banks of the Gran and the philosophy of Carnonte was saved. There came out of it this incomparable book, in which Epictetus was surpassed: this manual of the resigned life, this Gospel of those who do not believe in the supernatural, which has not been able to be understood until our time. A true eternal Gospel, the *Meditations* will never grow old, for it affirms no dogma. The Gospel has grown old in some of its parts: science no longer allows the naive concep-

tion of the supernatural which constitues its foundation. In the *Meditations,* the supernatural is only a tiny, insignificant stain which does not affect the wonderful beauty of the background. Science could destroy God and the soul, but the *Meditations* would still remain young with life and truth. The religion of Marcus Aurelius is, like that of Jesus was at times, absolute religion: that which results from the simple fact of a high moral conscience faced with the universe. It is not of one race, nor of one country; no revolution, no progress, no discovery will be able to change it.

These lines do an admirable job of describing the impression that may be felt by Marcus' readers. They must, however, be qualified and made more precise. Like many other historians who followed him, Renan was wrong about the meaning which the famous dilemma "Nature or atoms" had for Marcus. He thought it meant that Marcus was completely indifferent to the dogmas of Stoicism (Nature) or of Epicureanism (atoms). According to Renan—and this, he thought, was the secret of the eternal youth of the *Meditations*—Marcus discovered that the moral conscience is independent of all theories about the world and of all definite dogmas, "as if," in Renan's words,[3] "he had read Kant's *Critique of Practical Reason.*"

In fact, as I have noted, the meaning of this dilemma is entirely different. In the first place, Marcus did not invent it: it was traditional within the Stoic school. Moreover, the Stoics had elaborated this reasoning in order to establish irrefutably that, even if Epicureanism were true—a hypothesis which they excluded absolutely—one would still have to live as a Stoic. In other words, one would still have to act in accordance with reason, and consider moral good to be the only good, even if, all around us, everything were nothing but chaos and chance. Such a position does not imply skepticism—quite the contrary. Yet the fact that the Stoics constructed such an argument is extremely interesting. By imagining that their physical theories might be false, and yet people would still have to live as Stoics, they revealed that which, in their eyes, was absolutely essential in their system. What defined a Stoic above all else was the choice of a life in which every thought, every desire, and every action would be guided by no other law than that of universal Reason. Whether the world is ordered or chaotic, it depends only on us to be rationally coherent with ourselves. In fact, all the dogmas of Stoicism derive from this existential choice. It is impossible that the universe could produce human rationality, unless the latter were already in some way present within the former. The essence of Stoicism is thus the experience of the absolute nature of moral conscience and of the purity of intention. Moral conscience, moreover, is only moral if it is pure—that is to say, if it is based upon the universality of reason, which takes itself as an end, not in the particular interest of an individual or a state. All Stoics, and not just Marcus Aurelius, could have subscribed to the twin Kantian formulations of the categorical imperative:

> Act only in accordance with the maxim which is such that you can wish, at the same time, that it become a universal law.

> Act as if the maxim of your action were, by your will, to be erected as a universal law of Nature.[4]

We must not say, therefore, that "Marcus writes as though he had read the *Critique of Practical Reason,*" but rather that Kant uses these formulas because, among other reasons, he has read the Stoics.

With these qualifications, Renan was right to say that we find in the *Meditations* the affirmation of the absolute value of moral conscience. Can we speak of religion here? I do not think so. The word "philosophy" is enough, I think, to describe the purity of this attitude, and we ought to avoid mixing with philosophy all the vague and imprecise implications, both social and mythical, which the notion of religion brings with it.

An eternal Gospel? Renan thought that some parts of the Christian Gospel had grown old, whereas the *Meditations* would always remain young. And yet, are not some of Marcus' pages—the religious ones—also very distant from us? Isn't it better to say that all gospels grow old, to the same extent that they have been fashionable—in other words, to the extent that they have reflected the myths and collective representations of the time and milieu in which they were written? There are some works, however—among them both the Gospel and the *Meditations*—which are like ever-new springs to which humanity comes to drink. If we can transcend their perishable aspects, we can sense in them an imperishable spirit which calls us to a choice of life, to the transformation of ourselves, and to a complete revision of our attitude with regard to human beings and to the world.

The *Meditations* call us to a Stoic choice of life, as we have seen throughout this book. This obviously does not mean that the work is capable of leading us to a complete conversion to the dogmas and practices of Stoicism. Yet, insofar as we attempt to give meaning to our lives, the *Meditations* invite us to discover the transformation which could be brought to our lives, if we were to realize—in the fullest sense of the term—those specific values which constitute the spirit of Stoicism.

It could be said, moreover, that there is a universal Stoicism in humanity. By this I mean that the attitude we call "Stoic" is one of the fundamental, permanent possibilities of human existence, when people search for wisdom. For instance, J. Gernet[5] has shown how some aspects of Chinese thought were related to what we call Stoicism. They obviously developed without Greco-Roman Stoicism having exercised any influence on them whatsoever. This phenomenon may be observed, among other places, in Wang-Fou-chih,[6] a Chinese philosopher of the seventeenth century, who writes:

> Vulgar knowledge (that which limits itself to what one has seen or heard) is constituted in the egotism of the self and is far from the "great objectivity" [*ta kong,* a term which has both a moral and an intellectual meaning].

We can glimpse that this "great objectivity" is entirely analogous to Marcus' method of physical definition, which also consists in liberating oneself from an egoistic point of view, and in placing oneself within the perspective of universal Nature. As Gernet comments:

> Morality and reason are one. Once the sage has enlarged his spirit to the dimensions of the universe (*ta sin:* the exact equivalent of the term *megalopsuchia,* or "greatness of soul") and "made his person an object of the world," he is able to grasp the spirit of the "Great Transformation"; that is, of the life of universal exchanges by which the beat of the world is marked.

The sage's "great objectivity"—or, as we could say, the expansion of his spirit to the dimensions of universal Reason—inspires a moral attitude which is entirely Stoic. We can see this in the following passage from Wang-Fou-chih:[7]

> The good man waits for what destiny reserves for him, and is not saddened by death. He uses his particular capacities as far as he can, and develops the good dispositions of his nature [which is a reflec-

tion of the celestial principle of order], so that he does not sin against the relevant norms.

We can recognize another theme that we have encountered in Marcus Aurelius in Tang Zhen, another Chinese philosopher of the same period who has been translated by Gernet: the opposition between the puniness of human beings, lost in the cosmos, and the transcendence of the moral conscience, which makes it equal to the universe:

> In the immensity of the space and time of the universe, man resembles a speck of dust blown by the wind, or a tiny spark of light. What makes him equal to it, however, is the perfection of his fundamental goodness, and the nobility of his moral effort.[8]

Among the numerous attitudes which human beings can adopt with regard to the universe, there is one which was called "Stoic" in the Greco-Roman world, but which could be called by many other names, and which is characterized by specific tendencies.

In the first place, the "Stoic," in the universal sense in which we understand him, is conscious of the fact that no being is alone, but that we are parts of a Whole, constituted by the totality of human beings as well as by the totality of the cosmos. The Stoic constantly has his mind on this Whole. One could also say that the Stoic feels absolutely serene, free, and invulnerable, insofar as he has become aware that there is no other evil than moral evil, and that the only thing that counts is the purity of moral conscience.

Finally, the Stoic believes in the absolute value of the human person. It is too often forgotten, and cannot be repeated too much, that Stoicism is the origin of the modern notion of "human rights." I have already cited Seneca's fine formula on this subject:[9] "man is a sacred thing for man." Yet how could I fail to cite also the remark of Epictetus, when someone asked him how he should put up with a clumsy slave (I, 13, 3):

> You are the slave! So you can't put up with your brother, who has Zeus as his ancestor, and who, as a son, was born from the same seed as you and, like you, descends from on high . . . Don't you remember whom you are ordering around? Your kinsmen, your brothers by nature, and progeny of Zeus.
>
> —But I've got rights with regard to them because I bought them; they don't have any with regard to me!

—Can you see where you are looking? You see the earth, a pit, and you see only these miserable laws, which are the laws of the dead. Don't you look to the laws of the gods?

Epictetus uses the mythical, imagistic representation of the filiation of all human beings from God, which may seem antiquated to a modern audience. Yet when he talks about Zeus—and, as we have seen, the same thing holds true of Marcus Aurelius—he is thinking first and foremost of reason. What Epictetus means is simply the following: this slave is a living being like you, and, like you, a man gifted with reason. Even if human laws refuse to recognize that he is your equal, the laws of the gods, which are the laws of reason, recognize his absolute value. We people of modern times think that we have abolished these laws of the dead, but in the last analysis they still dominate the world.

V. Goldschmidt[10] was right to point out that another aspect of what could be called "eternal Stoicism" is the exercise of concentration on the present instant. This consists, on the one hand, in living as if we were seeing the world for the first and last time; and, on the other, in being aware that within this lived present of the instant, we have access to the totality of time and of the world.

⁂

The reader may rightly object at this point: the fact that there is a kind of universal, perennial character to this peculiar attitude which we call "Stoic" may perhaps explain why, despite the distance which separates us from them, we can still understand the *Meditations,* and, better yet, find rules for our thought and action in them. Yet this doesn't explain the unique fascination that they exert upon us. Could we not say that if this book is still so attractive to us, it is because when we read it we get the impression of encountering, not the Stoic system, although Marcus constantly refers to it, but a man of good will, who does not hesitate to criticize and examine himself, who constantly takes up again the task of exhorting and persuading himself, and of finding the words which will help him to live, and to live well? To be sure, these are spiritual exercises, carried out in accordance with a specific method. Yet, in a sense, we are present at them: we catch them *in actu,* in the very moment in which they are being practiced.

In world literature one finds lots of preachers, lesson-givers, and censors, who moralize to others with complacency, irony, cynicism, or bitterness; but it is extremely rare to find a person training himself to live and to think like a human being (V, 1):

> In the morning, when you have trouble waking up, let the following thought be present to you: "I'm getting up to do the job of a human being."

One must admit that there are few hesitations, fumblings, or searchings in these exercises which follow a canvas that Stoic philosophy and Epictetus have drawn in advance with precision. The personal effort appears rather in the repetitions, the multiple variations developed around the same theme, and the stylistic effort as well, which always seeks for a striking, effective formula. Nevertheless, we feel a highly particular emotion when we enter, as it were, into the spiritual intimacy of a soul's secrets, and are thus directly associated with the efforts of a man who, fascinated by the only thing necessary—the absolute value of moral good—is trying to do what, in the last analysis, we are all trying to do: to live in complete consciousness and lucidity; to give each of our instants its fullest intensity; and to give meaning to our entire life. Marcus is talking to himself, but we get the impression that he is talking to each one of us.

ABBREVIATIONS

Birley: A. R. Birley, *Marcus Aurelius* (London, 1966); 1987².

Breithaupt: G. Breithaupt, *De M. Aurelii Antonini commentariis quaestiones selectae* (Göttingen, 1913).

Casaubon: *Marci Antonini Imperatoris De Seipso et Ad Seipsum libri XII,* Guil. Xylander . . . Graece et Latine primus edidit, nunc vero . . . notas et emendationes adjecit Mericus Casaubonus (London, 1643). Greek text with Latin translation.

Dalfen: J. Dalfen, ed., *M. Aurelii Antonini ad Se Ipsum Libri XII* (Leipzig: Teubner, 1979, reprinted 1987). Greek text only. A critical edition with an excellent index of vocabulary; but Dalfen, in my view, wrongly considers too many passages to be interpolations.

Diels-Kranz: *Die Fragmente der Vorsokratiker,* Greek and German by Hermann Diels, edited by Walther Kranz, 3 vols. (Berlin, 1954–). Contains the Greek text with German translation of the pre-Socratic philosophers, such as Heraclitus, Democritus, and Empedocles.

Farquharson: *The Meditations of the Emperor M. Aurelius,* ed. with translation and commentary by A. S. L. Farquharson (Oxford, 1968). Greek text with an English translation; rich commentary.

Fronto: cited simultaneously in two editions: M. Cornelius Fronto, *Epistulae,* ed. M. J. P. van den Hout (Leipzig: Teubner, 1988); *The Correspondence of Marcus Cornelius Fronto,* ed. and trans. C. R. Haines, 2 vols., Loeb Classical Library.

Galen, ed. Kühn: *Claudii Galeni Opera omnia,* ed. C. G. Kühn, 20 vols. (Leipzig, 1821–1833). Greek text with Latin translation. Some of Galen's works have been published in newer editions by various editors; these are indicated in the notes.

Gataker: *Marci Antonini Imperatoris de rebus suis, sive de eis quae ad se pertinere censebat libri XIII commentario perpetuo explicati atque illustrati,* studio . . . Thomae Gatakeri (Cambridge, 1652). Greek text with Latin translation. The Latin commentary is extremely rich, but sometimes a bit prolix.

Grimal: P. Grimal, *Marc Aurèle* (Paris: Fayard, 1991).

Renan: E. Renan, *Marc Aurèle et la fin du monde antique* (Paris, 1882). Often reprinted. The edition I cite is in the collection entitled "Le livre de poche," "Biblio/Essais," no. 4015 (Paris: Librairie générale française, 1984).

Stobaeus *Anthol.*: K. Wachsmuth and O. Hense., eds., *Ioannis Stobaei Anthologium,* 5 vols. (Berlin, 1884–1912).

Stoïciens: Les Stoïciens, trans. É. Bréhier, ed. under the direction of P. M. Schuhl; Bibliothèque de la Pléiade (Paris: NRF, 1962). Contains French translations of texts by Cleanthes, Diogenes Laertius, Plutarch, Cicero, Seneca, Epictetus, and Marcus Aurelius.

SVF: H. von Arnim, ed., *Stoicorum Veterum Fragmenta,* 4 vols. (Leipzig, 1905–1924). Contains only Latin and Greek texts.

Theiler: W. Theiler, ed., *Kaiser Marc Aurel: Wege zu sich selbst* (Zurich, 1951–). To date, this is the best edition of the Greek text of the *Meditations,* as well as the best translation (in German).

NOTES

1. The Emperor-Philosopher

1. On these factories, see H. Bloch, *I bolli laterzi e la storia edilizia romana* (Rome, 1947 [1968²]), especially pp. 204–210, 331; Margareta Steinby, "Ziegel-stempel von Rom und Umgebung," in *Paulys Realencyclopädie,* Supplement, XV, 1978, col. 1489–1591.

2. On the relationship between these births, mintings of coinage, and impe-rial propaganda, see K. Fittschen, *Die Bildnistypen der Faustina Minor und die Fecunditas Augustae* (Göttingen, 1982).

3. Cf. E. Champlin, *Fronto and Antonine Rome* (Cambridge, Mass.: Harvard University Press, 1980), pp. 139–142.

4. James F. Gilliam, "The Plague under Marcus Aurelius," *American Journal of Philology,* 82 (1961): 225–251.

5. Cassius Dio, LXXII, 36, 3.

6. F. Lot, *La Fin du monde antique et le début du Moyen Age* (Paris, 1951), pp. 198–199.

7. See the works of E. Renan, A. R. Birley, and P. Grimal.

8. On this aspect of ancient philosophy, see P. Hadot, *Exercices spirituels et philosophie antique* (Paris, 1992³) [English translation: *Philosophy As a Way of Life,* Chicago, 1995]; Hadot, preface to R. Goulet, ed., *Dictionnaire des philosophes antiques,* vol. I (Paris, 1989), pp. 11–16.

9. J. M. Rist, "Are You a Stoic? The Case of Marcus Aurelius," in B. F. Meyer and E. P. Sanders, eds., *Jewish and Christian Self-Definition,* vol. III (Lon-don, 1983), p. 23.

10. It is true that the Christian apologist Justin, a contemporary of Marcus Aurelius (cf. André Wartelle, *Saint Justin, Apologies* [Paris, 1987], pp. 31–32), at the beginning of his *Apology,* gives the title of "philosophers" to Marcus Aurelius and to Verus. Melito of Sardis, another apologist (cf. Eusebius of Caesarea, *Ecclesiastical History* IV, 26, 7) associates Commodus with the philosophical repu-tation of his father, Marcus Aurelius. In both these cases, it was obviously because of Marcus that his associates were dignified with this title. On the notion of "philosopher" in the Imperial period, see the excellent work by J. Hahn, *Der Philosoph und die Gesellschaft* (Stuttgart, 1989).

11. Fronto, *Ad Antonin. Imper., De eloquentia,* 2, 15, p. 143, 19 Van den Hout; vol. II, p. 70 Haines.

12. *Historia Augusta, Marcus Aurelius* (hereafter *MA*), II, 1: "*Fuit a prima infantia gravis.*"

13. Fronto, *Ad Marc. Caes.,* II, 16, p. 34, 2 Van den Hout = vol. I, p. 150 Haines.

14. According to the *Historia Augusta (MA* IV, 9, vol. I), Diognetus or Diogenetus was Marcus' painting teacher.

15. See J. Taillardat, *Les Images d'Aristophane* (Paris, 1962), p. 268, §474; n. 2.

16. *Historia Augusta, MA,* II, 6.

17. Seneca, *Letters to Lucilius,* 18, 5–7; 20, 9; Pliny the Younger, *Letters,* I, 22, 4; Musonius, 20, in A.-J. Festugière, trans., *Deux prédicateurs de l'Antiquité, Télès et Musonius* (Paris, 1978), pp. 123–124.

18. Cf. Strabo, *Geography,* V, 47.

19. Cf. Polybius, *Histories,* I, 32, 1; Plutarch, *Agesilaus* 2; *Cleomenes* 11, 3–4; Dionysius of Halicarnassus, *Antiquities of Rome,* 2, 23, 2, 1.

20. Plutarch, *Lycurgus,* 16, 12.

21. F. Ollier, *Le Mirage spartiate,* 2 vols. (Paris, 1933–1943). Cf. E. N. Tigerstedt, *The Legend of Sparta in Classical Antiquity,* 2 vols. (Stockholm, 1965–1973).

22. Musonius, in Festugière, *Deux prédicateurs de l'Antiquité,* pp. 52; 124.

23. Cf. Plato, *Symposium,* 219b; Xenophon, *Memorabilia,* I, 6, 2.

24. *Historia Augusta, MA,* III, 3.

25. Cassius Dio, LXXII, 35, 1.

26. Themistius, *Orationes quae supersunt,* ed. G. Downey and A. F. Norman (Leipzig: Teubner, 1969–1974), vol. I (*orat.* 17), p. 307, 28; vol. II (*orat.* 34), pp. 218, 6; 226, 9.

27. I. Hadot, *Seneca und die griechisch-römische Tradition der Seelenleitung* (Berlin, 1969), pp. 167–168.

28. Epictetus, *Discourses,* IV, 8, 12.

29. Fronto, *Ad Antonin. Imper.,* I, 2, 3, p. 88, 4 Van den Hout = vol. II, p. 36 Haines.

30. Fronto, *Ad Marc. Caesar.,* IV, 13, pp. 67–68 Van den Hout = vol. I, p. 214 Haines. On the idea of conversion, cf. A. D. Nock, *Conversion: The Old and the New in Religion from Alexander the Great to Augustine of Hippo* (Oxford, 1933); P. Hadot, *Exercices spirituels,* pp. 175–182.

31. It is highly improbable that Marcus, as a Caesar, should have been the assessor of Aufidius.

32. E. Champlin, "The Chronology of Fronto," *Journal of Roman Studies,* 64 (1974): 144ff.

33. R. B. Rutherford, *The Meditations of Marcus Aurelius: A Study* (Oxford, 1989), p. 106 n. 41; H. Görgemanns, "Der Bekehrungsbrief Marc Aurels," *Rheinisches Museum für Philologie,* 134 (1991): 96–109; P. Hadot, in *École Pratique*

des Hautes Études, Ve Section. Annuaire XCII (1983–1984) (hereafter *Annuaire EPHE*), pp. 331–336.

34. H. Görgemanns ("Der Bekehrungsbrief Marc Aurels," pp. 102–108) shows that this description contains an allusion to the wrath of Achilles in the first book of Homer's *Iliad*. The irony was intended by the young Marcus, in order to attenuate the pain he was inflicting upon his teacher Fronto, by allowing him to glimpse his growing love for philosophy.

35. Cf. the formula *"Silent leges inter arma"* ("laws are silent during wars"), in A. Otto, *Die Sprichwörter* (Hildesheim, 1962), p. 192, and cf. Plutarch, *Agesilaus,* 30, 4.

36. *Les Stoïciens, textes traduits par E. Bréhier, édités sous la direction de P. M. Schuhl* (Paris, collection de la Pléiade, 1964), p. 68 (§163); cited in what follows as *Stoïciens.* On this philosopher, cf. I. Ioppolo, *Aristone di Chio e lo stoicismo antico* (Naples, 1981).

37. Cf. *SVF,* vol. I, §§383–403.

38. Seneca, *Letters to Lucilius,* 94, 2; Cicero, *On Ends,* III, 50; IV, 43; 79.

39. On this point, correct what I said about Aristo in P. Hadot, *Exercices spirituels,* p. 130, and in *Annuaire EPHE* XCII.

40. *Historia Augusta, Antoninus Pius,* X, 4.

41. [There is an untranslatable play on words here, between the French "tendu" and "détendu." —Trans.]

42. *Historia Augusta, Antoninus Pius,* X, 5.

43. *Historia Augusta, MA,* III, 2.

44. *Suidae Lexikon,* ed. A. Adler, vol. I (Stuttgart, 1971²), §235, p. 341.

45. Philostratus, *Lives of the Sophists,* II, 557. This Lucius is obviously not Lucius Verus, Marcus' adoptive brother, as is supposed by Grimal (p. 89), but a philosopher about whom Philostratus tells other anecdotes as well, within the same context. Note Marcus' tolerance of Lucius' uninhibited speech; cf. Rutherford, *Meditations,* p. 89.

46. Fronto, *Ad Antonin. Imper., De eloquentia,* I, 4, p. 135, 3 Van den Hout = vol. II, p. 50 Haines.

47. Ibid., 2, 1, p. 144, 2; 5, 4, p. 151, 22 Van den Hout = vol. II, pp. 66; 83 Haines.

48. See G. W. Bowersock, *Greek Sophists in the Roman Empire* (Oxford, 1969), pp. 53–54; Philostratus, *Lives of the Sophists,* II, 5, 571.

49. *Historia Augusta, MA,* III, 2; III, 3.

50. Galen, *De praecognitione = Galen, On Prognosis,* ed., Engl. trans., and commentary by V. Nutton (= Corpus Medicorum Graecorum, V, 8, 1), Berlin, 1979, p. 82, 6. In his review of R. MacMullen's *Enemies of the Roman Order* (*Journal of Roman Studies,* 59 [1969]: 265), O. Murray puts forth the hypothesis that Marcus' friend and teacher is the same Claudius Severus mentioned by Galen—that is, Marcus' own son-in-law.

51. On these sessions, see P. Moraux, *Galien de Pergame: Souvenirs d'un médecin* (Paris, 1985), pp. 83, 101.

52. Fronto, *Ad Amicos*, I, 14, p. 180, 2 Van den Hout = vol. II, p. 10 Haines.

53. Fronto, *Ad Anton. Imper., De eloquentia*, 2, 11, p. 140, 6 Van den Hout = vol. II, p. 62 Haines.

54. Fronto, *De feriis Alsiensibus*, 6, p. 230, 14 Van den Hout = vol. II, p. 10 Haines.

55. Cf. Rist, "Are You a Stoic?"

56. Fronto, *Ad Marc. Caesar.*, V, 24, p. 73, 7 Van den Hout = vol. I, p. 196 Haines.

57. Fronto, *Ad Antonin. Imper.*, I, 3, 2, p. 91, 21 Van den Hout = vol. 2, p. 120 Haines.

58. *Historia Augusta, MA,* XXIII, 5.

59. On Galen's testimony, see the remarks of V. Nutton in his commentary on Galen, *On Prognosis,* pp. 163ff., as well as Hahn, *Der Philosoph und die Gesellschaft,* p. 29 n. 42; pp. 148ff (on philosophical life in Rome during Galen's time). On the careers of these personages, see G. Alföldy, *Konsulat und Senatorenstand unter den Antoninen* (Bonn, 1977); Bowersock, *Greek Sophists in the Roman Empire,* p. 82.

60. Persius, *Satires,* III, 54.

61. Galen, *In Hippocrat. Epidem.*, VI, ed. Wenkelbach/Pfaff (Berlin, 1956²), p. 206 = vol. XVII B, p. 15 Kühn. The conclusions drawn from this text by Dailly and van Effenterre, in "Le cas Marc-Aurèle," *Revue des études anciennes,* 56 (1954): 365, are risky to say the least. Remarks on Imperial fashions in hairstyles may be found in J. Marquardt, *Das Privatleben der Römer* (1886; reprinted Darmstadt, 1980), vol. II, p. 602.

62. Cassius Dio, LXXII, 35, 2.

2. A First Glimpse of the Meditations

1. Cassius Dio, LXXII, 24, 1; cf. A. S. L. Farquharson, *The Meditations of the Emperor Marcus Aurelius* (Oxford, 1968), vol. I, p. xiv.

2. Themistius, *Oratio 6 (Philadelphoi),* 81c.

3. Aurelius Victor, *Book of the Caesars,* 16, 9; *Historia Augusta, Avidius Cassius,* III, 6–7.

4. Nicephoras Callistos Xanthopoulos, *Ecclesiastical History,* III, 31, in Migne's *Patrologia Graeca,* vol. 145, col. 960.

5. *Suidae Lexikon,* ed. A. Adler (Stuttgart, 1967²), vol. III, §214, p. 328, 24.

6. *Arethae Scripta Minora,* ed. L. G. Westerink (Leipzig [Teubner], 1968), vol. I, p. 305.

7. Ibid., vol. II, p. 105, 5 (= *Meditations,* I, 7, 7); *Scholia in Lucianum,* ed. H. Rabe (Leipzig [Teubner], 1906), pp. 189, 207 (= *Meditations,* VIII, 25; 37).

8. Cf. P. Meyer, "Des Joseph Bryennios Schriften, Leben und Bildung,"

Byzantinische Zeitschrift, 5 (1896): 10, who points out several literal citations from Marcus in the writings of this fifteenth-century author.

9. Ioannis Reuchlin, *De arte cabalistica libri tres* (Hagenau, 1517), p. xxxv verso (quoting *Meditations,* IV, 36, designated by the formula *"in libro ad se ipsum tertio,"* as well as VII, 23); p. xlviii verso (quoting IV, 28, 2, where the verb *haploun* is understood not in the sense of "to simplify oneself," but "to get rid of," "to free oneself": *explicare se*). On the manuscript of Marcus used by Reuchlin, cf. L. Bergson, "Fragment einer Marc-Aurel-Handschrift," *Rheinisches Museum,* 129 (1986): 157–169.

10. *Marci Antonini Imperatoris de rebus suis, sive de eis quae ad se pertinere censebat libri XII,* commentario perpetuo explicati atque illustrati studio Thomae Gatakeri, Cambridge, 1652.

11. Cf. P. Hadot, "Préface" to the *Dictionnaire des philosophes antiques,* published under the direction of Richard Goulet, vol. I (Paris, 1989), p. 10.

12. P. Moraux, *Galien de Pergame: Souvenirs d'un médicin* (Paris, 1985), p. 153; L. Brisson, M.-O. Goulet-Cazé, et al., *Porphyre, La Vie de Plotin,* vol. I (Paris, 1982), p. 283.

13. *Arethae Scripta Minora,* vol. I, p. 305.

14. *Anthologia Palatina,* book XV, §23, in *The Greek Anthology,* XII, 135: "If you want to vanquish sadness, open this blessed book and go over it carefully; with its help, you will easily persuade yourself of this oh so fruitful truth: whether past, present or future, pleasures and pains are naught but smoke."

15. *Suidae Lexikon,* ed. A. Adler (Stuttgart, 1967^2), §214, vol. III, p. 328, 24.

16. See Meric Casaubon's edition of Marcus Aurelius: *Marci Antonini Imperatoris De seipso et ad seipsum libri XII* (London, 1643), *Prolegomena,* pp. 12–14 (unnumbered pages), citing the second edition of the *Editio princeps* (1568).

17. See Casaubon, pp. 2–3 of his notes, which are at the end of the work.

18. Gataker, p. 24.

19. Caspar Barthius, *Adversariorum Commentariorum Libri LX* (Frankfurt, 1624), Book I, ch. 2, pp. 22–24.

20. J.-P. de Joly, *Pensées de l'empereur Marc Aurèle* (Paris, 1773^2), pp. xxxiv–xliii.

21. Farquharson, pp. lxiv–lxvii.

22. Renan, pp. 157–158.

23. G. Misch, *Geschichte der Autobiographie,* I, 2 (Bern, 1951^2), p. 449.

24. P. A. Brunt, "Marcus Aurelius in His Meditations," *Journal of Roman Studies,* 64 (1974): 1.

25. Fronto, *Ad Marc. Caesar.,* II, 8, 3, p. 29, 2 Van den Hout = vol. I, p. 138 Haines.

26. Brunt in *Journal of Roman Studies,* 64, p. 3 n. 12; R. B. Rutherford, *Meditations,* p. 29 n. 90.

27. Cf. Photius, *Library,* vol. II, codex no. 175, pp. 170–171 Henry.

28. Aulus Gellius, Preface, §2.

29. Plutarch, *On the Tranquillity of the Soul,* I, 464F.

30. Augustine, *Soliloquies,* ed. and trans. P. de Labriolle, in *Oeuvres de saint Augustin,* 1st series, V, *Dialogues philosophiques,* II, *Dieu et l'Ame* (Paris, 1935), p. 25.

31. Porphyry, *Life of Plotinus,* 8, 4.

32. See E. Arns, *La Technique du livre d'après saint Jérôme* (Paris, 1953), pp. 47–48 (quoting the *Patrologia latina,* vol. 25, 1118A).

33. Brunt in *Journal of Roman Studies,* 64: 1, quoting Cassius Dio, LXXII, 36, 2.

34. T. Dorandi, "Den Autoren über die Schulter geschaut: Arbeitsweise und Autographie bei den antiken Schriftstellern," *Zeitschrift für Papyrologie und Epigraphik,* 87 (1991): 11–33, especially pp. 29–33.

35. On the meaning of this term, see Arns, *Technique du livre,* pp. 18–22.

36. J.-P. de Joly, *Pensées de Marc Aurèle,* pp. xxxiv–xliii.

37. Brunt, "Marcus Aurelius," pp. 1–15; G. Cortasso, *Il Filosofo, i libri, la memoria. Poeti e filosofi nei Pensieri di Marco Aurelio* (Turin, 1989), pp. 60; 1a n. 11 (bibliography).

3. The Meditations as Spiritual Exercises

1. Epictetus, *Discourses,* I, 3, 1; I, 18, 20; II, 16 (title); III, 10, 1.

2. Victor Hugo, *Quatre-vingt-treize,* III, 2, 7.

3. *Stoïciens,* pp. 48 (§§100–101)[= Diogenes Laertius, *Lives,* VII, 101–102], 271 [= Cicero, *On Ends,* III, 8, 27ff.]; *SVF,* vol. III, §§29–48; Epictetus, *Discourses,* IV, 1, 133.

4. I am following here the division of the text proposed by Theiler, but I retain, with Dalfen, the reading *mimos.*

5. *Stoïciens,* p. 97 [= Plutarch, *On Stoic Self-Contradictions,* 9, 1035Aff.] =*SVF,* vol. III, §68.

6. Cicero, *On the Laws,* I, 7, 33; I, 12, 33, carries out the same linkage between the idea of common law and that of the community among reasonable beings.

7. Lucretius, *On the Nature of Things,* III, 1024–1052; F. Villon, *Ballade des dames du temps jadis,* in Villon, *Poésies complètes* (Paris, Livre de poche, Lettres gothiques, 1991), p. 117. Cf. G. B. Conte, "Il trionfo della Morte e la galleria dei grandi trapassati in Lucrezio III, 1024–1053," *Studi italiani di filologia classica,* NS, 37 (1965): 114–132, especially p. 131 n. 2.

8. *Stoïciens,* p. 58 (§134) [= Diogenes Laertius, *Lives,* VII, 134]; *SVF,* vol. II, §§299–305.

9. On the use of Greek in Rome, cf. Quintillian, *Instit.,* I, 1, 12; I. Hadot, *Arts libéraux et philosophie dans la pensée antique* (Paris, 1984), p. 248.

10. As is the view of J. M. Rist, "Are You a Stoic?" in Meyer and Sanders, eds., *Jewish and Christian Self-Definition.*

11. Aulus Gellius, *Attic Nights,* VII, 1, 7; VII, 2, 1.

4. The Philosopher-Slave and the Emperor-Philosopher

1. On quotations in Marcus Aurelius, see the excellent study by G. Cortassa, *Il Filosofo, i libri, la memoria. Poeti e filosofi nei Pensieri di Marco Aurelio* (Turin, 1989).

2. See, for example, A. A. Long, "Heraclitus and Stoicism," *Philosophia,* 5–6 (1975–1976): 133–153.

3. Cf. M. Conche, *Héraclite, Fragments* (Paris, 1986), pp. 68–69 (fr. 11 Conche = fr. 73 Diels/Kranz). See G. Cortassa, *Il Filosofo,* pp. 41–54. [Cf. Charles H. Kahn, *The Art and Thought of Heraclitus* (Cambridge, 1979), fr. v., pp. 30–31. —Trans.]

4. Cf. Conche, p. 333 (fr. 96 Conche = 71 Diels/Kranz) [= fr. cvi, pp. 76–77 Kahn —Trans.].

5. Ibid., p. 71 (fr. 12 Conche = 75 Diels/Kranz) [= fr. xci, pp. 70–71 Kahn].

6. Ibid., p. 65 (fr. 10 Conche = 72 Diels/Kranz) [= fr. v, pp. 30–31 Kahn].

7. Ibid.

8. Ibid., p. 297 (fr. 85 Conche = 76 Diels/Kranz) [= fr. xli, pp. 46–7 Kahn].

9. We could add to this list the theme of the cosmic seasons: IV, 23; IX, 3; IX, 10 (a reminiscence of Heraclitus); cf. Conche, p. 198 (fr. 51 = 100 Diels/Kranz) [= fr. xlii, pp. 48–9 Kahn].

10. Cortassa, *Il Filosofo,* pp. 65–70: Empedocles, frr. 27–28 Diels/Kranz. Cf. Horace's well-known remark about the Sage (*Satires,* II, 7, 86): "And, round and spherical, he finds everything within himself."

11. Cf. Cortassa, *Il Filosofo,* pp. 107–113; Democritus, fr. 3 Diels/Kranz. Analogous criticisms of this dictum are to be found in Seneca, *On Peace of Mind,* 13, 1; *On Anger,* III, 6, 3; as well as in Plutarch, *On Peace of Mind,* 465c.

12. Democritus, fr. 115 Diels/Kranz. Cf. Cortassa, *Il Filosofo,* pp. 115–117.

13. Democritus, testimony 49 Diels/Kranz = Galen, *De elementis ex Hippocrate, libri II,* ed. G. Helmreich, Erlangen 1878, I, 2, p. 3, 20 (Vol. I, p. 417 Kühn).

14. This is the interpretation of Cortassa, *Il Filosofo,* pp. 109–113.

15. This is the interpretation given by Theiler in his translation of this passage.

16. Diogenes Laertius, VI, 83. The translation proposed by L. Paquet, "Every *human undertaking* is naught but smoke" (*Les Cyniques grecs: Fragments et témoignages* [Paris: Livre de Poche, 1992], p. 164), certainly does not correspond to what Marcus understood.

17. It is not known to which precise anecdote Marcus is alluding; cf. Cortassa, *Il Filosofo,* p. 57.

18. Cortassa, *Il Filosofo,* pp. 129–139.

19. Ibid., pp. 141–145.

20. On the possibility of moral progress, see I. Hadot, *Seneca,* pp. 76–77; and on the difference in the seriousness of faults, ibid., pp. 144–152. Cf. Seneca, *On Clemency,* IV, 3: *"Peccavimus omnes, alii gravia, alii leviora."*

21. Cortassa, *Il Filosofo,* pp. 125–128.

22. Ibid., pp. 147–162.

23. Cf. P. Hadot, "'Only the Present Is Our Happiness': The Value of the Present Instant in Goethe and in Ancient Philosophy," in *Philosophy As a Way of Life*, pp. 217–237.

24. Aulus Gellius, *Attic Nights*, I, 2, 1–13; II, 18, 11; XV, 11, 5; XVII, 19, 1; XIX, 1, 14.

25. Lucian, *The Ignorant Book-Collector*, §13, in Loeb Classical Library edition, vol. 3, p. 192.

26. Galen, *De libris propriis*, in *Opera omnia*, vol. XX, p. 44, 10 Kühn.

27. Origen, *Against Celsus*, III, 54, 23; VI, 2, 15; VII, 53, 13; 54, 24.

28. Simplicius, *In Epicteti Enchiridion*, pp. 45, 35; 116, 48 Dübner.

29. Lucian, *Demonax*, §55, in Loeb Classical Library edition, vol. 1, p. 168.

30. See the excellent article by S. Follet, "Arrien de Nicomédie," in R. Goulet, ed., *Dictionnaire des Philosophes Anciens*, vol. I (Paris, 1989), pp. 597–604; see also P. A. Stadter, *Arrian of Nicomedia* (Chapel Hill: University of North Carolina Press, 1980). Some of Arrian's works may be found in A. G. Roos and G. Wirth, eds., *Flavii Arriani quae extant omnia*, vol. II: *Scripta minora et fragmenta* (Leipzig: Teubner, 1968).

31. P. A. Stadter, *Arrian*, p. 14; J. H. Oliver, "Arrian in Two Roles," in *Hesperia*, Suppl. XIX: *Studies in Attic Epigraphy, History, and Topography presented to Eugene Vanderpool* (Princeton, 1982), pp. 122–129.

32. Follet, in *Dictionnaire des Philosophes Anciens*, vol. I, p. 597; *Suidae Lexikon*, vol. II, p. 117 Adler.

33. A new edition of the Greek text is currently being prepared by G. Boter. The text and English translation, ed. and trans. W. A. Oldfather, is available in the Loeb Classical Library.

34. See Follet, p. 602.

35. Ibid., p. 599.

36. Themistius, *Oratio* 34.

37. [A consul *suffectus* was one elected upon the death or abdication of a regularly elected consul. —Trans.]

38. A summary of the various positions adopted, as well as a bibliography on the question, may be found in Follet, in *Dictionnaire des Philosophes Anciens*, vol. I, p. 602.

39. J. Souilhé, *Épictète, Entretiens*, vol. I, Introduction, p. xxix.

40. [The French words used here are "lecture" and "leçon" respectively; they both derive from the Latin *lectio*, "reading." —Trans.]

41. Aulus Gellius, *Attic Nights*, I, 26, 1–11.

42. Photius, *Library*, codex 250, 111, vol. VII, p. 189 Henry.

43. This too often repeated opinion is refuted by I. Hadot, "Épictète," in *Encyclopedia Universalis*, p. 36.

44. Aulus Gellius, *Attic Nights*, XIX, 1, 14.

45. Ibid., I, 2, 6.

46. Farquharson, vol. II, p. 446.

47. On the quotations of Epictetus in the *Meditations,* see G. Breithaupt, *De Marci Aurelii Antonini commentariis quaestiones selectae* (Göttingen, 1913), pp. 45–64.

48. H. Fränkel, "Ein Epiktetfragment," *Philologus,* 80 (1925): 221.

49. In my forthcoming edition of Marcus Aurelius, I hope to return to Fränkel's demonstration, as well as to the more general problem of the fragments of Epictetus in Marcus.

50. "La physique comme exercice spirituel, ou pessimisme et optimisme chez Marc Aurèle," *Revue de théologie et de philosophie* (1972), pp. 225–239, reprinted with corrections in P. Hadot, *Exercices spirituels,* pp. 119–133.

51. Philo of Alexandria, *On the Special Laws,* II, §46.

52. *SVF,* vol. I, §360 = Clement of Alexandria, *Stromata,* II, 21, 129, 5.

53. I, 12; III, 1, 2; III, 16, 2; VI, 22; VI, 26, 3.

54. *SVF,* vol. I, §§351–357; cf. *Stoïciens,* p. 68 [= Diogenes Laertius, *Lives,* VII, 160 —Trans.].

55. H. Görgemanns, "Die Bekehrungsbrief Marc Aurels," *Rheinisches Museum für Philologie,* 134 (1991): 108, is of the view that the name of Aristo—famous for his eloquence and therefore nicknamed "the Siren"—is only emphasized in the letter to Fronto which speaks of Marcus' "conversion" to philosophy in order not to hurt Fronto's feelings. Fronto, on this hypothesis, would have been more offended to hear of his rival Junius Rusticus or of the *Discourses* of Epictetus, which Fronto's literary taste held in low esteem.

5. The Stoicism of Epictetus

1. Émile Bréhier, *Histoire de la philosophie,* vol. I (Paris, 1928; reprinted 1991), p. 266.

2. Seneca, *Letters to Lucilius,* 20, 2–5.

3. *SVF,* vol. I, §179 (= Johannes Stobaeus, *Anthologium,* II, 7, 6, vol. II, p. 75, 11 Wachsmuth). On the transcendence of the accord with oneself in comparison with the things with which the living being is in accordance, cf. Victor Goldschmidt, *Le Système stoïcien et l'idée de temps* (Paris, 1979⁴), p. 129.

4. *SVF,* vol. II, §§625; 596–632.

5. Cf. P. Hadot, "La figure du sage dans l'Antiquité gréco-latine," in *Les Sagesses du monde,* ed. G. Gadoffre (Paris, 1991), pp. 11–18.

6. Cf. O. Luschnat, "Das Problem des ethischen Fortschritts in der alten Stoa," *Philologus,* 102 (1958): 178–214; I. Hadot, *Seneca,* pp. 72–78.

7. Cf. P. Hadot, "La division des parties de la philosophie dans l'Antiquité," *Museum Helveticum,* 36 (1979): 201–223.

8. Bréhier, *Histoire de la philosophie,* vol. I, p. 266.

9. Cf. Cicero, *On the Limits of Goods and Evils,* III, 21, 72–73.

10. Plutarch, *On Stoic Self-Contradictions,* 9, 1035aff. = *SVF,* vol. II, no. 42 = *Stoïciens,* pp. 96–97.

11. *SVF* II, no. 41 = Diogenes Laertius, VII, 40, 9–10.

12. *SVF* II, 38 = Posidonius ap. Sextus Empiricus, *Adversus mathematicos,* VII, 19, 1–2 = *Against the Logicians,* I, 19, vol. II, p. 10 Bury.

13. *SVF* II, 53 = Chrysippus ap. Plutarch, *On Stoic Self-Contradictions,* IX, 1035e2–4.

14. Diogenes Laertius, VII, 41. See also ibid., 39, where mention is made of philosophical *doctrine,* and not of *philosophy.* Cf. P. Hadot, "Philosophie, discours philosophique et divisions de la philosophie chez les stoïciens," *Revue internationale de philosophie* (1991), pp. 205–219.

15. See Plutarch, *On Stoic Self-Contradictions,* 9, 1035aff.

16. Émile Bréhier, in his "Préface" to A. Virieux-Reymond, *La logique et l'épistémologie des Stoïciens* (Chambéry, n.d.), p. v.

17. A. Bonhöffer, *Die Ethik des Stoikers Epictet* (Stuttgart, 1894; reprinted 1968), pp. iii–iv; Bonhöffer, *Epictet und die Stoa* (Stuttgart, 1890; reprinted 1968), p. v.

18. Epictetus, *Discourses,* II, 17, 40; II, 19, 9; III, 2, 13–16; 21, 7.

19. Epictetus, *Manual,* I, 1.

20. [Throughout, the term which Pierre Hadot has rendered in French as "domaine" or "forme" is the Greek word *topos. Topos* literally means "place," but the ancient rhetorico-philosophical discipline of *topics* (one thinks of the works entitled "Topics" by Aristotle and Cicero) has been excellently defined as follows by the Swiss philosopher A.-J. Voelke: "A discipline which permits the orator to find what it is appropriate to say, in accordance with the situation in which he finds himself, and the goal he has set himself. In particular, topics provided a repertoire of points of view, or places, susceptible of providing a basis for a variety of forms of arguments." *La Philosophie comme thérapie de l'âme: Études de philosophie antique* (Fribourg, Suisse/Paris, 1993), p. 2. —Trans.]

21. Plato, *Republic,* IV, 436bff.

22. Plutarch, *On Moral Virtue,* III, 441C–D.

23. See Epictetus, *Discourses,* I, 4, 12; III, 2, 1.

24. *Stoïciens,* p. 30 (§39) [= Diogenes Laertius VII, 40, vol. II, p. 150 Hicks —Trans.].

25. Cf. H. Throm, *Die Thesis* (Paderborn, 1932), pp. 88, 118; P. Hadot, "Philosophie, dialectique, rhétorique dans l'Antiquité," *Studia philosophica,* 39 (1980): 147.

26. A.-J. Voelke, *L'Idée de volonté dans le stoïcisme* (Paris, 1973), p. 97.

27. This point, I believe, should suffice to refute the objections set forth by D. Pesce, in his *Il Platone di Tubinga* (Brescia, 1990), pp. 55ff.

28. *SVF,* vol. III, §68 [= Plutarch, *On Stoic Self-Contradictions,* 9, 1035c — Trans.].

29. On these types of reasoning, see *Stoïciens,* pp. 1339–1340, notes to p. 824.

30. After a general introduction (chapter 1), the reader proceeds to the discipline of desire (chapters 2–29); the discipline of action (chapters 30–51); and the

discipline of assent (which is only mentioned in passing; see chapter 52). The *Manual* then concludes with a series of sayings which must always be kept "at hand" (chapter 53); cf. M. Pohlenz, *Die Stoa*, vol. 2 (Göttingen, 1955), p. 162.

31. On these attempts, cf. P. Hadot, *Exercices spirituels*, pp. 150–153.

6. The Inner Citadel, or the Discipline of Assent

1. *Stoïciens*, p. 32 (§49) [= Diogenes Laertius, *Lives of the Eminent Philosophers*, VII, 49. Cf. the translation of Long and Sedley vol. I, §33D, p. 196; §39A, pp. 236–237 —Trans.].

2. Ibid., p. 33 (§51ff.) [= Diogenes Laertius VII, 51ff; cf. Long and Sedley vol. I, §39A, pp. 236–237; §40P; Q, p. 248; 39D, p. 238; 40A, pp. 241–2; etc. —Trans.].

3. Aulus Gellius, *Attic Nights*, XIX, 1, 15–20.

4. *Stoïciens*, p. 489 (= Cicero, *On Fate*, XIX, §43).

5. *SVF* II, 98 (= Sextus Empiricus, *Against the Logicians*, II (= *Adversus Mathematicos*, VIII), §397, vol. II, pp. 446–447 Bury [Loeb Classical Library]).

6. Plutarch, *On Moral Virtue*, 3, 441c.

7. *SVF* II, 846 (= Damascius, *Commentary on the Phaedo*, §276, p. 167 Westerink).

8. Goldschmidt, *Système stoïcien*, pp. 120–121.

9. I base this translation of *ou pantos* on the versions of such previous translators as A. Politian, W. A. Oldfather, M. Meunier, and W. Capelle.

10. Sextus Empiricus, *Adversus Mathematicos*, VII, 234, 2 – 235, 4 = *Against the Logicians*, I, vol. II, §§234–235, p. 126 Bury (LCL).

11. Seneca, *Letters to Lucilius*, 78, §14.

12. Seneca, *On the Constancy of the Sage*, X, 4.

13. Seneca, *On Anger*, II, 4, 1f.

14. Ibid., I, 16, 7.

15. Empedocles frr. 27–28 Diels-Kranz; Horace, *Satires* II, 7, 86.

16. *Stoïciens*, p. 44 (§88) = *SVF* vol. III, §4 [= Diogenes Laertius, *Lives*, VII, 88 —Trans.].

17. Aristotle, *Nichomachean Ethics*, X, 7, 1177b26.

18. Paul Claudel, *Vers d'exil* ["Verses from Exile"], VII.

19. Plotinus, *Enneads*, I, 1, 13, 7.

20. Pascal, *Pensées*, §460, p. 544 Brunschvicg.

21. Ibid., §793, p. 695.

22. *SVF* III, §171 = *Stoïciens*, p. 133 *ad finem* [= John Stobaeus, *Eclogae*, II, 88, 1ff. Wachsmuth; Cf. Long and Sedley 33 I, vol I p. 197 (translation); vol. II p. 200 (Greek text, commentary, and further literature) —Trans.]. Cf. Voelke, *L'Idée de volonté*, pp. 50–55.

23. *SVF* III, §265 = *Stoïciens*, p. 45, §92 [= Diogenes Laertius, *Lives*, VII, 92–93 —Trans.].

24. R. Schaerer, *La Question platonicienne* (Paris-Neuchâtel, 1969), p. 100.

25. É. Bréhier, "Préface" to A. Virieux-Reymond, *La Logique et l'épistémologie des Stoïciens*, Chambéry, p. v.

7. The Discipline of Desire, or Amor Fati

1. Cf. Voelke, *L'Idée de volonté*, pp. 131–133.

2. *Stoïciens*, p. 44, §§87–89 = *SVF* III, 4 [= Diogenes Laertius, *Lives*, VII, 87–89 —Trans.].

3. On the identity of living according to nature and living in accordance with the *logos* (Marcus Aurelius VII, 11), cf. *Stoïciens*, p. 44, §86 = *SVF* III, 178 [= D.L., *Lives*, VII, 85–86 —Trans.].

4. Anatole France, *Le Livre de mon ami*, XI, in *Oeuvres*, vol. I (Paris, La Pléiade), p. 515.

5. *SVF*, vol. II, 509 [= Johannes Stobaeus, *Eclogae*, I, 8, 40, p. 106, 5ff. ed. Wachsmuth = Arius Didymus, *Epitome*, Fr. Phys. 26, ed. H. Diels (*Doxographi Graeci*, Berlin, 1879, pp. 461f.) = Long and Sedley fr. 51B, trans. vol. I, p. 304; Greek text and commentary vol. II, pp. 301–302 —Trans.]. On this problematic, cf. J.-J. Duhot, *La Conception stoïcienne de la causalité* (Paris, 1989), pp. 95–100.

6. H. Bergson, *La Pensée et le Mouvant* (Paris, 1934), pp. 168–169.

7. Cf. Simplicius, *Commentary on Aristotle's Categories*, p. 407, 3 Kalbfleisch: "for them, the future is determined."

8. This interpretation of Stoic ideas about the present, the past, and the future is based on that of Émile Bréhier, *La Théorie des incorporels dans l'ancien stoïcisme* (Paris, 1962³), pp. 58–59.

9. Goldschmidt, *Système stoïcien*, p. 195.

10. *Pace* E. R. Dodds, *Pagans and Christians in an Age of Anxiety* (New York, 1970), p. 9, and Rist, in Meyer and Sanders, eds., *Jewish and Christian Self-Definition*, pp. 38–39.

11. Homer, *Iliad*, XX, 127; XXIV, 209, 525; *Odyssey*, VII, 197.

12. Cf. Pierre Boyancé, "Remarques sur le Papyrus de Derveni," *Revue des Études Grecques*, 87 (1974): 95.

13. Plato, *Republic*, 617b ff.

14. *SVF* II, 913 [= Stobaeus, *Eclogae*, I, 79, 1 Wachsmuth —Trans.].

15. *SVF* II, 914 [= Diogenianus in Eusebius, *Evangelical Preparation*, VI, 8, 9, 1—10, 5 Mras. —Trans.].

16. Good accounts of this theory are contained in É. Bréhier, *Chrysippe* (Paris, 1951), pp. 114–127; S. Sambursky, *The Physics of the Stoics* (London, 1959), pp. 11–17. Cf. *Stoïciens*, pp. 167–169 (= Plutarch, *On Common Notions, 37,* 1077–1078).

17. *Stoïciens*, p. 169 [= Plutarch, *On Common Notions* 1078D-E —Trans.].

18. Hubert Reeves, *Patience dans l'azur* (Paris, 1988), p. 259.

19. Francis Thompson, *The Mistress of Vision* (Aylesford: St. Albert's Press, 1966).

20. Euripides, fr. 898, in A. Nauck, ed., *Tragicorum Graecorum fragmenta* (Leipzig: Teubner, 1889; repr. Hildesheim: Olms, 1964).

21. Nietzsche, *Ecce homo. Why I am so Intelligent,* 10 [= *Friedrich Nietzsche: Sämtliche Werke, Kritische Studienausgabe herausgegeben von Giorgio Colli und Mazzino Montinari* (Berlin/New York: Walter de Gruyter, 1988), vol. 6, p. 297, 24–29; cf. Friedrich Nietzsche, *On the Genealogy of Morals and Ecce Homo,* ed. and trans. Walter Kaufmann (New York: Vintage Books, 1967), p. 258 — Trans.].

22. Nietzsche, *Nietzsche Contra Wagner, Epilogue,* I [= vol. 6, p. 436, 15–19 Colli/Montinari; cf. *The Portable Nietzsche,* selected and translated by Walter Kaufmann (New York: Viking Press, 1954), p. 680 —Trans.].

23. Nietzsche, *Posthumous Fragments,* late 1886–Spring 1887, 7 (38) [= vol. 12, pp. 307–308 Colli/Montinari; cf. *Friedrich Nietzsche, The Will to Power,* translated by Walter Kaufmann and R. J. Hollingdale, edited by Walter Kaufmann (New York: Vintage Books, 1968), pp. 532–533 (no. 1032) —Trans.].

24. Nietzsche, *Posthumous Fragments,* Spring-Summer 1888, 16 (32) [= vol. 13, p. 492, 31—493, 7 Colli/Montinari; cf. Kaufmann/Hollingdale, pp. 536–537 (no. 1041) —Trans.].

25. William Blake, "Auguries of Innocence," in G. Keynes, ed., *Blake, Complete Writings* (London, 1966), p. 431.

26. Seneca, *On Benefits,* VII, 3.

27. *Stoïciens,* p. 140 (= Plutarch, *On Common Notions,* VIII, 1062a).

28. Seneca, *Letters to Lucilius,* 74, 27.

29. On these notions, see P. Hadot, "Only the Present," in *Philosophy as a Way of Life,* pp. 63–75.

30. Ludwig Wittgenstein, *Tractatus Logico-Philosophicus,* 6.4311.

31. Seneca, *Letters to Lucilius,* 16, 4.

32. This has been the view of scholars from Renan to J. M. Rist (in Meyer and Sanders, eds., *Jewish and Christian Self-Definition,* p. 29).

33. Here I am following the text of Theiler.

34. Aristotle, *Protrepticus,* fr. 2, pp. 27–28 in W. D. Ross, ed., *Aristotelis Fragmenta Selecta* (Oxford, 1955).

35. Seneca, *Letters to Lucilius,* 16, 4. In this passage, we can recognize several of Marcus Aurelius' hypotheses: an impersonal providence (= hypothesis 4 in our diagram); a personal providence (= hypothesis 5); and chance (= hypothesis 1). On these various hypotheses, cf. W. Theiler, "Tacitus und die antike Schicksalslehre," in *Phyllobolia für Peter von der Mühll* (Basel, 1945), pp. 35–90 [reprinted in Theiler's *Forschungen zum Neuplatonismus* (Berlin: Walter de Gruyter, 1966) — Trans.].

36. Cf. M. Frede, *Die Stoische Logik* (Göttingen, 1974), pp. 98–100; Aulus Gellius, *Attic Nights,* XVI, 8, 14.

37. Chrysippus, in Aulus Gellius, *Attic Nights*, VII, 1, 7–13.

38. Cicero, *On the Nature of the Gods*, III, 35, 86. See also II, 66, 167: the gods are concerned about great things, and neglect the minor ones. Cf. Philo of Alexandria, *On Providence*, II, §102: the cataclysms brought about by the natural transformation of the elements are only accidental consequences of fundamental natural processes.

39. Cf. Marcus Aurelius' use of the word *toioutos* in *Meditations*, V, 8, 4, where the cosmos is described as "such-and-such" a body, and destiny as "such-and-such" a cause. See also IV, 33, 3.

40. Pascal, *Pensées*, §77, trans. W. F. Trotter (New York: E. P. Dutton, 1958), no. 77, p. 23.

41. [The word translated here as "reasons" is the Greek *logos*, which has a wide variety of meanings, including "formula," "definition," "proposition," and "account," to name but a few. —Trans.]

42. *Stoïciens*, p. 59 (§§135–136); *SVF* vol. II, §1027 [= Diogenes Laertius, *Lives*, VII, 135–136; cf. Long and Sedley no. 46B, vol. I, p. 275 (translation); vol. II, p. 272 (Greek text and commentary) —Trans.].

43. Seneca, *Natural Questions*, I, Preface, 3.

44. Cleanthes, *Hymn to Zeus*, translation by A.-J. Festugière, *La Révélation d'Hermès Trismégiste*, vol. 2 (Paris, 1949), p. 313; see also *Stoïciens*, p. 8.

45. Seneca, *Natural Questions*, II, 45, 1.

46. Ibid., II, 45, 2–3.

47. Ibid., II, 46.

48. Epictetus, *Discourses*, I, 12, 8; I, 20, 15; Marcus Aurelius, *Meditations*, III, 16, 3; X, 11, 4; XII, 27, 2; XII, 31, 2 (on the identity of following Reason and following God).

49. Cf. P. Hadot, "Introduction" to *Plotin, Traité 50* (Paris, 1990), p. 68.

50. Origen, *Against Celsus*, IV, 74; cf. *SVF*, vol. II, §§1156–1157.

51. H. Bergson, *Les Deux Sources de la morale et de la religion*, p. 343 (the phrase quoted is the last sentence of this work).

52. Cicero, *On the Nature of the Gods*, II, 66, 165–166.

53. On this passage from Marcus Aurelius, see the remarkable article by André-Jean Voelke, "Santé du monde et santé de l'individu: Marc Aurèle V, 8," *Revue internationale de philosophie*, 1991, pp. 322–335. These pages are all the more moving in that, as he was writing them, the author was quite aware of his own imminent death.

54. *Kaiser Marc Aurel und seine Zeit*, ed. Klaus Stemmer (Berlin, 1988), p. xii.

55. R. B. Rutherford, *Meditations*, p. 68.

56. Seneca, *Letters to Lucilius*, 107, 2.

57. Plotinus, *Enneads*, Treatise 38 (VI, 7), 22, 31.

58. In *Nietzsche Contra Wagner*, "Epilogue," I.

59. *Journal de l'abbé Mugnier* (Paris: Mercure de France, 1985), p. 221 [= the diaries of the French clergyman Arthur Mugnier (1853–1944); the princess in

question is Mugnier's Romanian correspondent Martha Bibesco (c. 1887–1973) —Trans.].

60. Note the "view from above" mentioned in the citations from Nietzsche quoted above. On the theme of the "view from above," cf. R. B. Rutherford, *Meditations,* pp. 155–161, 251; P. Hadot, "La terre vue d'en haut et le voyage cosmique," in J. Schneider and M. Léger-Orine, eds., *Frontières et conquêtes spatiales,* Dordrecht, 1988, pp. 31–39 [trans. in Pierre Hadot, *Philosophy As a Way of Life* (Oxford, 1995), pp. 238–250 —Trans.].

61. Seneca, *Letters to Lucilius,* 102, 21.

62. In the Loeb Classical Library edition, ed. and trans. A. M. Harmon, vol. 2.

63. This was the theme of a well-known eighteenth-century novel, *Le diable boiteux,* written by Lesage ["The Limping Devil." Alain René Lesage, author of *The Adventures of Gil Blas de Santillane,* wrote this work in 1707. For an English translation, see *Asmodeus; or, The devil on two sticks* (London, 1841) —Trans.].

64. Lucian, *Dialogues of the Dead,* vol. 7 of the Loeb Classical Library edition of Lucian. *Charon* is in vol. 2.

65. Epictetus, *Discourses,* III, 22, 24; E. Norden, *Beiträge zur Geschichte der grieschischen Philosophie* (= *Jahrbücher für classische Philologie,* 19. Supplementband) (Leipzig, 1893), pp. 375–385.

66. Arthur Schopenhauer, *The World as Will and Representation,* trans. E. F. J. Payne (New York: Dover, 1966) (first edition, 1958), vol. 2, p. 444. [The Latin motto may be translated "Always the same things, but in a different way." —Trans.]

67. Lucretius, *On the Nature of Things,* III, 944.

68. See Epictetus, *Manual,* chap. 17: "in the drama of the world, you play the role the Director wants you to play." On this theme, cf. Goldschmidt, *Système stoïcien,* pp. 180ff.

69. Immanuel Kant, *Critique of Practical Reason* (Hamburg, 10th edition, 1990), p. 186 [emphasis by Hadot —Trans.].

8. The Discipline of Action, or Action in the Service of Mankind

1. Fronto, *De feriis Alsiensibus,* III, 7, p. 216, 11 Van den Hout = vol. 2, p. 12 Haines: "Si quempiam condemnas, parum cavisse videtur."

2. I have borrowed this translation from I. G. Kidd, "Posidonius on Emotions," in A. A. Long, ed., *Problems in Stoicism* (London, 1971), p. 201; see the article by Kidd in the same collection: "Stoic Intermediates and the End for Man." See also I. Hadot, *Seneca,* pp. 72–78; and in V. D'Agostino, *Studi sul Neostoicismo,* the chapter entitled "I doveri dell'etica sociale in Marco Aurelio," pp. 120–140; Goldschmidt, *Système stoïcien,* pp. 145–168.

3. *Stoïciens,* p. 50 ("Le convenable") [= Diogenes Laertius, *Lives,* Book VII, 107–110 —Trans.].

4. See Cicero, *On the Limits of Goods and Evils,* III, 5, 16ff., together with the remarkable commentary of Goldschmidt, *Système stoïcien,* pp. 126–132.

5. Seneca, *On Benefits,* IV, 33, 2.

6. Cicero, *On Duties,* III, 13, 15ff. On these casuistic problems, see I. Hadot, "Tradition stoïcienne et idées politiques aux temps des Gracques," *Revue des Études Latines,* vol. 48, pp. 161–178.

7. Cicero, *On Duties,* III, 12, 51–53.

8. Cf. Voelke, *L'Idée de volonté,* pp. 73–75.

9. Marcus Aurelius, IV, 1, 2; V, 20, 2; VI, 50, 2; Epictetus, *Manual,* 62, 2; Epictetus, quoted by Marcus, XI, 37, 1. For Seneca, see the texts cited in the following notes.

10. Seneca, *On Peace of Mind,* XIII, 2–3.

11. Seneca, *On Benefits,* IV, 34, 4–5.

12. Ibid.

13. Cicero, *On The Limits of Goods and Evils,* III, 6, 22.

14. Seneca, *On Providence,* II, 1, 4.

15. Seneca, *On Benefits,* II, 10, 1.

16. Ibid., II, 10, 3.

17. *SVF,* vol. III, §45 [= Servius, *Commentary on Virgil's Aeneid,* I, 604 — Trans.]. Cf. Seneca, *On the Happy Life,* IX, 4: "(virtus) ipsa pretium sui"; Spinoza, *Ethics,* V, proposition XLII.

18. Here, I am following the text of Farquharson.

19. Matthew 6:3.

20. Plotinus, *Enneads,* I 4, 10, 26ff.

21. Seneca, *On Benefits,* IV, 34, 4; *On Peace of Mind,* XIII, 3.

22. Cicero gives a history of this exercise in his *Tusculan Disputations,* III, 13, 28ff.; cf. I. Hadot, *Seneca,* pp. 60–61.

23. Philo of Alexandria, *On the Special Laws,* II, §46, 6–10.

24. I owe this excellent expression to Mireille Armisen-Marchetti, "Imagination et méditation chez Sénèque. L'exemple de la *praemeditatio,*" *Revue des Études Latines,* 64 (1986): 185–195.

25. Seneca, *Letters to Lucilius,* 98, 6.

26. Immanuel Kant, *Foundations of the Metaphysics of Morals,* 2nd section.

27. *Stoïciens,* p. 49 [= Diogenes Laertius, *Lives,* VII, 105–107 —Trans.]. Cf. É. Bréhier, *Études de philosophie antique* (Paris, 1987), pp. 135–138.

28. Seneca, *Letters to Lucilius,* 89, 14.

29. "Their" representation. We can render the Greek text more explicit in this way, both because of the context and because of the parallel in Epictetus, *Manual,* §61.

30. *SVF,* vol. III, §262; Philo of Alexandria, *Allegory of the Laws,* I, §87; cf. Marcus Aurelius, I, 16, 5.

31. Cassius Dio, LXXII, 34, 4.

32. Plato, *Laws,* VI, 756e–758a; Aristotle, *Nicomachean Ethics,* V, 6, 1131a–b.

33. Herodian, *History of the Empire*, I, 2, 2. Herodian is thinking in particular of the marriage of Lucilla, widow of the emperor Lucius Verus, with Claudius Pompeianus. It appears that this marriage was pleasing neither to Lucilla nor to her mother, Faustina.

34. *SVF*, vol. III, §125.

35. Plato, *Republic*, 617e1; 620d8; *Phaedo*, 107d7.

36. Louis Lavelle, *L'Erreur de Narcisse* (Paris, 1939), p. 111 [trans. W. T. Gaird-ner, *The Dilemma of Narcissus*, London and New York, 1973. Lavelle (1883–1951), professor of philosophy at the Sorbonne and the Collège de France, proposed a spiritual version of existentialism. —Trans.].

37. Socrates in Aristotle, *Nicomachean Ethics*, VII, 3, 1145b21–27; Plato, *Protagoras*, 345d; *Gorgias*, 509e; *Timaeus*, 86d.

38. Galen, *De animi cuiuslibet peccatorum dignotione et curatione* , ed. W. de Boer, *Galeni de animi cuiuslibet peccatorum dignotione et curatione* (= Corpus medicorum Graecorum, vol. 5.4.1.1 [Leipzig: Teubner, 1937]), p. 53 De Boer = vol. V, p. 77 Kühn.

39. Seneca, *On Clemency*, III, 4.

40. Lavelle, *L'Erreur de Narcisse*, p. 196. Cf. J. de Romilly, *La douceur dans la pensée grecque* (Paris, 1979).

41. Epictetus, *Discourses*, III, 22, 54.

42. Matthew 25:40.

43. Seneca, *On Clemency*, III, 3.

9. Virtue and Joy

1. *Protagoras*, 325a; 329c; *Republic*, 487a5; *Phaedo*, 69b2; *Laws*, I, 630–631 and XII, 963.

2. *Stoïciens*, pp. 44–46 [= Diogenes Laertius, *Lives*, VII, §§87–93]; 56–58 [= D.L., *Lives*, VII, §§125–131]; *SVF*, vol. III, §§262ff.; §§295ff.

3. *Orphei Hymni*, ed. G. Quandt (Berlin, 1955), Hymn 10.

4. K. Smolak, "Der Hymnus des Mesomedes an die Natur," *Wiener Human-istische Blätter*, 29 (1987): 1–13.

5. Cicero, *On Duties*, I, 4, 11; I, 5, 15. These notions are developed throughout the bulk of Book I.

6. On apparent conformity with nature which is linked to pleasure, and leads us astray, see Cicero, *Laws*, I, 31.

7. Seneca, *Letters to Lucilius*, 59, 16–17.

8. Aristotle, *Nicomachean Ethics*, X, 4, 1174b33.

9. Seneca, *On the Happy Life*, IX, 2; cf. *Stoïciens*, p. 46 (§94) [= Diogenes Laertius, *Lives*, VII, 94 —Trans.].

10. Seneca, *On the Happy Life*, XV, 2.

11. *Stoïciens*, p. 53 (§116) [= Diogenes Laertius, *Lives*, VII, 116 —Trans.].

12. Ibid., p. 166 (= Plutarch, *On Common Notions*, 35, 1077b).

13. Ibid., p. 44 (§88: the easy flow of life)[= Diogenes Laertius, *Lives,* VII, §88 —Trans.].

14. Plato, *Laws,* IV, 716a1.

10. Marcus Aurelius in His Meditations

1. Renan, p. 274.

2. Ibid., p. 267.

3. Ibid., p. 30.

4. Ibid., p. 34.

5. P. Wendland, *Die hellenistische-römische Kultur in ihren Beziehungen zu Judentum und Christentum* (Tübingen, 1972⁴), p. 238.

6. J. M. Rist, *Stoic Philosophy* (Cambridge, 1969), p. 286.

7. P. Petit, *La Paix romaine* (1982³), p. 194: "Marcus Aurelius, a Stoic philosopher of the superstitious rather than the rational type, despite the traces of a rather negative despair at the end of his life."

8. Dodds, *Pagans and Christians,* pp. 8, 29 n. 1.

9. Ibid., p. 29 n. 1.

10. *Historia Augusta, MA,* V, 2.

11. Cassius Dio, LXXII, 36, 1.

12. Grimal, p. 53.

13. Philostratus, *Imagines,* I, 30, 4, 8–9 Benndorf/Schenkl.

14. R. Dailly and H. van Effenterre, "Le Cas Marc Aurèle," *Revue des études anciennes,* 56 (1954): 349–350.

15. Cassius Dio, LXXI, 6, 3–4.

16. Cassius Dio, LXXII, 36, 2.

17. Dailly and van Effenterre, in *Revue des études anciennes,* 56: 354.

18. T. W. Africa, "The Opium Addiction of Marcus Aurelius," *Journal of the History of Ideas,* 1961, pp. 98–99. See my refutation of this article, "Marc Aurèle était-il opiomane?" in *Mémorial André-Jean Festugière* (Geneva: Cramer, 1984), pp. 33–50.

19. Galen, *De antidotis,* I, 1ff., in *Opera omnia,* vol. XIV, p. 2ff. Kühn.

20. Galen, ibid., I, 7, p. 42 Kühn; II, 17, p. 201; II, 9, p. 155; cf. P. Hadot in *Mémorial André-Jean Festugière,* p. 38.

21. Galen, *Ad Pisonem de theriaca,* 2, vol. 14, pp. 216–217 Kühn.

22. T. W. Africa, in *Journal of the History of Ideas,* 1961, p. 102, n. 78.

23. Ibid., p. 101.

24. Thomas De Quincey, *Confessions of an English Opium-Eater* (New York: Heritage Press, 1950; 1st ed.: London, 1821), p. 60.

25. Seneca, *Letters to Lucilius,* 99, 10; 49, 3.

26. *Greek Anthology,* book VII, 472.

27. *SVF,* vol. 2, §762 = *Stoïciens,* p. 178 [= Plutarch, *On Common Notions,* 44, 1083B-D —Trans.].

28. Plato, *Cratylus*, 402a; cf. A. A. Long, "Heraclitus and Stoicism," *Philosophia* (Academy of Athens), 5–6 (1975–76), p. 153.

29. Plutarch, *On the Disappearance of Oracles*, 39, 432a.

30. Ovid, *Metamorphoses*, 15, 179.

31. Plato, *Republic*, 486a, quoted by Marcus Aurelius, *Meditations*, VII, 35.

32. Philo of Alexandria, *On the Special Laws*, III, 1–2.

33. Maximus of Tyre, XXII, 6, p. 91 Dübner.

34. Ovid, *Metamorphoses*, XV, 147.

35. For example, Seneca, *Natural Questions*, I, praefatio, 7–13.

36. *Metrodori Epicurei Fragmenta*, fr. 37, ed. A. Körte, in *Neue Jahrbücher für classische Philologie, Supplementband*, XVII (1890), p. 557.

37. Cicero, *Dream of Scipio*, 3, 16. Cf. A.-J. Festugière, *La Révélation d'Hermès Trismégiste*, vol. II (Paris, 1949), pp. 441ff.

38. Pascal, *Pensées*, section II, §72.

39. P. Rabbow, *Seelenführung. Methodik der Exerzitien in der Antike* (Munich, 1954), p. 85.

40. J. Dalfen, "Formgeschichtliche Untersuchungen zu den Selbstbetrachtungen Marc Aurels," inaugural dissertation at the University of Munich (Munich, 1967).

41. M. Alexandre, "Le travail de la sentence chez Marc Aurèle: philosophie et rhétorique," in *La Licorne, Publications de la Faculté des lettres et des langues de l'Université de Poitiers*, 1979/3, pp. 125–158.

42. R. B. Rutherford, *The Meditations*, pp. 126ff.

43. Fronto, *Ad Antonin. Imper., De eloquentia*, 4, 8, p. 140, 8 Van den Hout = vol. II, p. 79 Haines.

44. Fronto, *Ad Antonin. Imper.*, IV, 1, p. 105, 4–6 Van den Hout = vol. I, p. 305 Haines.

45. [Here Marcus is quoting Hesiod, *Works and Days*, 197ff. —Trans.]

46. W. Williams, "Individuality in the Roman Constitutions: Hadrian and the Antonines," *Journal of Roman Studies*, 66 (1976): 78–82.

47. Breithaupt, pp. 15–16, cites the parallel with the titles placed at the beginnings of the third and fourth books of the *Odyssey: Ta en Pulōi; Ta en Lakedaimoni* ("The things that happened in Pylos"; "The things that happened in Lacedaemonia"). As far as Marcus' titles are concerned, this would correspond to "That which was written at Carnutum."

48. Theiler, p. 307.

49. Breithaupt, p. 39.

50. Theiler, p. 307. Should we attach any importance to the fact that Reuchlin, in 1517, cites a passage from book IV as if it belonged to book III? Cf. above, Chapter 2, n. 9.

51. On the grammatical problem, see Theiler, p. 307.

52. Theiler, p. 347.

53. [Villon's poem *La ballade des Seigneurs du temps jadis* consists of a series of

stanzas, each of which ends with the refrain "Mais où est le preux Charle-maigne?" —Trans.]

54. *Historia Augusta, Lucius Verus,* VIII, 7–11.

55. On Caninius Celer, see G. W. Bowersock, *Greek Sophists in the Roman Empire* (Oxford, 1969), p. 53 (cf. *Historia Augusta, MA,* II, 4, p. 136; Philostratus, *Lives of the Sophists,* I, §524). The Hadrian mentioned by Marcus cannot be the rhetor Hadrian of Tyre, as Dalfen believes (p. 69), for the rhetor Hadrian died well after Caninius Celer, and was still alive when Marcus was writing (cf. Philostratus, *Lives of the Sophists,* II, §590).

56. See P. Courcelle, *Recherches sur les Confessions de Saint Augustin* (Paris, 1968), pp. 12–29.

57. Cf. P. Graindor, *Un milliardaire antique: Hérode Atticus et sa famille* (Cairo, 1930); W. Ameling, *Herodes Atticus,* 2 vols. (Hildesheim, 1983).

58. On the documents we possess about this trial, see J. H. Oliver, "Marcus Aurelius: Aspects of Civil and Cultural Policy in the East," in *Hesperia,* Supplement XIII, 1970. For a French translation of the documents, see S. Follet, "Lettre de Marc Aurèle aux Athéniens (EM 13366): nouvelles lectures et inter-prétations," *Revue de philologie,* 53 (1979): 29–43. On the first of these trials, see Fronto, *Ad Marc. Caesar,* III, 3ff.; p. 37, 5ff. Van den Hout = vol. I, pp. 59ff. Haines. On the relations between Marcus and Herodes Atticus, see Bowersock, *Greek Sophists,* pp. 49, 94–100.

59. Fronto, *Ad Verum Imper.,* I, 6, p. 111, 17 Van den Hout = vol. II, p. 154 Haines.

60. Fronto, *Ad Amicos,* I, 3, p. 173, 28 Van den Hout = vol. I, p. 280 Haines.

61. Fronto, *De feriis Alsiensibus,* 4, p. 234, 13 Van den Hout = vol. II, p. 18 Haines.

62. R. B. Rutherford, *Meditations,* p. 229.

63. On the first book of the *Meditations,* see the excellent book by F. Marti-nazzolli, *La "Successio" di Marco Aurelio* (Bari, 1951).

64. *Historia Augusta, MA,* XXIX, 10.

65. See R. B. Rutherford, *Meditations,* p. 132.

66. Renan, p. 36.

67. *Historia Augusta, MA,* XXIX, 6.

68. On Marius Maximus, see R. Syme, *Emperors and Biography* (Oxford, 1971), pp. 113–114.

69. Cassius Dio, LXXII, 34, 4–5.

70. Ibid., 30, 2.

71. *Historia Augusta, MA,* XX, 5.

72. Cassius Dio, LXXII, 34, 4.

73. *Historia Augusta, Avidius Cassius,* I, 8.

74. *Institut. Justin.,* III, 11, 1, quoted by W. Williams, in *Journal of Roman Studies,* 66: 80; cf. G. Cortassa, *Scritti di Marco Aurelio* (Turin, 1984), p. 574

(Greek and Latin texts with Italian translation of all the works of Marcus Aurelius).

75. On these figures, see R. MacMullen, *Enemies of the Roman Order* (Cambridge, Mass., 1966), pp. 1–94.

76. The emperor Julian compares the figures of Cato and Dio of Syracuse, because of their unhappy fate (*To Themistius*, 3, 256a).

77. Plutarch, *Dio*, 5, 8, 960b; 7, 1, 960e; 8, 1, 961b; 17, 6, 965a; 47, 1–9, 978–979; 52, 1–3, 980–981.

78. Seneca, *On the Constancy of the Sage*, VII, 1; *On Providence*, II, 9ff.

79. Plutarch, *Cato the Younger*, 67–68, 792–793.

80. Epictetus, *Discourses*, I, 2, 19; IV, 1, 123.

81. On these questions, see P. A. Brunt, "Stoicism and the Principate," *Papers of the British School at Rome*, 43 (1975): 7–35; R. B. Rutherford, *Meditations*, pp. 59–80 (an excellent study of "The Stoics and the Empire").

82. Cassius Dio, LXXII, 33, 2.

83. *Historia Augusta, MA*, XXII, 3; VIII, 1.

84. Herodian, *History of the Empire*, I, 2, 4; and cf. F. Millar, *The Emperor in the Roman World* (London, 1977), pp. 271–271. In his preface to the Loeb edition of Herodian (p. lxxx), C. R. Whittaker emphasizes the relations between the ideology of Herodian and the tradition which goes back to Claudius Severus.

85. *Historia Augusta, MA*, XII, 1.

86. See P. Hadot, "Fürstenspiegel," *Reallexikon für Antike und Christentum*, vol. VIII, fasc. 60 (1970), pp. 555–632.

87. R. B. Rutherford, *Meditations*, p. 108.

88. *Historia Augusta, Antoninus Pius*, XII, 6.

89. *Historia Augusta, MA*, VIII, 1.

90. Since Alexander and Philip were great conquerors, the context forces us to conclude that the Demetrius mentioned here is not the statesman and Aristotelian philosopher Demetrius of Phaleron, but the Macedonian conqueror Demetrius Poliorcetes, the "taker of cities." The reading "of Phaleron," attested by manuscripts A and T, is a gloss which has been incorporated into the text, as had been suspected by H. Schenkl and G. Cortassa.

91. Cicero, *Orator*, I, 230.

92. Cicero, *Letters to Atticus*, 2, 1, 8; Plutarch, *Phocion*, 3, 2, 742f.

93. Seneca, *Letters to Lucilius*, 95, 33.

94. G. Ville, *La Gladiature en Occident des origines à la mort de Domitien* (Rome, 1982), pp. 462, 482.

95. *Historia Augusta, MA*, XXIII, 5.

96. Cassius Dio, LXXII, 29, 3.

97. Reading *hosē pronomeia* (*pronoia* AT).

98. Vaclav Havel, *Méditations d'été* (Paris, 1992), p. 137 [published in English as Vaclav Havel, *Summer Meditations*, trans. Paul Wilson, New York: Vintage Books, 1993 —Trans.].

Conclusion

1. Nietzsche, *Human, All Too Human,* II, §168; vol. 2, p. 446 Colli/Montanari.

2. Renan, p. 166.

3. Ibid., p. 162.

4. Immanuel Kant, *Foundations of the Metaphysics of Morals,* 2nd section [= p. 421 in the edition of the Königliche Preussische Akademie der Wissenschaft (Berlin, 1902–1938) —Trans.].

5. J. Gernet, *Chine et christianisme* (Paris, 1991²), p. 193.

6. J. Gernet, "La sagesse chez Wang-Fou-tche, philosophe chinois du XVIIᵉ siècle," in *Les Sagesses du monde* (Paris, 1991), p. 103.

7. Ibid., p. 103.

8. Tang Zhen, *Écrits d'un sage encore inconnu,* trans. L. Gernet (Paris, 1991), p. 97.

9. Seneca, *Letters to Lucilius,* 95, 33.

10. Goldschmidt, *Système stoïcien,* pp. 216–218.

INDEX

✳